Explore with Monitor: Book 1
Lessons for Freeing Yourself

Harvey and Julie Grady

iUniverse, Inc.
New York Bloomington

Explore with Monitor: Book 1
Lessons for Freeing Yourself

iUniverse books may be ordered through booksellers or by contact-
ing:

iUniverse
1663 Liberty Drive
Bloomington, IN 47403
www.iuniverse.com
1-800-Authors (1-800-288-4677)

ISBN: 978-0-595-47484-4 (pbk)
ISBN: 978-0-595-91756-3 (ebk)

Printed in the United States of America

iUniverse rev. date: 12/31/2008

Acknowledgments

Our gratitude extends to those who helped set the foundations on which the Monitor work is built: Edgar Cayce, Jane Roberts and Seth, Wayne Guthrie, Bella Karish and E.C., Alice Ann Bailey and Djwal Khul, and many others who contribute to deeper understanding of ourselves and our world.

Equally cherished are those who have shared in the patient process of building a structure of fascinating and useful information: many friends involved in the early lessons with Monitor (listed alphabetically by last name): Bob and Diane Anderson, Judith Anderson, Julie Ann Bartelone, Arzani and Doug Burman, Gertrude Davis, Donna Franquemont, Mary Gibbons, Lois Kelley, Jane Kephart, Mary McCarthy, Helen McCormick, Lois McCoy, Todd Metcalf, Jan Ost, Mardel Phillips, Jean Paul Setlak, Francene Shoop, and others too numerous to name, but whose contributions are also valued.

We appreciate the competent work done by Harvey's daughter, Margaret Grady, in designing, printing, and mailing the monthly lessons of *Explorations in Creative Consciousness* that are partially compiled here in book form. We hope to continue beyond this book with a series of books that share the entire set of Monitor lessons.

Our thanks go to Elmer Green for his continued encouragement, penetrating wisdom, and contributing the Foreword of this book. Without his urging, the Monitor material might not have been compiled in book form.

Much love has gone into this book, including the artistic work of Ann Nunley, whose cover image, "Dahlias," portrays the healing mystery of our creative lives.

May you be nourished by the Love and wisdom you find here!

Table of Contents

Figures

Experiential Exercises

Foreword
by Elmer Green, Ph.D.

Author, The Ozawkie Book of the Dead

Monitor's message about personalities and Souls, as outlined in this book, is psychologically unique in its description of the semi-autonomous Selves of a person, and in its suggestions for dealing with these Selves, bringing them to spiritual consciousness and integrated action.

Monitor's taxonomy of the Selves will no doubt become a feature of Psych 101 classes within a decade or two, but its transcendental source may not be openly recognized. The reason: Monitor speaks of the Soul and High Self of a *living* Planetary Being, in whom we live and move and have *our* being, and for most humans that idea is further out than the Land of Oz.

However, the basic concept is simple. *That Being is the sum total of Life on this planet.* Humanity is its conscious left and right cortex, so to speak, and Gaia is the living substance out of which we, and all other things, are made, including the mineral kingdom.

For those familiar with psychological jargon, this Being can be thought of as the *collective* High Self and *collective* Soul of the Jungian *collective* unconscious **plus** Gaia. In AmerIndian terminology, the Planetary Being is called "Father Sky" and "Mother Earth." Interestingly, according to the Ancient Wisdom, Humanity and Gaia both are "Father Sky" and "Mother Earth" amalgams.

The importance of these ideas to us individually lies in the fact that each one of us is a cell of the Planetary Being (as above, so below) and has an individual share of the planet's spiritual and mundane *parts*. And *these* parts of us—the conscious, subconscious, and superconscious Selves—must be integrated, not only for our individual well-being but also for Humanity as a whole. As we integrate ourselves, "save" ourselves, so to speak, we help "save" the entire planet. That's the challenge.

In the Ancient Wisdom it is said that Humanity is the mind of this planet and has successfully developed INTELLIGENCE, the third aspect of Divinity. Hopefully, Humanity will soon demonstrate LOVE, the second aspect of Divinity, and do so quickly enough to ease the planet's pain (our pain) as it goes through its crisis (our crisis) of Integration.

But allow me to backtrack and explain why I am comfortable with these concepts, and with the idea that there really **is** a Monitor—separate from Harvey Grady.

In 1938, when I was a student in the Institute of Physics, University of Minnesota (Minneapolis), I met an "Irish yogi" by the name of Will J. Erwood. He, like Harvey Grady, was a channel for a transpersonal Source. When I had a chance to talk with this Source, "he" called himself The Teacher, and before I could ask questions he proceeded to tell me everything of importance that had happened to me since the age of three.

He told me where I had lived, where I went to school, what I had learned, and what I was interested in. He discussed my talents and trainings, and remarkably, he told me of my inner hopes—things that I had discussed with no one, not even my parents. And still more impressive, he told me, in detail, many of the sleeping dreams I'd had in the previous few months.

Having established his credentials as a Source, you might say, he asked if I had any questions.

That was the first of weekly discussions that went on for five years. Interestingly, The Teacher always referred to himself as "We." When I asked why he never said "I," he explained that he was the spokesman for a group of Teachers who worked as a unit. And since they were literally of ONE MIND, he said, it was more appropriate to say "We" than "I."

Eventually, when I asked him who **he** was, and why he used a pseudonym instead of a real name, he laughed and said it was because personalities have problems with names. If he used a name that I might think of as significant in history, then **I might NOT believe** what he told me because of authority. And if I did, he said, **that would be MY mistake.**

And if he used a name that I had never heard of, or one that was of little importance in history, then **I might NOT believe** what he said, for non-authority reasons. And if I did, **that also would be MY mistake.**

The only way to decide if something is likely true or false, useful or not useful, he explained, is to *test it in your own life.* You must evaluate every idea *for yourself,* on the basis of your own **experience.** If you do, you will eventually **know** what IS, not simply "believe" something, or "think," or "hypothesize," or "feel." *If you learn to discriminate in this way,* he said, *you will develop a solid basis for planning and for action, and to an important extent, be able to shape your own future.*

Since the time of those conversations with The Teacher (whom, over the years, I sometimes met as an inner Instructor at turning points in my life, starting in 1920), I've used his **experiential** guideline for evaluating all psychic and spiritual "information" that has come my way.

Most important to me, The Teacher's guideline was the same, I eventually discovered, as that given by Aurobindo (the great Indian sage), by the Dalai Lama, by The Tibetan (Djwal Khul, the Instructor of Alice Ann Bailey), by Koot Humi and Morya and Djwal Khul (the three Instructors of H. P. Blavatsky), by Jesus, and **now,** by Monitor. Very interesting.

Subsequently, a criterion which I added for discriminating between "psychic" sources was whether or not they agreed with the tenets of the Ancient Wisdom as expressed by the above Teachers.

The first quick test, though, I learned from The Teacher's example. If a channeled source identifies itself with anything other than a pseudonym, such as Seth, or Genesis, or Yaveth, or Lazaris, etc., or makes **any** claim to *historical authority,* I immediately suspect that **that** source is a *cosmic entity* (using Aurobindo's phrase) rather than a *Kosmic Being.*

By *cosmic* is meant everything **below** the subtlest causal "plane" of substance and consciousness (the "frequency domain" of the immortal High Selves of humans). And by *Kosmic* I mean the High Self plane **plus** every more-subtle gradation of substance and consciousness "above" it, whatever its name or plane. That includes, of course, the Tibetan VOID.

One more definition: I have found it useful to think of **Universal** as the sum total of Kosmic and cosmic. It, therefore, includes **everything** that is manifest. The Universal is the Brahma of India, sometimes referred to as "The Divine Mother."

Another useful criterion for discriminating between cosmic sources and Kosmic Sources is the presence or absence of **flattery.** Cosmic sources often tell psychics, channels, and their followers how powerful and important they are in the working out of "God's plan."

On the other hand, sometimes by making use of feelings of inferiority in the channel and followers, cosmic sources tell their listeners how **unimportant** they are—worms in the dust, etc., or how "low in the scale of evolution they are." *Accepting* that *glamour*—the inverse of *accepting flattery*—is, of course, just as bad. Maybe worse.

In other words, **flattery or its opposite**, coming from a channeled source, or coming *directly*, psychically, is an indication to me that the source is **cosmic**, lacks Kosmic Love and Goodwill, despite its possible protestations, which are often punctuated with a spray of words like "love, unity, goodwill, integration, God, spirit," etc.

Significantly, the two greatest *collapses* of New Age organizations, which I remember (in groups which originally had worked for world spiritual unity and the development of human potential), were the direct result of the president of each organization disregarding the advice of anyone who had a **physical** body and following, instead, the flattering advice of channeled "guidance" which told them that the turning point of the Millennium depended on their doing such and such.

Subsequently, against the protests of *human* advisors, the presidents of both organizations boldly organized expensive conferences (PIVOTAL conferences, the channeled "guidance" said, in both cases) that would anchor God on the planet and prepare Humanity for The Second Coming. Both organizations suffered total wipe-out bankruptcies and died.

Also, I have noticed that *cosmic sources usually lack a sense of humor,* especially about themselves and the message they are trying to put across. Humor, which usually contains an element of objectivity, is corrosive to cosmic self-esteem and raises questions for which these sources have no graceful answer. The Beings whom I have learned to respect as Kosmic Sources, on the other hand, are quick to laugh, even about themselves. *They enjoy humor and seem especially to appreciate its glamour-canceling effects.* Humor clears the air.

Returning to my experience of Monitor: Having read all of The Tibetan's writings (the books of Alice Ann Bailey), most of Rudolf Steiner, most of

Manly Hall, all of Aurobindo, almost all of early Theosophy (H. P. Blavatsky, A. P. Sinnett, Col. H. S. Olcott, Annie Besant, and C. W. Leadbeater, including three readings each of *Isis Unveiled* and *The Secret Doctrine*), and all of W. Y. Evans-Wentz, and two or three hundred other books on religion, spiritualism, and occultism—and after having thrice read *The Mahatma Letters to A. P. Sinnett,* and also having obtained a Ph.D. in traditional psychology—*having done all that, it was fascinating to read Monitor's transcripts and observe how beautifully and skillfully he integrated the main features of the Ancient and Modern Wisdom, filling in chinks between systems, extending and linking ideas* (oddly enough, always in support of modes of thought which I already had come to value as representative of Kosmic Sources), *and expanding the overall picture of Earth's evolution to include extraterrestrials and their contribution to the development of the Planetary Being.*

In short, I was inspired by Monitor's words, and my criteria for identifying Kosmic Sources were more than met.

But more than just saying good things, every Teacher is confronted by difficulty in communication, how to get ideas across in a form that an audience can understand. *(As Alfred Korzybski said, in* Science and Sanity, *if you put it in words, it's already wrong.)* Monitor solved this communication problem in a unique way by combining short lectures followed by study group **Questions and Answers.**

Though most of the people who attend Monitor's sessions live in Arizona, what they ask are the questions of the whole planet. Customs, cultures, politics, and religions may differ land to land, but in one form or another, spiritual seekers everywhere ask, *"How am I related to God? How can I solve my personal problems, spiritually? Where is my Soul? Why do I have trouble believing? How can I become **aware** of Divinity? What is the Divine PLAN? What is God's <u>will</u>? How can I be of service to humanity?"* And also, *"Why doesn't God answer my prayers?"*

Some of Monitor's questioners open with, *"This may seem simple, but what I'd like to know is . . ."*. But Monitor made it clear that **no** question is simple or naive. In fact, simple questions are often the most profound. And also, if one person has that question, so might a million others.

Interestingly, like The Teacher, Monitor always refers to himself as "We," and for the same reason. "We" refers to the fact that Monitor is the spokesperson for a "data bank" of other individuals like himself who *together* function like an on-line Library of Congress, actually an on-line Library of Kosmos and cosmos, the Universal Library.

According to Monitor, more than 100 minds and memories are linked in a network (Internet in the sky?) that can call up information on almost any subject. How can this happen?

For Jungian theoreticians it's no great mental leap to hypothesize that Carl Jung's idea of the collective unconscious can be extended to include what in India is called the **akashic record,** the Collective Mind and Memory of the Planet.

In Indian and Tibetan tradition, the akashic record is the memory of everything (physical, emotional, mental, and spiritual) that has happened in the Life of the Planetary Being since its beginning, *and also includes in thought-form* **structure** *(which is part of the akasha)* **everything** *that the Planetary Being is considering for the future.* Interestingly, therefore, the future includes **everything** that is in the mind of Humanity and Gaia **right now,** as well as everything that humans, Gaia, angels, and Teachers are **planning.**

That is why Monitor and other Kosmic Sources can get precognitive glimpses of future events. It might be said that they have access to God's Mind.

Reading the akashic **future** isn't as simple as reading the akashic **past,** however. The reason: *The **future** is in a state of flux. It might be said that details of God's Plan in time and space are fluid because God hasn't yet made up His/Her Mind.*

The Universe appears to be a grand still-being-designed tapestry, and since the Mind of the Universal Weaver includes the Mind of our Planetary Being, which in large part is comprised of the Mind of Humanity, partial responsibility for what is woven on Earth depends on what Humanity wants, consciously and unconsciously.

This idea is important for precognition theory because in regard to the still-being-designed Tapestry of Reality, Humanity can change things. In thinking about this, I recalled a relevant passage from Koot Humi in *The Mahatma Letters to A. P. Sinnett* (page 4):

> . . .the world of 'esotericism,' with its laws based upon mathematically correct calculations of the future—the necessary results of the causes **which we are always at liberty to create and shape at our will** . . .

In other words, the future is moldable. And what happens depends to a degree on what **we** and everyone else on the planet, consciously and subconsciously visualize.

[To digress for a moment, The Mahatma Letters to A. P. Sinnett *were not channeled, like Monitor's transcripts, but were handwritten in the 1880s by two Teachers, Koot Humi and Morya, who lived in physical bodies in southern Tibet. Many of the* Letters *were "magically" delivered to Sinnett by chelas (student monks).*

Some Letters, *however, were literally apported, made to disappear in Tibet and reappear in India, occasionally in Post Offices where stamps were then canceled in the usual way, with the PO's location and date. And after that, they were reapported to Sinnett's location, covering 1000 miles or more in a few minutes.*

One Belgian physicist, who went to India to study this anomalous phenomenon, said that to him it seemed clear that super-physical forces were involved. Otherwise much of the British postal system in India would have to be thought of as an accomplice of the Theosophical Society.

After Sinnett died (1921), the Mahatmas' letters were found by A. T. Barker and in 1923 compiled for printing. The printer was Rider & Co., London. Further information is available in the Readers Guide to the Mahatma Letters to A. P. Sinnett *(G. E. Linton and V. Hanson, Theosophical Publishing House, Wheaton, Illinois, 1972).*

In 1974, while in London, I examined the **original** *handwritten letters in the British Museum, where they have been carefully preserved.]*

A few more words: With a hundred hard-disk memories in a PC computer network, businessmen nowadays can get answers to economic questions in ways that would have seemed miraculous a few years ago. And the old statement, *"As below, so above,"* makes it easy, by analogy, to imagine Monitor speaking with one MIND for an entire group. He literally is the MONITOR for a multi-entity memory bank. The fact that MINDS rather than disks are his resources makes it simpler, in some respects, than a computer net. There are no start-up glitches or hard-disk crashes.

Now it is well known in India that anyone with a Universal Library Card (that is, anyone who has developed through the agency of the High Self a connection with the akashic record) can get information on **any** subject. The problem is, though, as in any library, even though you check out a book, you may not be fluent in its jargon. Even a Master Teacher doesn't know **everything.**

To handle this problem, Monitor's working group includes experts on almost any subject a human can think of, and when a question is asked, the appropriate Source comes online, so to speak, to provide an answer.

Once, when a member of the study group asked a recondite question about the percentages of different kinds of beings who lived in Lemuria, Monitor answered something like, *"Just a moment—while we consult the Statistics Department."* That's a bit of Kosmic humor.

And now, enjoy exploring *Explore with Monitor.* It is a great trip, far more interesting and exciting than any astronaut or cosmonaut excursion in physical space. *Bon Voyage!*

Elmer Green, Ph.D.
Lakewood Hills, Kansas
7 November 2007

Introduction

I want to share with you some background about my experience with channeling that led to this series of discussions with Monitor. Before Monitor began talking through me on April 10th, 1991, much had already taken place that you may wish to know about.

I began to channel intentionally in 1972, at age 32, by communicating first with specific aspects of my own subconscious and superconscious levels of mind, then later with nonphysical Teachers. This journey began an exploration of my own being, which led to the discovery that my personality was being developed as an instrument for communication with higher levels of consciousness. I was told that I needed training. I recognized and accepted that need. My personality required stretching, purification, clarification, and refinement. What better place to begin than "know thyself"?

My High Self acted as an inner teacher, guiding me past barriers of fear that I previously did not know existed below the surface of my awareness. Many times the thoughts—"I can't do this. I'm not capable. I'm not worthy."—passed through my mind. They made repeated appearances before I grasped the fear behind them. My High Self, called "Joseph," guided me to such realizations, yet I needed to take action by connecting the feeling of fear (constricting my throat) with the limiting thought. As those blocking fears yielded to understanding, Joseph took me on inner journeys to build awareness of my personality.

Going beyond the fear barriers constituted a major part of my training. Long acquaintance with my High Self definitely assisted. In childhood I had expanded awareness and encountered a number of nonphysical beings. During those encounters I frequently asked questions and received answers in my mind. The answers proved quite helpful. One day, when I was ten years old, it occurred to me to consider who supplied the answers. So I mentally asked, "Who or what are you?" The answer essentially said, "I am your Higher Self. Consider me a guardian angel, if you wish, yet I am part of you and you are part of me." Because that mental voice had consistently helped me, I called it "Helper." Giving it a name made it easier to converse mentally. Many times I questioned the information that Helper supplied, yet discovered that it knew far more than I did. Its information was frequently validated by my experiences.

Even though I lost contact with my High Self in high school and college, when besieged with formal education that seemed to have no place for Higher Selves, that contact was re-established when I was 23. My book, **Growing Up Psychic**,[1] presents many of those childhood and young adulthood experiences of spiritual disconnection and reconnection. So when I began intentional channeling in 1972, I already trusted my Higher Self and sought greater access to its guidance.

In the late 1960s the work of Drs. Wayne Guthrie and Bella Karish of the Fellowship of Universal Guidance in Los Angeles prepared me for the concept of "Inner Selves." Their pioneering work with the "Three Selves" concept combined the Hawaiian Huna approach with Edgar Cayce's description of human consciousness.[2] Wayne and Bella's psychic counseling method provided a more detailed view of the personality, which I found practical. In 1965 Bella gave me a reading, called a "Three Selves Evaluation," introducing me to my "High Self" Joseph and my "Male Basic Self" Samson. During the reading Bella channeled each of those Selves. Because I was not prepared to hear their mental voices directly, they spoke to me through Bella.

Following that reading, I established my own mental communication with Joseph and Samson. My inner dialogues with them confirmed and added information to what the reading had revealed. Their names, which had been presented through Bella, were symbolic and changeable, yet handy to use in calling them to talk with me or in thinking about them.

On the inward journeys guided by Joseph, I retained full ability to respond to situations. If I didn't want to go where I was being led, I balked. Even though I closed eyes for most of those journeys, I could open them any time that I wanted. Remaining fully alert, I allowed Joseph to guide me only as far as I was willing to go. I often stopped when Joseph would have preferred for me to continue. Exercising my will in ways contrary to Joseph's gave me a sense of empowerment. I felt reassured that no sneaky devil or demon was ensnaring me.

Growing Up Psychic: A Spiritual Journey, by Harvey Grady, Center for Human Potential, 1995.

Pathways to Your Three Selves, by Wayne A. Guthrie and Bella Karish, Fellowship of Universal Guidance & Zivah Publishers, 1989.

In fact, I was extremely cautious about maintaining proper spiritual protection and concerned that someone or some thing might try to control or possess me. Bella and Wayne had stressed the need for developing channels to maintain proper spiritual protection. Consequently, I consistently began and ended Lessons with prayers for protection, God and Christ's guidance, and "only the highest good." In taking the risk of exploration into (for me) unknown realms, I felt as prepared as possible. Joseph led me into past life recalls, visits to higher planes, and better understanding of my own personality and its path of growth.

Like a translator of foreign languages, my vocabulary required expansion to describe the inner landscape of the personality and the interactions of Inner Selves. Beyond that, the vocabulary had to depict the continuity of our lives as they undulated in and out of physical existence. Words had to be found for description of nonphysical regions of existence, in which we live, move, and evolve into unity with our Souls and ultimately with God.

How do you develop such a vocabulary? For me, the process involved willingness to explore realms of consciousness with a skeptical, questioning mind and a stubborn adherence to spiritual values represented by a "universal Christ." Not the "limited Christ" of a particular church, defined by the interpretations of other persons. To me, that approach seemed like eating food already chewed by others. I needed to make my own contacts with Higher Consciousness as did Arjuna, Moses, and Mohammed, wrestle with my own angel as did Jacob, and find my own way to Enlightenment as did Gautama, the Buddha. I found it crucial to seek "the Highest," asking it to guide and protect me in searching for better connection with it.

From infancy I had experiences of communication with nonphysical beings. Childhood encounters with human, angelic, and devic beings who did not have physical bodies had stimulated my curiosity and commitment to systematic research. My first encounter with Yeshua, or "Jesus" as the world now knows him, occurred during my early teens. These experiences are presented in my booklet, **Encounters Through the Veil**, for those who are interested.[3]

Encounters with nonphysical beings—whom I see, feel, and communicate with telepathically—had led me to brief encounters with "a universal Oneness" whose Being encompasses all other beings. From It I received Love, communion, nourishment, and encouragement to enjoy and gain understanding of the mysteries of Life, realizing that my comprehension was incomplete, yet part of the process of evolution. As stated in the **Book of Tao,**

Encounters Through the Veil: A Boy's Adventures in Nonphysical Realities, by Harvey Grady, Center for Human Potential, 1995.

The Tao that can be told is not the eternal Tao.
The name that can be named is not the eternal name.
The nameless creates the beginning of heaven and earth.[4]

Our search for understanding guides us to direct encounters with beings and Being Itself. None of us owns "the ultimate Truth." Making such a claim requires a combination of arrogance and ignorance. For me, I humbly do the best I can in the moment to express little comprehensions or let them be expressed through me by others more skilled. These "little truths" lead us like a trail of bread crumbs to greater comprehensions. What we learn is limited by what we *live*, and so we are required to "walk our talk" before we are ready to receive greater understanding.

These considerations are embodied in my "Master Teaching Source," a Soul-related group of thousands of beings who guide the evolution of my personality and who identify themselves by the enigmatic name of "Tao." I regard myself as only one of many who serve with the motive of wise Love, not claiming possession of ultimate Truth. I consider the words that I speak, or are spoken through me, as able to stand on their own merit. They deserve to be questioned, tested, and evaluated for validity in the lives of those encountering them.

In 1972, my sources of channeled information talked about the value of opening up new models of channeling. They said that channeling involved our ability to receive information and absorb wisdom. Wisdom can be transmitted, but we don't always absorb it because it may exceed the limits of our beliefs. Our beliefs about ourselves and our reality need to be expanded. They said that much channeled energy and information would be presented to the world by the end of this century and beyond.

I wanted to explore the process of channeling. I'd studied most of the Edgar Cayce material, the Seth books, and some channeled books from other substantial sources. I had been exposed to the actual practice of channeling as done in a spiritualist church, and then to the channeled therapeutic work of Wayne Guthrie and Bella Karish in Los Angeles. I had many questions about channeling. What is the process? How does it work? So I asked these questions and channeled answers in limited private moments, either isolated at home or when driving a car on trips between cities in Arizona.

My job at the Arizona Department of Corrections entailed frequent travel in helping communities organize their own juvenile delinquency prevention programs. I took a battery-powered tape recorder in the car, asked questions out loud, and voiced the information that came in response. While channeling at home, it was more efficient to sit down at a typewriter and

---

Tao Te Ching, A New Translation by Gia-Fu Feng and Jane English, Vintage Books, 1972.

type the questions and answers. Often one of my four children interrupted the flow, and I attended to their needs before returning to the typewriter. However, those interruptions gave me practice in maintaining a focused attunement. They also demonstrated to me the value of remaining flexible in meeting the needs of the moment and using the highest possible attunement in performing even the most mundane tasks.

The information said, right from the beginning, that every human channel is less than perfect. We won't find 100% transmission of accurate information. We won't receive 100% transmission of the total energy available from sources of higher consciousness, because a single person is normally incapable of receiving the full range of channeled consciousness. It said that one of the most important aspects of the channeling process involved the formulation of questions. A question creates a *bridge* for communication from our surface mind to the deeper levels of personal and collective mind. A question sends a request into the conscious universe and draws back information, wisdom, and energy in response.

The sources I channeled said that any single person could bring through only a limited amount of a transmitted response to a question. If we got more than one channel functioning at the same time in harmony, more of the total information and energy available could be presented. I hope to include multiple channeling in this *Explorations* process later on. We can experiment some day with a "Channel Panel!"

Much of the channeling presented to the public has involved a one-way transmission of information, where people easily become spectators. Being a spectator is a limiting role. I prefer a seminar type of exchange to encourage development of human potential, a two-way discussion that draws out the best in us. Isn't each one of us a channel? Don't we channel everyday in the act of living? What we call channeling, which I call "on-stage" channeling, involves attuning and focusing our attention to a higher level of consciousness than we normally do in daily living. Each of us can do "off-stage" channeling in daily life by asking for the "highest balanced attunement" as we go about our normal tasks.

When I channel, I first say a prayer for spiritual protection and attunement to the Highest through Love for all involved. Then I move my awareness up through the top of my head and expand it, giving other aspects of my being room to function. I deliberately connect with my High Self, the "guardian angel" of my personality, which I sense as a bright white star about three inches above the top of my head. When connected with the High Self, I experience a profound communion filled with Love, wisdom, serenity, poise, expanded mental awareness, and often a delightful sense of humor. Next, I relax and allow the High Self to make connection with the Teacher who needs to exchange information and energy.

The Teacher directs information and energy through my physical body and the voice centers of my brain. My role is to relax and let it happen. As the channeling takes place, subtle energy expresses in and around my body. The energy expands to include every person in the vicinity. Each person acts like an antenna that draws signals from the universe. Some persons in the room get filled with stimulating energy. Some may feel tingling or warmth. Others may feel like going to sleep, while others might find themselves seeing auras. The energetic transactions seem as important as the information exchanged.

My wife, Julie, conducts the group lessons with Monitor. Who is Monitor? As you read Lessons one and two, you will find out about Monitor just as we did. My High Self and Master Teaching Source, Tao, had encouraged me to initiate a weekly group channeling series open to the public, focus discussion on one topic a month, and call the series *Explorations*. They had even suggested the first topic, "Personality and Soul." They said that a new development would take place, but deliberately remained vague about it. My job involved being flexible and accepting of what needed to take place without my foreknowledge. My experience of the night before and the actual introduction of Monitor at the first *Explorations* Lesson on April 10, 1991, is related in the first chapter of **Growing Up Psychic**. Part of that account is presented after this Introduction.

From 1972 to April 10th, 1991, the main Teachers who channeled through me were Tao and Michael (the Archangel). Tao's energies during channeling opened me up and began a process of conditioning my chakras and my physical and subtle bodies. When Michael first came through me in 1976, the conditioning process became more intense, bringing out physical, emotional, and mental impurities. My training and experience in counseling and holistic medicine provided me with tools for aiding the purification process. Daily meditation, prayer, healing work, and service for others assisted the conditioning of my chakras and bodies.

Michael encouraged me to give personal and group readings for friends. By constantly testing the accuracy and validity of the information channeled, my confidence in channeling grew more confirmed. From 1976 to 1991 Michael gave hundreds of problem-solving, health, research, and life readings, many of them for persons I had never met except by letter or telephone. Feedback from those persons demonstrated the accuracy and helpfulness of the readings, giving me incentive to continue in the challenging role of a channel.

In April 1991, as previously mentioned, Monitor was introduced as the major Teaching Source of my readings, and the *Explorations* series was launched. A **Commentary,** interspersed between the early Lessons, describes my experience of channeling Monitor for the first time and offers my interpretations of Monitor's ideas.

Another feature of this book offers **Tools for Exploration**, a set of experiential exercises suggested by Monitor for class members and readers. Readers may photocopy the exercise pages for recording their own experiences as they perform the exercises for expanding their consciousness. For quick reference, a list of experiential exercises is offered following the **Table of Contents**

A **Glossary** is provided after Chapter 9 to provide readers with definitions of terms that Monitor uses, and at the end of the book an **Index** offers a way to study all references in this book to specific subjects, ranging from "Adic plane" to "Zodiac."

The format for these Lessons remains much the same as when they began. Prior to channeling, we discuss the scheduled topic to formulate questions and different points of view about it. We encourage a dynamic exchange between Monitor and participants, which creates a seminar-type atmosphere. In a seminar, various points of view are expressed and considered, which stimulates our thinking about the topic. Most participants do not passively assume that Monitor presents "ultimate Truth," but find themselves examining ideas they have not previously considered.

The *Explorations* series of lessons are intended to stimulate our thinking, expand our awareness, refine our vocabulary, and motivate us to connect more reliably with our own Higher Consciousness. We are invited to explore, and where that leads us remains *our* choice and *our* opportunity!

MY EXPERIENCE CHANNELING MONITOR

FOR THE FIRST TIME

(excerpted from the book, Growing Up Psychic, *by Harvey Grady)*

Sitting still in the padded old rocking chair so it did not creak, I sensed the living Light above my head. At first it seemed like white mist, then as my awareness moved upward through the mist, it clarified into the unmistakable presence of my radiant High Self. Bathing in its timeless benevolence, any sense of physical time had already been left behind. An eon could go by with no difficulty here, and I wouldn't care because the joy, vitality and serenity of that Godly presence was more like home than the physical world.

A stirring occurred in that pure White space. A light-golden swirl appeared around us, me and the High Self, signaling the arrival of Tao, my wise and cryptic Master Teacher. After brief greetings, Tao assumed a more crystalline configuration and asked permission to channel. The High Self and I assented simultaneously, so Tao began speaking to the group of people assembled in the living room.

TAO: We come to you as Tao to introduce Monitor, which is a name presented for a group which will endeavor to present information more in line with human experience than has been presented by many of the sources originating from levels of awareness far removed from human expression. We introduce Monitor.

"We introduce Monitor." The words resounded from a far-off distance, as I happily floated in the presence of the High Self. A minor part of my mind noticed the word "Monitor" with interest. So, that was the name chosen to label the new source now assembling to channel through my physical body. How interesting! "Monitor" implied the act of watching, observing, keeping track of things. Like a brain wave monitor in the intensive care unit of a hospital. Or like the TV screen monitor of a computer where information was displayed. That part of my mind enjoyed solving puzzles. It wondered what this "Monitor" would be like.

It did not have to wait long for the answer. As the light-golden crystalline structure of Tao liquefied and withdrew, a multi-colored swirl replaced it. Like a faceted jewel, where red, orange, yellow, green, blue, indigo, and lavender facets were positioned in a matrix of rich golden Light, this new collective consciousness took over where Tao left off. Once positioned for channeling, the multi-hued facets extended out through the room and far outside like a gigantic lens. They handled the transition smoothly, assuming full control over the speech and language mechanisms of my body as though they had done it before.

MONITOR: We will function as a team in bringing clear understanding to you and to those beyond these walls in terms of language and metaphor. We will bring in various sources, as it seems appropriate.

First, let us consider the concept of "Personality and Soul." "Personality" is a term that has wide usage now throughout the world as individual human beings become more aware of their Being. Psychology is evolving from rudimentary levels of understanding and beginning to consider the possibility that human beings are more than physical organisms. Those in psychology who entertain the concept of mind as more than the brain are open to consider models whereby mind may be better understood.

Well, these new guys sounded competent. They used precise, understandable language, which I appreciated greatly, considering that much published channeled material did not. So that part of me relaxed, willing to relinquish its partial control over the channeling. Easing out even farther above my physical head, which was now busy speaking to the group in the living room, I let the High Self lead me somewhere very pleasant and removed from the scene of channeling. There I remained willingly in my expanded mental body, enjoying a rejuvenating stay among colorful living cloud-forms in golden light emanating from everywhere.

Chapter 1

Personality and Soul

Lesson 1

April 10, 1991

TAO INTRODUCES MONITOR

TAO: We come to you *as Tao* to introduce "Monitor," which is a name presented for a group who will endeavor to present information more in line with human experience than has been presented by many of the sources originating from levels of awareness far removed from human expression. We introduce Monitor.

MONITOR: We will function as a team in bringing clear understanding to you and to those beyond these walls in terms of language and metaphor. We will bring in various sources, as it seems appropriate.

First, let us consider the concept of "Personality and Soul." "Personality" is a term that has wide usage now throughout the world as individual human beings become more aware of their Being. Psychology is evolving from rudimentary levels of understanding and beginning to consider the possibility that human beings are more than physical organisms. Those in psychology, who entertain the concept of mind as more than the brain, are open to consider models whereby mind may be better understood.

PERSONAL RESEARCH

As we consider "mind," we review our *experiences* with mind. Let us consider some of our common experiences. We are aware that we wake and sleep. What part of us goes to sleep and then *awakens*? Is that part of us who goes to sleep the same as the one who awakens? What happens to that part of us during sleep? Is it dormant, or is it active in some other way? These kinds of questions are gradually being addressed in psychological research.

Yet the most significant psychological research that we recommend here is that which we, as individuals, may conduct by ourselves. Consider what we might do tonight in terms of *personal research*. Tonight, before going to sleep, we can pay attention to our sense of awareness, our sense of beingness or consciousness. We can note how we feel physically, emotionally, mentally, spiritually, before going to sleep. We might even write some notes about those qualities to remind us at a later time. Then, in the morning when we wake up, we can pay attention again to what we are feeling and experiencing physically, emotionally, mentally, and spiritually. If we make more notes, we can then compare the qualities of our experiences *before* and *after* sleeping.

This method provides useful research, a personal research which is quite valid from our perspective, for an individual is fully capable of asking relevant questions for testing different ideas or concepts and arriving at conclusions based on one's own experience. *Personal research* becomes the individual's pathway to the achievement of what you term "higher states of consciousness" and ultimately "spiritual mastery."

We can begin in daily experience to question: "What is our consciousness?" "What is this concept of *personality*?" "What does it mean?" As we deal with the concept of personality, we have a basis of experience to consider what might be meant by the term "Soul." If we skip considering personality, we miss an opportunity for achieving a deep and rich understanding of *Soul*. The reason for this is, we suggest, that *we achieve awareness of Soul through awareness of our personality*.

Many people feel uncomfortable with their personality and seek to find a better state of being. That can lead a person to create *illusions* and a state of *division* in which one paradoxically seems to exist in a lower state of being and longs to be in a higher state of being. This approach is guaranteed to be frustrating. We suggest an alternative approach that involves *exploring our personality and finding within it the presence of our Soul*.

INDIVIDUATION—LIFE ESSENCE ENTERS FORM

From our perspective, which originates in the causal plane, we have this view: that *each person is an expression of the whole universe* – all of Life – which is intelligently and coherently organized and which lives and functions as a single unit. Each person offers a unique expression of the Whole of Life, and each person is endowed with *identity*. Let us give a metaphor to illustrate what we mean by "identity."

If the entire universe – which is alive and may be described as the creation of God or Divinity – is considered as a jewel, the jewel is fulfilled as it develops facets. Here we describe each individual being as a facet of the jewel. Each facet reflects the light and energy and substance of the entire jewel, yet each facet has its own distinct identity, its own uniqueness.

This concept of identity allows the consciousness of the universe to explore itself creatively. The universe, if anything, is creative! It moves and changes and explores. Much of what it does involves reflecting from one facet to another in the way that light reflects within a jewel. The light is shared by all facets of the jewel, and this light may be a metaphor for what we term "mind."

We offer a simple definition of *mind* to begin with, and allow a more sophisticated definition to emerge from our discoveries. We *define* "mind" *as the Life of the universe reflecting one facet to another*. When we define facets as identities, we need to indicate that Life in the universe is free to explore these facets of identity. Some of the Life of the universe does so, and some chooses not to. The Life that explores the facets of identity may be called "Life experiencing identity forms." Here we deal with the concept that Life, as an energy, may inhabit forms.

A *form* is a container or a vehicle for Life to express within and through. When Life does that, it gains a unique perspective that the form provides. Forms have different vibratory qualities. The Life that expresses in one form gains a unique perspective of the vibratory quality that vibrates within the whole of the universe. The Life that inhabits another form gains another unique and valuable perspective, and so a need exists for Life, which explores the facets of identity, to *move* from form to form.

In a planet such as Earth, a variety of forms are provided for Life to experience. Each one in this room may be described as Life experiencing their specific *human form*, which comprises only one of thousands of forms that the Life uniquely *you* has explored and continues to explore.

You use words associated with *physical* awareness, *emotional* awareness, *mental* awareness, and *spiritual* awareness. You are most comfortable with *physical* words. *Emotional* words are developing, but lack the variety and precision of your physical words. Your *mental* words appear even more vague. Your *spiritual* words have poetic value more as inspiration than designating specific spiritual referents. So, in talking about concepts, we will endeavor to utilize physical terms, analogies, and metaphors to encourage more accurate development of your thinking.

EVOLUTION OF LIFE IN THE WORLD OF FORMS

First, we will talk about how Life enters form as it explores the facets of identity. On a cosmic level throughout the universe, we begin with what we call "Cosmic Identities," which we identify as twelve in number, each of which distinctly differs in quality. From the twelve there emanate a vast number of more restricted forms of identity that we term "Monads." So, you see, we describe two *levels* of identity, Cosmic Identity and Monad Identity. Life flows first into the Cosmic Identity level and from there extends itself into the Monad level. And where is the Soul? Where is the personality in this picture of things?

Life experiencing on a cosmic level seeks to find and express *unity* with all other facets of Life. The twelve aspects of Cosmic Identity, in their evolution, find that they do not easily unify. What they attempt to accomplish cannot be accomplished in that level of form. Therefore Life in a Cosmic Identity level seeks expression in the Monad level. The Monad level is more limited in scope and thus provides opportunity for Life to achieve the expression of unity not achievable in the Cosmic Identity level. Alas, on the Monad level, unity is not truly achieved, and so Life extends itself once again to what we term the *Soul Identity* level. In the Soul level, Life expresses in ways that involve experiences with solar systems and planets. Life explores many avenues and dimensions of expression.

If you take the image of a tree, the tree extends many roots into the earth. Without those roots, the tree lacks sufficient sustenance to survive. You can use this metaphor to understand how Life develops in the universe.

The Creator creates Life and gives it freedom of expression. Life diversifies, with roots reaching out from the Cosmic Identity level to the Monad level. The roots need to reach out even more, so they create further branching of roots, which become Souls. The Souls create even more branchings termed "personalities" and "sub-personalities." Throughout this scheme, we find the unity of Life flowing through all of the roots just as the Life of the tree flows through all of its roots.

Consider now the process of *growth*, for you know that a tree begins with a seed. The seed extends roots, and when the roots extend far enough, the seed projects what ultimately becomes a trunk. The trunk extends branches. The branches extend leaves, and we may perceive an order and a beauty in the process of growth. We suggest that the Cosmic Tree of the Kabbala,[5] and other ancient symbolic systems of understanding, represent this growth of consciousness throughout the universe.

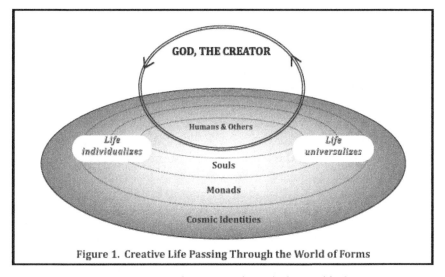

Figure 1. Creative Life Passing Through the World of Forms

Figure 1. Creative Life Passing Through the World of Forms

HOLISTIC VIEW

Each of us represents a vital part of that consciousness. Each one of us constitutes part of the Cosmic Tree. Each is unalterably connected to the Whole of Life and is part of an effort by all Life to achieve an expression of unity. Through diversity, each of these roots and branches and leaves of the Cosmic Tree expresses only what each one can uniquely express. Sometimes those expressions involve harmonious purposes.

Purpose becomes a key part of the picture. Life expressing *creates* purpose. Purpose becomes the expression of some form of intent. "Intent" and "purpose" appear as words with similar meanings. You could say that the purpose of a tree may be to grow and be itself. That statement describes the purpose of the tree in isolation from all that surrounds it. Human beings have often defined Life forms in that manner, which can be described as "isolationist" and "reductionist" thinking. We prefer to encourage, in our discussion, holistic ways of thinking that recognize that a tree offers an expression of the whole of the universe. We say that *the purpose of the tree involves expressing the universe through its growth and unique being.*

A single leaf in a mulberry tree, or a mesquite tree, reflects qualities that would not be possible if beings in a distant solar system were not expressing the behavior that they *are* expressing. The quality of a drop of water in the ocean would not be the same if the ocean currents were not flowing in their

---

Kabbala: a set of mystical teachings written and compiled by certain Jewish rabbis and based on esoteric interpretations of the Scriptures.

particular configuration, if the winds were not blowing in certain patterns, if the Earth was not turning, and the sun was not bathing the Earth in its radiance on a regular basis. And if that sun was not moving in its own orbit with other suns around a center of gravity, the quality in that drop of water would not be the same. Each part of the whole reflects the whole, and each part *affects* the whole through its actions.

Consider the quality of God, a Creator who presents the gift of freedom to creation. *Consider a Creator who enables each tiny part to affect the whole.* Would you consider that this Creator has a sense of trust? And consider that all of the universe is contained within its Creator. The Creator is also affected by the actions of each tiny part of its creation. How the Creator is affected and how the Creator affects each one of us remains largely a mystery, but we introduce that as a concept here in order that we may effectively look at the whole as it affects the parts.

When we apply this kind of thinking to consideration of personality and Soul, we identify certain factors. First, we find the *stream of Life* that flows from the Creator to the universe in the Cosmic Identity level to the Monad level to the Soul level to the personality level. We discover a stream of expression of Life that needs to be recognized. The personality reflects the whole of the universe, yet is strongly influenced by the Soul who creates it. The Soul becomes a very important consideration for the personality.

SOUL EMBODIMENT IN A PERSONALITY

When Life inhabits a form, Life creates an *identity* based on its experience of that form. When a Soul inhabits a human personality, the Soul is affected to a large degree by its vivification of that personality. The Soul becomes greatly invested in the personality, and its investment goes through stages of development. We will briefly describe that process.

When a Soul activates a human personality, the Soul has to focus its awareness. This has been described by some teachers as the Soul entering into a state of meditation where it focuses its awareness and directs some of its Life force into a human personality. The human personality becomes a Soul infusion of a body form that has its *own* evolution in Earth. The human body is invested with the Life force of a Soul. They interact, and in one lifetime of one body, the Soul begins to grow accustomed to the experience of embodiment.

Several embodiments or human lifetimes are required before the Soul truly feels comfortable inhabiting a human body. The Soul then trusts the consciousness expressing in that personality to undergo a process of growth, and consequently the Soul becomes more dormant. It allows its Life force to evolve *through* the personality.

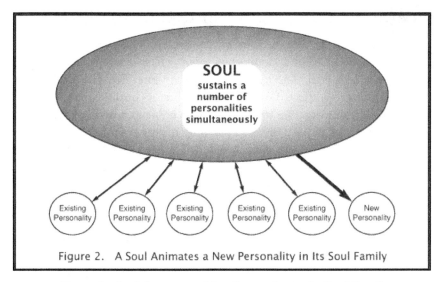

Figure 2. A Soul Animates a New Personality in Its Soul Family

Figure 2. Soul Animates a New Personality in Its Soul Family

A newly embodied Soul finds itself drifting around almost in a dreamlike state. It often finds itself having accidents or unintended experiences. It might wander through a forest bumping into trees, stumbling over bushes and rocks. A newly embodied Soul needs to have those kinds of experiences to make it alert and responsive to *physical* expression. It develops a strong physical system of responses.

We find here the development of what psychologists term "instinct," which in many ways is strongly related to the *animal* qualities of the body. A personality, at first, has no instincts, but as its experience grows, it develops them. It learns to rely more and more on *instincts* for survival and pursuit of its interests. It develops *interests* that initially are focused on maintaining survival and then, with subsequent embodiments, on achieving higher needs.

SUBCONSCIOUS MIND

We find portions of a personality that are continued from one physical embodiment to another. These may be described as "subconscious mind" *from the viewpoint of the Outer Self.* The subconscious mind of a personality brings with it memories of its past embodiments. One embodiment adds to another embodiment's experiences, and the subconscious portion of a personality gains sophistication. The personality evolves, becoming competent in a number of areas. As it evolves, it allows the new Body Self to depend on it.

COMPARING CONSCIOUS AND SUBCONSCIOUS MINDS

Therefore, David, as a personality, consists of an *Outer Self*—which is unique to his body—and a *subconscious mind*, which is unique to all of the bodies it has inhabited. The experiences of the Outer Self give it a certain vibratory quality. It is affected strongly by the vibratory qualities of the physical body itself. The subconscious mind of David is influenced by all of the bodies it has inhabited and so has a different vibratory quality than the Outer Self.

We speak of these as two levels of mind. They function that way because they have different bases of experience and vibratory qualities. In David they may function quite independently at times, with one level of mind going about its business and the other level of mind going about its separate business. If the two happen to agree on purposes or goals, they may work together in harmony. But if the two disagree on purposes or goals, a conflict of purpose arises in David's personality.

At times the Outer Self might win the conflict. It would win most often in situations where a distinct *physical gratification* could be achieved. The Outer Self of David might see a cookie, and its purpose of eating the cookie would prevail, even though David's subconscious mind might prefer some other creative project.

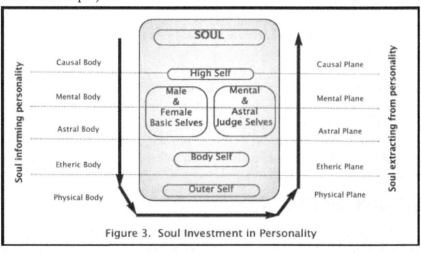

Figure 3. Soul Investment in Personality

Figure 3. Soul Investment in Personality

The subconscious mind tends to prevail by *subterfuge*. When David goes to sleep tonight, his Outer Self will be largely dormant, not totally, but approximately 80–90% dormant. During that time his subconscious mind can create experiences for the Outer Self that will influence the Outer Self's desires for the coming day. If his subconscious mind desires to pursue a creative project, tonight it could well propagandize his Outer Self during the sleep state, and tomorrow David's Outer Self would wake up and feel a strong desire to pursue that creative project. The subconscious mind has many means at its disposal to accomplish *its* goals.

INTRA-PERSONAL COMMUNICATION

If the two levels of mind function independently with little common agreement, we find a great waste of mind and Life. If they do communicate with each other, they can achieve much more.

Now we invite you at this point to consider how well do you, as Outer Selves, communicate with your subconscious minds? How do you approach your subconscious minds? Do you have a way?

We assure you that your subconscious minds have ways of communicating with you! Once you become aware of your subconscious minds, you can have a great influence over them, because subconscious minds generally have enough experience to realize the value of cooperating with the Outer Self, so we ask you to consider what you might do about that.

SUPERCONSCIOUS MIND

We also find a higher level of mind, which we term the "superconscious mind." This level of mind functions as a *guide* for the Soul's expression of Life in a human personality. The superconscious mind has extensive experience. It understands the promises and pitfalls of embodiment. The superconscious mind guides the experiences of the Outer Self and subconscious minds of the personality. It functions as a teacher and a guide and comprises an essential part of the personality.

It has accepted the assignment of responsibility for assisting the Subconscious and Outer Selves in their development. Its job is accomplished when the personality achieves spiritual mastery. At that point the human personality has become so aware of its Soul and so filled with its Soul's activities that the personality, in effect, is absorbed within the Soul.

Now some of you may be saying to yourselves, "I don't want to be absorbed. I want to remain myself." Some of you might say, "I don't want to be a cluster of components. I want to be whole. I want to be unified." We recognize these as valid concerns, yet we present this point of view to you even though it may be controversial in some respects, because we want you to consider how you are functioning.

Is your awareness, day by day, the awareness of an isolated being like the tree considered in isolation from the universe? Or do you have awareness, at times, of your *connection* to the whole of the universe? Of your connection to the Creator? How do you value these awarenesses?

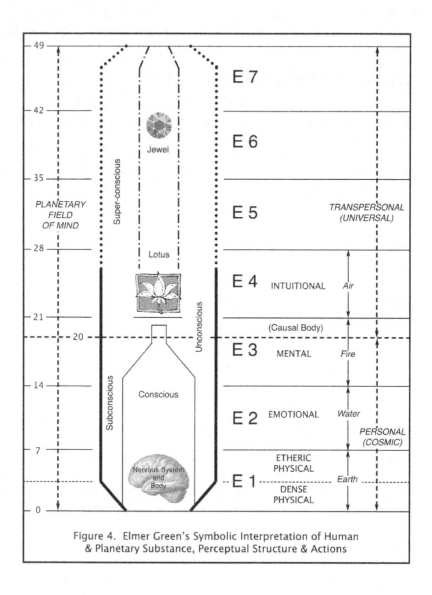

Figure 4. Elmer Green's Symbolic Interpretation of Human & Planetary Substance, Perceptual Structure & Actions

Figure 4. Elmer Green's Symbolic Interpretation of Human & Planetary Substance, Perceptual Structure and Actions

Some of you may find these experiences quite uplifting and giving your Life special meaning or a certain brightness. Yet some of you may experience such times of connectedness so infrequently as to wonder if that experience is even possible. We encourage you to explore such experiences. How might you do that?

We encourage you to ask the aspects of your mind that go *beyond* the Outer Self, "Please help me be aware of my connection to all of Life." Who knows? If you ask, you may actually *receive* the experience that you ask for. If you do not ask, you will follow a path of experiences which will lead you there eventually, yet if you value your connection, why *not* ask?

We have endeavored here to sketch a picture of Life evolving through form. We have indicated a hierarchical relationship of consciousness through a personality given freedom, yet ultimately subsumed by its Soul. We have spoken little of the Soul because we have focused first on a preliminary description of the nature of the personality. We remind you that truly understanding the personality takes the first step toward understanding the Soul.

QUESTIONS

We are preparing now for questions. We would like to ask you to question what we have presented. We find that questions open the belief configurations of minds. One is not ready for an answer if one cannot even formulate the question. Therefore, the questions that you ask will all be reasonable and worthy of serious consideration. We now invite your questions on the subject of personality and Soul.

THREE LEVELS OF CONSCIOUSNESS

MARGARET: I have studied methods of defining the structure of Being which, in a general way, are very similar to what you've outlined here. Is there some underlying pattern that flows throughout all our beings that comes to be defined similarly in many different cultures and modes of thinking?

MONITOR: We are not quite certain what you're asking, but will begin with this response. We find an essence of Life that flows from the Creator to the Cosmic Identity to the Monad to the Soul to the personality, a common essence, a common set of qualities. If you ask in that regard, that is our answer.

If you mean a common pattern in different people, we would say, indeed, that we find common patterns that relate to the causal patterns active in and beyond this planet. These you recognize perhaps by the term "archetype." Would you like to proceed with your question?

MARGARET: Yes, I was trying to stay away from specific examples, but that's not going to work. I was thinking specifically about Jung's description of personality and also a body of work known as the "Three Selves" concept of personality and Soul. They both seem to be structured around the idea of three different aspects of expression. Once again, as you have spoken this evening, you have outlined at the personality level three different aspects of expression, and I'm trying to see the connection among all of these systems.

MONITOR: Probably the connection or similarity among these systems involves the human personality's ability at this time to *grasp* three levels of consciousness. To describe consciousness in terms of, let us say, 144 levels, would simply overwhelm most human beings. We suggest that you be open to this: that *three* levels represents a teaching decision based on the teacher's estimate of the student's capability to comprehend. As the student becomes more capable, more elaborate descriptions of consciousness will be presented.

TIME

ARZANI: When you spoke of past lives as an experience of the subconscious mind, I've also heard the concept that all lives are happening at once, and that the past is only our perception because we live in time. I haven't been able to conceptualize what it would be like if everything happened at the same time, because in the models that have been explained to me we are learning and resolving more in each lifetime. Is this all happening at once? It doesn't make sense to me. Could you explain?

MONITOR: You raise the question of time, which is not yet well understood on the human level. A being's perception of time depends on the identity form it occupies. From the viewpoint of the Outer Self of a human being, which is based primarily on physical body structure, time has one definition. The Outer Self experiences time in the way that its physical body experiences it.

However, because the Outer Self is vitally connected with consciousness ranging all the way back to the Creator, the Outer Self may be capable of experiencing time as it is experienced by *other levels* of form, such as the expanse of time experienced by the subconscious mind or the superconscious mind or the Soul. Many of your "mystical experiences" of timelessness occur through the Outer Self's connection with higher levels of its Being.

A Soul experiences all of its embodied Outer Selves essentially at the same time. Let us provide a metaphor for understanding this. A tree experiences the functioning and Life of all of its roots and all of its leaves at the same time. For the tree, that is normal awareness. For the root, it is not. If it tapped into the *tree's* awareness, the root would be stressed, yet may enjoy the tree's awareness momentarily. Thus the Outer Self may enjoy the *Soul's* sense of time, but only for brief moments. Does this assist you at all?

ARZANI: I think I'll have to tap the tree to understand it!

MONITOR: We find no substitute for the experience. For example, from our perspective, which is a superconscious perspective, we can experience you in all of your lifetimes in a single moment. This is why those who develop higher awareness are able to tap past life experiences and even future experiences.

Do you have further questions or statements? Perhaps someone would like to express a point of view.

"EGO" AND "OGE"

DAVID: Could you elaborate on the personality and the unconscious mind and then explain why the ego state of consciousness is predominant, and why the unconscious is unable to more regularly manifest itself or take on a personality?

MONITOR: The term "ego" is quite interesting and one to which many people refer. We define *ego as the accumulated focus of physical embodiment in the subconscious mind which becomes impressed upon the Outer Self.* It represents, in large part, a type of *inertia.* Much of the structure of consciousness referred to as "ego" represents the fundamental needs to survive, be safe, etc. Ego, when described as an entity itself, is misleading because it is more appropriately described, from our point of view, as *a portion of the subconscious mind and a portion of the Outer Self.* The two aspects in many instances function independently, yet represent a common source of *resistance* to Life and extending one's identity into new areas of risk.

We suggest that you consider the term "Oge" *(pronounced oh-gee)* which is ego spelled backwards. The term "ego" has taken on a certain power, and we would like to suggest that its power be seen in perspective. "Oge" could be described as that force in the subconscious mind and Outer Self that seeks *progress*, the opposite of resistance to learning. Oge impels one to grow and seek new experiences, entertain risks, and express the essence of Life. Consider that concept.

SLEEP

MARGARET: At the beginning of your discourse about what happens between the time we go to bed and the time we wake up in the morning, the dream time or sleep time, you merely alluded to what happens during that period. Could you be more specific as to what really goes on during that time? Is it the same for everyone, or always the same for an individual?

MONITOR: During sleep, the Outer Self goes into some degree of dormancy, which is largely physiological. The Outer Self continues to function, but turns in a different direction than it normally faces when it consciously inhabits the body. If the Outer Self did not change direction, it would not sleep. Yet the body requires sleep. The forces of personality and Soul require that the "child" of their mating—the Outer Self—be dormant to different degrees.

Some persons suffer from insomnia, where the Outer Self goes dormant only to perhaps five percent. Persons who have deep sleep without dreams or any memory of what occurred during that time may achieve dormancy up to approximately ninety eight percent. The Outer Self needs to *release its control* for the benefit of the body so that the physiological process of regeneration may take place. The central nervous system must be temporarily deactivated, which allows the autonomic nervous system to perform its role in regeneration.

DREAM POSSIBILITIES

The dream state, which the Outer Self often experiences, consists of a variety of possible experiences. The dream state is mediated, one hundred percent of the time, through the subconscious mind, which never sleeps, nor does the superconscious mind. The superconscious mind assists the Outer Self in developing its capabilities and achieving access to wisdom. It assigns the subconscious mind the task of assisting the Outer Self in dream states.

Dreams at times consist of symbolic experiences that the Outer Self may recognize in its own mode of experience. In dreams, the Outer Self may see, hear, smell, taste, and feel things it recognizes. These experiences are supplied by the subconscious mind to enable the Outer Self to grow. At other times, the subconscious mind may propagandize the Outer Self, seeking to bring about certain alignments or develop certain desires in the Outer Self. This amounts to a form of manipulation that is quite common in human experience.

Since the subconscious mind strongly depends on the Outer Self for fulfillment of its subconscious goals, times occur when the subconscious mind has adventures which you term "out-of-body experiences," which means that the subconscious mind moves away from the physical body and encounters experiences in other levels of reality. On some occasions the subconscious mind intentionally shares such adventures with the Outer Self to see what the Outer Self will do with them. On other occasions the subconscious mind performs actions and intentionally does *not* share them, but somehow the Outer Self receives impressions about them.

Beyond these possibilities, the superconscious mind at times directly impresses experiences, symbolic or otherwise, upon the Outer Self during the dream state. In most cases, the Outer Self is deeply impressed. Such dreams appear vivid and clear. Occasionally the Soul impresses on the Outer Self dream experiences that have a similar quality to those produced by the superconscious mind.

POLARIZED VERSUS UNIFIED PERCEPTION

The Outer Self responds to an order established by the rotation of the planet, which provides alternating periods of light and darkness. It learns to function in terms of *polarized* actions, such as acting and then receiving. Polarized action forms the basis for the Outer Self's experiences and, to some extent, for the experiences of the subconscious mind as well.

The superconscious mind functions from a *unified* level of consciousness where polarization is resolved. So does the Soul. The Outer Self has difficulty recognizing the unified whole of experience and tends to relate more easily to experiences expressed in polarized form.

The Outer Self tends to see light and think in terms of light. It sees darkness and thinks in terms of darkness. It has difficulty conceiving of darkness and light at the same time. The lower portion of the subconscious mind *fears* this polarized quality of perception. The higher portion of the subconscious mind looks beyond the *polarization of perception* and quite easily sees light and darkness at the same time.

PARADOX IN DREAMS

Those who become spiritual Masters and yet communicate with physical human beings often talk in terms paradoxical to normal human polarized perception. Their use of *paradox* expresses a quality of unified perception. When the Outer Self in the dream state experiences paradox, the symbols in the dream experience make sense to the Outer Self *only* in the dream state. When it awakens, the dream symbols seem ridiculous and nonsensical. The Outer Self thinks, for example, "I was riding a purple cow into a supermarket? Now that makes no sense at all."

In such experiences the Outer Self is being challenged. Its perceptions are being deliberately stretched and reordered. Such experiences should be *sought*. A wise person might ride a purple cow into a supermarket!

As paradoxical experiences occur, the Outer Self gains a greater sense of confidence and allows itself a greater openness to consider different modes of perception. This attitude encourages the Outer Self to be more open for understanding.

This ability to remain open has been termed "negative capability" by the poet Keats, who recognized in the plays of Shakespeare an ability to entertain vastly different points of view. Negative capability is more appropriately considered as *positive capability,* for it represents growth of the Outer Self.

The Outer Self directly experiences alternating periods of being awake and then asleep, periods of activity and periods of oblivion. That oscillating sequence gives a particular rhythm to the Outer Self, giving it opportunity to *start fresh* each day and so help break the Outer Self from its tendency to remain the same.

CONTINUITY OF CONSCIOUSNESS

Consider the value of continuous experience, when the Outer Self becomes willing to accept its dream state experiences and consider them as real and important as its waking state experiences. The Outer Self who pursues this path achieves a continuity of consciousness and expands its ability to accept a wider range of experiences, including subconscious and superconscious experiences. The Outer Self, who actually achieves continuity of consciousness, learns its lessons at least one hundred times faster than the Outer Self still in broken consciousness.

Do you have any questions or comments?

JULIE: No. We thank you for sharing. You have given us much to think about.

MONITOR: We thank you for receiving us. We look forward to our next discussion.

We bless each one, and we leave you now.

> **TOOLS FOR EXPLORATION**
> Exercise 1

PERSONAL RESEARCH QUESTIONS

1. *Before* going to sleep at night, pay attention to your sense of awareness. Ask yourself these questions:

   "How do I feel physically?"
   "How do I feel emotionally?"
   "How do I feel mentally?"
   "How do I feel spiritually?"

2. *After* waking in the morning, pay attention to your sense of awareness. Repeat the same questions:

   "How do I feel physically?"
   "How do I feel emotionally?"
   "How do I feel mentally?"
   "How do I feel spiritually?"

3. Compare the answers describing your awareness *before* and *after* sleep.

   The most noticeable difference between the two times is:
   (Complete each of the following sentences)

   My awareness focused *more* upon these states:
   (Circle the words that apply)

   Physical   *Emotional*   *Mental*   *Spiritual*

   My awareness focused *less* upon these states:

   (Circle the words that apply)
   Physical   *Emotional*   *Mental*   *Spiritual*

4. I feel *most comfortable* describing these states:

   (Circle the words that apply)

Physical   *Emotional*   *Mental*   *Spiritual*

I feel *least* comfortable describing these states:

(Circle the words that apply)

Physical   *Emotional*   *Mental*   *Spiritual*

5. I have *learned* in doing this exercise that:

EVALUATING THE FIRST LESSON

An hour and a half later, the High Self returned me to the physical body still sitting in the chair. The body and chair felt hot. As I slid back into it, I felt hot. Perspiration ran down my back. Like a fading coal when the fire has gone out, the physical body glowed with residual energy from Monitor. The energy nourished the body, replenishing it so that it was not tired. Yet my arms and legs wanted to stretch, so I moved them while Julie completed the prayer for closure of the channeling. Opening my eyes, I found them slightly out of focus, and then I remembered the eyeglasses nearby. I had taken them off for the channeling.

Putting on the eyeglasses enabled me to notice that everyone in the room seemed sluggish. I took a drink of water to ease the dryness of my throat, then asked the group to share their experiences, thoughts, or opinions. One friend, Margaret, replied, "Wow! That's all I can say." The rest of the group laughed. I felt some concern—what did their reaction mean? What had happened while I was away?

Donna said, "Monitor talked like a college professor. Some of it I could follow, but other parts went over my head." Oh oh, maybe this new Teacher was like other channeled Teachers who spoke in vague generalities, avoiding specifics where they could be pinned down—so-called "teachers" like stereotype politicians who wanted to win votes by telling voters only what they wanted to hear. If Monitor was like that, I would need to confront my High Self about this new Teacher's qualifications. I did not want to sponsor that kind of channeling!

A third person spoke up, "Sure. Some of it went over our heads, but it made us look up into places we've never dreamed of. Now I want to learn more about it."

That sounded better, giving me some relief. I asked the group, "What stood out for you in Monitor's talk?"

A lady in back said, "Oh, their description of each individual's mind as a jewel with facets reflecting the Light of God. That image just sparkles. I can see it so clearly!"

"Yes," exclaimed the man next to her. "Just as each Soul is a facet of God, so is each personality a facet of its Soul."

Another woman vibrantly added, "And so is each Self a facet of the personality. The Light of God shines in all of the facets. We're like jewels embedded in jewels, aren't we?"

Their responses pleased me, since they had been deeply moved by Monitor. I asked the group, "Who else wants to share?"

One woman, who normally stayed quiet in group discussion, replied, "I simply couldn't stay awake." The man on the couch laughed, "You weren't the only one. At one time I noticed that half the group had their eyes closed. Maybe they were not asleep, but sure looked like it. I think the energy from Monitor became so intense that it put us into an altered state of consciousness."

"Yes," I said, "I couldn't stay awake either." We all laughed.

After more discussion, we realized that Monitor had not revealed much about themselves, so we agreed to ask questions about Monitor to start off next week. I felt better about the Lesson and looked forward to reviewing a typed transcript of it so that I also would know what had been said. Everyone left, perking up as they talked, and leaving Julie and me to clean up after the meeting.

As we put away chairs and picked up empty paper cups, Julie told me that she had been as zonked by Monitor's energy as anyone else. She had been sitting in a chair beside me during the channeling, so her energy field had strongly interacted with the field established by Monitor. To relax and ground ourselves, we watched the CNN news at ten. She was ready to sleep after the news, but I wasn't sure if I could. Yet sleep came easily despite the one and a half hours of trance.

WHO IS MONITOR?

The following Wednesday evening at seven we were ready with questions. Julie and I asked the group to formulate questions about Monitor and the on-going topic "Personality and Soul." When I slipped into the Light connection above my head, Monitor was already prepared for us.

Lesson 2
April 17, 1991

QUESTIONS ABOUT MONITOR

MONITOR: Welcome again. We come to you as Monitor.

MARGARET: Monitor, can you explain to us who you are? Are you a single being? A composite being? Where does your information come from?

JULIE: I also wanted to ask if you are willing to answer personal or individual questions about the topic of Soul and Personality.

MARGARET: And are you also willing to entertain a conversational format here, rather than a lecture format?

INITIAL DESCRIPTION OF MONITOR

MONITOR: Yes to all of the above.

We are a composite consisting of 153 individuals who are working on various levels to bring information and process it so that you may understand it in terms with which you are comfortable. Understand that part of the information is processed by you as energy, or energetic experiences. Consequently, it is of value for you to understand and note what you experience energetically during these times of sharing.

We apologize for what you considered our lengthy statements last time. We were, in that process, establishing a number of linkages within the people here and also within this area of time-space. A certain place may become sensitized or programmed for certain functions. We are programming this area, this place, for communication, a very rich form of communication.

We are individuals, yet we work together. We coordinate well because we are so closely matched in consciousness. Therefore, when one of us has a need, others sense it and help to fulfill the need for that individual.

Our sources of information consist of all of the sources that have been tapped through this kind of process for human beings throughout their history. That includes the so-called "Halls of Wisdom" or "Temples of Wisdom" which give access to references—the closest term in the human context is "books." Yet it also includes individuals, very wise Beings, whom at times we ask for information. Once you understand that, you can realize that it will be no difficulty for us to represent the views of various Teachers.

We promote the concept that *truth is a search, a journey that each being makes.* Each being learns, not just through mental perception, but also through *emotional perception*—what you call "material and spiritual perception." Therefore, the journey involves much more than hearing a lecture. It requires Life to experience itself. A being's perception of truth changes as the being itself changes.

Once again, we draw your attention to the flow of energy that is already underway within this group. As you notice how the energy affects you, you may wish to comment on it later. And if you have questions about it, we will be happy to respond to them on an individual basis.

Part of our information comes from what you call the "Akashic Records." We also find certain amounts of information already present in your own pools of wisdom and knowledge. So we retrieve the information requested from what appears to us as the best source. We check it or match it with what exists in your pools of knowledge. In that way, we can better translate what we have to present into appropriate words and energies. We translate them in ways that you are likely to accept. That doesn't mean that we will present only information that you *can* accept. You can tell that from the previous Lesson.

In that Lesson, we were attempting to stretch your minds, to get you to think in terms of certain types of structure that relate to personality and Soul and beyond. Each of you feels like you're connected to the Whole, at least at times. Even when you don't feel it, we can assure you that you *are*. As you explore that experience of connection within your own being, you can make discoveries.

ENCOURAGEMENT TO IMPROVE CONCEPTS

We made the statement that *knowing your personality represents the best way for you to become acquainted with your Soul.* So, how do you become acquainted with your personality? You notice yourself. You notice others. You observe and question. You have free access to such experiences; they are all present for you. But you encounter your greatest limitations in the ways that you *think* about those experiences. Your concepts of personality and Soul seem quite limited to us. Therefore, part of our purpose involves helping you consider other concepts with which you may interpret your experiences.

We assure you that each of you is free to arrive at your own conclusions. We have no desire to coerce. We enjoy encouraging you, but we're very aware that your development depends on the *clarity* of your own effort, the *clarity* of your own purposes, the *clarity* of your own motives. Human beings in this time have difficulty achieving such clarity because of inadequate concepts. They often confuse the structures and dynamics within their own beings and so fail to achieve the clarity that's possible.

We think we've said enough about this. Did we answer all of your questions?

MARGARET: I think so. I have some additional questions about who you are.

MONITOR: Go ahead.

FURTHER DESCRIPTION OF MONITOR

MARGARET: Of the 153 beings who work together, have you all at some time been humans on this planet? Are you human now, wherever you are? Do you also work with other groups like ours at other places around the planet?

MONITOR: Of our group, only 23 have *not* been in a human body. We utilize those who have been in the human body for those tasks that most require familiarity with human consciousness. We reach beyond the human kingdom, of course. Once you move beyond the narrow scope of the human kingdom, you realize that Life involves *the combination of several lines of evolution.*

All of the beings in all of the lines of evolution are ultimately required to work together in harmony and thereby achieve the Unity of Consciousness which allows all of Life to return to Oneness with the *Creator* of Life. And that becomes the gift that all of us may give to our Creator when we are *willing* to create that Unity.

We reach out to all of the different species or kingdoms of Life as we have need. We do not function solely with this group. As a highly trained team, we are engaged in a number of activities. We may not discuss all of them, but can indicate that we work through at least *four other channels* similar to this channel at this time.

Our activities are not limited to the physical plane. We function in *all* the planes and so are involved in activities virtually impossible to describe to you. You would not have enough reference to understand.

Did we answer your question?

MARGARET: Yes, you did. Have some of you, or all of you, completed your return journey back to the Source and then come back to us to do this, or are you somewhere along the way?

MONITOR: One hundred forty six (146) of us have completed our journey or, as you would say, "graduated" from the course of humanity. Several of us are still completing those tasks, and they comprise an important part of what we do.

Other questions? Comments?

DONNA: Are you all in the spirit world, or are some embodied presently?

MONITOR: We, of course, as all of you, *all* exist in the spirit world. What does not? We have three members physically embodied at this time, and those members are utilized in several ways. One of the most important ways they serve entails their ability to sleep at appropriate times. As they sleep, we may openly utilize the faculties of their subconscious minds to tap many different areas of awareness and knowledge throughout that level of the subconscious. These three members are positioned around the planet so that at least two of them are asleep at *this* time.

SHOCK WAVES IN CONSCIOUSNESS

MARGARET: What is it you tap from their subconscious?

MONITOR: It's difficult to describe. We monitor *currents* of consciousness, much as you might monitor the wind or breeze. These currents constantly change and shift. They do follow habitual routes, but at times move in unexpected directions.

Remember that each one of us, including everyone in this room, takes part in the whole of consciousness. We monitor in these ways to be alerted to what you might describe as "shock waves" that might be moving through some levels of consciousness.

An example of a shock wave would be the atrocities taking place in Iraq, Somalia, and Mali. The *pain* of one being radiates through the whole Planetary Being and even beyond. When beings such as you, or beings such as we, set aside our fears and become free to be as sensitive as we naturally are, we are subject to the shocking pain generated by the thoughtless cruelty that still permeates so much of humanity. So we monitor these currents and, when a shock wave is detected, take protective action to cushion the reactions of the channel and the rest of us involved. Our desire is that the information come across clearly. The shocks distract.

These kinds of "productions" are not undertaken lightly, as you can imagine. Much is accomplished in the total field of consciousness as these productions are achieved. Therefore we protect the channel, you, and ourselves, ensuring a degree of quality in our time together.

Other questions? *[Pause]*

PERSONALITY AND "EGO"

Let us ask *you* a question. What is a personality? Who would like to answer that? Is someone brave enough to respond?

LINDA: Possibly the lower self or the ego.

MONITOR: Ego?

LINDA: I don't know your term for it, but that's *my* term for it.

MONITOR: Yes, you see, new views of the personality are emerging, which is one of the most interesting aspects of humanity, because these views are really not that old in your time. They reflect your capacity for self-awareness.

The Psychopathology of Everyday Life, by Sigmund Freud, included in The Standard Edition of the Complete Psychological Works of Sigmund Freud, Hogarth, 1954.

The term "ego" was introduced by Sigmund Freud and perhaps has been more accepted as a term by people throughout the planet than the rest of his terms.[6] Yet ego accounts for only a *small* part of the personality, from our perspective. You are welcome to your own perspective!

Yet we find that ego is composed of part of the subconscious mind and part of the Outer Self, the *resistant* part of both levels of mind. *Ego wants to maintain the status quo* and therefore resists the changes that inevitably come. So ego is definitely worth knowing about inasmuch as it has importance as the *internal resistance* of the personality. Yet there's much more to find in the personality.

We appreciate your sharing that concept and we accept different points of view. Would someone like to share another point of view or another picture of the personality?

EGO AND JUDGE SELF

ARZANI: What is the ego as compared to the concept of the "Judge Self?"

MONITOR: The "Judge Self" concept is a very clever approach because it's difficult for the average human being to relate to ego. Ego is somehow vague and difficult to define in any given moment. The average human being, however, can notice his or her *resistance* in a given experience, but ego remains vague.

The "Judge" image allows one to relate to it as something alive, as something with whom you can *communicate*. It is more holistic or fulfilling, because it is more like Life itself, whereas the image of ego tends to be dehumanizing, tends to be like a material object, *a hunk of lead in the middle of the personality.* So we recommend the concept of a Judge Self as a better way for people to deal with resistance in themselves.

MARGARET: Are you saying then that the Judge Self is equivalent to the ego?

MONITOR: It largely overlaps what is meant by ego. Again, we may look at different definitions. Freud had his definition. *A Course in Miracles* has another definition, which, in our opinion, is more substantive than that offered by Freud.[7]

"OGE"

We introduced a term in our last conversation that involves taking the word "ego," spelling it backwards and calling it "Oge." *[pronounced oh-gee.]* We encourage you to be aware of the *resistance* within yourselves, of course.

A Course in Miracles, Foundation for Inner Peace, 1975. The Course includes a text, a workbook for students and a manual for teachers, all derived from the work of Helen Schucman and William Thetford.

Yet we urge you to be even more enthralled and thrilled with *the part of you that seeks to grow and to progress, which we call Oge.*

GIFTS AND TALENTS

JULIE: Would personality be, in part, our individual and unique use of our gifts and talents?

MONITOR: Well, in terms of individual expression of *being*, yes. That's a little loose in definition because it might also include a farmer plowing a field. The farmer would be using a gift. So we say, *using the gift of Life that is focused in and around your physical body,* as opposed to using machinery as a means of expression.

BODY AWARENESS

Much of your awareness is based on *physical* sensing. Only in the last, let's say, 1,100 years of human history have human beings become more comfortable in physical experience. Before that, many times they did *not* feel that they were truly there, or truly fit within physical experience. We have seen a strong resistance to accepting the physical body.

We encourage you to *accept your bodies, all of them, not just the physical.* You will learn a great deal about your other bodies as you learn about your physical body, because the physical body is patterned on the etheric, astral, and mental bodies, and the mental body is patterned on the causal body, which is also patterned on even higher bodies.

We talked about "identity forms" last time, which is a pretty abstract term. We distinguished between Life that is experiencing a body and Life that is not – in other words, the Life of "Spirit" which does not individuate and flows through the universe interacting with beings in forms. Since you occupy a physical body, you can experience your awareness of it, using your perceptual senses.

Now, when you are aware of your body, what do you notice?

MARGARET: How it feels.

MONITOR: How it feels and *how it functions.*

At this point in time human beings are still quite ignorant about the functions of their bodies. We see a growing movement, an emerging perspective that encourages human beings to understand the functioning of their bodies and learn how to help them function.

For example, Arzani has learned how to use visualization to stimulate her immune system. The immune system, for most persons, functions in whatever way it will. They have little conscious influence over it. Yet Arzani has learned how to stimulate her immune system. We see this as part of an encouraging trend because, as persons learn how to make their bodies function better, they automatically open up energetic pathways in their bodies and so achieve greater consciousness.

A *lie* has been perpetuated for hundreds of years that the physical body is bad, that it is somehow the opposite of Spirit, which is *good*. We think that's plain balderdash. It confuses many people.

We encourage you to explore your bodies, become aware of your bodies, really feel them. We find that most people don't even take the time to feel their bodies.

Your body is like a window to the universe. Your body remains as connected with the Creator as anything else. *If you want a telephone to call God, use your body.* It's already wired up!

It's a shame that so many people try to get out of their bodies, because they don't recognize the value of what they have. It's a *gift!*

AWARENESS BEYOND HABITS

ARZANI: I have a question about that. You mentioned the Course in Miracles. As I interpret it, the Course in Miracles says, "to get out of your body," and I wonder where is that coming from? Do you know the source of that information and why it gave that information?

MONITOR: The interpretation we prefer, to which you allude, is that it's saying, "Get out of your *habits*," because most of your habits remain subliminal to you. You're not always aware of them, and so they tend to run your lives. When you're functioning one hundred percent by habit, you're like a robot. Therefore, most systems promoting spiritual enlightenment give you ways to *break out* of your habits. And you become most aware of your habits by observing your physical habits.

Human beings, as yet, are just barely aware of their *astral* existence. They're still struggling with, "Are emotions real? Are desires real?" No one prominent has said yet, to our knowledge, "I *feel*, therefore I am!" We find a distrust, a widespread discomfort, yet in time it will be overcome. One of the reasons for this distrust is due to many traumatic experiences occurring to beings presently embodied in the *astral* plane.

As you identify your habits, you are more likely to identify first your *physical habits* – how you eat, how you exercise or fail to exercise, how you sleep, how you wake. All of those things are more easily recognizable for you. But the Course in Miracles puts emphasis on awareness of your *emotional* and *mental* habits. How better to get you started than to direct you in that way? Yet you'll notice that there's a great deal of focus on noticing your physical experience.

Does that address your question?

ARZANI: Well, I've finished *A Course in Miracles*, and I get very distressed when I read that my body is "not real" and those kinds of things, because I'm working so much on healing my body that I don't want to discount it. But you don't feel that it's harmful to work within "the Course"?

MONITOR: We understand why it was said that way. Somebody has to encourage the human beings, who are presently physically embodied, to move beyond their toothpaste, cereal, nail polish, and car. We find it important to focus attention beyond the body, yet believe that *the most natural pathway to focus attention* lies first in the *body*. In the physical body you have *all* of the energies present, *all* of the levels active through the causal level and beyond.

You need to learn how to identify your causal body by going *through* your physical body. Yet you need more concepts to consider. You need to be aware that such possibilities exist. If you don't know that such possibilities even exist, you might not credit them when you observe them.

WHAT IS A PERSONALITY?

What is a personality?

HELEN: It's the combination of the subconscious and the conscious minds working together.

MONITOR: We support a view that includes conscious and subconscious minds as two levels of one mind. How did we distinguish between them in our last discussion?

We talked about the Outer Self as being largely localized or identified with the physical body. When the physical body dies, the Outer Self shifts into a new kind of existence and is absorbed by the subconscious mind. This transition, by the way, is *not* an unpleasant process at all!

The subconscious mind is that mind which continues to exist through many physical bodies and which began its existence even before it inhabited a physical body. It will exist after its final physical body is laid to rest.

The interchange between the short-term focus of the Outer Self and the long-term focus of the subconscious mind is most important for human beings. When human beings are trapped in the concept that they *only live once,* they have very limited options for fun and freedom. If they realize that they *live as long as they need* to live, and then some, they have much more freedom and fun!

So the Outer Self and the subconscious mind represent two very important parts of the personality, but we would add a third, the *superconscious mind.*

The superconscious level of mind allows for organized growth. With the help provided by the superconscious mind, you *[indicating one person]* can grow, and you *[indicating another person]* can grow without destroying each other. If it was up to the limited consciousness of your Outer Selves, you would probably destroy each other. In some cases, if it was left up to your subconscious minds, you might still destroy each other. But with the *superconscious mind,* you are protected. True, sometimes some people's bodies are destroyed, yet that experience follows their plan of growth, and it occurs always with the consent of their superconscious mind.

If you look at all three levels of mind and include your Body Consciousness—the consciousness that exists within the cells, molecules, and atoms of your body—you have a complete set of elements for the human personality. Are you following us?

HELEN: You're saying that a personality consists of the subconscious, the conscious, the superconscious, and all the cells and atoms, etc., of the physical body?

MONITOR: That's right. Consider the personality as a "package" of consciousness, a group of vibratory, living *entities* who are held together by a purpose. Its purpose lies where the Soul comes in, because the personality wouldn't exist if it wasn't for meeting its Soul's needs. The glue that holds them all together is the *Soul,* yet the Soul amounts to more than glue. It has its own life, which you glimpse in visions and dreams. When you're at your most poetic, most expanded and lofty states, you get a sense of what your Soul is like everyday.

SOUL'S ENTRY AT BIRTH

JULIE: When does the Soul enter the physical body?

MONITOR: At varied times. The Soul enters the physical body through the subconscious and superconscious levels of mind, and that arrangement varies.

The superconscious mind surrounds the new physical body, even from the time that it consists of a single sperm and ovum. The superconscious mind may introduce the subconscious at any point after the moment of conception.

The superconscious mind must have established a specific relationship with the new physical body. You could call it "sponsorship" of the new body at the time of conception.

At the time of conception, a number of vibratory conditions happen to set the whole pattern for that body and its personality. The Soul of the incoming personality remains the strongest influence. The subconscious and superconscious minds comprise the next strongest influence. After that, the influence of the *mother,* and next the influence of the *father.* Lastly, the influences of *environment and heredity.*

The Soul enters at conception, but the body may not be fully endowed with mind until later, sometimes after birth. The subconscious mind is given free will and latitude within the boundaries of a plan of growth. The subconscious mind may willingly accept assignment into that new body. Yet, at other times, it may panic, reject it, and back out. By rejecting the assignment, the subconscious mind may compromise the body, either in terms of the body dying —if the Soul or superconscious mind decides that it is a lost cause—or the body may continue, but in a disabled state, mentally and physically disabled. In any event, the Soul benefits from the experience.

The Soul is experiencing this planet so that it may develop, grow, and contribute what it has to contribute to this planet. Some theories of the Soul portray it as somewhat selfish or self-centered, coming to this planet like a hummingbird comes to a flower to get what it wants and then departs. But we would like you to consider the Soul as being very *sensitive* to the interrelationship of all of Life. The Soul, in our view, comes as much to *contribute* to the planet as it does to *gain* from the planet.

So, the Soul enters at conception, but the full mind of that new person may not enter until even after birth and, in some cases, long after birth. Those cases may be considered autistic, insane, retarded, or some such category.

ABORTION

ARZANI: How does abortion fit in to this view?

MONITOR: What do you mean?

ARZANI: If a woman chooses to abort a child, is that part of the Soul's purpose, and she's acting from that? Or could she actually abort the plan of a Soul who meant to embody in this planet?

MONITOR: Yes, she *can* abort a plan of an incoming Soul. That degree of freedom is allowed. The mother has *an opportunity to accept* the incoming Soul and its plan. All of that plan is communicated to her telepathically, Soul to Soul and superconscious mind to superconscious mind.

The mother gains full awareness in her deeper being of the purpose of the incoming Soul who would be her child. She has freedom, on all levels of consciousness, to accept it or not. If she *accepts* it, she provides a unique act of service. Yet certain circumstances might indicate to her that it is not wise or prudent to have a child. Therefore, she has the right to seek abortion and deny the incoming Soul *its* opportunity.

The incoming Soul is *not* at a loss. It finds the next available satisfactory opportunity to enter physical form. Abortion, therefore, *does* involve removal of Soul. The incoming Soul knows what the mother is thinking and feeling. It is very aware.

The Soul accepts no *negative* experience into itself. It is so complete, so whole, that it accepts each experience as nourishing. So abortion does *not* place any undue handicap upon the Soul denied physical birth.

Are you following what we say?

JULIE: Is it just the personality that suffers, then?

MONITOR: The personality of the *mother* suffers, usually tremendously.

SUFFERING

JULIE: Or in *any* negative experience, it is the personality that does the suffering, but not the Soul?

MONITOR: Indeed, the Soul is always *satisfied.* The personality suffers, but we would clarify that *not all* of the personality suffers. The *superconscious mind* has achieved enough wholeness that it no longer suffers. It serves without suffering. The *subconscious mind* may suffer greatly, particularly in its lower aspects. And the body-mind or the Outer Self certainly suffers until it learns better.

HOW TO FIND YOUR SOUL

EILEEN: Can you describe what is meant by the Soul, and how we, as personalities, can bring the Soul into our lives?

MONITOR: We recommended last time that human beings can best approach their Soul through understanding their own personalities. Consider this statement in light of a simple analogy. If the Soul is like a human being and extends its hand into the water of a fishbowl to experience what is offered by the fishbowl, then the hand in the water is like a personality.

If you're a hand in water, you first need to become aware of yourself. Then you need to become aware of the role of a "hand" by observing what other hands do in those conditions. As you become aware, you realize that you're suspended somehow in the water. You don't know how you are suspended unless you extend awareness up your arm and into the rest of the body, which is analogous to the Soul. As you study yourself as a hand, you may discover that you have certain structural qualities that reflect the qualities of the Soul.

The *structure* of a personality reflects the structure of its Soul. It's not *exactly* the same, any more than a hand is exactly the same as the whole body. Yet the type of tissue, the chromosome structure, the DNA structure, would be the same in the hand as in any part of the body. The *signature of the Soul* is found in the personality.

Now, *how* does the hand extend awareness up the arm to the rest of the body? By thinking of itself as *more than a hand.* Simple, isn't it? If we don't take that step, we don't make it.

Are *you* more than a physical body? Yes, we hope so. Are you *more* than a set of emotions? Yes. Are you *more* than a mind that thinks erratically? Yes. You begin to understand the *structure* of your experiences – *how* you experience and *what* you experience. These steps enter new territory for human beings.

Much help is being provided throughout the planet to help human beings find *words* to express these kinds of observations—*the observations of self-awareness.* Yet we must counteract the absurd lie that *human beings are alone and isolated.* From our perspective, this statement has never been true, yet has been part of the experience of persons who *believe* that lie is true. Each person needs to realize that his/her act of *disconnection* creates the experience of isolation, and conversely, his/her act of *connection* establishes the truth that no one is ever alone.

So you may consider the idea that you have *structures in your consciousness* that you can objectively determine by examining your own personal experiences and the experiences of other persons. But you will also find confusions in human thinking patterns that make your interpretations wishy-washy and clarity difficult to achieve. This is one of the reasons why so many spiritual teachers emphasize meditation as a way to become clear, a way to know God. By the way, if you want to know God, you've got to know your *Soul* first.

A SOUL SEEMS LIKE GOD

To a human being the Soul seems like God. It appears vast and unlimited in power compared with the usual powers of a human being. When persons have what they call "God experiences," they are usually having *Soul* or *superconscious mind* experiences. Human beings, at this stage – and we apologize if this disappoints you – are not yet *able* to have God experiences, except as you consider that God participates in *all* experiences. Isn't God experiencing the experience through *you?*

If each human being remains connected to God directly by a stream of Life force, then you may regard yourself as God experiencing Life in the experience of a specific personality. You are never alone, yet you might *feel* alone. You feel alone because somehow you believe that you *are* alone. The pain of isolation eventually motivates you to seek beyond yourself and discover your *unbroken* connection with your Soul and, through your Soul, with God.

SEARCH FOR SELF UNDERSTANDING

So you begin by understanding what's going on in your personality. When you do things like explore yourself, you learn about your *structure* and your *functions* also. Consider your functions by asking, "What am I good for?"

Consider the question, "What are *you* living for?"

HELEN: Experiencing.

MONITOR: Experiencing. Exactly. That's a beautiful answer!

Human beings often load themselves down with all kinds of burdens: "We're here to save the world!" "We're gonna save the universe!" or "We're gonna save God!" or something that feels *heavy.* Well, that's very fine; but if you're here to experience *freedom,* you'll be a lot happier, and your Soul will be better nourished than if you're trudging through endless drudgery. Pursuit of freedom reveals your *constraints* – what restricts your freedom.

EXPANDING AWARENESS TO OUR SOUL

In seeking understanding of your personality, you seek *freedom.* In seeking freedom, you can *meditate* to expand your awareness, to build awareness of your physical being, your emotional being, your mental being, *and* your spiritual being. You learn that your spiritual being is intricately involved in all of the other dimensions of your being, yet you may recognize *it* only after exploring *them.* You learn that your spiritual being participates in your physical, emotional, and mental activities, yet exists in a higher level. In our analogy of the hand in the fishbowl, you discern that you are *not* the water, nor the fish, nor the fishbowl, but a hand placed into that setting by a greater being.

When you start being aware of your *spiritual* being, you're developing awareness of your *Soul.* In Earth, the Soul functions effectively *above* the level of mind. The arrangement may be different on other planets. In Earth you may be aware of something that is *not* mind, *not* emotion, and *not* the physical body.

Doesn't that sound paradoxical? You need to accept physical experience so you'll know what it is. When you know what it is, you can distinguish between physical experience and *non*physical experience. When you can tell the difference between them, you can realize more clearly where your *Life essence* resides. Do you find that you *are* your physical body, or are you something else? Do you discover that your Life essence resides somewhere else beyond the physical plane?

If you truly accept your emotional experience, you know what that is. You can distinguish between emotional experience and *spiritual* experience. At this point in human evolution we find that most people are confused about that point. They often confuse emotionality or sentimentality with spirituality. They go to church. They sing a beautiful song with tears in their eyes. They feel their heart expand, and they think that's a spiritual experience. Well, it might be, but they're responding to the *emotional* aspect of it.

We're not criticizing that. We're trying to give examples for you to understand what we're saying. The emotional experience is very important. As you become well aware of your emotions, you will be able to allow them to set you *free,* to go beyond them so that you can rise to a *higher* level of awareness.

Each of us has the gift of awareness. Our awareness can expand limitlessly. We can be aware of physical reality, emotional reality, mental reality, spiritual reality, Soul reality, and beyond. We can be *aware!*

Now we may not be able to talk about it in human language very well, because language has been very limited in those areas. Consequently, we have difficulty getting a clear interpretation of what we've experienced of the Soul. But we can assure you that, as you develop greater awareness of your Soul, it's essentially what you know as awareness of God. A sense of infinite mercy, infinite compassion, infinite power, infinite knowledge – these qualities all describe your Soul. That's what you *are,* and you're *even more* than that!

SOULS AND THE PLANETARY BEING

What seems infinite to you is focused on the level of planetary evolution and has much to do with the evolution of Planetary Consciousness – the single living Entity who animates a *world*. Souls come into a planet to experience, participate with, and contribute to that Planetary Being.

Your concept of Planetary Being has only recently been revived and will be a very important concept for you as *you* evolve. If you wish to contribute to your planet, *get to know your Soul* because your Soul will guide you to do exactly what is needed for the Planetary Being's benefit. You'll be guided. You'll do just what is helpful, automatically.

As human beings at this stage of development, you can be in contact with your Soul one moment and lose contact the next, which leaves you in a state of confusion. Keep trying to connect your awareness with your Soul. That's the essential path of growth we are suggesting. Every spiritual system or religious institution in this planet has, in some way, attempted to motivate people in that direction.

We've been talking for a while. We thank you for being with us again. We invite you to come back. We encourage you to come back because we'd like you to develop a deeper sense of understanding. And if you do come back, we can get more acquainted with each other, and understanding can develop. So we thank you very much.

EVALUATING THE SECOND LESSON

After the channeling, Julie and others filled me in on what they had learned about Monitor. It struck me as odd that we should attach such importance to the details of the form side of Life when the crucial factor lay in its essence. What difference did it make if the group called Monitor consisted of 153 or three individuals? In our commercialized society I could imagine a marketing war in which someone declared that a channeled source of 194 individuals was better than a source of 82 individuals. Did a larger group necessarily imply better quality of information? Not to me. Yet some people might see it that way.

What meant more to me than numbers was experiencing the energetic quality of the information source. I had encountered an impressive intelligence in Monitor. The highly refined quality and patterning of the Monitor energy field still impressed me. I had met it twice at the onset of channeling. The quality of light-gold energy that formed the core of the Monitor energy field reminded me of earlier encounters I had with Jesus and Mary whom I recognized as very highly evolved beings. Such an energetic quality instantly elicited a response of deep trust, even with one's life, because it radiated such pure Life itself. Its quality was unmistakable, like the feel of a gold coin.

Yet the practical demonstration of what we were doing in the Explorations Lessons lay in the information and how it was presented by Monitor. I asked the group, now stirring about after the channeling, "What were the highlights of the Lesson?" Many in the group still did not realize that I was not privy to the information shared. I did not know what had been said during the time of channeling.

Their greatest curiosity was aroused by the idea that three of Monitor's members were encased in physical bodies. That seemed intriguing. I found it fascinating to consider the idea of utilizing three persons in physical bodies located in different parts of the globe as sensors "monitoring" the field of consciousness for shock waves. Such a cautionary measure felt consistent with the quality of Monitor's actions.

No experiential exercise was given during this Lesson. In reading the transcript, Julie and I noticed that Monitor had made some provocative statements. I interpret some of them as follows:

> *To know our Soul, we must first know our personality.*

> *We may productively focus attention first on our physical body, learning about it and the subtle nonphysical energies that express through and around it, before seeking to focus attention beyond the physical body. We need our physical body to correlate with perceptions and measurements of our nonphysical bodies.*

> *Our personalities may be seen as "packages" of living nonphysical entities held together by the purposes of our Souls.*

> *These component "entities" comprise the superconscious and subconscious levels of our mind. Each of these levels of mind consists of Selves who have evolved through prior existence to this lifetime.*

> *The Soul invests itself in the physical body of a baby in successive stages from just before conception to later than birth. It invests itself through the subconscious and superconscious levels of mind. The superconscious mind invests itself first by bringing the sperm and ovum together. The subconscious mind invests itself later, bringing a full investment of the Soul into the baby.*

> *Even after the superconscious mind has started the process of conception and gestation, the subconscious mind may in some*

cases panic and back out, causing death to the baby. If this happens early, a miscarriage results. Following birth, the baby may die from known or unknown physical causes.

In some instances where the subconscious mind does not wish to invest itself in the baby, the superconscious mind keeps the physical body alive, but its mental development lags. The subconscious mind is encouraged to enter, but if it continues to refuse the opportunity, the superconscious mind or Soul may release the physical body through death and seek another physical conception.

A mother who chooses abortion has freedom to accept the baby or not. If she decides in favor of birth, she provides a unique act of service to the incoming Soul. If she decides to have an abortion, she has the right to deny that opportunity for birth to the incoming Soul. The incoming Soul is not at a loss if the prospective mother removes its opportunity. It merely finds the next available opportunity, which can be with the same or a different mother.

Abortion involves removal of the beginning investment of the incoming Soul and its superconscious mind, but not its full investment, because the subconscious mind usually delays entering the baby until the mother makes her decision.

We tend to interpret our mystical experiences as perceptions of God, when they usually involve perceptions of the Soul or superconscious mind of our own personality.

Our Souls look like God to us, because they exhibit infinite mercy, compassion, power, and awareness. Yet God, the Creator of the universe, exists on a vastly greater scope. When we gain Soul awareness, we achieve a more realistic view of God.

Our Souls invest themselves in Earth for two purposes: (1) To assist in the evolution of the Planetary Being of Earth; and (2) To evolve themselves.

When we, as personalities, grow closer to our Souls, we learn to express their qualities of mercy, compassion, power, and sensitivity in meeting the needs of all forms of Life in Earth.

Monitor said that they intended to stimulate our thinking. By furnishing us with definite, provocative statements and asking us to consider crucial questions, they had certainly stimulated us!

Lesson 3
April 24, 1991

WELCOME

MONITOR: We come again as Monitor. We welcome you all! We've enjoyed our exchanges. We especially appreciate any questions you have that we might address. Yet we invite the rest of you, who hear the question, to consider *your* answers as well. From our perspective, we are all evolving beings, all children of the Creator, and so we *all* have something worthy of sharing. We view Creation as a process happening in every moment, and so we especially value what you have to offer.

SUBCONSCIOUS MIND AS SOUL PROJECTION

MARGARET: Last week and the week before, you described the subconscious mind as the repository of experiences from past lives. Yet some viewpoints describe the subconscious mind as being a blank page, empty and waiting for us to write upon it. How do these two concepts correlate with each other?

MONITOR: We appreciate your contrasting these different points of view. In jest, we say that those who view the subconscious mind as a blank page have not yet learned how to read!

In our view, the subconscious mind is most appropriately described as the aspect of the embodied personality that goes beyond the boundary of any single embodiment or lifetime. It evolves through Earth experience on behalf of the Soul. The Soul is able to experience Earth through this projection of itself, which functions much as a robot or a space probe, an intelligent extension of the Soul.

The Soul is unable to place its wholeness, its fullness, into the polarized vibrations of the lower planes of Earth and must *project* itself as a polarized extension. The subconscious mind becomes the continuous part of that projection, maintaining from one lifetime to another.

Those who say that the subconscious mind is like a blank page are actually considering the "conscious mind" or "Outer Self." We see the Outer Self as beginning as a blank page within the womb. We ascribe that viewpoint to the conscious mind, not the subconscious.

Further, the subconscious mind amounts to *more* than the repository of various lifetimes or embodiments, since Subconscious Selves have experience in planes of existence other than physical embodiment.

When a human being is born, the Soul has chosen to embody. Its projection, the subconscious mind, enters the fertilized egg and animates it by impregnating it with energies or codes which unfold throughout that lifetime. This energetic imprinting creates the special shape and purpose of that lifetime, which is, after all, for the benefit of the Soul and the Planetary Being.

So when you approach your subconscious mind, we urge you to use respect because the subconscious mind of your personality has much greater experience than *you,* the Outer Self.

Now this presents a difficult consideration for some Outer Selves because they wish to perceive themselves as *the* center of power, awareness, and purpose of the personality. While such desires are noteworthy and have some practical value, the Outer Self remains rather limited in its abilities. It may, nevertheless, serve as *coordinator* for many activities, linking different aspects of the subconscious mind with each other and with the superconscious mind.

We find a number of divisions in the subconscious mind, much as you would find a number of petals in a rose. However, the subconscious mind functions as *a whole being* in terms of Soul experience.

The Soul is a whole being, much in the way that you sense that God is a whole being. You have experiences of *wholeness,* of mystical unity, which give you evidence of the nature of God. Such experiences also reveal the nature of the Soul.

The subconscious mind *reflects* the wholeness of the Soul. How do you, as a personality, know when you contact and experience your Soul? You know you have Soul contact when you have the unmistakable feeling of Wholeness, Oneness, and a sense of expanded being that has room for all your experiences and then some.

Soul contact can be much more complex than that, but this constitutes a point which is relevant to most of you. You achieve Soul contact through your subconscious mind's linkage with your High Self who, in turn, links with your Soul. Consider your subconscious mind not as a blank page, but as an evolving image of your Soul.

Did we answer your question?

ASTROLOGY AND PAST LIVES

MARGARET: Yes, you did. In our system of astrology, a person's moon sign is said to relate to the subconscious mind and the working out of past life experiences. Can you comment on how we, as individuals, can use our knowledge of that to help us work out karmic patterns from past lifetimes?

MONITOR: Indeed, because Life development in Earth and other planets is composed of vibratory energies, you may consider the analogy of a *pool* of water as a way to understand how these vibratory energies operate in individual lives and connect one lifetime with another.

In one lifetime, let us say, you create certain waves. Some of those waves radiate out, strike the nearer shore, and rebound during that lifetime. Other waves take longer to strike the distant shore and return. They may return in a later lifetime. But all is conditioned on the vibratory balance of the pool. The Earth itself, as a living entity, is such a pool of energy. What is created by any single expression of Life affects all of Life in that pool or *planetary energy system.*

The relative positions of planets and stars create vibratory effects in Earth's energy field. When you are embodied in that field on a physical level, you are subject to that type of effect or "coding." The various bodies of a person receive an energetic impact from a veritable symphony of vibratory forces emanated by the changing positions of planets and stars. A person's bodies are *coded* by the emanations of individual planets and stars and also by their combinations. The coding of Jupiter and the coding of Leo constitute examples of this.

Just as a code entered into a computer causes the computer to take certain actions, astrological codes predispose persons to take certain actions. The coding of Jupiter brings a specific range of influences or tendencies. The coding of other planets brings other characteristic influences. These influences may be observed by detailed study over long periods of time.

Your astrology is evolving into a viable system that has a more scientific basis. Astrologers need sufficient time and aware experience to refine the system by observations. So astrology is unfolding in the physical plane. In the other planes of Earth, astrology applies just as well and is practiced at even higher levels of competence. It is only a matter of time until, in the physical plane, it becomes a very precise tool.

Astrological influences continue to affect a personality, whether they are embodied in the physical, etheric, astral, or mental planes. The vibratory codings are continuous. When a personality leaves the physical plane and later returns to it by birth again, its timing is carefully chosen to provide those vibratory conditions compatible with the vibratory conditions of the ending of an earlier lifetime, from where the same lessons are continued.

Let us say that Margaret has a lifetime in Rome, 2nd Century AD, with the name of Marcellus. In that lifetime Marcellus died on August 17th. The astrological vibrations are noted at death to allow for continuation of the energy patterns of that lifetime. Five lifetimes later, Margaret's Soul decides that it will re-embody as Margaret in the 20th Century. It decides that what was left unfinished in the lifetime of Marcellus needs to be continued and possibly completed in the lifetime of Margaret. The Soul chooses a birth time on or close to August 17th. It might not be the exact date, but a date that matches relevant astrological vibratory patterns of the August 17th on which Marcellus died. In that way, vibratory conditions may be continued to permit continuous learning of lessons, but not necessarily from lifetime one to lifetime two. Many times a Soul skips several lifetimes before it continues a lesson or a theme again.

SOUL'S PROGRESSION OF LESSONS IN DIFFERENT LIFETIMES

The Soul uses a process that can best be explained by the metaphor of weaving a braid consisting of several strands. In that braid of interweaving themes, a Soul may best evolve in overcoming the growing resistance expressed by the Subconscious and Outer Selves of its embodiments. The resistance may be appropriately termed "Ego." So the Soul may develop other directions of development that affect the subconscious mind and allow it to overcome the resistance it has built up regarding a specific course of learning.

Let us say that Margaret's subconscious mind has resisted learning lessons of power. The gladiator, Marcellus, used power and understood it in limited terms. The subconscious mind of Marcellus resisted a broader definition of power. By waiting five lifetimes and developing other themes, other competencies such as Love and fellowship, the attitude toward power from the time of Marcellus can be modified. Then, as the Soul reintroduces the theme of power in the lifetime of Margaret, the subconscious mind becomes much more receptive to change and learning advanced lessons of power.

A FURTHER DESCRIPTION OF THE MONITOR GROUP

JULIE: If we may change direction, Monitor, you mentioned there were several individuals in your group who were unembodied. Are they angels?

MONITOR: Some are, some are not.

HELEN: As a follow-up on that, what are they, if they have never embodied and are not angels?

MONITOR: They are Souls. Within the structure of planet Earth, Souls come both to observe and participate. As they chose to participate, they can enter activities in the causal plane, which do not require entanglement in the Earth's karmic plan. They simply assist the plan *from the outside,* so to speak.

Many such beings assist in the Earth's evolutionary process. Some of them, known as *Buddhas,* come to share the radiance which they have the capability of sharing. They share it in an appropriate way that the beings of Earth may best accept. Much of their focus lies not on individual human, devic, or elemental beings, but on the Planetary Being. In a sense, they come as midwives or healers to assist the evolution of the Planetary Being. They function on appropriate levels of consciousness and act from beyond the Soul level. They function from the Monad level.

Souls who participate in Earth have the opportunity to embody in the mental, astral, etheric, and physical planes. Once they embody in a particular plane, they remain there for a course of learning. Souls who enter Earth understand that their involvement will take what, to a personality, seems like *eternity,* but to the Soul seems like an experience of intensity. Since the Soul experiences all of human time simultaneously, *intensity* offers perhaps the best way to describe the Soul's experience.

THREE PHYSICALLY EMBODIED MEMBERS OF MONITOR

JULIE: Are the physically embodied three beings in the pool known as Monitor aware that they are part of Monitor?

MONITOR: Not on a conscious mind level. Subconsciously and on the Soul level, indeed, they cooperate fully with the plan. Having that knowledge in their Outer Selves would be counterproductive for accomplishment of their plans. We wish you to know, moreover, that *some of you* in this room function in a similar fashion for different groups.

Souls work *in groups* more than they work individually for the benefit of Planetary Consciousness.

GROUP WORK ON SOUL AND PERSONALITY LEVELS

When their evolution began, human beings were quite group-oriented, but oriented in the sense of *animal herd instinct.* Development of *individualized* human consciousness took a considerable portion of human history to accomplish. It was achieved in the later portions of the civilization of Ibez and the earlier portions of the civilization of Mu. The process of refining individualized consciousness was pursued until 1400 AD, when it moved to extremes and was redirected towards *individualized group consciousness.* This present tendency toward individualized group consciousness gives you ability to create a more highly articulated consciousness in a group.

In contrast with the group consciousness of early Mu, you are much more capable of thinking of diversities, interweaving different ideas and approaches as you work together as a group. In the early times of Mu that was not possible. Individuals then came together with little ability to think *independently.* They depended on the guidance of a higher Spirit to direct their activities. Most often, one personality emerged as a leader, with the rest of the group as followers.

That pattern often worked quite harmoniously. But, at the present stage of human evolution, it is no longer possible nor desirable, since individuals have reached the development of *interdependence.* Each personality is now able to reach to its Soul and beyond, to bring Soul radiance through it, and to share it on the human level, building *world consciousness.*

The collaboration of personalities requires individual choices. Therefore you find only relatively small-sized organizations promoting collaborative activities. It would be paradoxical at this stage of human evolution to find a large-sized organization promoting interdependent activities.

MARGARET: Monitor, I had a realization of what you are talking about. On a trip to South America I was traveling through high country and noticing that farmers there were farming in much the same way that they had farmed for centuries. They did it because they didn't know what else to do. In our country some people are starting to return to the land after living in cities, but now they make a conscious choice to go back to the land. Yet the people in South America aren't there out of a conscious choice. They seem to be operating from instinct. Is this an example of what you mean?

INTUITIVE GUIDANCE

MONITOR: Exactly. Psychology describes the process as *moving from animal instinct to intelligence.* From our perspective, present human intelligence constitutes a temporary phase since it is largely ego-based. A great benefit will occur when it perishes. Intuition will replace the present type of intelligence and be vastly superior, since *intuition functions through Soul contact.* As more of you become activated by intuition, the word "intuition" will be differentiated into approximately 200 separate actions, for which you now lack words.

Your Soul is keenly aware of its context, its environment composed of all the Life forms throughout the planet. If you receive its intuitive guidance, you are guided to live in a way that is of maximum benefit to the whole of consciousness of the planet. An individual *without* Soul contact acts in ways harmful to the planet. The learning involved in transitioning from disconnected intellect to Soul-connected intuition entails the pursuit of various purposes and then discovery of the limitations of those purposes. Purposes realized by intellect are, of necessity, limited and will eventually phase out of human evolution to be replaced by purposes activated through the Soul's intuitive processes.

When you examine those persons who, in historical perspective, have made the greatest contributions to the benefit of Planetary Consciousness, you find examples to use in examining intuitive processes. On the other hand, many persons who are presently valued as making historical contributions have functioned through intellect to a greater degree. In a later time their contributions will appear diminished. For example, the inventor of the gasoline engine will be seen as making an apparently positive contribution that, due to limited consciousness, led to widespread pollution. The idea was karmically proper, yet *not* for the benefit of the entire planet.

You will find that the contributions of those who selflessly assist others are, for the most part, intuitively guided. We do not speak here of those who are codependent or neurotic in their roles of helping and healing others. We speak of those who work with genuine intuitive guidance and who are clear enough to receive it.

Are there questions?

SOUL-INFUSED PERSONALITY

JULIE: Some of things you've just said may apply to the next question: Will you describe a "Soul-infused personality?"

MONITOR: How would you recognize a person who not only is in close contact with his/her Soul, but also activated by his/her Soul? What would he/she look like? How would he/she function?

A description of a Soul-infused personality depends on the context in which the Soul is embodied. At this point in time, most Soul-infused personalities remain unknown, working anonymously for the maximum benefit of Planetary Consciousness. They function with intuitive guidance and generally stay quiet. They do not seek fame, glory, power, or money.

They have left those illusions behind. They function in an extremely sensitive way to those around them and those throughout the planet.

When they are awake, they function in an Outer Self mode and interact with other people and creatures. They are largely unassuming, but may, on occasion, exhibit the power of Soul when the Soul chooses, not when the personality chooses.

An example of this situation may be found in the prophet Elijah, as written in the *Bible*. Elijah, as a Soul embodied in a personality that was quite advanced for its time, challenged the 400 priests of Baal and the wicked queen Jezebel to a showdown of "which God was the true God?" In that demonstration, the one man, Elijah, was allowed to demonstrate the power of his *Soul*, which in his awareness seemed to be the power of the unnamable God, the One God. And in that circumstance, he outpowered the 400 priests of Baal.

Elijah's personality became destabilized by that expression of power and went about chopping off the heads of the 400 priests of Baal, which was *not* an action of his Soul or his God. It was the action of the personality – to be more specific, the Mental Judge Self of Elijah. Then, as a personality in other embodiments, he was required to suffer and realize how insensitive his action had been. Does this illustrate an example of the power of the Soul? We believe it does. Does it to you?

A Soul uses its abilities to *benefit all of Life*. So the power of the Soul may affect the weather, bring healing, or change the fertility of the soil and seed. It may influence devic, elemental, and angelic beings, and even what you term "extraterrestrial" beings. A Soul exercises its powers with utmost sensitivity to the benefit of the entire consciousness of the planet.

Some personalities, who act as shamans, magicians, or sorcerers, may perform some of these acts occasionally. Some of these people may function at a Soul level, while others do not. Those who function at a Soul level are able to perform their acts of power as their *Soul* chooses to act.

Those who perform such feats with less power and consistency function with higher powers of mind—what their subconscious mind is able to accomplish—but do not necessarily act on behalf of their Soul. *Soul-activated sorcerers* produce nothing but benefit, while personality- or subconscious mind-activated sorcerers may produce great damage.

Consider the implications, then, of a personality and how it connects with its Soul. Consider the implications for your planet.

Questions?

EXPERIENCE OF WHOLENESS

TODD: When a personality fuses with its Soul and has the experience of wholeness which you spoke of earlier, is that the same experience universally when *any* being experiences its wholeness, or does each Soul experience its wholeness in a different way?

MONITOR: The experience of wholeness is similar to striking the key of Middle C on a million different pianos. Each manifests in the key of C, yet each piano produces its own unique situation and quality. Does this answer your question?

TODD: Yes, and I have one more. Would the Soul striking the key of C experience itself as *all* of the middle Cs on *all* of the pianos?

MONITOR: It may, but not initially. Because a *resonant* phenomenon takes place between a personality and its Soul, that particular *connection* gains precedence. Once the resonance has stabilized within its personality, a Soul – and even the personality, to the degree in which it is capable – may experience the resonance of its union with other Souls.

Does this answer your question?

TODD: Would it experience that resonance as *itself*?

MONITOR: As a wave in the pond. The wave is not separate from the pond, yet holds its unique position.

TODD: Okay.

FEARLESSNESS

ARZANI: I have a question about fearlessness. In my own experience, the only time I can experience fearlessness is when I feel connected with my Soul, because I believe that the Soul doesn't carry experiences of fear from other lifetimes. I wonder if there are other kinds of fearlessness that are not dependent on Soul contact. For example, would a war hero experiencing fearlessness be in a Soul state, or is there another state of fearlessness besides the Soul experience?

MONITOR: We would say first that what you describe as your own experiences are true instances of Soul contact. We affirm what you have said, that the Soul does *not* directly experience fear.

In the case of the war hero, it may be Soul contact or an altered state of consciousness in which the subconscious mind dominates the conscious mind or Outer Self. Remember that the subconscious mind may be aware that it is virtually indestructible. The war hero may tap the subconscious mind, which is aware that it does not perish with the death of the body and therefore exhibits fearlessness. It is even possible that if the subconscious mind is sufficiently clear, the hero may tap the superconscious mind, the High Self part of his being, which is beyond fear, as is the Soul.

Soul contact is not always the cause of fearlessness. However, approximately 90% of it derives from Soul contact, because the subconscious minds of human beings are generally too prone to fear at this time.

PLANETARY TRANSITION AND FEAR RELEASES

At this time of transition, the Planetary Consciousness is moving into a sudden change, a realization, in which its pulsation and distribution of force will be reorganized for the better. It will provide a much clearer context for human development.

In the present time, which leads to those changes, a great deal of fear is purposely being forced to the surface. The Hierarchy definitely promotes the expression of fear throughout humanity and at times throughout the elemental and devic kingdoms. Fears must be released, even though the process seems quite distressful, in order to produce sufficient purification so that the Higher Consciousness, soon to enter in obvious ways to your world, may clearly manifest.

As the Higher Consciousness enters, those beings who express fear will experience energetic reactions equivalent to being set on fire. Much work will be done by various individuals qualified to work with what we may describe as "Divine Fire," or "Soul Fire," which is a particular form of Higher Consciousness transmitted from the Soul to and through the personality which may be used to *burn off* their fears. That process will not be accessible to all human beings. It will be limited only to those whom the Hierarchy deems ready. But understand that in these times you *are* experiencing greater amounts of fear than at any previous time in human development.

Questions?

THE "11/11" EVENT ON JANUARY 11, 1992

ERMA: Does this have anything to do with the "11/11," January 11th of 1992, and the crop circles in England?

MONITOR: It does, but we would note that this date in '92 represents but one step of a series of steps leading to a major shift of consciousness within the Planetary Being. What you refer to relates to those activities from beings of higher dimensions, those you term "outerspacial beings" who assist in the purification process. Do you follow us?

ERMA: Yes, thank you.

MONITOR: Thank you!

PERSONALITY AND SOUL CONNECTION

JULIE: One of the questions we have is "How did we manage to get so disconnected, and did we ever have a mind-body connection?"

MONITOR: The mind and body have *always* been connected. The difficulty has been in the personality's achieving sufficient quiet, stillness, order, and patterning to connect with its Soul. The personality has never been separated from its Soul. Being separated would mean its extinction, which is simply not done.

The personality is connected to its Soul by an energetic bridge, which we call the "sutratma" or "lifeline," that is always present to the personality. Yet the personality must be sufficiently still, clear, and organized to allow the sutratma to bring comprehensible vibrations from the Soul.

The practice of meditation has been of great assistance in clearing the channel between personality and Soul. Yet meditation *alone* is not sufficient in most instances, since the personality must be fully activated, fully involved, fully alive, fully *at risk* to be sufficiently patterned for openness to its Soul. In other words, one must walk one's talk. One must live what one conceives. Only thinking or feeling is *not* sufficient to manifest Soul through the personality.

SEXUAL ABUSE

JULIE: Another question along another line is "Why is there so much sexual abuse at this time?"

MONITOR: We find that the increase in sexual abuse at this time is due to extremely fragmented social forms of separating feeling from thinking, separating awareness of the body from cognitive thinking. The fragmentation of European culture, carried into the American and Latin American cultures, has provided ingredients for increased violence.

Sexual expression represents a fundamental desire for *Life,* for the expansion and continuation of Life. It also represents the *celebration* of Life when a person is open to be as intimate with another person as it may be with its Soul.

During this era, the amount of stimulated fears has complicated the situation and produced a *greater incidence of sexual abuse* in this time than since the time of the Roman Empire.

TODD: Could you clarify the point you were trying to make about the separation of the cognitive and the feeling? What process would mend that, what would bring it to its whole state?

MONITOR: Fragmentation of the personality is overcome by enabling it to extend its awareness of itself so that it may begin to grasp more of its totality, more of its wholeness.

An example of fragmentation is a businessman who has clear objectives for business, status, power, and the like, yet who knows *not* his own feelings. His feelings accumulate and emerge in impulsive acts that are quite irrational. The businessman may be frozen in a *male* mode and most likely releases his emotional accumulation when dealing with females, who represent the opposite polarity that the male needs in order to achieve a sense of wholeness. Therefore, sexual abuse occurs. And once it has, it may easily become habitual because the man has not learned how to unify *himself.* He is trapped in fragmentation.

Appropriate assistance to such a person allows him to explore awareness of his body sensations, that he may *feel* and experience all that his body does. Thus he may allow perception to flow instead of blocking it with rigid patterns of thought. Cognitive thoughts are particularly fragmenting, since man's intellect is capable of operating in circles. So those who are very cognitively organized are often the most fragmented.

Does this begin to answer your question?

TODD: Yes, it does.

MONITOR: Once a person explores the feelings of his body, he begins to change the structure of his mind. We have said before that the body is one of the best places to begin to understand the personality, and that the personality is the best place to begin to understand the Soul. The Soul manifests within the body as well as the mind.

TODD: So your suggestion for a sexually abusive person is that by accepting more of his feelings, they would be more integrated into him rather than projected out and acted out impulsively and abusively.

MONITOR: Indeed. He will feel his impulses and understand them. He does *not* need to project them outside of himself, which is done as an act of *fear* in an attempt to retreat or run away from the impulses.

TODD: Does the rejection of sexuality, as was done in the Victorian Age, contribute to the increase in sexual abuse?

MONITOR: Absolutely. It is of that and similar trends we speak.

ARZANI: For the woman who has been abused as a child, do you have some advice on how to help her with her healing?

MONITOR: Indeed. It is much the same as we have just recommended, that she observe her body, experience her body, its sensations of pleasure and discomfort. That she find, within her body, sufficient *space* for allowing the memories of trauma to emerge. As they emerge, they may be released. If they do not emerge, they remain embedded or encoded. Seeking wholeness in her experience necessitates body awareness.

Let us indicate what we mean.

BODY AWARENESS OR HEALING BY SOUL INFUSION

We invite you now to pay attention to your left foot. Extend your awareness and focus it in your left foot. How much awareness do you have of your left foot? Do you feel sensations of warmth and coolness? Do you feel sensations of pressure? Do you feel sensations of pulsing as your blood circulates? Do you feel the movement of cells within your foot? Or do you consider your foot as being stationary and solid? We assure you it is not.

As you put your attention into your left foot, you become aware of how little awareness you have, at first. As you repeat this exercise a number of times, you become aware of each of your toes, which you may not now be capable of doing. You may also become aware of various other parts of your foot, ranging from external skin to internal tissue. Potentially, you have awareness of every cell in your foot.

Now consider that this exercise puts you in a position analogous to that of your Soul, who attempts to bring sufficient awareness into the personality until it can resonate with the Soul and so allow the Soul to have full awareness *through* the personality. You could describe the outcome of this exercise, if you carried it to its conclusion, as having a personality-infused left foot, much as we describe a Soul-infused personality.

Do you understand now that the personality's *awareness* gives the Soul *access* to the personality? If your foot totally ignored its connection with the rest of your body, it would leave you quite crippled. And indeed, many humans experience crippled bodies as a means of helping them become aware of how they need to be *responsive* to their Souls.

You, as a personality, may best encourage the growth of consciousness in your left foot by focusing on it, bringing your Life essence into manifestation there, and being so aware of it that your left foot enhances its consciousness and seeks its source.

In this exercise, you find a give and take. Soul must initiate the process, and personality must respond. As a personality gains sufficient ability to be aware of itself, it is directed toward its Source.

Consider the cells in the left foot to be antennae capable of receiving signals. At first they point in all directions, picking up signals, Life impulses from all sources. Only a few antennae are directed toward the personality, and so they respond only slightly to the personality's awareness and desires. Through evolution, as the cells redirect themselves toward the personality, like antennae pointing toward it, they respond to *its* desires.

As we advance this analogy, you can see that you, as a personality, become more directed towards your Source, your Soul, so that you may respond to your Soul's desires. Your responsiveness increases, degree by degree, until your personality and Soul unite, and the lesser form of the personality is subsumed within the greater form of the Soul. And lest you be concerned that something is lost in the process, we assure you that it is a most glorious experience, where nothing essential is lost.

MARGARET: What would it be like to continue that process of infusing different parts of the body with personality consciousness? Could we eventually create that same sort of unity between the mind and the body that we seek to create between personality and Soul? And if we could create that kind of unity, how would it express itself?

MONITOR: As greater and greater awareness of what is going on within the body and the mind. You cannot have one without the other. Some persons explore development of body consciousness and, in so doing, develop their minds. Others explore the nooks and crannies of their minds and are ultimately led back into body consciousness. The astral body, the mental body, and all of your bodies become more known, accessible, and increasingly subject to the intentional control of the personality. You describe such a process as "mastery."

Did we answer your question?

MARGARET: Yes. Last week you talked about Arzani having control of her immune system. So it's this kind of example expanded to the entire body, that's the state we could achieve?

MONITOR: Indeed. For example, you are challenged with the healing of your eyes. In that challenge, you have opportunity to open intentional awareness of the consciousness of your eyes, which includes the eyes as a total mechanism and their components. As you gain that awareness, you gain greater capability of generating healthy tissues and balanced function within your eyes.

You are being motivated to such a course of learning by your High Self. Realize that you may find as much of your Soul within your eyes as you find within a sacred text. It is a matter of opening your awareness.

Have we become a little heavy?

[The group laughs.]

BIRTH

JULIE: Here's a quickie question. "Why does birth hurt?"

MONITOR: Because it represents the lesser option. In the formulation of the human race, people were given the option to manifest other beings, which you know as "babies," through the act of creation as it is practiced in the higher planes of existence. And indeed, that did occur for a time. But the presence of fear led to a shutting down of those capabilities associated with androgynous being. As human capability for androgynous being diminished, the lesser option became the common practice, which involves physical birthing.

In the first wave of Souls embodied in Earth, beings were materialized in adult form. Later, the concept of having babies was adapted from the elemental kingdom and utilized as the last option for human beings.

The birth of a baby is still complicated by the presence of fear, which increases the experience of pain for both mother and child. As human beings learn to give birth *free of fear,* maintaining a presence of radiant Love, pain is greatly reduced. Yet physical birth always involves some amount of pain. As human beings evolve to spiritual mastery, the process of physical birth is no longer needed. That change depends upon humans' ability to manifest androgynous consciousness once again.

JULIE: Is there anything you would like to add before we close?

SOUL-GENERATED DREAMS

MONITOR: Yes, we challenge you all to dream tonight. Of course, you *will* dream, but we challenge you to ask that your dreams be guided by your *Souls* and that you be assisted to *remember* your dreams. This is a practice not in current usage, but was used in ancient cultures such as Egypt, the Minoan civilization, and areas of ancient Greece. Soul-generated dreams will give you much of value.

Ask to have your Soul give you a dream, and ask that you be assisted to remember the dream. We encourage you to make written notes of your dreams or record them in some fashion. You may find that a Soul-generated dream is familiar or quite different in quality from your usual dreams. That finding varies from person to person.

As you sleep, you may develop *continuous consciousness,* which greatly aids the ability of your conscious mind to relate to your subconscious mind, superconscious mind, and Soul. As you develop continuity of consciousness, your Outer Self expands its capability, and you lose that frustrating tendency to *forget* what you have learned. You gain greater ability to recall and retain those positive lessons that have been learned throughout the history of your Soul's embodiments.

As you accomplish this, you are no longer as vulnerable to performing acts of negative karma. Your sensitivities are enhanced, and so you are guided in the paths of wisdom and harmlessness.

We suggest that you experiment, not simply for one night's dream, but dream for a period of nights, allowing yourselves sufficient opportunity for experiencing a Soul-generated dream.

CONCLUSION

We believe that we have complicated your lives enough, and we thank you all for being patient with our sometime laborious explanations. If you were sitting in this chair, you would find yourselves having the same problems.

We thank you, and we depart this evening.

TOOLS FOR EXPLORATION
Exercise 2

SOUL-GENERATED DREAMS

1. Before going to sleep, mentally ask your Soul to give you a dream. Also ask to remember it. *You might say something like, "I ask that my Soul give me a dream tonight. I also ask for help in remembering it when I awake."*

2. Upon waking in a quiet, peaceful manner, allow any dream memories to surface before engaging in physical activity, such as getting out of bed and going to the bathroom.

3. Write notes and make sketches (if helpful) in a dream notebook, capturing what you remember of the dream.

4. Repeat this process for several nights, perhaps for one month, keeping notes on all dreams that you have recalled during that period.

5. Review your dream notes and select those dreams that seem to be Soul-generated. Write down in your dream notebook the qualities that you feel distinguish these dreams from the others.

6. Even though you might not be totally certain that you have had one or more Soul-generated dreams, you have initiated communication with your Soul. Like any beginning dialogue, be aware that you may receive responses from your Soul in dreams that occur later on, or in significant life experiences.

7. Notice the *qualities* of such responses and compare them with the qualities of your possibly Soul-generated dreams. Do their qualities seem similar and compatible? Your personal research of your Soul has begun!

WHAT HAVE WE LEARNED ABOUT "PERSONALITY AND SOUL?"

The third Monitor Lesson completed the topic, "Personality and Soul." What had we learned? We considered the following ideas that Monitor had stated as facts. These statements were difficult to verify as actual facts, just as most psychological "facts" are difficult to verify. Yet they offered a broader, more inclusive framework for approaching an in-depth understanding of personality and Soul. Through personal research we can apply and test these statements as assumptions useful for increasing our own understanding of the topic:

A human personality is created and maintained through hundreds of physical lifetimes by a Soul who exists in a causal body.

A Soul utilizes its personality as a projection of itself into the lower planes of existence, which it cannot enter directly, due to the polarization of Earth's lower plane energies.

A Soul's causal body contains and animates the physical, etheric, astral, and mental bodies of the personality it projects.

Each personality reveals the qualities of its Soul.

The vibratory qualities of a Soul may be paranormally perceived through observation of its projected personality.

In studying a personality in depth, we can gain knowledge of its Soul through normal perception. By scientific observation and analysis, we can identify personality traits and characteristics, then correlate them with paranormal observations of Soul qualities to arrive at a preliminary point of understanding of the Soul.

By studying many personalities, we can attain general knowledge about Souls.

Individually, we can develop a deeper understanding of our personality by noticing the thoughts, emotions, desires, and behaviors originating beyond our conscious mind (the Outer Self).

By exploring our subconscious and superconscious levels of mind, we can gain a more complete comprehension of our personality.

We are likely to discover that our subconscious mind is not unified, but fragmented into compartmentalized "Selves." These Selves can be alienated, co-existing, conflicting, competing, or cooperating with each other.

We can use a variety of methods to identify, communicate with, and gain rapport with our Subconscious Selves. These methods include dream work, hypnosis, meditation, guided imagery, dramatization, and inner dialogue.

We can gradually overcome the fragmentation and compartmentalization of our minds by such methods, developing a continuity of consciousness that maintains our awareness through sleep and waking.

We can explore the qualities of our Soul.

Chapter 2

Creativity

Lesson 4

May 1, 1991

MONITOR: We are present again as Monitor. As you listen to the birds, the bells, and the wind, consider what is within them that is similar to the word "creativity." Our theme, this month of May, is *Creativity*. Obviously that means that we thoroughly understand *Personality and Soul,* so we move ahead! If you don't mind too much, we will interweave the two subjects.

DEFINITION OF CREATIVITY

What is creativity? The ultimate creativity is the creation of Oneness of Being. But, of course, most of us are not yet too competent at doing that, so we get involved with other forms of creativity. It may be instructive, in light of our previous discussion about personality and Soul, to talk about *who* can be creative within the personality.

The conscious mind, or Outer Self, can be creative. The subconscious mind, in all of its aspects, can also be creative. Each aspect is capable of creativity. The superconscious mind, of course, is very creative. What about the Body Self, can it be creative? And we say definitely so. How far down can you take that on the scale of being? And we say that the systems and organs within the physical body do have a range of choices and can be creative. The cells of the body can be creative. The molecules and atoms within the cells can be creative, and indeed even subatomic entities can be, and are, creative. So just within the range of the human personality we find much opportunity for creativity. Yet there is much to understand about it.

As we understand creativity better, we can be more fulfilled. The term "fulfillment" innately requires creativity. One cannot truly be fulfilled without being creative. Why? What would *you* say? Let's provoke you a little.

MARGARET: It seems that the pattern of creativity is carried from one level to another. We are created, and we need to continue that creative energy. If we don't, then we've blocked a flow of energy.

MONITOR: And so you're suggesting that fulfillment . . .

MARGARET: Fulfillment comes in the act of passing that energy on in the form of a new creation.

MONITOR: Indeed, a form of advancement. All of you *are* creative as personalities, whether you consider yourselves so or not. We can tell.

When we look at the nature of creativity, we begin to realize an investment of being which an individual must make in order to be creative. In understanding that investment, and how it occurs, one may better appreciate the nature of fulfillment.

Understand that as Life expresses itself in the process of individuation, each facet of that individuation is called upon to be creative. It is called upon to accept its existence in the form in which it has been placed, and it must learn to fulfill and exceed the form. In so doing, the individual Life essence proclaims its nature, that it is *more* than the form. And indeed, that states in the microcosm what occurs in the macrocosm. For the universe, as it fulfills its expression, enables its inhabiting Life essence to exceed the form of the universe, and thus return to the Creator as a gift.

Consider that the Creator imbues all of Life with the gift of creativity, and that Life expresses that creativity to the fullest degree possible in its evolution, eventually achieving that unity, that Oneness of Being, which allows the universe to be gifted back to its Creator.

Now let's examine the word "creativity" and then we will respond to more questions.

Creativity involves action, which may be *inner* action or *outer* action. An action, in order to be creative, must be more than simple habit, routine, or rote. An action, in order to be creative, must be of *conscious* intent, not of accidental origin, but a consciously intended expression of the being performing the act.

We distinguish between actions that are repetitive and those that introduce new qualities, new elements, and new fusions of consciousness. We will make a puzzling statement at this point and say that *it is consciousness that creates qualities.*

DONNA: Would you explain that?

MONITOR: Later we'd be happy to. We'd like to puzzle you with that for a while. One way you can respond to that puzzle is to begin to ask the questions evoked within you, which begins an internal process to provide you with answers to that question.

DONNA: What kind of qualities are you referring to?

MONITOR: All of the qualities that human beings and all other beings within the universe experience.

Now consider consciousness. You might ask, "What consciousness?" And that leads you to understand what we're talking about. Understand that the Creator gave the gift of free will, or the will to choose, to all of Life. As Life manifested within the universe in the form of Cosmic Identities, those identities made choices, and the rest of the universe unfolded. Those choices created a diversity from a unity, and the challenge involves regaining that unity.

In other words, by analogy, a cloud becomes rain and disperses itself into the environment. But in time, the action of weather draws the moisture to the sky, and it reforms as a cloud. That image portrays a cycle that the universe is in the act of performing.

Consciousness *creates* quality. Consider the underlying need of all Life to merge in voluntary unity, achieving a state of Oneness. The universe functions in such a way that no unit of consciousness is separate from the whole of consciousness. Creativity, therefore, involves the *flow* of Life, in various manners, from one Life form to another. As that flow occurs, creativity is made more possible and likely. When that flow or *exchange* of Life is impeded or blocked temporarily, the manifestation of creativity is made less likely.

Now consider, if Donna was going to be creative, Donna would not find it possible, nor would anyone else, to be creative solely by herself. Her creativity would *necessarily* link her with other Life forms, whether it be connection with other human beings, with aspects of her subconscious or superconscious levels of mind, or other beings beyond the human species. Creativity necessarily links Donna with other Life forms.

CREATIVITY AS WAVE PHENOMENA

Consider creativity as a wave phenomenon, which is a useful form of thinking developed in physics. The wave involves many particles, never one particle. One particle, however, can generate a wave, which involves other particles as well as itself. Creativity necessarily involves more than one Life form. It involves a *transaction*, a flow, an exchange. For example, the creativity of the Greek poet was recognized as inspired by a muse, which we recognize as a devic entity. A collaboration occurred between that devic entity and the human entity, and the result was the creation of a poem.

The poem, of course, was far more than words, spoken or written. The creation of the poem was a *wave form*, an energy pattern involving the entire universe. The universe resounds to a single act of creativity. Again, the part cannot be separated from the whole.

Are you following some of this thinking?

DONNA: We're trying!

MONITOR: Well, we're deliberately trying to stretch you.

JULIE: You're doing a good job!

ERMA: Would it mean that, if someone had an idea somewhere, it could be transferred to many others at the same time?

MONITOR: Indeed, it would almost automatically be transferred to others who were receptive to that wave action, or to that vibration.

Do you notice that vibration in the distance? *[Coyotes howl in the neighborhood.]* Can coyotes be creative?

ERMA: You bet!

MONITOR: Indeed, all Life forms may be creative. That is a fundamental choice, is it not? To be creative, or stuck in a rut?

ERMA: How about the theory of you thinking of someone and the phone rings, and there they are. Is that the idea, too?

MONITOR: Absolutely. We find a *transmission* of thought, of personal energy, which informs you that the call is coming. Usually, for human beings in this time of development, their conscious mind, or Outer Self, is insulated against such knowledge. The insulation occurs because the Outer Self may not consider such knowledge possible and may be so focused on certain activities that it simply does not pay attention.

So, *paying attention* to develop awareness becomes the first step for creativity. Creativity results from internal actions of paying attention to experience. The experience may occur in the present moment, through memory, or through precognition. All of those modes of attention can generate creativity.

SOUL EXPRESSION IN ART

Many great artists have first built their skill of paying attention. When Van Gogh painted "The Irises," those lilting flowers in a pot on a table, he paid deep attention to those irises. His attention was so profound that he expressed qualities of his Soul in his act of creation. And you, as admirers of that painting, recognize that quality. Now that's one example of quality, where the personality may express the quality of its Soul. Wherever that Soul quality is expressed, a power emanates.

This might be more easily noticed in works of art, which you recognize as acts of creativity. When you participate in a painting, a sculpture, a play, a dance, you experience from your facet what another facet of consciousness has experienced and communicated.

Those who believe that the sculpture is simply the physical form, shaped by the artist, fail to understand the essence of Life. For if you perceive with open eyes the manifestation of Life through the sculpture, you see that it is far more than a physical form. The sculptors who perform the most profound works of art are those who achieve the greatest states of linkage, or unity of consciousness, in their acts of creation. Their achievement in consciousness creates a clarity that reflects throughout the Life expression of that work of art. The clarity is reflected in the physical as well.

Although they may fail to recognize it, human beings are more impressed by the *nonphysical* qualities of art than by its physical qualities. They do not yet feel comfortable with nonphysical terminology. In time, they will.

In a garden, a rose bush that is tenderly and creatively nurtured by its gardener, also may manifest Soul quality and express such a beauty, such a power, as the sculpture, the painting, or the symphony. Again, it involves an act of conscious creation on the part of the gardener and on the part of the rose. Notice there the *collaboration* among Life forms.

We ask Jeff, do you improvise with your music?

JEFF: Yes.

MONITOR: And when you improvise, do you plan it out ahead of time or do you explore and allow it to happen?

JEFF: Explore and allow it to happen.

MONITOR: And then you may find yourself being moved by the music.

JEFF: Yes.

MONITOR: Consider the flow or the exchange of Life that takes place in that action. Jeff allows his mind to shift its focus of attention. In that moment, Jeff's mind focuses on – let us call it – a *realm* of music, creating a connection like a funnel. As long as Jeff holds it open with his attention, the funnel draws the music to and through him and his instrument. The music consists of far more than combinations of sounds. The music expresses the consciousness manifest in the creation.

QUALITIES

We talked earlier of qualities, attempting to puzzle you. Let us explain a little more of what we mean. When you appreciate the song of the birds, what facets of consciousness are involved?

First of all, you may be aware of your consciousness, the conscious mind (or Outer Self) of the human being. You can consider your conscious mind as having a vibratory pattern. Then consider that the consciousness of the bird, which fulfills its own creative expression, has its own vibratory pattern. As the vibratory patterns of the bird and your conscious mind meet, like two waves meeting on the surface of water, they interact, and in that interaction each perceives qualities. The qualities arise from the expression of consciousness, of Life in action.

Of course, the interaction is more complex than that, because the air that carries the physical sound of the bird's song is also alive and also consciousness. Its consciousness – or vibratory pattern of the Life within the air – joins that interaction and lends its quality to the experience of the conscious mind of the human and the bird.

Looking at it from another aspect, the consciousnesses of the human and the bird affect the consciousness of Life within the wind. In this way you may recognize the constant exchange and transaction of Life. An exchange of Life takes place, not only among facets of consciousness, but between each facet and the Whole of Life. This is why when you sneeze, the universe responds.

MARGARET: What do you mean by that?

MONITOR: The universe cannot help but respond, for all Life is one. Consciousness reacts. It cannot fail to react.

MARGARET: For every action there is an equal and opposite reaction. That's one of the laws of matter.

MONITOR: What you're stating is a law of physics devised by Isaac Newton. We would modify that statement to say that *for every action, there is a reaction of the whole.*

In other words, the universe may be considered as a total energy system, a *living* energy system that expresses intent at all levels of manifestation. When Margaret sneezes, the universe, including distant nebulae, responds. All parts of the universe cannot help but respond. Luckily, not much in the way of dramatic response is required. What would you think, Margaret, if your sneeze produced a supernova?

MARGARET: The universe would be gone by now!

INTENT

JULIE: You mentioned the intent. The intent behind the action has a great deal to do with the effect created, I imagine.

MONITOR: The intent has a tremendous amount to do with what is created, and with the qualities created. Once you consider each facet of consciousness as inseparable from the whole of consciousness of the universe and its Creator, you may begin to value intent in terms of *how well the intent seeks to benefit the whole.*

As human beings you have had the experience of being taught in your social structures how to be self-centered. In so doing, much instruction has been imparted to you about using purposes and intents that benefit solely yourself. This form of self-centered intention excludes the whole – the universe that surrounds you. The universe is excluded from a self-centered intention.

The Buddha teaches that a human being is wise if he or she acts with intent that blesses *all* of Creation. This has been stated in various forms. One form states that one should seek to be harmless, that one should seek to be supportive and nurturing of all Life, with which we certainly agree. It has also been expressed in other forms, but we would like to cast it in these terms: as human beings, your intent may be expressed *creatively* or *repetitively.* Your intent, expressed creatively, is much *more* powerful than when expressed repetitively.

CREATIVE VERSUS REPETITIVE INTENT

As you cycle in repetition, your Life force essentially diminishes in expression. You lose vitality. You don't lose it totally, but your vitality has no real means of expression, since Life itself is creative in its own nature as a gift of the Creator.

Now consider your intention, expressed creatively as inclusive of all Life. If your intent conveys blessing, benefit, and nourishment to all Life, you are *structuring* your consciousness to interface with the Whole of Life. As you continue to do that, your consciousness *becomes* whole. It achieves successive states of Oneness to greater and greater degrees. Conversely, as your intention *excludes* the Whole of Life, your consciousness is structured accordingly.

Intention, based on a *fragment* of the whole, structures consciousness into being a fragment of the whole. Consciousness, whose intent expresses the Whole of Life, structures its consciousness into the Whole of Life. Now that expresses the *core opportunity* in all acts of creation.

JULIE: Could we have an example of that?

MONITOR: Certainly. Who would like to give an example? We'd like to encourage an example from the group.

MARGARET: Well, I could give an example around the publishing that my partner and I do. If we were to publish a book, and if our intent in doing that was to satisfy the ego of the author or to satisfy our own need to make money, then our intent would be a limiting intent. But if we publish the book in order to truly share a message with the entire world, and that is really the intent behind it, then we are not limited in our intent and can tap into the whole consciousness.

MONITOR: This offers a good example, in our opinion. A counter-example would be a publisher who seeks to meet his or her own need to the exclusion of all other needs. In the short term, that publisher might actually accomplish the goal, but then what happens? What actually happens is that the publisher separates herself or himself from the whole to the extent of the energy invested in that intent.

Consider Mother Teresa, who expresses her universal intent by making a simple statement, "Accept each person as Christ." She says that the person most in need is essentially the Christ. So she focuses her intent on those most in need, but she does not exclude those who are *not* hungry or homeless or ill. She has become quite skilled at treating virtually all humans as Christ. Now if you were the Christ, how would you feel about Mother Teresa?

MARGARET: I'd love it!

MONITOR: You would feel like she recognized *you*. To state it another way, if Erma was talking with Nancy, and Erma noticed that Nancy was aware only of Erma's left elbow, how would Erma feel?

MARGARET: Self-conscious about her left elbow.

MONITOR: She would feel somehow deficient in the exchange of Life with Nancy. Erma would recognize that what she *is* essentially was not recognized by the other person. In that exchange, we find an experience of absence, of opportunity lost.

Consider how the Christ Consciousness must feel about humanity. Consider how the Buddha Consciousness must feel.

Within this context, consider creativity for those who are more enlightened are challenged to use their creativity to help those less enlightened. How do they help? They help them to be more *creative!* And remember that creativity begins with expansion of awareness, of attention, becoming aware of what you were not aware of before and placing your attention into areas of consciousness that are new to you.

STIMULATION BY PLANETARY CONSCIOUSNESS

Times have occurred in the history of Earth where the Planetary Consciousness was relatively stable in its expression. During those times, such as the time of the Dark Ages in Europe, the individual human being was moved more by the impulse of Soul to be creative.

In this present time, the Planetary Consciousness is extending itself into new areas. It is opening itself in new ways, and you have not only the stimulus of your own Souls, but also the stimulus of the Planetary Consciousness, which is itself creative at this time. At times you experience that stimuli as *pressure,* which you naturally tend to resist. Your natural tendency is to maintain a homeostasis within your present form. However, that will *not* be allowed. This suggests one reason why a deeper understanding of creativity has particular value for you at this time.

As we talk tonight, we make coherent statements about creativity here and there, deliberately leaving vague areas in between. We do not want to explain it all so clearly that you will not have questions.

MARGARET: I have a question.

MONITOR: Wonderful!

CHAOS

MARGARET: One of the qualities that many people notice about the creative process is that at the beginning it seems to be very chaotic. I'm wondering if chaos is inherent in the nature of creativity, or if there are ways to create which don't arise out of chaos, but come another way.

MONITOR: Chaos is necessary as an early stage of creativity, and sometimes as a later stage. We describe the human experience of chaos as its *perception of a changing order in which the new pattern is not yet perceived.* Chaos involves the human perception of what seems to be no pattern. When a human being fails to perceive a pattern, he/she feels somewhat distraught at not being able to surmise a purpose. Not knowing the purpose makes a human being feel insecure. But we reassure you that your experience of chaos is a blessing in disguise, for if you did not experience chaos, you would not be creative.

ATTENTION AND AWARENESS

Let us go into this in more detail to illustrate a point. What is attention? What is awareness? *Attention* may be described as a function of mind where the mind has relative stability. Attention results when the mind is sufficiently ordered to reflect on itself and its environment. *Awareness* may be described as systematic linking of various moments of attention.

Let's say at this moment that you place your attention on the sound of the wind chime. During the time you have been listening, your minds have shifted from paying attention to the chime to numerous other experiences. You may have been listening to your heartbeat, to your neighbor moving, feeling your leg itch, remembering that you need to go to the bathroom, or whatnot. Your attention has been placed on the wind chime in a sporadic manner.

If you were to describe this in linear time, you were paying attention to the wind chime perhaps for one second, at first, then you shifted away for several seconds, returned to the wind chime again for maybe half a second, shifted away for several more seconds, then returned to the wind chime, and so forth. Your attention is constantly moving. *Your awareness represents the attempt of your mind to maintain a sense of pattern with your experience of millions and billions of attentions.*

Now creativity, especially for human beings, must begin with building capability for paying attention. If a person pays continuous attention for one minute, he/she becomes vastly more creative. If he/she pays continuous attention for twenty minutes, he/she approaches enlightenment. Within spiritual disciplines, the common thread that is taught involves developing *continuous focus of attention*, for that permits greater awareness.

If you were aware of any one brick in the fireplace, you would have no idea of fireplace, because your attention would be limited to a one brick capacity. If you spent hour after hour, day after day, year after year, contemplating that brick, your attention would automatically shift to another brick, and you would have awareness of two bricks. Once you're aware of two bricks, you open to the possibility of many bricks in association with each other.

You might not, at that point, be aware of the fireplace, but you would be getting closer to that awareness. Ultimately your attention would provide you with enough awareness of what you were contemplating so that you would become aware of the fireplace. All that time the fireplace has been fully formed and present right in front of you.

In this way we illustrate the importance of developing your capability for paying attention. As your attention capability grows, your awareness automatically grows. As your awareness grows, you become aware of the Life within and around you. Do you understand how that is a creative process?

MARGARET: How does our attention get from one brick to two bricks to many bricks? What's the process that causes the attention to expand?

MONITOR: The mind, which has the intention of being attentive to the brick, creates a flow of Life or, if you wish, an attunement between the energy patterns of the mind and the brick. That flow automatically produces awareness of other bricks that have similar energy patterns to the original brick. The flow brings about an automatic extension of awareness.

MARGARET: So the link that's established between the mind and the brick takes on a Life of its own, and expands to the second brick and the third.

MONITOR: Yes, a natural flow of Life is established. You see, Life seeks to be One in the manifested universe, because Life is One, although manifested forms may not realize that. The wave may not realize that it is created by the ocean. Life will flow to connect all forms.

TALENT

ARZANI: I have studied art, dance and music for ten years, but I've never expressed any of them in the way that Jeff expressed his experience with music. I find that I express myself more creatively in teaching and writing. Can you explain how talent occurs, and how we are assigned particular talents?

MONITOR: Talents are primarily creations of the subconscious mind and the superconscious mind interacting. The conscious mind (Outer Self) may sense the need for development of a talent, yet it is the subconscious mind that develops the capability from lifetime to lifetime. The intent of the creativity lies primarily within the subconscious mind.

The subconscious mind may express a very self-centered intention or a universal intention. The subconscious mind also may seek to make itself a channel for higher levels of mind.

When you, as an Outer Self, seek to express a talent, it is helpful to know what part of your subconscious mind is involved in expression of that talent. Once you identify that expression with an aspect of your subconscious mind, you may ask that aspect what it seeks to accomplish, what is its intention. As the Outer Self, you may seek to support accomplishment of that intention, and allow that talent to express. Or, you may block it.

If you block, you will experience conflict with that aspect of the subconscious mind. In time, the subconscious mind will have its expression, whether it is through your Outer Self, or whether it needs to push the Outer Self aside, or whether it needs to wait until another embodiment with a more cooperative Outer Self. It is wise for the Outer Self to realize that the talent expresses the subconscious mind far more than the conscious mind.

This is one reason why in writing or teaching, as you mentioned, you find yourself making statements or expressions for which you have no conscious intent. The intent comes from your subconscious or superconscious levels of mind.

In this time of Planetary Consciousness, talents are encouraged. The expression of much that has lain beyond the reach of the Outer Selves of humanity will be exposed to them so that they may cooperate with the transformations of consciousness being forced on individuals by transformation in the Planetary Consciousness. As expression of subconscious material is encouraged, the Outer Self is wise to cooperate.

PRAYER

ERMA: If St. Teresa of Avila were here with her prayer work today, and had the ability to see on television the disasters all over the world, could her prayer work make a difference? Could her prayers turn things around?

MONITOR: Very definitely so. Consider what is "prayer work." Prayer work involves your conscious mind perceiving a need, and then asking all of Life, which you may call God or Creator or some other name, to meet that need. Prayer offers a very powerful form of creativity. If one reaches to the Source of Life itself, one's consciousness, that has occupied multitudinous fragmented forms, may be stimulated by direct appeal to the Source of Life itself.

Prayer asks for intervention in a perceived course of action by God, or by some being representative of the nature of God. St. Teresa, being quite accomplished in the creativity of prayer, had a very powerful effect on world events. The Flow of Life would emanate from her, exchanging with higher elements of consciousness within the planet, the solar system and beyond, throughout the universe, until it contacted the Source, the Creator. The Creator's response changes the quality of consciousness of all aspects of Life involved in that prayer.

In this type of action, prayer involves a request for healing. Prayer may also involve other actions, but we speak primarily of this, since that was the intent of your question.

PRAYER THROUGH ART

An artist may create a work of art as an act of prayer. In that case, the work of art functions as an act of prayer not only as the artist creates it, but as each person perceives it. This principle functions with Tibetan prayer wheels, for example, because the intention in the creation of a prayer wheel is that it generates the prayer of its creator every time it is spun.

ASSIGNMENT IN CREATIVITY

How would you like to be creative in this coming week? We encourage you to consider that, in light of tonight's sharing. You may wish to spend some time discussing this. How would you like to be creative?

We would like to begin next week by asking you to share how you've been creative and what you have experienced during moments of creativity. What have you felt? What have you been aware of? What has resulted from your creativity?

We've given you several ways in which you may be creative, ranging from paying attention to a single brick to calling upon the Source of Life to heal. You may write a poem, create a statue, bake a cake, avoid hitting a pedestrian. You have many opportunities. Consider that in each act of creativity you experience something new, a new sense of qualities that derive from your transaction with other facets of Life.

Consider this image. It's too good for us to pass up! If you wish to conduct an interesting experiment, select an ant pile, go out each day, as much as you can, and spend ten minutes putting your attention on the ants and their activities. As you do this, the quality of your consciousness and the consciousness that you represent affects the quality of consciousness of the ants, the pebbles, and plants in that vicinity. If you do it long enough, you may observe visible changes in the behavior of the ants and at times even in the appearance of the ants. This is roughly what occurs when Great Beings come to Earth. They pay attention to human beings, and the quality of human consciousness is changed.

We thank you, and we wish you well in your discussions about creativity. We leave you now.

TOOLS FOR EXPLORATION
Exercise 3

DIRECTING ATTENTION AT ANTS

Monitor's premise states that your consciousness may affect the consciousness around you, even the behavior of ants. By focusing your attention on a group of ants, Monitor says that you can alter their behavior, even if you do not try to impose your intention on them. The following experiment gives you a way to explore Monitor's premise.

1. Find an ant pile where you can comfortably sit or stand nearby.

2. Spend at least ten minutes observing the ants, placing your attention into them and their activities until you are well aware of their behavior.

3. Observe the same ant pile at least five times, or as many times as you wish until you notice how your consciousness may possibly affect the observable behavior of the ants.

4. If you wish, you may want to experiment with changing your state of mind in ways that might affect the behavior of the ants. For example, you might visit the ant pile when you are agitated and upset, and at another time when you feel calm and meditative. Do you notice any difference in the behavior of the ants on those occasions? Do they appear more or less active when you are agitated?

5. Do they appear more or less active when you are calm?

6. What differences do you observe in their behavior?

7. Realizing that other influences might also affect the ants' behavior, what do you conclude from this experiment?

8. Write down what you have learned in doing this exercise.

Lesson 5

May 8, 1991

MONITOR: We welcome you as Monitor.

We have begun the subject of creativity and hope you have some questions. We could, of course, talk all night and lull you all into a deep sleep, which would be very refreshing for you. What questions do you have?

ARZANI: I have a question, but it's not about creativity. Is that okay?

MONITOR: Go ahead.

PROTECTION

ARZANI: It's a question about the prayer we began the Lesson with, the Protection Prayer. I have a difficult time with the concept that we need protection and that we need to separate out some things and send them away. I've always felt protected anyway in my life. Is that a personal preference of the channel, or do *you* feel it's important to say a protection prayer?

MONITOR: Is there a need for protection in such an endeavor as this? And we say, "Yes." The action behind protection is selectivity. If you would like to hold a meeting in your house and allow any person to enter, you would be inviting in possibilities that would range from those who would treat you honorably to those who would not.

When you host the kind of activity that focuses upon the sacred or the special, you naturally desire to have participants who are open to that kind of experience, who have a sense of understanding about it, and who have the necessary decorum to allow that event to take place. If you were to attempt to conduct a sacred ceremony with a group of hyperactive five-year-olds, wouldn't you find it difficult? So we learn to be selective.

Selectivity is based upon the desired goal of your action. The desired goal of *this* action is to have free interaction among the parties present, those in physical form and those of us who are not, allowing an exchange of information and energy. This goal seems quite innocent and beneficial, yet we assure you that there are beings, *not* in the physical body, who seek to disrupt and distort such a simple exchange. They are motivated to take that action because they have their own concepts of what order should be, what all of you and all of us *should* be doing. They would force their concept upon us, and prevent us from doing what we wish to do.

Protection, in these circumstances, amounts to a matter of organization. It is *not* something that promotes fear, although some people may feel fear at the mention of "negative" or "evil" beings and energies. If you feel fear, you feel fear, and it is wise for you to know that. Some of you may not feel fear, but wonder why is this precaution used. It is used because we, and our associates, the Teachers of the channel and his partner, have advised them to use such precautions. Does that answer your question?

ARZANI: Yes.

DIFFERING VIEWS

MONITOR: You do not have to agree with our viewpoint. Disagreements of viewpoint are often very stimulating. One of our prime objectives in these sharings is to stimulate thought on your part and our part. We are perfectly willing to entertain a different viewpoint than that which we express, and at times we may even be guilty of expressing contradictory points of view.

SUBATOMIC ENTITIES

JULIE: Anyone else have a question? Could we start with some questions from the information you shared last week? You mentioned a term, "subatomic entities." Could you share with us what you mean by "subatomic entities?"

MONITOR: We will share briefly, because you would have difficulty understanding what, to us, would be a full description. Your scientists have viewed energy and matter as inanimate, lacking in consciousness. They have viewed consciousness as being some kind of by-product of the actions of matter. We understand why they take this point of view, because their type of science has been organized in ways that avoid the power structures of religious institutions. The irony is that scientists, in many cases, have created their own power structures that are just as dogmatic as religious institutions. You have been influenced, as children in school, by the viewpoint that matter is inanimate. Our viewpoint is that matter *is* animate; it is fully alive and active, growing and *creative* – there, we used the term – as you are on your level of existence.

Thus, we can describe a subatomic particle or a wave as an "entity." You can have "quark" entities, "neutron" entities, "gluon" entities, etc. You can imagine that, within the atoms, they have prejudices and troubles like yours, and indeed they do. The underlying challenge of Life, on all levels of expression, is to voluntarily find the basis for unity and act in ways that are beneficial to all of Life. Part of the structure of matter in this planet is prevented from full expression because of such biases upon the subatomic level.

There are beings at that level that live and have their own patterns of fulfillment. Again, we cannot describe much about that. We would not make much sense to human beings. But let us assure you that, from our vantage point, there are beings that are in many ways remarkably similar to yourselves, existing on a scale of size that is more than a quadrillion times smaller than your size. These subatomic entities are not truly small, because size is a function of your human consciousness. Even the devic beings, who work with you on this planet, are not limited by your concept of size.

HUMAN CONSCIOUSNESS

Understand that you have certain organizing mechanisms in the consciousness of your bodies and Outer Selves, which give you a very structured, limited appreciation of time, space and much of Life. That structure has been developed purposefully so that the special learning conditions available to human beings may be effectively utilized.

You need to understand that you are *cosmic* beings, cosmic citizens. You have traveled throughout the universe and come to this planet for a particular type of experience. It is your Soul that has traveled, and most of the rest of your being is what has been developed by your Soul in this planet. A human being is like the tip of a pin that the Soul inserts into Earth experience. Your Outer Self comprises perhaps *one tenth of one percent* of the total consciousness within your being, and yet the irony is that we are talking to you within that framework. It is incumbent upon us to find ways of expression that make sense to you, as pinpricks of consciousness.

We do not mean, in any way, to devalue your status, because it is quite desirable among many Souls who wish to be in your places. You have excellent opportunities for learning within these structured, limited conditions of human existence. We emphasize that, even though your consciousness is very tightly focused, each human being has access to its Soul, its Monad, its Cosmic Identity, and its Creator, for no one is separated from the wholeness of existence. How was that for a creative answer?

GROUP: Very good!

MONITOR: We're like politicians. We always have a way of getting across the point that *we* want to make. What else do you dare ask us?

PURPOSE OF HUMAN EXISTENCE

CONNIE: So what is the purpose of human existence, since it's so limited?

MONITOR: The purpose of human existence is to experience these very limited, extremely focused conditions of consciousness, in order to test the will. The Creator has given free will to all of Life, even to human beings. Your will is your opportunity to choose, to make decisions based upon your experience.

Many conditions throughout the universe are very loose in their restrictions. Great freedom exists in many planets and star systems for Souls to experience a great variety of conditions. Yet Souls also need to experience intense *limitation*. When a Soul is given great freedom, it tends to focus on that which it desires and avoid that which it wants to avoid. Planets such as Earth provide the opportunity for Souls to *focus upon that which they most wish to avoid*. Now isn't that a dandy explanation of the purpose of human existence?

You are here to experience that which you most wish to avoid. And if you do that, you gain great freedom, because freedom always originates within the will of a being, no matter on what level of Life that being expresses. Freedom is achieved from within, not from without.

ONENESS

We have spoken of the ultimate expression of creativity as being the individual being's creation of Oneness with all Life and with the Creator. How can that Oneness be accomplished? Only through a being's acceptance of *all conditions* of Life. A being must accept that which it does not wish to accept at first. It must accept that which it most wishes to avoid in order to approach a state of Oneness.

This entire solar system, of the star called Sol, deals with *polarized* consciousness. The whole purpose of polarized consciousness is to give you experience of the *extremes*, the light and the dark, the good and the bad, the holy and the evil, so that you may choose. If you choose to avoid large portions of the experience offered within polarized consciousness, you're missing the point and essentially acting in fear. As you learn to act in Love, you learn to accept that which is "dark" to your perception, that which is "evil" to your perception. By that act of acceptance you learn, you gain, and you incorporate more of the wholeness of your own being. If every part of the universe reflects the Whole of the universe, then what do you gain by avoiding that which you fear? So you can see perhaps more clearly why Souls come to Earth and other planets like it.

AVOIDANCE

LINDA: I had a simple thing go through my mind when you were talking about avoiding something. I had to give a speech from the pulpit, and I did not want to do it. I did it, however; but it was a real stretch for me. Then I found out I have to do it again. I really prefer not to. I would prefer to avoid it. I know this is just a simple statement of avoidance. I'm not sure what my question is.

MONITOR: You are aware that you have the fear of giving that speech or sermon. For human beings, the first act of awareness takes place as an internal action. The first action of creativity begins with your act of paying attention to your experience. As you pay enough attention to your experience, you begin to notice. You develop an awareness of what you are experiencing *and* what you are creating.

Your fears about this task originate in some experiences, some from earlier in this lifetime, but primarily from other lifetimes, as we see it. They derive from experiences in which you spoke what, to you, was "truth," and you were persecuted for your open statements, not once but three times. So, from our perspective, it is no wonder that your guiding consciousness would bring about such experiences in this lifetime to enable your Male Self to face and overcome his fears from past persecution.

Now this presents a useful example. If your Male Self was *reactive*, he would simply allow the fear to drive him. He would not face the fear, but allow the fear to move him aside from the chosen path of ministry, of teaching, of healing. And he would be intensely frustrated. However, your Male Self, who is part of your subconscious mind that has existed in other lifetimes, has chosen to be creative, and in being creative, *is* recognizing his fear and assisting you to recognize that fear.

As your personality becomes mobilized to overcome the fear, you have the opportunity in physical experience to demonstrate that you have overcome the fear. You do that by completing your assignment, by giving the talk, despite the fear. In so doing, your conscious mind is being creative, and the Male aspect of your subconscious mind is also being creative.

The sense of resistance, which you still feel, represents what is called your "Judge Self" who comprises that aspect of the subconscious mind that is most fearful of persecution. Your Judge Self has not been willing to demonstrate its creativity, so your challenge remains perhaps a little heavy for you. But we are certain that you will prevail in your demonstration of creativity. In overcoming the habit of fear, you will assist your Judge Self. Your Judge Self will reluctantly have to admit that you spoke in public and were *not* persecuted. You were not killed. You were not imprisoned. So perhaps it may consider that hope exists for its creative expression.

Once you understand these dimensions within your personality, you can begin to see how the aspects of you, who are most free to receive and express Light and Love, can help those aspects of you that are still quite bound in fear. And that's a challenge worthy of a human being.

CREATION OF SOULS

DONNA: I have a question about Souls. Have all Souls been created, or are new Souls now being created? How does that work?

MONITOR: That's an interesting question because you will find different sources giving different answers. We have a chance to be controversial no matter which way we answer.

When viewed from the perspective of what you call "linear time," Souls are still being created. Outside of linear time, from the perspective of the superconscious mind and that which is higher in vibration, all of Creation is still taking place. In that sense of time, all Souls have been created. But from another sense of time, all Souls have not been created. This sounds paradoxical. From your human vantage point, Souls are still being created. Yet it is possible for you, in a state of mystical enlightenment, when the awareness of your personality becomes illuminated by the awareness of your Soul, for you to perceive all Souls as being fully present.

In this way we try to illustrate difficulties in human comprehension of such subjects. The presence of fear, which permeates the collective and personal expressions of mind within humanity, creates a number of distortions of perception and interpretation of human experience.

SOUL-ACTIVATED PERSONS

One of the greatest breakthroughs in human understanding will occur, beginning in the next century as relatively small numbers of human beings become activated by their Souls. These Soul-activated personalities will be able to present, simultaneously around the planet, very similar versions of wisdom, which goes into such realms as we are talking of now. At the present time humanity is struggling with intellect, which is primarily dominated by fear. The intellectual attempt to understand such subjects is futile. Such understandings may only be approached through intuitive mind. The intuitive intellect *is* developing.

INTUITION

We, in our manner of presentation, purposefully encourage the development of intuitive intellect. We accept your mind structure, as it exists, and we nudge it towards intuitive activity. We supply you with statements that your intellect may grasp to a point, and then we tickle your minds to reach into intuitive abilities to complete what is otherwise an incomplete picture. So we are clever! We admit it.

As you wrestle with this material, you will often get intuitive insights, and we certainly wish you to share them, for that is clear evidence of your growth. As you grow, as individuals and as a group, you make it more possible for all of humanity to grow in a similar way.

THE CREATOR

CONNIE: You have frequently used the term "the Creator," and I'm not sure if we're into a semantics thing here, but I get a picture of this single entity that is responsible for all of us. I find myself with a great deal of dismay, because my belief is that "We are God, God is us, we are God." So I want that clarified.

MONITOR: We respect your point of view and agree with it. We have not said anything truly to the contrary. You must realize that if you were to describe God, or the Creator, you would have to describe that beingness in a way which reflects its essence and yet its complexity. Human beings seem capable of grasping the essence, that there is a Life, and that Life is intelligent, beneficent and creative. What human beings have difficulty with is understanding how that Life manifests. We use the term "Creator" because most human beings may more easily relate to that, yet it is important to remind ourselves that *each expression* of Life is also the Creator, expressing a unique facet of Life. Indeed, all life forms comprise parts of the Creator, or of Life expressing. *All co-create!*

If you approach the description of yourself in a similar way, you have to describe what is the essence of Connie. You describe how that essence of Connie manifests in Life forms. You look at the various bodies which that essence occupies. You look at the mental body and describe its structure, and look at the astral body and describe its structure. If you're not aware of those bodies, they would have little meaning for you. If you *are* aware of the physical body, you can describe the essence of Connie as a little toe, as an intestine, a thyroid gland, or an eyelash. Each of those *forms* of expression is created, and all co-create the physical body and the other bodies. So we agree with you. We just wanted to explain in a way that might stimulate you.

INVESTMENT OF BEING

JULIE: You said that to be creative, an individual must make an "investment of being." Could you help us better to understand what that investment of being is, and tell us how to make it?

MONITOR: Oh, that's an excellent question! If you view yourselves as being in one of two modes, *reactive or creative*, you may approach a worthwhile understanding of this concept of investment of being. If you are reactive, you maintain your habit pattern. You stay stuck in the rut of repetitive existence, which is your right, if you choose that. Staying in that rut requires no investment of being beyond what originally led you to choose that rut. At that point you've made a creative choice and you chose a rut. Once in the rut, you could be reactive and remain there without making any further investment of your being, of your Life force. Of course, through the mechanisms of the Law of Karma, you will run yourself down to a point of pain and restriction where you will seek something better. Then, at that point, you may be willing and motivated to make another creative choice.

When you make a creative choice, you must invest your Life force, your being, in a *new* expression. If you have been learning how to ride a horse in the Western style, you express yourself in that style. That expression takes conscious intent, conscious attention, awareness and persistence to learn that style. Having learned the Western style of riding a horse, you then might choose to learn the Eastern style or the British style, which would require you to make another investment in conscious change. Your investment in creativity always involves a conscious intentional action.

Let us say this in a different way. We've talked about Linda and the lesson of her Male Self in facing and overcoming his fears of public speaking, especially in an arena of religious spiritual import. Linda, as the Outer Self, may simply remain reactive and allow the fear, which plays on the Subconscious level, to dominate her will so that she would not take steps to challenge that pattern of fear. However, her superconscious mind has arranged these circumstances to benefit the Male Self of the subconscious mind. The Male Self recognizes this and therefore chooses to be creative, to break that pattern. He assists Linda, the Outer Self, to value creative change, and thus assists Linda to support his position. At this point, neither the Male Self nor Linda have convinced the Judge Self of the value of that approach. Therefore, the Judge Self stays in its rut and does not seek creative change.

Within the personality of Linda, there are forces moving toward creative change by overcoming the pattern of fear. But she also experiences resistance from the Judge Self. This illustrates that each Self within the personality has its own range of free choice. No Self within the human personality has a total freedom of choice. Each Self has a limited range of choice available to it, appropriate to its level of evolution.

Human beings often desire to have god-like powers, and indeed they do. But as many stories have illustrated, people easily misuse those powers because they do not have the wisdom to use those powers for the benefit of all of Life. The proper path for a person to develop such powers is through linkage with its own Soul. As the Soul asserts itself through the personality and the personality surrenders itself to its Soul, then god-like powers may be expressed with the wisdom of the Soul. Human beings who have accomplished this are called "Masters," "Avatars," and at times even "Gods and Goddesses."

Creativity is essential for the achievement of such states. A person cannot simply be "good" by following the rules and achieve such illumination. The Buddha taught such wisdom clearly, through example and precept. Human beings are required to take risks. Creativity always involves some measure of risk, especially when you recognize that the concept of "risk" derives from the experience of fear. People learn to grow from fear into Love. Within Love, a being need not experience risk, yet is free to experience risk inasmuch as that being retains contact with fear.

BENEFITS OF FEAR

We ask you to appreciate the benefits of fear. Fear consists of a response generated from the mental level to the astral level to the etheric and physical levels of existence. Fear represents the mind of the Self that feels exposed and at risk. The exposure may be to the threat of destruction, loss of capability, or loss of status. Fear acts as an alarm that causes the mind of the Self to become attentive. It represents a very useful reflex as part of the instinctual pattern that human beings have adopted. So fear, in its essential function, is really quite useful. It offers a call to *pay attention.*

In the course of human history, many illusions have been generated around the experience of fear. These illusions cause the Self to believe that its fear presents a valid perception of the threat of destruction, or other threats. But the illusions are false, and fear functions as an *alarm* calling for attention.

Illusions – created largely in the lower levels of the mind and most active in the astral forces of emotions, desires, attitudes, and expectations – create a *false* perception of threat. These illusions, producing and sustaining what we call a "dysfunctional fear reaction," have become a habit for human beings and some devic beings in Earth. This dysfunctional pattern of fear has complicated matters for the Spiritual Hierarchy. It is, therefore, important for each being present in this planet to recognize fear as an appropriate alarm, and distinguish it from the dysfunctional habit of reacting to illusions.

How's that for a provocative statement?

ARZANI: You were talking about how you are stimulating us with your teaching, but I get a sense, when I leave here, that you are doing something more than speaking. I feel like my Soul has been activated, and I don't think it's through my mind. Is that a secret?

MONITOR: Are you saying that your Soul may be activating and bypassing your mind? We're teasing you.

ARZANI: I just feel like you're doing something more than talking.

MONITOR: Why would we do that?

ARZANI: Because you love us!

LOVE

MONITOR: Indeed. And what is Love? We have talked of fear in terms of creativity, and if properly understood – you notice how smoothly we're reintroducing the discussion – and if properly understood, you notice that fear is a call to awaken and pay attention to your experience and *potential* threats. Fear may be a very proper part of creativity. Yet to be frozen in fear, in the dysfunctional fear reaction that we have mentioned, limits one to reactivity, not creativity.

Love represents the harmony of being throughout all of the universe, plus the Being of that which we call "Creator," which permeates all of the universe. Love offers a vibratory influence that all beings, in all forms of Life expression, can experience. It presents *a call to unity,* the unity which already exists within the Creator, and the unity which will exist as each facet of individuated Life voluntarily chooses to create Oneness and unity of being with all of the universe. Love offers a call to unity that moves Life in all forms. Love moves both individuated Life and non-individuated Life, or that which you term "Spirit."

Love *invites* creativity. If you seek to be Loving, you seek to be sensitive to the Life around you. In being sensitive, you pay intense attention to that Life. You develop awareness which expands your own sense of being, and as you invest your being in that expansion, Life force flows through you, carried on the vibration of Love to the Life form you are loving. That creates Oneness of Being for the one who Loves and the one being Loved. That Oneness of Being foreshadows greater expressions of Oneness.

You are challenged to Love your own personality. You find a much more difficult challenge to Love another personality. Yet you do this and more, because of the tremendous transforming quality of Love. Love moves one to be more than his or her Life form. A human being is moved by Love to be more than a human being. A human being may become something advanced, like a cactus, or an ant! *[Laughter from group.]* Notice how we enjoy ants. A human being moves beyond its normal limits, and with Love cannot help being creative.

We have mentioned Vincent Van Gogh, and how his intense Love caused his Soul to express in his paintings. As you enjoy his paintings, you are stimulated by the Soul quality that emerges from his work. His contact with his Soul causes you to have contact with *your* Soul. The critics call that "uplifting," and it is.

JULIE: Yet his personality seemed to be quite distorted. Is there a need to work on the personality? How does that help? Or is it not important to work on the personality?

MONITOR: Vincent Van Gogh had a rather distorted personality, one that was certainly not well integrated, but was productive and intensely focused by his Love. He found that gaining the Love of human beings was extremely difficult, and yet had such need to express Love that he expressed it in the way he knew best, in one of the ways that was perhaps safest for him. When he attempted to express his Love to human beings, they often were frightened and withdrew or persecuted him. He could express his Love in paint on a canvas and be rewarded with a creation of "Beauty and Truth." The Truth is the expression of his Soul, the qualities of his Soul's consciousness. When the poet Keats talks about Truth and Beauty, this is essentially what he means.

Of course, we recommend that human beings seek contact with their Souls, for that leads them to spiritual mastery. For the Soul to fully express in a human being, its personality must be fully integrated.

Van Gogh and other creative persons of his type represent an intermediate stage of development and not the final stage. The final or more fulfilled stage of integrated personality may be seen in that of the Master Yeshua (Jesus), the Master Buddha and others within this planet that have not achieved such notoriety. Does this answer your question?

CONNIE: What about Einstein in relationship to Vincent Van Gogh. Was he advanced or connected with his Soul?

MONITOR: Einstein was indeed connected with his Soul. Much of his connection was achieved intuitively. He had the ability to move beyond the limits of conventional intellect and let his intuitive mind express itself in concepts that could be expressed mathematically. Mathematics, when properly undertaken, represents a wonderful expression of intuitional understanding. Einstein was not a fully integrated personality in in our view, but definitely more integrated than Van Gogh. Einstein was capable of functioning in a way that demonstrated to human beings in his lifetime that people of good will could act in ways that benefit the entire planet.

Much of his value, for the world of his time, came from the fact that he moved beyond *national* allegiance. In his actions of risk, in defying the order of Nazi Germany and – if you truly knew, but it has not been published – his acts of defying the similarly repressive elements of the United States of America, you would see that his challenges brought him in contact with his Soul. Einstein maintained his sense of integrity and was severely beaten for it in the later years of his life, and this story has *not* been told. Ultimately, perhaps, it will be told, but the government of the United States is not yet prepared to let that be known.

BEYOND FORMULAE

You have been presented with a concept within the Christian religion, that you must do as Jesus did in order to achieve Oneness with God. In one sense, we agree with that statement, but in another we disagree. If you focus yourself on your Soul, and allow your Soul to express through you in your daily living to the degree that Jesus did, you will indeed achieve that Oneness. But you are not necessarily called to do exactly what Jesus did. In fact, if you were to imitate exactly the actions of Jesus, you would be repetitive and not creative. Each person must find his or her creative path to express Oneness. No formula exists for you. You must be creative. You must *invest* your being. You may feel the need to surrender your Life, but you do not necessarily have to in order to achieve Oneness with your Soul, and therefore Oneness with higher being, and ultimately with God, the Creator.

You must find your own way. How do you do that? How do you create Oneness? How do you now relate to fear? How do you now express Love?

We think this is a dandy place to stop. We ask that all of you be blessed, and we leave you for tonight.

Lesson 6

May 15, 1991

MONITOR: We come to you again as Monitor. What do you notice as we enter the vibration of your group? Many times we allow a short time of silence upon entry, when we are already present but not yet speaking. We ask you to notice what you feel and sense during that time of entry.

VIEWPOINTS

Having looked at creativity from different points of view, we have identified certain fundamental components. We have looked at it from the viewpoint of human consciousness and given you some glimpses of creativity as it operates in consciousness other than human. We have given you the challenge of creating Oneness of Being, where your being voluntarily joins with other beings expressed in other Life forms.

Donna may contemplate a rose, and creatively extend her attention to the point where her awareness blends with the awareness of the rose, causing a flow of Life between Donna and the rose and the rose and Donna. That's an example of Oneness of Being. Scott may so attune himself that he may become at one with Donna, and in so doing create a Oneness in the flow of Life between their two beings.

The flow of Life offers another way to regard creativity. It links two Life forms energetically. It involves more than a flow of communication. It represents the flow of Being itself. It concerns more than a flow of words, more than a contact of eyes, more than a touching of fingers. It expresses a contact of Being which transcends the Life forms involved.

Your realizing of such experiences has great value, for in such experiences you gain a sense of your Creator, of the Creative Process that is active in your being and all beings. Those who are your spiritual leaders manifest such creativity. To do so, they must overcome their fears. They face their fears; they feel their fears; and they act for the highest good. They act for the benefit of all of Life. If you wish to be like them, you must face your fears as well.

We have noted some items that we wish to bring to your attention again. We've also given you suggestions for how you might be creative. Would anyone like to share their experience of creativity? No matter how trite it might seem, each experience has value and may instruct others. Who would like to share?

A CREATIVE EXPERIENCE

JULIE: Well, I'll start off. I tried a new way, for me, of painting or using color this past week that was without any plan or form to it. And I noticed quite a bit of fear arising when I did it, because I guess I had expectations. I keep thinking I've gotten rid of expectations, but there must have been some because I felt annoyance and fear about it. I wasn't happy or satisfied with the work. I remember you said last week that with creativity comes chaos. It felt chaotic to me, and it wasn't a lot of fun.

MONITOR: You are indeed engaged in a creative process. To experience chaos means that you are stretching beyond the former patterns of your mind. So your mind will be exposed to new patterns. "Chaos" is an appropriate word for describing the transition from old to new patterns. We have also described creativity as involving risk. Have you felt the risk?

JULIE: Yes, very much so. Very uncomfortable.

MONITOR: Human beings are called on to take many risks in relationships. Many choices are forced by relationships. Relationship draws an individual out, causing exposure of those aspects of self that the individual would prefer not to expose. Yet that exposure gives opportunity for the individual to become aware of and release old patterns that have not been previously recognized or understood.

The artist in Julie has encountered a relationship with color and paint, and experiences a sense of risk because the color and the paint function in new ways that exceed old limits. So there is an aspect in Julie who reacts in fear and feels out of control. Julie, what aspect do you feel reacts that way?

JULIE: Well, in terms of Self Integration, the Judge Self, the fear self, the part that says it should look a certain way. The part that has expectations.

MONITOR: We agree. And the Mental Judge Self wishes to be safe, right, and perfect. When it cannot, it feels disturbed; it feels in the midst of chaos, which leads us to appreciation of the concept of *surrender*, which has great value if one understands "surrender to what?" If one surrenders to chaos, one more readily discovers the new order, the new pattern in what appears to be chaos.

What changes is the mind that perceives. As our perceptions change, the reactive patterns – the habits that our mind maintains – also have opportunity to change. Therefore a creative person changes more rapidly than a person who avoids creativity.

ARTISTS

An artist has a great opportunity to experience creativity, and so the role of artist has been, throughout human history, a position of opportunity for personal change. The statement has been made that the artist is the "sensitivity of the race." It has also been said that the artist functions years ahead of the time in which most other people function. We say that the artist lives more in the present, and that other people, who are not as creative, function more in the past, in their habits.

OVERCOMING FEAR PARALYSIS

JULIE: Monitor, I know individuals who get so paralyzed with fear that they cannot function. Could you give some method or suggestion for breaking through that stuck place?

MONITOR: We talked last time about the dysfunctional fear reaction which may paralyze individuals or cause them to continually flee or continually fight some foe. We distinguished it from the healthy reaction of fear that is an in-built condition of the human body. Healthy fear properly functions by sounding an alarm, giving a warning to cause an individual to pay attention.

Dysfunctional fear results from an individual accepting illusions as truth. A common illusion is the feeling that one is helpless. Doesn't the belief in helplessness create actual helplessness? If an individual does not perceive options of positive action and positive change, he/she chooses not to change, but remains the same, choosing to stay in a rut. A person who is paralyzed by fear is not truly paralyzed, but simply believes he/she is paralyzed.

Consider where fear originates. In those instances, fear originates in the subconscious mind, not the Outer Self. One of the aspects of the subconscious mind has bought the illusion of helplessness and experiences such fear of helplessness that the other Selves are convinced of its truth. Yet if one of those Selves chooses to act creatively, the illusion of helplessness immediately begins to crumble.

The strategy for change, in assisting a person paralyzed by fear, involves assisting one of their Selves to become creative, to initiate significant change, even if on a small scale. The Self who persists in its illusion of helplessness blinds itself to learning. It may be assisted through prayer, through the helpful energies and ministrations of some other Self or person, yet it must come to the point where it chooses creative action and moves beyond the illusion. Does this make any sense to you?

JULIE: Yes. Thank you.

SETH

MARGE: I would like to ask if the entity, Seth, is in this family of Monitor.

JULIE: In the 153 beings comprising Monitor?

MONITOR: We would say, "No." The entity, Seth, represents a composite similar to our composite, but is not present in our grouping. It is, however, still active in the planet and functioning through a small number of channels at this time.

MARGE: Thank you.

MONITOR: Have we put you all to sleep? If so, we hope you have beautiful dreams!

VIBRATORY LEARNING

ERMA: Is it possible to be quiet and just be in the presence of another personality to share creativeness?

MONITOR: Indeed, yes. Much important learning and change in consciousness occurs when one person experiences the presence of another person. Without exchange of words, the consciousness of one affects the consciousness of the other.

Persons may benefit from being with certain individuals of vibratory capability. Those individuals may be other human beings, devas, angels, or what you term "extraterrestrials," travelers from other solar systems.

Much of the time, as your Outer Self sleeps at night, your Subconscious Selves do exactly that. They go to be with some Being whose presence provides them with the vibratory qualities they need. Because most of the personality does not use spoken language, it learns primarily through direct contact. You may describe that contact as telepathy, but it consists of more than that. It involves Being in contact with Being, which represents more than mind in contact with mind.

We have suggested, if you are truly intrepid, that you find an anthill and spend time with the ants. We're not suggesting that you let them crawl all over your precious body, but simply by being present with the ants, you will find the consciousness of the ants changed by contact with your consciousness. Conversely, your consciousness may be changed by their consciousness.

Consider what's happening in this room at this moment. Notice what you feel, notice what you sense. Who would like to share what they're experiencing?

GROUP: A great sense of peace.

MONITOR: What else do you experience?

GROUP: Oneness.
Acceptance.
Heightened awareness.
A difference in physical vibration.

MONITOR: A difference in physical vibration. Indeed, you are experiencing contact with us, and we are experiencing contact with you.

You have learned, throughout human history, to consider yourselves as lesser beings than those of us who no longer occupy physical bodies. This offers a prime example of illusion. Why would that make you lesser beings? We, on our part, are affected vibratorily by you to a high degree. In order to perform our mission well, we have sufficient numbers of individuals who allow us to adjust our reactions that stem from contact with you. Our sensitivity is such that we may be greatly affected by you.

GROUP CONSCIOUSNESS

Such sharings as this allow for dispersal of fear patterns and illusions. If some are dispersed this evening in our company, that makes it easier for other groups around the planet. What they accomplish also makes it easier for us. The Hierarchy promotes greater numbers of such exchanges at this time. It emphasizes group activity, because group activity now provides individuals within the group greater access to their Souls.

The consciousness of your Soul is focused on the maximum benefit of Life in this planet and beyond. Your Soul will not act in ways that fail to benefit all of Life in this planet. How then do you, as personalities, become attuned and in harmony with your Souls except by learning to *be like* your Souls, learning to *embody* the qualities of your Souls?

Experience in a group such as this creates a collective consciousness that enables each individual present to be more experienced in, and accepting of, contact with their own Soul. In other words, this is a way of creating Oneness. We consider it important that you and others understand the importance of group process, group consciousness, as a bridge between the individual personality and its Soul.

ONENESS WITH SOUL

Creativity functions in many ways. If we restate the ultimate challenge, creativity involves the creation of Oneness of Being. The *crucial* Oneness of Being – that needs to be accomplished within the next two hundred years of physical time – lies in developing rapport between personality and Soul. That rapport will never be developed by following rote formulae. It may only be approached by the individual personality acting creatively. Such creativity entails risks, where a personality meets those experiences that it most wishes to avoid. As a personality accepts, as an experience, that which it wishes to avoid, that personality gains sufficient wholeness, sufficient vibratory capability in the structure of mind and body, that it may achieve rapport with its Soul. Hallelujah!

GROUP: *[Laughter]*

LIFE WORK OR CAREER

DORIS: What about creativity as connected with life work and life purpose?

MONITOR: A person, who manages to make his/her life work a work of creativity, experiences many advantages. The person who makes his/her life work one of dull repetition has disadvantages. A creative practitioner or career person enjoys a greater range of experiences, *including* those experiences that they most wish to avoid. Thereby, they grow; they flourish! Their creativity deepens, broadens in scope, becomes more rich, and touches people more profoundly. The person who acts as a dilettante in creativity lacks such inspiration and impact.

To choose to be creative, we must be willing to experience *risk*. The more we create, the more we risk. Obviously, we find elements in the human personality that resist risk. They want to be safe. They wish to be secure and so drag their feet, causing the personality to become stretched like a rubber band, which is what you term "stress."

A good strategy to use is that of a *rhythm* of creativity. In such a rhythm, a personality assesses itself, evaluates its *needs*. On any given day, one aspect of the personality may wish to be creative, to move onward in its expression of Divinity. However, another aspect of the personality may wish to remain safe, stuck in a rut. If the personality ignores one side or the other, it gets ineffective results. If the personality establishes a rhythm which says, "This is the time to be creative," those aspects which desire safety may be safe on the following day or evening, when it's time to cease creative work. If a person meets the needs of both progressive and regressive aspects, a rhythmic balance may be achieved.

Each Self in the personality has its own needs. Its needs are as valid as the needs of the entire personality, just as the needs of one human being are as valid as the needs of the Planetary Being. The validity holds true no matter what the scale of being, because all Life is One Being. All Life expression involves God-in-the-making. So, an effective creative strategy meets the needs of more venturesome aspects and then the needs of the more timid aspects of the personality.

Much of your Life experience is already structured in rhythms that allow for the release of fear. The fear we speak of here involves a dysfunctional fear reaction based upon illusion.

Doris, if your Female Self is fearful that she may not be allowed to be creative, her fear will block her creativity, will it not?

DORIS: Yes.

MONITOR: If you try to force her into creativity, you will have mediocre results, and you will experience increased stress, tension and difficulties. If you recognize her fear, allow her to express her fear, and help her to overcome her fear by assisting her to identify an illusion, she has an opportunity to free herself from that illusion. With your support, she may move beyond that limit into new heights of creativity. Any comments?

LIFE AND DEATH FORCES

SCOTT: To what degree is creativity the same as the Life force? If creativity is a result of the Life force, to what degree is it the result of the Death force? Eastern philosophies often require a negative polarity for each positive force.

MONITOR: You express something that we would like to underline. Creativity may be regarded as *the flow of Life*. That flow of Life generally causes the indwelling being to exceed the limits of its form. Life inhabits form for the purpose of growth. Form gives Life opportunity to individuate, to become a unique expression of the Whole. The form teaches and then must be discarded.

Creativity is required both in the entry of Life into the form and its exit from the form. Creativity may be viewed as the flow of Life *into, through, and out of* the form. The form may be viewed as the structure of a human being, or you could view form as the human being's job, relationship, or lifetime.

Does creativity have an opposite polarity? Yes, *reactivity*. Creativity involves the ability to choose new options. Reactivity represents the ability to choose the same options over and over again.

The drawbacks of creativity are the flushing up of fear, exposure to risk and death – which is not so bad, by the way. The drawbacks of reactivity include no advance in consciousness, inability to have true death or release from form, and extreme limitation of experience. Creativity brings risk. Creativity brings death, in the sense of release from form. And what is so bad about that? Haven't you all, as children, been elated to have school end?

SCOTT: Is creativity an end in itself, if the end appears to destroy its source? For example, a civilization survives by destroying its natural environment. It creates a negative entropy which uses up its resources.

MONITOR: Most of Life does *not* function by negative entropy, which is understood as a breakdown or disintegration of highly evolved systems into less evolved systems. Most of Life evolves into higher systems, which is a process that has only now been recognized by your scientists. Specifically we speak of Ilya Prigogine, the Belgian scientist who has written of his observations of atomic, molecular, and biological processes that evolve into higher systems of order, in what might be called integration or "positive entropy."

Yet negative entropy, or disintegration, must also take place in the balancing of planetary Life. The Planetary Being represents a consciousness in change, moving through its own dynamic process of development. As Planetary Consciousness goes through a particular change, the death of thousands of human beings may result. The destruction of its component beings, in that instance, may benefit the Planetary Being. As the Planetary Being evolves through positive entropy, human beings may experience negative entropy. The human beings released through death may also benefit by release from bodies of lower vibration into bodies of higher vibration, made possible by the evolving Planetary Being.

SCOTT: Is the aim of Eros, the name that Freud gave to the Life force in humanity, to establish and continue the existence of humanity?

MONITOR: Yes, we believe so, although the concept of Eros, as defined by Sigmund Freud, represents to us a partial statement of the action of positive entropy in human beings. His concept, as we interpret it, fails to indicate that the Life force functions in a range of expressions, or in a variety of Selves in the personality. In addition, Freud's concept of Thanatos, or the Death force, we find to be the result of illusion. Therefore, it lacks the status, in our view, of his concept of Eros. We find that the dysfunctional fear reaction produces Thanatos through the illusion of death as the end of Life.

Creativity *contradicts* Thanatos. Although creativity often assumes a destructive role, it *continues Life* rather than ending it. For example, consider the painter, Pablo Picasso, whose work evolved through numerous changes. He periodically sensed that his modes of expression, such as his paintings of the Blue Period, were becoming stale and repetitious. He actively destroyed such stale paintings. He applied paint in ways that effectively destroyed what many people would have called masterpieces. He took risks. He divested his being, his Life force, from old forms and reinvested in chaos, and thereby arrived at new modes of expression.

Destructiveness may be an active form of creativity. Does not the Hindu tradition credit the Destroyer as well as Creator and Sustainer? When one employs the destructive form of creativity, one simplifies by prioritizing options and eliminating most of the options in order to focus on one option. In that way, one may focus one's power creatively and achieve new depths of expression, new discoveries. Such creative choices are best used in a rhythm that alternates creative and destructive modes.

Does that address your question?

SCOTT: I think so. I think, as we experience the world, a lot of what we term "creative" eventually ends up destroying us. But I guess if that means creative transformation to some other form, then it makes sense.

MONITOR: Indeed, it does.

EGO AND FEAR

SCOTT: So the Ego, in itself, needs to be destroyed, which is the need for security, or the need for any kind of reassurance of the future, that needs to be destroyed.

MONITOR: Yes, we have defined Ego as a fear reaction, resistant to change, existing within conscious and subconscious minds.

Human beings are challenged to grow beyond fear. As long as a personality occupies an unglorified physical body, he/she will experience fear. In that condition, which is the normal condition for human beings at this time, we recommend that one recognize the fear reaction as a warning, examine its merit, and go beyond the fear into action.

The fear may *not* be avoided. It may only be denied and suppressed for a time. Fear accumulates, if denied and suppressed, and creates an obstacle, a shell, a boundary, which effectively isolates a person from its Source.

GLORIFICATION

Once a person has faced fear multitudinous times and acted more and more in terms of the creative forces of Love, then he/she changes the vibratory status of their body, and ultimately the body becomes *glorified*. "Glorification," as we use the term, means that the body moves beyond the positive and negative polarization state of physical matter. A glorified body vibratorily achieves a *synthesis* of positive and negative energy states. The synthesis produces a unified state that is not polarized.

Having a glorified physical body gives a person the opportunity of functioning in a state that is harmonious with higher levels of being and certainly that of the Soul. The Soul exists only in a harmonious, unified state. When the Soul is allowed, by the personality, to create a glorified body, a human being becomes something more than a human being.

The norm, at this time of human history, consists of human beings occupying *unglorified* bodies. The norm in the future will be that of human beings occupying *glorified* bodies. How glorious is your body?

GROUP: *[Laughter]*

HELEN: How can a glorified body remain on Earth and not have the polarization of positive and negative?

MONITOR: A glorified body exists in the primary act of creation of the Earth, which was originally created in a unified state. Its energy was not polarized initially. The state of polarization may be described as an overlay on the original non-polarized state.

We have stated several times that each person present is connected as a personality to their Soul. Their Soul is connected by a chain of being to the Creator. Each person represents a direct extension of the Creator at this moment. If you do not experience that in its fullness, you are living in illusion based on fear.

Your fears, therefore, become the *material* of your lessons. You learn lessons of discovering and releasing fear throughout most of your lifetimes on Earth. When you have completed that curriculum, your body achieves glorification. Your Inner Selves achieve a synthesis that produces the clear channels needed for glorification of the body.

Glorification of the body has happened more times in human history than your history notes. Your historians and news reporters do not even expect glorification to occur; yet it does, and has throughout human history. As more and more human beings achieve glorification, that process becomes easier for all other human beings still involved in the curriculum of fear.

Creativity leads to the release of your human form. The body, which you know as your physical body, ceases to exist and is transformed into a unified etheric body, which exists in a unified etheric Earth. And if we use more ether, you will sleep very peacefully!

GROUP: *[Laughter]*

JULIE: Thank you, Monitor.

Lesson 7

May 22, 1991

MONITOR: We welcome you again as Monitor.

As you have been listening to and experiencing us, and as we have been listening to and experiencing you, we have exchanged a flow of Life. That flow has, indeed, been creative. Have you noticed creativity within yourselves? We warned you last time that we would ask this question because we do care that you make some attempt to apply, test, and make the information yours. Have you noticed creativity within yourselves? We would like to hear some of you share your sense of creativity.

JULIE: Anyone have a creative experience? Donna.

DREAMS INVOLVING CREATIVITY

DONNA: May I share a short dream that followed the last meeting? Someone in Harvey's group was painting murals. Someone would paint one on the wall for me, if I had room for it. We came to my house, not where I live now, but could not find a free wall on the first floor. We then went to the recreation room, and there was room for the mural. I never did see the mural, but someone was about to paint it on the wall. Is there any comment on that?

MONITOR: We believe that the dream was talking to you about actions in your subconscious mind. You could view them as Subconscious Selves who are guiding and assisting you to transform walls. What are "walls" to you?

DONNA: Well, they either keep things in or keep things out, I guess.

MONITOR: Indeed. For you and other human beings, walls create a certain kind of structure in which you live. Walls may keep you in or keep you out. Walls, therefore, represent structures, within your life or your belief system, which limit. Now the act of painting a mural upon the wall does what?

DONNA: It takes creativity.

MONITOR: It takes creativity. And the mural is a picture, is it not? A design that would transform the wall from a limitation to a structure of beauty, perhaps. The wall would certainly change its character for you. Now within the dream, did you not have difficulty seeing the mural yourself?

DONNA: No, I didn't see the mural. I did have difficulty because I didn't see the mural.

MONITOR: This would indicate perhaps that the mural was being created on a subconscious level, which is normally beyond the sight of the conscious mind. The wall, or the structure, or the limitation, was one that involved the area of recreation, did it not?

DONNA: Yes.

MONITOR: Your niece has ideas about this. You might consult her as to what it means. You may find, like many other persons, that one becomes compulsive and overdoes responsibilities and obligations and has difficulty simply being. We recommend being as a creative activity. When you become so wrapped up in activities, you are conscious mainly of your human or, let us say, mortal existence, which is only one facet of your being. Most people exclude awareness of all other aspects of their being when they're busy. This is why so many spiritual teachers recommend forms of meditation that involve, fundamentally, providing oneself the opportunity to allow the normal limitations of self-perception to fade away and to permit greater awareness of self. If you, as a human being named Donna, are 90% spiritual being, 3% mental being, 1% emotional being, and 1% material being, then when you are engaged in being aware only of your physical existence, you miss 99% of your being.

Due to dysfunctional fear reactions – which many people learn quite well – most people are quite motivated to retain awareness of only 1% of their being. They prefer to *ignore* 99% of their being because their fears tell them it would be too much for them to handle. Their psychological defenses would be overwhelmed, outflanked by exposure to a greater sense of being. This is why you might say that walls have a purpose, to hold one in or keep one out.

We have mentioned the creative aspect of becoming one with other beings, other forms of Life. One form of dealing with walls, from that perspective, entails sensing a wall, becoming so aware of the wall that one includes it within one's being, creating a Oneness of Being between person and wall. In that process, a person removes the wall as an obstacle or limitation, and beingness becomes greater in the flow of Life between person and wall. A mural, painted on a wall, represents a person's investment of creativity in that wall, and so that wall becomes more than a limitation. Does this make any sense to you?

DONNA: Yes, it does. Thank you.

MONITOR: Thank you for sharing your dream. We enjoy dreams. We find that dreams represent realities and ways of expressing realities that the people of this time greatly need in order to exceed the narrow boxes of understanding so prevalent now.

HELEN: Monitor, since you enjoy dreams, would you like another?

MONITOR: Oh, indeed!

HELEN: This one I believe happened before we got into the subject of creativity. In the dream I was in the midst of remodeling my house, and everything was getting done.

MONITOR: One's house represents what to you?

HELEN: Well, it could be the physical body, but it can also, I think, be the entire set-up of all the bodies.

MONITOR: Indeed, it could have multiple meanings. And so representing the place and the conditions in which you are living, the house was being remodeled, changed. Notice the term "remodeled." If you consider your consciousness, at that time, as being modeled, it was being introduced to a new model. The word "model" suggests "mode." It suggests a means or a way of acting or of living. Therefore, changing your ways of acting or living had significance. Now in your dream, where was the remodeling taking place? In the front, in the back - what part of your house?

HELEN: The main floor and also upstairs.

MONITOR: The upstairs would represent what to you?

HELEN: Spirit, I think.

MONITOR: Spirit or Higher Consciousness would be a reasonable interpretation, in our opinion, and that remodeling might take place on levels perhaps out of sight of the Outer Self, as the previous dream related. You may be well assured that the dream represents a change occurring in consciousness *beyond* your Outer Self. In the dream, how did you react to the remodeling?

HELEN: Oh, I was very excited about it, very pleased.

MONITOR: That presents a positive and a creative response. Some people would be upset. Some people would be frightened of remodeling. We appreciate your acceptance. Is there anything further about the dream you would wish to explore?

HELEN: I think there was a lot of work being done on the floors.

MONITOR: And what would the floors represent to you?

HELEN: Foundation, understanding.

MONITOR: Foundation, understanding, indeed. Understand what we are saying, that changes in understanding have already taken place within your subconscious mind, and will become apparent to your conscious mind.

TIME STREAMS

It may help you to consider that actions within the subconscious mind operate on a different set of "time streams" than occurs within the time stream of the Outer Self. We speak of time as "streams" because of the nature of consciousness, which utilizes the ability to choose among options. Time, therefore, is subservient to the need of the person to make choices.

You might not notice any effect of time change as an Outer Self, but if you were experiencing Life from the viewpoint of the subconscious mind, you would experience parallel, diverging, and converging streams of time. Now this perhaps sounds obscure to you, but we will attempt to give you a glimpse into the perspectives of the subconscious mind in this regard.

The subconscious mind that you glimpse in your dreams as illustrated by these two dreams, deals with several probable streams of time. Each stream of time contains a series of events. The subconscious mind explores the consequences of choices. If, for example, Helen considered abandoning her house because it is being remodeled, the subconscious mind would react to that thought as it is expressed by the Outer Self. If that thought occurred during a particular day, the subconscious mind would explore the various possibilities that choice led to. The subconscious mind also explores other possible choices, depending on its own background and creativity. Once its investigation is complete, the subconscious mind might feed back to the Outer Self the most desirable choice, or the least desirable choice, and its consequences to the Outer Self by means of a dream experience. In this way, a helpful exchange occurs.

DREAMS AS COMMUNICATION

To the Outer Self, dream experiences often seem quite different than the Outer Self's normal mode of experience. Helen, in her dream, might run into a giraffe wearing pink tights, which she would normally not expect when she was awake. The subconscious mind would be using such an image either to communicate some definite meaning or to gain the attention of the Outer Self sufficiently that the Outer Self would retain memory of the dream.

You must understand that your subconscious minds are frequently frustrated at the Outer Self's lack of grasp of sleep experience. It is as though the Outer Self were a child being taken on a journey, and the child falls asleep at many of the most important places. The subconscious mind learns early within the childhood of the physical body that it does little good to keep waking up the child, because the child becomes confused and disturbed.

So the subconscious mind strategically chooses sleep experiences that are carefully selected and presented to the Outer Self.

We do not want to leave you with the impression that this is all the subconscious mind does, because this represents perhaps 2% of the activity of the subconscious mind. It has many other interests and activities taking place. Yet the subconscious mind does have a greater flexibility with streams of time than the Outer Self. The Outer Selves of people, who become capable of sensing the future or the past, gain that capability through the cooperation of some aspect of the subconscious minds. Now are there some questions or comments?

CARL JUNG

ARZANI: After last week's meeting we were discussing Carl Jung, and we wanted to know your opinion about how integrated his personality was, how evolved his teachings were, from your perspective.

MONITOR: We find that one of the great values of Carl Jung was his ability to communicate information received from beyond his "conscious mind." His experience was carefully structured to allow him to be made aware of various degrees of the subconscious mind, or various levels. He, as an Outer Self, did well to pay attention to that plan. He performed his mission in an excellent manner.

This aspect represents what we would suggest, from our perspective, his greatest contribution to humanity, opening the doors to the so-called "unconscious mind." We find, however, that he did not go through those doors as far as many individuals are today going. So we find advancements being made, important advancements that provide a greater sense of direction and a greater indication of the landscapes of subconscious and superconscious minds.

We appreciate his contribution, and state that he remains quite active in the pursuit of passing on information to many individuals who are students of his. We speak here especially of students who are in a physical body. One advantage of his contribution is that he assisted his students to remain open to what would come through the unconscious mind, and so he especially has access to his students. Does this answer your question?

ARZANI: Yes.

DREAM FROM FEMALE SELF

JULIE: Any other questions? Mary.

MARY: Okay, if I could ask you to digress a little bit. I had a dream a couple of nights ago that was particularly confusing. I woke up right afterwards and knew I should write it down, but it had an ominous feeling to it, so I didn't do it. I had a feeling that I was getting some kind of a message that I had a limited amount of time to complete something, and that the numbers, which were like fifteen or sixty days, stuck with me as I tried to recall the dream later. Its message was I just better get about my business and hurry up because I had a limited amount of time to do this. It had a very ominous feeling to it, so I concluded that I might die, or something like that. I got later that it could also indicate change. The other remembrance from the dream was that there was a ring in it that had a number of diamonds and rubies. It wasn't a ring that I am familiar with. I think that ring has shown up in several different dreams. It had a very clear message, but I didn't get it.

MONITOR: Do you recall whether the ring was a woman's ring or a man's ring?

MARY: It was a woman's ring.

MONITOR: Very good. Then this gives you a clue that your Feminine Aspect or your Female Self was attempting to encourage your completion of a task within the time designated. We find that the ominous tone was simply her insistence that it be done, and we find that her insistence is well placed. She has been concerned that you, the Outer Self, would continue to be distracted.

The ring represents a past life experience where she had authority, so that sense of authority was present in the dream. It appears that the presence of authority was such that you interpreted it as a sign of impending doom, which we assure you it is not.

If you were to ask her, within your mind, what assignment needs to be completed, she would find it much easier to remind you.

Understand that the subconscious mind communicates normally in a telepathic manner. When it communicates telepathically with the Outer Self, the Outer Self is often not receptive. The Outer Self is too often focused with need for words of language. As the Outer Self gains experience in meditation, it becomes more accepting of telepathic communication. The subconscious mind, which is often frustrated by its difficulties of communicating, will then renew efforts to assist the Outer Self in accomplishing what it needs to for the optimal benefit of the being.

This dream is not an ominous dream, simply a weighted reminder.

CARL JUNG AND ARCHETYPES

MARY: I want to get back to Carl Jung. He talked a lot about integration of a person and, in fact, didn't think he was fully integrated even at the time of his death. Is creativity one of the most difficult parts to integrate?

MONITOR: Not at all. Creativity is actually *a process of integration*. We have described it as a flow of Life from one being to another, or from one Self to another, one aspect of a personality to another aspect of that personality. It definitely *assists* integration.

We find that Carl Jung was not fully integrated at the time of his physical death. In our opinion, he is now much more integrated.

We also raise a question that we have not heard, yet deserves addressing, "What is the relationship between creativity and the concept of archetypes?" We thought you would never ask, so we ask the question. The concept of archetypes was a contribution of Carl Jung, yet, in our opinion, his descriptions of archetypes seem rudimentary.

Many persons now have come to believe that they are shaped and driven by archetypes. The image they present is that of themselves as small objects being driven by the enormous power of planetary archetypes. We do *not* agree with this image. We do agree that the experience of being driven by archetypes does occur to human beings, but not as a consistent experience.

The archetypes that Carl Jung talked about represent patterns in the causal plane of the planet. Those causal patterns consist of vibratory patterns, configurations of vibrations in the causal plane. The significance of these patterns is that *they structure the vibrations of the mental plane.* It is the mental plane vibrations that affect human, devic, and elemental beings. These archetypes represent vibratory *predispositions*. They flow throughout the entire energy field of the planet. They permeate all parts of the planet.

A human being may find himself, or herself, subjected to those patterns at times through the vibratory action of the mental plane on the mind of a human being. That interaction, that effect of the archetype takes place in the subconscious mind of the human being, not within the Outer Self. The Outer Self is too insubstantial to be affected by the archetype. The subconscious mind, however, is sufficiently substantial to be affected, and so one aspect of the subconscious mind may be driven by one archetype, while another aspect of the subconscious mind may be driven by another archetype.

A more proper description of the effect of archetypes on a human being would be a *dance of archetypes* in the subconscious mind. Much as you conceive of the motion of planets and stars relative to the Earth as having cycles and seasons of vibratory effects, so may you consider the cyclical effects of archetypes.

Creativity, for a human being, involves the ability of the subconscious mind to move into and out of an archetype experience. Furthermore, when a subconscious mind is in the midst of the archetype experience, it may use creativity to further intensify or dramatize the archetype by expressing it more fully.

JULIE: Could you give us an example of that?

MONITOR: We may not easily give an example of the subconscious mind, but we can give an example that illustrates the effect of the subconscious mind's dance with archetypes.

In the early portion of this century, you know of a woman named Isadora Duncan who was a great expresser of her subconscious mind. She expressed both male and female aspects with dramatic flair. Her Female Aspect was extremely aesthetic in her expressions, which were perhaps best expressed in dance. In this instance, the Female Self of Isadora Duncan was able to express the archetype of Divine Lover, the Goddess, or that aspect of the Divine Feminine.

You may also find an example in General George Patton, whose Male Self expressed the warrior archetype. George Patton possessed sufficient intelligence, as an Outer Self, to allow his Male Self to express its intuition, its wisdom, and thereby save many lives of soldiers. Does this assist you?

CREATIVE VISUALIZATION

DONNA: In the Ancient Wisdom text that I have here, it says, "You can have what you want. You can do what you want. You can be what you want." Is this brought into manifestation by creative visualization?

MONITOR: Indeed, although not all people are equally competent at visualization. Some people will simply act, and their actions become their visualization. If a person is attempting to manifest a quality or situation, that person is required to create the vibratory conditions he or she is seeking to manifest. Vibratory conditions are created within the mind and emotions of that person before they may be manifested in the energy field external to that person. Just as the baby comes forth from the body of the mother, so the manifestation must come forth from the bodies of the manifestor. If the manifestor has only a vague notion of what he or she is to manifest, the manifestation will be equally vague. If the manifestor has the specific notion of what is to be manifested, then he or she may manifest that, yet get in trouble because he or she has perhaps not acted for the highest good.

We have mentioned that one of the greatest expressions of creativity involves exercising sensitivity to the needs of all of Life. The Buddha described this as "harmlessness" or as benefit to all of Life, to the Whole. Therefore, when you seek to manifest, you may avoid difficulty by asking that the manifestation be done in a way that benefits the Whole of Life. Realize that you, as Outer Selves, grasp only a small portion of Life, of reality, and so you are wise to allow your Higher Consciousness to guide you, in manifestation especially.

MANIFESTATION

JULIE: Monitor, at one time a spiritual teacher named Frida Waterhouse shared with me that her view was that there were two paths that we could walk. On one path you asked God specifically for what you wanted and accepted it, and God would give it to you. The other path was to surrender to the higher wisdom and trust that everything you needed was provided. And she also said that we needed to choose one path or the other, and whichever path we chose, to choose it without guilt. But we couldn't walk both paths at the same time. And I'd like your view on that, on her view.

MONITOR: We, in general, agree. The person who chooses to ask God for whatever he/she wishes to manifest acts from a certain set of conditions. Those conditions involve the disposition of the subconscious mind of that person. The subconscious mind needs to explore personal empowerment or individuation, and so needs the experience of receiving that which it asks for. In that way they learn the value of asking for that which is for the greatest benefit to the Whole of Life. They learn that lesson by experiencing the consequences of seeking to benefit themselves and not the Whole of Life. That experience shows them that they are part of the Whole and cannot successfully divorce themselves from the Whole. Once that path has been followed to its final point, they have the other path open to them as an option. Do you understand us?

JULIE: Yes, thank you.

FRIDA WATERHOUSE

ARZANI: I wonder if you are you familiar with Frida Waterhouse on your side?

MONITOR: Indeed, yes.

ARZANI: How is she?

MONITOR: She is quite well and in the process of re-embodying within this year. She is enthusiastic about these times of change in the planet and wishes to participate in these changes.

JULIE: Thank you. Any other questions?

MONITOR: We warn you, if you do not ask questions, we will talk!

SELF-AWARENESS

JULIE: I have one. I have one! One exercise that you suggested was noticing our reactions to whatever is going on, and to notice if we're being reactive or creative. And so I've been doing that, paying attention to feelings and what's going on. It seems that my reactions are a lot stronger, even the reactive ones. The more attention I pay when I work with them, the stronger and more reactive they become. Is this a step forward or backward?

MONITOR: We congratulate you on opening to an awareness of the real strength of your reactions and creations. Previously you, as most human beings, have throttled back your awareness and thereby have been largely driven by the strength of reactions and have limited your ability to create. When you and other persons open yourselves to sense fully the patterns in you of habit, of reaction, you are able to create more effectively. How can you alter that which you do not sense?

JULIE: You can't. Any other questions about creativity?

DREAM ABOUT EXPOSURE

LINDA: I have a question about a dream I had. I had an idea what it was saying and I'd like to check it out. I was doing some work in my nightgown. I have this rose-colored nightgown. It's my very favorite, but it's so old I'm going to have to throw it away before long. In my dream I was working, doing a lot of physical work with a lot of people, when I realized that I didn't have any underwear on. I'd been working for a couple of hours. And then I thought, "It's a little late to think about that since I've just been out here working for two hours. You can see through it anyway. Oh well, it doesn't really matter." And the dream ended. For a moment there I was feeling a little embarrassed. So I feel that I'm releasing or letting go of a lot of stuff.

MONITOR: We find, Linda, that this relates to your concerns about giving sermons. It helps you to understand that even though you are willing to do the work, you at times feel exposed and vulnerable in your Male Self. We have spoken to you of the times of persecution in past lives that he experienced. This dream is showing his progress.

LINDA: Thank you.

MONITOR: And consider the color, rose, as a color of comfort and also suggestive of the action of the kundalini force that accompanies the progress of the subconscious mind. You are likely to have experiences in the second and third chakra areas, involving the kundalini experience, which will not be traumatic, but the product of natural growth beyond fear.

LINDA: Thank you. Today in class they were asking for volunteers for speakers throughout the summer, and I cringed and said, "No, I'm not going to do this." One title, "First things first," just grabbed me, and all the time I heard this inner voice nudging me to volunteer for that. It came to me that Spirit was nudging me so that I can conquer this fear, but I was just holding back.

MONITOR: Your High Self is doing the nudging, and your Male Self is gradually progressing.

GONAD CHAKRA

MONITOR: Let us now introduce a couple of statements concerning the relationship of creativity to the chakras. This dream, through the rose color, suggests the action of creativity in the first chakra at the base of the spine. The dominant color in that chakra may be described as red or crimson. Through the infusion of the White Light entering through the aerial circuit which links the chakras, the first chakra becomes rose-colored. The action of creativity in that chakra lies in the use of will, primarily in the subconscious mind, in accepting the forces represented by White Light, thereby changing habit patterns and becoming creatively altered by those forces.

The subconscious mind manages the chakras, and in this instance within Linda, the first chakra is managed by her Male Self. We find that his choice to overcome his fears allows him to accept more completely that presence or that pattern of energy that you may term "the Christ." He was one of those who went forth preaching the new and heretical gospel of Gnostic Christianity and was punished and killed for that activity. The trauma caused him to question his acceptability, his worthiness to receive the presence of the Christ. We find that, in this lifetime, the testing has provided him with opportunity to go beyond the walls of fear, which had previously limited his behavior.

FEAR WALLS

As in the previous dream discussed by Donna, we discussed the function of walls as limitations. If a person wishes to avoid an experience, he/she creates a wall that blocks that experience from happening. That is an example of the action of fear. We have previously said that planet Earth is a very good place to experience that which you most wish to avoid. In Earth one creates a wall, then another opportunity presents itself. One creates walls until one has thoroughly imprisoned oneself. After a sufficient time of boredom, that person seeks any way out of that prison and becomes motivated to remove walls.

What happens when a wall is removed? Fear is experienced, and one is challenged whether or not to proceed through the opening in the wall or to retreat back into one's prison. And if one proceeds, one meets that experience which they had wished to avoid and thereby, in the meeting, is transformed. In the meeting one becomes more whole, more complete, more fulfilled. How else is wholeness achieved except by one's willingness to meet what one most wishes to avoid?

The Male Self, in Linda's situation, remained in the prison of his fears, sheltered safely within walls on all sides, until gradually, in the last two lifetimes, he was willing to move through walls. In this lifetime, his fear patterns are greatly diminished, but still present. As he continues to give talks, those fears will totally disperse.

GROUP NAME

DONNA: Does Monitor have a name for our group?

MONITOR: Because we normally do not use human language, we do not have a name, but what you might term an image, a construction for the group. If we used words, we would use the term "Explorations Group."

We see each of you as expressions of the Creator, just as we are. We see you as equals with this difference – you are functioning in deep sea diving suits, while we wear skimpy bathing suits on the deck of the ship. We can enjoy the breeze. We can enjoy the skies. We can watch the dolphins jumping above the waves while you wrestle underwater with giant clams!

We thank you once again. We encourage you to share experiences, as well as dreams, and to bring questions. You may consider some areas that we have just touched on this evening – the relationship of creativity to archetypes and chakras.

We bless you, and we leave you now.

Lesson 8

May 29, 1991

MONITOR: We welcome you again as Monitor. Do you have something to ask or something to share?

JULIE: We welcome you, Monitor. Would anyone like to share anything? I have a question, but would anyone would like to share anything first?

MONITOR: You'd better get your question in!

CONSEQUENCES OF AVOIDANCE

JULIE: You've said before that we are here to learn what we most want to avoid. What happens to us mentally, emotionally, physically and spiritually, if we do continue to avoid what we're supposed to be learning? How does it affect us in mind and body and experience?

MONITOR: An excellent question. Consider: what energy are you creating when you are in the process of avoiding? In a word, fear. Fear, as an energy, radiates from you when you are fearful. It flows throughout your chakra system and tends to enclose your chakras in containers, shells, which dim the radiance of your chakras. In this way, the Life force is "hidden beneath a bushel," you might say, or hidden within shells. And you may have more than one shell of fear around a chakra. The fear piles on, layer after layer, as you continue to avoid what you have come to experience, to express and learn.

A person who persists in avoidance places himself in shell after shell of fear and becomes less able to interact with Life, less able to interact with other Life forms, less able to know himself, less able to feel, less able to think. In brief, such people turn themselves into zombies, not quite alive, yet not quite dead, in the sense that people think of death. You might call the person who is avoiding a "professional avoider," one who is a walking dead person, one who is given the opportunity for living, yet chooses to avoid that opportunity.

What consequence does that have in a single lifetime? Well it has, of course, the consequence of cutting oneself off from Love, from friendship, from fulfillment of any kind of creativity. That person will most likely create some form of illness through the action of his subconscious mind.

The subconscious mind of that person will probably be divided between that portion which seeks to live, express, and feel, and that portion locked in fear. The portion that seeks Life will attempt to create a physical illness as a way of forcing a change of circumstances, a drastic enough change that would allow the Outer Self of the person to begin to realize what they have created in fear. If the creation of illness doesn't work, then the part of the subconscious mind that is seeking Life seeks death, seeks removal from that physical body into a less restricted condition.

After physical death such a person, who has been locked in fear, is still locked in fear, yet the Outer Self is removed as a *separate* factor. It is absorbed within the subconscious mind, and that portion of the subconscious mind that has been seeking Life gains greater freedom. It has been said – rightly so, in our opinion – that the subconscious mind operates like the Outer Self after physical death. The part of the subconscious mind seeking Life has greater opportunity after physical death to seek assistance and create avenues for healing and positive change in that personality. The part of the subconscious mind that has been locked in fear needs assistance. If it is truly incapable of being persuaded to let go of the fear, it must receive assistance, and excellent forms of assistance are made available after physical death.

So we can assure you that the person, who has been locked in fear and had to die in fear, will be assisted and freed from a great deal of that fear, freed from a paralyzed state after physical death. Beyond that point, the aspect of the subconscious mind that has been locked in fear will need to re-embody. In re-embodiment it will face the same choices, but hopefully will have benefited from instruction as well as healing, in that interim between physical lives. When they re-embody, they will have additional resources and perhaps additional motivation to make decisions that help them face what they have sought to avoid. They may then be better empowered to learn their lessons and express what they have come to express. Does this address the question?

ILLNESS AND BODY CONSCIOUSNESS

ARZANI: Is illness ever given as part of someone's plan rather than as a reaction to fear?

MONITOR: Quite often illness is given as a part of a plan of growth, aside from questions of fear. Yet even then it is strongly related to fear. It is important that the indwelling mind of the physical body learn the limitations of the physical body. There are many advantages to those lessons. Illness assists that mind which has been using physical bodies — one after the other — as vehicles for experience, to relate to the elemental consciousness that comprises the physical body. The elemental consciousness evolves in its own right and has its own worth and eventual glorious destiny. It comes to a point of frustration in those persons who fail to recognize it, and comes to a point of recognition and opportunity for fulfillment in those persons who do contact, respect, and communicate with it in a sense of true equality. It is wise for each human being to learn of his/her own Body Self.

Have you talked to your liver lately? Have you asked your big toe how it feels about your lifestyle? Consider the possible advantages of such communication. You might assume, because you haven't asked such questions, that your Body Self doesn't care. We suggest that is *not* the case. Your Body Self gains in capability and complexity. It has much to offer in terms of preferences and opinions.

You would do well to take excellent care of your vehicles, but many times you fail to do so because of various distractions. Ask your Body Consciousness what it wishes to eat, when it wishes to eat, when it wishes to sleep, when it wishes exercise, and when it desires rest. If you ask with a sense of respect, as communicating with an equal, you will be pleasantly surprised with the response you may receive.

If your Body Self feels your respect, then when your body moves out of balance, such as getting a cold or some other dysfunction, you will receive very useful, pertinent information. If you have been ignoring your Body Self and ask, you might not receive a very pleasant reception. The horse that has been ridden by a demanding rider and has been spurred and forced beyond its normal limits of endurance will likely resent its rider. If you have taken good care of your horse, it will be inclined to take good care of you as the rider. Enough of this horsing around! Let's have some more questions or experiences. *[Laughter.]*

JUDGE SELVES

HELEN: If a person dies because of fears generated by his Judge Selves, does that same subconscious mind come back into another lifetime with the same Judge Selves to work on the same things they avoided?

MONITOR: Yes, that is the pattern, as we understand it.

HELEN: So if they haven't worked through those fears with those particular Judge Selves, they have to repeat?

MONITOR: Yes. The Judge Selves represent a great potential in each person that tends to be locked in a prison of fear. The Judge Selves fear! Unless they are aided sufficiently by other aspects of the personality, Judge Selves continue to stay in prison, not understanding that they may be released and that, with assistance, they may open the door of their cell and emerge into Light and Love. Consider that a Judge Self is like a person who has been raised by animals and needs a positive human example, a role model to emulate in terms of caring, loving, and cooperating. It needs to learn how to care about other aspects of self, how to love and how to cooperate. It learns through *example*, not precept. What a Judge Self does not learn in one lifetime or between lifetimes, it must re-embody to learn. The personality can develop this great potential, if it responds to the needs of its Judge Selves.

Look around you in this world and recognize the actions of fear in personalities in positions of leadership at all levels of government and enterprise. That fear is most certainly *not* the product of the Outer Self or

Surface Mind. The fear comes from the aspects of the subconscious mind who do not recognize or accept easily the action of Love.

When the Outer Self of a personality begins to achieve Love and success, one of its Judge Selves normally feels excluded and resents the happiness or fulfillment of the Outer Self. The Judge Self then seeks to destroy that happiness. It attacks the Outer Self in obvious or subtle ways. When it succeeds in its attack, a Judge Self feels a measure of empowerment and safety. If you wish to avoid such conditions, which are normal among humanity, then meet and positively address this shadowy part of your personality. This is definitely the agenda for growth for humanity at this time and for the next approximately two hundred years. This challenge represents "meeting that which you most wish to avoid."

OVERCOMING FEARS

LINDA: I just wanted to let you know that I've been looking at my actions of avoidance and fear since you've been talking about it the last few weeks.

MONITOR: Excellent, we're pleased that you've done this!

LINDA: And I did the talk again from the pulpit, and everything went very well. It just flowed.

JULIE: She got a standing ovation.

MONITOR: Do you accept this feedback from the universe?

LINDA: Yes, thank you. It was wonderful. I just felt the energy of Love coming from the people I was talking to. It was coming through, and I was giving it back to them.

MONITOR: Consider how well your Male Self and Mental Judge Self have learned to function together in overcoming their past challenges, the persecution from the past. They have learned well. Have you thanked and congratulated them?

LINDA: No, I didn't think about that or about how they might feel.

MONITOR: We suggest that you thank those aspects of you that have learned and demonstrated their learning through the action of speaking.

LINDA: Okay. I really thank them. The other thing I wanted to change, another fearful thing to me, was leaving the Science of Mind organization and my practice as a Practitioner. It was like saying, "I am not enough." So I've made that decision. I'm going to take the big leap, and I'll be ordained on Sunday.

MONITOR: We congratulate you.

LINDA: So I'm feeling real good about looking at my fears, just becoming one with them, and continuing to conquer them.

MONITOR: Conquering is one image; another image is that of alchemy. When we realize that fear is an expression of the One Life, we can realize that we may take that energy of fear, accept it as it is, and change it into a positive expression of energy, which may be Love, joy, endurance, or whatever positive quality we wish. This offers a very specific meaning for the term "alchemy." The concept is: use the Life force instead of denying or blocking it. Allow it to flow, yet use your creative ability to transform, to transmute fear into a positive expression of Life.

LINDA: Thank you.

MONITOR: Thank you for your accomplishments.

ILLNESS AND GOD

ARZANI: A friend asked me to ask this. She is dealing with cancer, and I had mentioned that I thought cancer was an excellent test. And she said, "God wouldn't do that to us. God loves us. God wouldn't give us something painful and terrible like that." How would you respond to her?

MONITOR: We ask the questions first: "Where is God?" and "Who is God?" We've stated our bias before, that God is present in all of Life. We certainly agree that some distant deity does not give a human being cancer. Yet the Life force, the Deity within that person, may certainly create cancer or other illnesses and challenges to assist the conscious and subconscious minds to make their choices. How does an evolving individual learn to accept wholeness and Oneness with all of Life except by exercising choices which accept Life as the individual finds it?

Many times an individual seeks to avoid those aspects of Life present in his life path, so illness is created when no other measure seems sufficient to bring that individual's attention to bear on what he needs to face, accept, and learn. How can any being learn what it does not even recognize or accept?

We have talked about the fundamental use of creativity in becoming aware. Once a person is aware of an energy, a Life force, a condition which it experiences, then he/she may accept and work creatively with it.

Next month we will be talking about "The Nature of Reality" and how human beings create their reality. This question borders on that topic.

ELEMENTAL CONSCIOUSNESS

ARZANI: One other thing that will keep me up, if you don't answer it. When you talked about the elemental consciousness as having its own destiny, what is its destiny?

MONITOR: Oneness with God. Just as any other expression of Life, the elemental consciousness follows its path of evolution, which leads it to the same destiny as all other forms of Life.

Consider that Life exists throughout the universe as threads of evolution that interweave and, together, create a tapestry of creative, evolving Life threads that at first may struggle, conflict, and compete, yet through that experience gain capabilities of sensitivity and action that allow for resolution of conflicts and achievement of Oneness.

We have spoken of creativity as being a flow of Life between Life forms. An example of this may be sculpture, which engages the spectator and gives him an impact of Life force created, in part, by the act of the sculptor. Creativity stimulates Oneness by stimulating the flow of Life force among Life forms. Did we answer your question so that you may sleep?

ARZANI: No! Is there an image I could give my own Elemental Being to stimulate it to be more willing to cooperate?

MONITOR: Rather than you providing an image, why not ask your elemental consciousness for its image of its destiny?

We find at this point in human evolution, primarily in Western culture, an assumption that the consciousness of the body dies. "Dust returns to dust." And in one sense that's true, but we challenge the assumption that the dust is *not* conscious. We see all matter as alive, and all energy as alive. All exists within the definition of consciousness, as we see it.

When a physical body dies and the Soul, who has been animating and utilizing the body as a vehicle, removes itself from that vehicle, its elements return to a natural state. As Life changing forms, the elements *retain* consciousness and will be reassembled in other forms of Life. The consciousness of the elemental kingdom moves from its identification with a specific form – such as a rock, a flower, a cloud, an ostrich, or a human physical body – to a greater sense of Life.

How does elemental consciousness evolve beyond the identity of its form? By experiencing form after form after form. Through this kind of repetitive experience, elemental consciousness becomes aware that it lives beyond the lifetime of any form. In its acceptance of that, it opens to a greater degree of vivification and thereby is raised through various pathways into higher expressions of consciousness.

Now does that answer your question so that you may sleep?

ARZANI: Yes, that's wonderful! Thank you.

LOIS: I'd like to know if we all came into Life with an equal gift of creativity, or if we had different degrees of ability.

MONITOR: Coming into Life may be described at different points. Do you mean coming into human life?

LOIS: Yes, and specifically this life.

MONITOR: We find that each spark of Life is free, within a certain range of limits, to choose its experiences. While each Soul has essentially equal access to creativity, we find that not all Souls are equally creative. That pattern carries over to the expression of the Soul as a human being. So we say, "No." We find that not all human beings enter into a particular lifetime with equal creativity. We do say that each has equal *access to* creativity, which each person must find within themselves. As we have said, creativity begins inside the individual. Does this answer your question?

LOIS: I think so. Thank you.

GAEL: Along this same line, is that how we explain something like a child prodigy, like Mozart?

MONITOR: Yes, the subconscious mind of the child prodigy is able to express what it has learned previously. All it has to do is to get the Outer Self, of the new body, to allow it to demonstrate what it has previously learned. So you find some prodigies expressing quite freely, and other prodigies expressing in fits and starts, an erratic pattern caused by the struggle of their Outer Selves to dominate subconscious talents.

GAEL: Thank you.

JULIE: How would you work with a recalcitrant Outer Self that struggles against creativity?

MONITOR: There may be several ways of working with it. The Outer Self may be guided to examine the effects of its own choices and helped to clarify whether it chooses harmony or conflict. The Outer Self may also, on a deeper level of exploration, become acquainted with the subconscious mind that seeks to express through it. When the Outer Self becomes acquainted with the subconscious mind, it has opportunity to participate positively through cooperating and thereby feels more included in the process.

JULIE: Thank you.

MONITOR: Understand that, in such opportunities in prodigies, the Judge Selves often intrude to sabotage the collaboration between conscious and subconscious minds. In such cases, the Outer Self, of necessity, needs to transform the Judge Selves into a positive force.

LINDA: I wonder if you could tell us some more practical ways to develop our creativity, and maybe some common blocks to it?

AWARENESS EXERCISES

MONITOR: Yes, we thank you for the invitation. We have mentioned that, for a human being, creativity begins with the use of attention. Therefore, exercises at strengthening ability to pay attention prove useful. An exercise for strengthening your capacity for paying attention might involve your taking this moment and paying attention to what you hear. *[Pause.]*

Now, if you wish, pay attention to what you smell. *[Pause.]* Now we have suggested the use of two of your senses. When you begin such an exercise as this, it is useful to develop the habit of periodically noticing what you hear, smell, see, feel, and taste. Doing so helps you gain greater accord with the elemental consciousness of your body who maintains the structures of your physical senses.

When you exercise those senses, you place yourself into contact with your elemental consciousness. As you do that, you may notice something that for most human beings seems extraordinary, which is that you may smell without a clear, functioning nose, if you have rapport with your elemental consciousness. You may see without functioning eyes and hear without functioning ears, in that type of rapport. Instances of people with unusual sensory perceptions are now being studied. We offer this as partial explanation of that kind of occurrence.

Paying attention to your sensory input becomes a profound method of change. When you focus your attention on a single sense or, if you prefer, on a single object such as a flower, your entire vibratory field alters. Patterns of vibratory organization take place, working through the aerial circuit and chakras, spreading throughout your energy field.

Your energy field reaches out, let us say, to the flower, incorporating the flower within the field, and so you may experience Oneness with the flower. The Life force flows between you and the flower in two directions, and a profound experience may be achieved simply by focusing attention.

We find that a human being often shifts attention so frequently that vibratory development cannot take place. Now this offers only one example of what may be done.

On a completely different level, a person who seeks to be creative through painting may find his creativity blocked, so that every reflex seems a trap. He experiences an emptiness, a lack of fulfillment in what, up to that point, has been fulfilling uses of color, form, whatever. At that point, that artist is at the edge of creativity. If the artist accepts the fear that comes with the invitation to create a new kind of order, if he is willing to venture into the experience of chaos, the creativity of that artist expands into new forms of expression. If the artist hesitates at the brink of chaos and tries to go back into earlier forms of expression, the fear within the artist grows, and the artist becomes an imitator of himself. Therefore, courage is required, because risk will be encountered. The artist who truly desires to be creative launches into chaos and allows whatever new expressions to emerge.

MARJORIE: I have another question, a short one. I have all these ideas for what I want to write, but nothing seems to come out, or it just comes in little starts, and then I go for a long periods of not doing anything. I wonder if you could give me any help?

MONITOR: Certainly. We're pleased that you share your challenge with others. We find that your Female Self, within your subconscious mind, greatly desires to express what she has learned and what she knows others will benefit from. We find your Male Self somewhat doubting and inclined to be more reserved or withdrawn from the process. We find your Mental Judge Self adamantly opposed to the Female's expression. The Judge Self acts out of fear, feeling unsafe with the creative process which, of course, brings change. It feels threatened by the process of change and so seeks to maintain the status quo. The Female Self manages to express in times of brief duration and has, at this time, essentially no true support within your subconscious mind. In effect, one aspect of the subconscious mind within you wishes to express, but two other aspects do not wish to express.

We recommend some possible strategies for change that allow creativity to unfold. One strategy involves the Female Self in dialogue with the Male Self to determine what the Male Self would accept as motivation for him to support the Female in her expression. A slightly different approach involves the Female Self asking the Male Self what *he* might want to express. The first option involves the Female in convincing the Male Self to support her expression. The second option involves the Female Self being willing to entertain collaborative expression which meets both her needs and his needs. Of the two options, we recommend the second for you at this time.

That would be the first step, which would accomplish greater amounts of creativity, but it would not eliminate the resistance of the Mental Judge Self. We suggest a second step, which involves the Male and Female Selves assisting the Mental Judge Self, who feels unsafe. If they assist the Judge Self, he may learn to trust them and accept that he will be safe in their care. If that is done, creativity will be allowed to flow with minimal resistance.

Perhaps what we describe is not completely clear to you because you may not have had experiences communicating with these Inner Selves, yet we assure you that this approach is quite feasible. Is this of help to you?

MARJORIE: Yes.

MONITOR: The concept here is that the needs of each Self must be considered. If each Self perceives that its needs will be met in a creative endeavor, it will be much more easily motivated to support that creativity. The problem in the flow of creativity arises when one or more Selves feel that their needs will not be met.

LOIS: Monitor, as she was stating her problem, I was identifying myself with her problem and thinking that I've been in touch with feelings of creativity in terms of writing and photography. My creativity has been intermittent. It seemed like part of me wanted to say that creativity really wasn't there, that I was only thinking that it was, that I didn't have that ability, yet it continued to resurge. I'd appreciate any insights that you could give.

MONITOR: We find within you, Lois, that your Male Self desires creative expression and your Female Self has not been fully supporting him, since she has doubts about her own participation. She is not clearly aware that she may participate and support the Male Self and yet retain her own worth, her own identity. She has accepted illusions, transmitted from the Mental Judge Self, that she would lose her identity and value if she assists the Male Self in his creativity.

You may heal this impasse by talking with your Female Self and encouraging her to realize that she has the power to be herself and assert her full value in whatever she chooses to do. You may help her consider that she may choose to do her own independent creativity, and she may just as well choose to support the Male Self in his creativity. She may also ask the Male Self to share a joint creative project. She has all options before her. You may also encourage her to question her sense of losing value by assisting the Male. She has accepted the illusion created by the Mental Judge Self, yet has the power to find the truth for herself. Do you understand us?

LOIS: I believe that I do. Thank you very much.

MONITOR: In conclusion of discussion about creativity, we hope that each one has gained some new insights about this subject. When we consider the personality and how it can be a full expression of one's Soul, we may consider taking creative actions to allow our Soul to express. Without being creative, the personality does not truly allow its Soul to express.

The human personality at this time is less creative than the Soul, just as the Soul, at this time, is less creative than its sponsoring form, the Monad, and so forth up the line of identity.

Creativity has great importance for human and Soul evolution. You may be assured that as you take the risks of being creative, you assist not only yourself and other Life forms in the planet, but you also assist your Soul and other Souls to achieve fulfillment in Oneness. Life, held stagnant within a form, affirms isolation and separation. Life expressed creatively, flowing among various forms of Life, expresses Oneness, the essential Truth of Life.

We believe this is a particularly solemn note on which to conclude. We thank you, and we depart.

TOOLS FOR EXPLORATION
Exercise 4

PAYING ATTENTION TO YOUR SENSES

Monitor recommends that we develop awareness by paying attention to our senses of hearing, seeing, feeling, tasting, and smelling. Without realizing it, we may have learned to dull our sensory perception. As children, our senses offer vivid perceptions, yet with acculturation they can be easily diminished as we pay attention to other aspects of living. Perform the following exercise for each of the five recognized senses.

1. In the present moment, pay attention to your hearing (seeing, feeling tasting, smelling).

2. What do you hear (see, feel, taste, smell)? Make notes. How many items do you list?

3. What sounds (sights, feelings, tastes, smells) seem most obvious?

4. What sounds (sights, feelings, tastes, smells) seem most subtle?

5. What changes as you shift attention from the most obvious to the most subtle sounds (sights, feelings, tastes, smells)?

6. Compare your notes about the senses. Count the number of items you listed under step 2. Which sense gave you the greatest number of different perceptions—the keenest sense?

7. Which sense gave you the smallest number of different perceptions—the dullest sense?

8. Focusing on your dullest sense in a series of three-minute periods, pay attention to **contrasting** perceptions:

    HEARING: loud - soft, noisy - melodious

    SEEING: bright - dim, colorful - colorless, distinct - indistinct

    FEELING: pain - pleasure, hot - cold, rough - smooth

    TASTING: sour - sweet, salty - bitter

    SMELLING: sour - sweet, distinct - indistinct

9. Notice the energetic flow between you and whatever you sense. What do you sense?

10. What have you learned from this exercise?

Chapter 3

The Nature of Reality

Lesson 9
June 5, 1991

DEFINING REALITY

MONITOR: We welcome you. We come again as Monitor, and this time with a very provocative subject, "The Nature of Reality." What do we mean by the word "reality?" We do not use words except when we talk with you and others who are in physical bodies. Therefore it is a strange convention to us to deal with the word "reality." We may approach it from different angles. We encourage you to share your thoughts and feelings, especially because your definitions of reality will be very useful to us in bringing insights.

Let us start off with one definition. We may introduce other definitions and are happy to consider your definitions. We define reality as "what a being experiences." How do *you* define it?

ERMA: I would ask if reality could be the other side of the veil, the side that you are from. Is that reality?

MONITOR: We're sorry we didn't realize that our veil was showing. All our efforts come to no avail.

ERMA: I love your humor.

MONITOR: Perhaps reality is humor. What other definitions?

JULIE: Some people say, "Don't believe it unless you can see it." Their reality is based on the belief in what you can see and touch and experience, and I probably believed that for a long time. That's one definition of reality.

MONITOR: Indeed.

MARLENE: *A Course in Miracles* talks about how forms and bodies and the Earth are like an illusion, and reality is just spirit, spirit like energy. Any insight on that?

MONITOR: We find that if we use the word "experience," that experience is associated with a particular being. The being could be you or someone else or one of us. It suggests that reality depends a lot upon the focus of a being, and this means that some understanding of the structure of a human being is required to have a decent understanding of what reality is, within the experience of a human being.

CONSCIOUS MIND AND PERCEPTIONS OF REALITY

When we talk much about structure, people tend to get restless. At this stage of human understanding, more awareness than ever before is developing about the nature of human structure. Each element of the structure of a human being experiences a different reality. Let us give an example. Let us say that Marlene, as a conscious mind, has a sense of reality derived from the ways in which she experiences Life at this time. Her big toe on her left foot has a distinctly different sense of reality than does Marlene's conscious mind. The big toe participates in its own ways of sensing life. It, too, is Life encased in a form. Its form is that of a big toe on the left foot, and it perceives reality from its structural perspective that is based upon the structure of the physical and other bodies, which give it identity and substance. The big toe is linked to the greater form of the bodies.

We know that you're used to thinking of physical bodies. From our point of view, physical bodies are not truly there. What we perceive are the etheric bodies, which truly generate the Life and the structure. From your point of view, the physical body is an experience that is very important in your growth to understand. Marlene, your big toe is just one part of your body. How do you relate to it? How do you experience it? You can look at it and see that it's still there. You can feel it, move it around and touch it against an object. You have various ways of experiencing your big toe.

How does the conscious mind experience the body? By interacting with the body. But what senses does the conscious mind utilize? What are its pathways for experience? Not the physical senses, because they are part of the body. Now consider this: How does the conscious mind of Marlene relate to her physical body? We've already ruled out the physical senses. Now, is that puzzling? We phrase it this way to encourage your sensitivity to the different aspects of structure that make up a human being.

How does the conscious mind become aware of the body that it inhabits? We suggest an analogy for you. When you drive your car, how are you aware of the car? You, as the driver, have certain pathways—in this case, the physical senses—which you use to grasp the steering wheel, turn the key, steer the car, and get to where you are going safely. What are the equivalent mechanisms for the conscious mind? They are what we term "etheric senses, astral senses, and mental senses." At this point you say, "Oh no, not a lot of other structures, because that all gets so confusing." And we say, yes, it can be confusing unless we can discuss them in some kind of order that allows you to begin to grasp what it is we're talking about.

The etheric body, from our perspective, provides the vehicle. The other energies—astral, mental and causal—that enable the Life force to enter and live within the physical body, all interact with the etheric body. From your perspective, you perceive an animated physical body. From our perspective, we see a radiant Life force, radiant with several kinds of energy, occupying an etheric body. The etheric body radiates with all of those Life energies and becomes a clear expression of them. The etheric body exists within a vibratory condition that produces, in effect, a shadow that you call the physical body. The irony is that you perceive through etheric, astral, and mental senses, and truly not at all with physical senses.

ETHERIC PERCEPTION

HELEN: The sensing that we perceive as a smell or sight or a feel, that sensing is in the etheric body?

MONITOR: That's what we are saying. The etheric form of the rose interacts with your etheric form, and in that exchange you experience what you term "fragrance." Perception can be considered as reception of information that makes sense to the entity. You *can* smell the fragrance of the rose etherically, astrally, and mentally. How are we ever going to explain those aspects to you? By proceeding step by step. The first step is that we encourage you to consider how you do perceive. And let us lay this one on you. How do you perceive that you live?

PERCEIVING LIFE

DONNA: On what dimension?

MONITOR: Well, that's an excellent point, isn't it?

HELEN: I'd say by the Grace of God.

MONITOR: (*Laughs.*)

ERMA: We wake up in the morning and find out we're still here on Earth?

MONITOR: Waking up depends upon a structure. The kind of waking up we believe that you mean infers that you are focused as a Life force within a physical body, and waking up means a shifting of electrical conditions within your brain. The brain chemistry alters, and motor elements of the brain cause your eyes to open and your conscious mind to wake up and resume functioning. You open your eyelids and begin to see that you are, once again, on planet Earth.

PHYSICAL PERCEPTION

You have been taught that you have a physical body and that the physical organs create your physical senses. From our perspective, that is not at all the case. We've mentioned, in one of these earlier conversations, the growing awareness among your scientists that a number of people upon your planet see without eyes, smell without functioning noses, and exercise senses of perception in parts of the body other than where sensory organs are located. For example, there are children studied by scientists in different parts of the world, who read books and see pictures with their hands, elbows, knees or bottoms of their feet. We cite this as evidence that your human sensory mechanism is not truly physical. If the mechanism was purely physical, how could such children read with the bottoms of their feet? Are their eyes in the bottoms of their feet? No.

Consider this mystery: How do you perceive? Most of you agree that your modes of perception give you experience. You experience the rose by seeing it with your eyes, by smelling its fragrance with your nose, by feeling its softness with your fingers. And so most human beings think that they perceive with their physical senses. That is not at all the case, from our perspective. We suggest that it's time for human beings to begin to examine more about how they perceive and function.

ETHERIC REALITY

MONITOR: What about the person who has left the physical body and exists within an etheric body between lifetimes? In that etheric body, the person opens eyelids, perceives Earth, and knows by what he perceives that he has not left Earth. It is all quite recognizable. The etheric body exists within an etheric world. That beautiful world you see of supposedly physical beauty is, from our perspective, an etheric world. That world provides the senses of the etheric body with constant information. And so, the person who has died from a physical body, and whose etheric body has moved out of the vibratory condition of the physical, functions within a harmonious environment of etheric energy. It blends perfectly, receiving and transmitting energies. It maintains a homeostasis, and is, in effect, a more accurate or substantial reality than physical reality.

How can we say "more accurate" or "more substantial" in this case? We say "more accurate" because etheric reality is that energy manifestation which interacts with the energies of the astral, mental, causal and beyond. All of these energies function together, converging and diverging. To use the metaphor of waves upon the ocean, all waves affect all other waves eventually, and so it is with the energies of Life that permeate all of space. We use the term "more accurate" to describe the interaction of the etheric energy with all of the other energies. It is our observation that physical energy does not truly exist; it is a by-product of etheric energy when it exists in a certain vibratory condition.

The physical body, the physical reality of the world in which you live, may be described as an undertone of the etheric body and etheric world in which you truly live. The etheric body and etheric world, for you, is what truly sustains you. And, therefore, we consider it more substantial than the physical world and body. If your etheric body is open and clears out the flow of Life energies, you will have a true sense of vitality. If it is blocked and limited in its access to the energies of Life, you will feel tired, exhausted, depleted, cut off. Your etheric body has been called the "vital body" quite appropriately.

SHIFT TO ETHERIC REALITY

Consider that you live in the etheric body. You perceive, in part, through the etheric body, and therefore it represents perhaps the most substantial structure for your life experience. Now, by means of prediction, we say that changes in vibratory conditions upon the planet are producing a gradual shift away from the customary undertone of vibratory conditions which give you physical experience. What this means is that your entire sense of reality is subtly and gradually changing. Eventually physical reality will no longer exist for you. In time, which is now predicted to be somewhere between 300-500 years from now, human beings will completely shift into etheric reality and out of physical reality.

We're harping on this point because we anticipate that many of your beliefs are phrased within an assumption that you experience through the physical senses. So we wish to give you pause to consider the validity of that approach. If you limit yourselves to physical perceptions, you want physical descriptions of energies and events that are not physical. This is something that every entity, such as we comprise, who accepts assignment to illuminate or teach human beings, is oriented to recognize as a physical bias. We are reminded in our training that you regard life as physical, therefore we use physical metaphors and analogies time after time.

Remember that physical experience reflects the relationship of etheric, astral, mental and causal energies. Physical experience provides a point of reference which is sufficiently low in vibration to provide a meeting point of Life forms evolving from higher levels of vibration, enabling them to come down in vibration to a point on the scale where they meet and intermingle with Life forms moving from lower levels of vibration in an upward path. As these flows of Life force meet and intermingle, they travel together upwards, and thus you have a system of evolution of what we term "elemental consciousness," linked with the evolution of other forms of consciousness. The physical level serves a wonderful purpose within the evolutionary scheme.

THE ETHERIC AS VEHICLE OF PERCEPTION

MONITOR: The etheric body is the vehicle for your so-called physical sensory perceptions. We have said that your physical senses do not, in truth, perceive. You have had a misconception concerning this. The bias in this misconception has been that physical matter exists and physical organs perceive. And we distinctly say, "Not so," that the etheric body is the vehicle of perception. Consider your senses. Do you hear etheric sound? Do you feel etheric matter and radiation? Do you see the structure of the etheric body and the etheric forms of all of nature around you?

If you answer "yes" to one or more of these questions, then we say that yes, indeed, you do have some useful knowledge of the etheric body and the etheric world. If you cannot answer "yes" to any of these questions, we say that you are operating with knowledge that you have read, based upon the experience of others. In this area of exploration, we say that you should be cautious with the reports that others have made about their experiences, that you should devote greater priority to having your own sensory experiences of the etheric body and its world. It really is not that far off for you; it is quite close. You live in it without noticing that you notice it. I suppose an appropriate analogy would be that the last thing that a fish notices is water.

We encourage you to practice hearing, feeling, and seeing etheric reality. As you gain that capability, you have a more secure grasp of reality on that level. As it is, you function within a misconception that you perceive reality when you have so-called "physical" perceptions. In our opinion, you see only the shadow of the reality, and therefore you are easily misled by distorted or misinterpreted perceptions.

A significant change will be taking place in the vibratory quality of the planet, and there will be a change in the number of human beings who perceive etheric reality. That indicates the trend. Wouldn't you like to be leaders of the trend? We certainly encourage you.

THE SENSES

Now, we would like to make a few statements about senses. When you consider your senses of hearing, feeling, and sight from a broader perspective, and you no longer limit them to being physical senses, you begin to open yourself to the possibility that you may use these senses on etheric, astral, mental levels and beyond. When your Life essence was invested in your human form, your senses were intended to play a vital role in your fulfillment of that form and your release from it. Therefore, your senses have never been limited. They remain quite open. Yet, the level of reality that they perceive depends upon how you have energized your form by expressing your Life essence within it. As the levels of kundalini evolve within your body and change its vibratory qualities, your senses open to a broader sphere of perception. And we would like to comment about the senses in a way that goes beyond any single reality such as etheric or astral.

Senses are involved in all levels of form. When Life enters a form to have experience, it enters into an enclosure. The enclosure is made of a type of matter. The enclosure serves to limit the Life experience and to channel that experience in certain ways. The enclosure of form serves the purpose of giving Life essence a unique perspective, for the Life essence encased in that form experiences Life from a unique vibratory condition. If you consider the Life essence as having a vibratory quality based upon its past evolution, it brings that vibratory quality into its individual enclosure, the form. The form itself has a vibratory quality that has been invested in it by the Divine force of Life forming the structure of matter. And so, within that condition, you have two vibratory forces working, producing a third vibratory force, which is called "consciousness evolving from form." That evolving consciousness needs a way to experience from its unique perspective what Life is, both within and outside of that enclosure. It needs a way to experience inside and outside conditions. The senses provide the means. With use of the senses, the indwelling Life essence may experience its vibratory qualities within the enclosing form and beyond the enclosing form.

Now, we speak of the senses in a way that may be somewhat obscure, but will have value in your future explorations. The sense of *hearing* provides the indwelling Life essence with awareness of inner processes in the form, and beyond the form with an awareness of the direction and placement of other Life forms. The sense of *feeling* provides, for the human being, the best sense of vibratory conditions within the Life form. Beyond the Life form, feeling provides a sense of quality and value of the expression of Life. The sense of *sight* provides the indwelling Life essence with an inner form of projection which you term "visualization" or "imagination" as a means to experience vibratory conditions within its form. Beyond the form, it provides a sense of proportion, of the placement of that form within a configuration of forms.

Consider the changes that may take place when an indwelling Life essence fulfills the human form. The senses of that being, especially the senses of hearing, feeling, and sight, become augmented. They become aware of realities beyond the reality of the physical/etheric. They perceive the etheric and begin to realize that the physical is but an artifact. They begin to experience the astral world, which is where they will spend a great deal of their further development. The astral plane has several levels within it that represent various vibrational groupings. When an advanced being extends its awareness sufficiently into the mental plane, it finds in the mental plane a series of levels based upon vibrational groupings. When that being extends its awareness into the causal plane, it does so through its structure located there, that which you call the "Soul," or in some cases the "Overself." That structure, that Life essence inhabiting the form of the Soul, is capable of perceiving many levels existing within the causal plane. As it nears its fulfillment, it develops sensory awareness of those levels of reality beyond the causal plane. The senses, therefore, represent an important thread of development as the indwelling Life essence experiences plane after plane. The senses represent the ways in which you experience reality, and therefore they deserve considerable attention.

CONTINUITY OF CONSCIOUSNESS

Consider what you sense and how you sense when you sleep. During sleep your conscious mind goes dormant, yet still has sensory experiences provided by the subconscious mind. It might share with you some of its experiences in planes other than physical, but your conscious mind tends to interpret them in physical terms. If you retain awareness in your state of sleep, you can receive instruction about yourself and the higher planes of your Life. This awareness is called "continuity of consciousness" wherein your conscious mind maintains continuous awareness while shifting through different mental states. Your physical/etheric body becomes dormant as it recharges, yet your conscious mind stays alert and open to experience what comes through the subconscious mind and the higher senses.

HELEN: Do *we* retain continuity of consciousness as we go into sleep?

MONITOR: You retain memory. If you were viewing your mind as a tape recorder, does your tape recorder continue functioning during the time of sleep?

HELEN: Partially.

MONITOR: It does partially, and therefore there is great value in your expansion of that capability. Recognize, as you stretch the capability of your conscious mind, how well your conscious mind relates to your subconscious mind. If your conscious mind can relax in the care of the subconscious mind, it will very naturally allow its awareness to flow into the subconscious mind, and the awareness of the subconscious mind will flow into it. That, of course, is one definition of dream experiences. As you do that with greater facility, you find that you will be aware of transitional movements, as though you were moving through some kind of space. As you move in such a manner, you find that the space that you are traversing is organized differently than what you are used to. If you accept that organization of space, you retain continuity of consciousness. If you reject that space, you lose continuity of consciousness.

We find that most human beings, at this time, simply ignore the time of sleep. Their memory ends as they go to sleep and begins when they awaken. What is in between is a blank for them. That condition may be greatly altered, for as human beings retain continuity of consciousness through the time of sleep, they begin to experience an expansion out of the etheric body and beyond the astral body and may experience the mental plane, which is a prime need at this time for humanity to experience. Humanity needs to develop sufficient mental capability to remain organized and consistent in its experience of the astral plane.

The astral plane is quite fluid in character and may easily disorient the human mind unprepared to handle it. It would be the equivalent of releasing a fish into a swiftly flowing stream so that the fish does not maintain its position but is swept downstream. Therefore, the human mind is in the process of developing sufficient mental capability to remain oriented in its experience of the astral plane.

DREAMS ON THE DIFFERENT PLANES

Some dream experiences may reflect mental plane experiences, and some dream experiences may reflect astral plane experiences. How do you tell the difference?

We suggest that you consider that mental plane experiences have great clarity and a sense of peaceful orderliness. They will not have a vague or cloudy quality. All features are quite clear and consistent.

Astral dream experiences are characterized by a cloudy quality in which forms shift and the situation changes and changes more. Within astral dream experience, many people have enough mental capability to experience segments of enactments, what we call "dramas," that are presented for the benefit of the subconscious mind and also of the conscious mind inasmuch as it is able to accept them. Within the astral plane, many drama presentations will be experienced. Those presentations will be made coherent largely through the efforts of a teacher who does have sufficient mental capability to use that type of presentation as a means of instruction. That type of instruction has been aimed primarily at the subconscious mind, and we assure you that those teachers, who are often our colleagues, are delighted to use that form of presentation as instruction for the conscious mind.

Dreams of etheric experience appear quite peculiar to human beings because it is as though you experience a reversal of form. In etheric experiences, from your point of view, you experience reversals of inside and outside, left and right, up and down, and sometimes reversals of light and dark and even coloration. This type of experience is normally quite disorienting to the conscious mind. The subconscious mind is accustomed to it, and so, if you, the conscious mind, can ride along with your subconscious mind and trust it, then you will be assisted through such experiences. After sufficient times of exposure, you will grow accustomed to that perspective. Etheric dream experiences will have a quality similar to mental dream experiences, but with a distinctly different quality associated with etheric expression.

LINDA: So does that mean that an etheric dream is like an out-of-body experience?

MONITOR: To the conscious mind all of these experiences appear to be out-of-body, because of the conscious mind's concept of body, which is illusory. In fact, these experiences are not out-of-body because they are sensed; they are experienced by the same senses that the conscious mind uses, only focused on other planes than physical.

ETHERIC SENSES

ARZANI: I was shocked when you first told us that the senses were primarily of the etheric body. Then I was meditating yesterday, and realized that all the experiences that I was having in meditation were all etheric senses. What I was seeing, what I was hearing, what I was feeling really had nothing to do with what was happening physically. It wasn't as shocking to me when I saw it in that perspective.

MONITOR: This is a good example of what we would term "discernment," which allows you to perceive more accurately. If you, like most human beings, consider an experience as physical, you will not be able to discern etheric experience. In other words, you confuse the two modes of experiences and actually mislabel most of your experience. That might seem a matter of low priority, for some of you have read books describing the various energy levels and you are quite open to accept that as a possibility. But we say that this habit of mislabeling etheric experience as physical experience provides a major obstacle to your growth.

When you can truly discern and recognize etheric experience, you bring a greater accuracy to your perceptive mechanisms, those ways in which your brains and nervous systems process your sensory perceptions. Your perceptive mechanisms are greatly affected by your ideas, your conceptions of reality. As a rather absurd example, we say that a person who has the idea that sunlight is green will actually affect his perception of sunlight. He will tend to *not* recognize the variations of sunlight, which you recognize as other colors and the blended totality of colors that is sunlight. If you wish to discern reality more accurately, it is important to distinguish between etheric experience and physical experience.

LOIS: Monitor, you said you would encourage us to practice hearing, feeling and seeing etheric reality. Perhaps you can give us some examples of that.

MONITOR: We find that it is easiest for some people to perceive etheric reality in terms of sight, yet for others the sense of hearing provides the best access, and even for others, the sense of touch. For you, Lois, we recommend the sense of touch as your best means of access to perceiving etheric reality. As you practice etheric touch, you will find that etheric sight and hearing will follow. Each person should use that sense which is most conducive to etheric perception. For you, Lois, etheric touch may be gained quite easily. As you practice it by holding your hands a distance of six to eight inches away from, let's say, your leg, you will find that you can sense etheric touch as you allow your hands to move roughly an inch closer and then farther away from the original position. As you hands move, you sense etheric touch.

Consider how you learn physical touch, or how to touch physical reality. You use your hands to touch a variety of physical objects. You touch smooth, sharp, jagged, rough textured objects, and learn how to tell one quality from another. And so it is in learning etheric touch. Practicing gives you a variety of etheric sensations that you will find are quite similar to physical sensations. In the initial phase of developing etheric touch, you will discover that etheric touch seems to be limited to only a few sensations, such as warmth, tingling, and a sense of current similar to electrical current. Yet as you continue practicing, you will notice that etheric touch has a greater variety of sensations to offer.

When you do physical touching, you place your physical skin against the surface of an object, and so it works with etheric touching. You place your etheric skin against the etheric skin of the object. You will note one major difference from physical touching, which is that your etheric skin can easily penetrate the etheric surface of the object. With physical skin and surface, you do not experience penetration; you experience compression. As you place your hand against the arm of your chair and apply pressure, your physical hand does not penetrate the arm of the chair significantly. Instead, you feel compression upon the skin of your hand. But with etheric touch, your etheric skin has no difficulty in penetrating the etheric surface of the arm of the chair. With etheric touch, you may feel the textures and qualities of the etheric object throughout its form. Therefore, you begin to realize that etheric reality does, in some respects, differ from physical reality.

We liken this comparison to the analogy we have used before, that physical reality is a shadow of etheric reality. Physical reality is more limited than etheric reality in some respects. In time your mathematicians, your physicists, will develop a set of mathematical relationships that describe the relationship between physical and etheric structures. Etheric structure will be found to have added dimension.

THE LOSS OF SENSES

JULIE: Monitor, what happens when you have a physical loss, like loss of sight, loss of hearing? What happens on the etheric level?

MONITOR: In most such cases, we find that the guiding consciousness of the individual has introduced that condition to assist development of the subconscious mind. Remember that we defined the subconscious mind as that part of the personality that continues from body to body, lifetime to lifetime. When the subconscious mind becomes too caught up in physical reality, much as though a person watching a horror movie becomes caught up in the reality of that movie and forgets where he truly is, the subconscious mind may become stuck in limited perception. The High Self then initiates the condition of blindness, deafness or numbness in order to assist the subconscious mind to detach itself from its obsession with physical reality. Other conditions may also prevail, but we believe this describes the most common occurrences.

ARZANI: If there's an amputation of the physical body, does it still exist in the etheric body?

MONITOR: Exactly. The etheric body may not be amputated by physical means. The physical body, of course, may be amputated by physical means, but the etheric body will remain quite intact. An analogy, which might help you to understand this, is that of a person who intends to speak a complete sentence, but who is interrupted and speaks only part of the sentence. The rest of the sentence remains in the form of an energy potential that could be manifested but is not.

We have deliberately avoided being overly complex in our description of reality. What we would like to share with you now is how we have managed to do that.

We have avoided concepts of time and space, as you have avoided asking about them, because you have been pulled through the knothole by various other sources who have stretched your concept of time and space into something approximately more accurate. Time and space are experiences of the energy and structure of the universe, based upon the sensory consciousness of the particular form that Life inhabits. You live in the form of human beings, yet your Life essence is quite unlimited. Yet, because your Life essence is currently experiencing the human form, that form defines your experience of time and space. If your Life essence was experiencing through the form of a devic being, you would have a distinctly different experience of time and space. If you were experiencing through the form of the Planetary Being or Logos, you would experience time and space in ways appropriate to that form.

In consideration of these statements, realize that within each one of you lies the vibratory consciousness which connects you with virtually any major aspect of Life in the universe. Each of you has originated as a Life essence in other portions of the universe and has traveled to this place and will travel on. Therefore, if you knew how, you could gain access to many other states of consciousness than the consciousness of a human being. Consider, however, that there is a distinct value in your exploring your human being consciousness. It offers you a unique perspective. It is an opportunity that your Higher Consciousness has deliberately chosen.

Your consciousness has much to offer. If you explore your own consciousness, you gain ability to explore grounds of experience that are certain to be fulfilling to you. You may know your Higher Consciousness, or you might say your "Soul" consciousness, as you know your personality more thoroughly. We do not advocate abandoning your personality in favor of some nebulous Soul. We recommend that you fully realize your own being in this form. You benefit from recognizing your perceptions of etheric experience and distinguishing them from physical experience. We suggest that you do not truly have physical senses, that your concept of physical being is of the reality of a shadow, that the more substantial level of perception is found on the etheric plane, and that your senses function etherically. Your senses may function on many planes, but they will not so function if you do not fully explore them. So, we advocate your exploration of your own being, as you find it, and de-emphasize elaborate descriptions of the reality of the universe.

COLLABORATIVE REALITIES

SUSIE: It's my understanding that we all share a common reality, which we call our physical environment, and that each of us simultaneously experiences our own individual space/time locations, and that we are also part of a larger cosmic reality. Are these the only three realities that we have in the three-dimensional plane?

MONITOR: No, they are not.

SUSIE: How many are there?

MONITOR: We may not adequately number them, but give this for your consideration. We previously mentioned the elemental consciousness of a cell. The living entity of a cell has its reality, its own individual reality, yet it is part of the accumulative collective reality of all of the other elemental Life forms in your body. And so, your body has a reality as a collective form. As your Life essence inhabits the body, it brings with it other energies and other awarenesses that have their realities. Taken altogether, you as a human being, have approximately 800+ realities to experience. Numbers, in this instance, are not very significant. What is more significant is that you realize that one individual is contained within a larger individual. For example, the living cell in your body is contained within the reality of your body. Your body, as an individual expression, is contained within the reality of your total personality. Your total personality, in turn, is contained within your Soul, and your Soul within your Monad, and so forth.

The nature of reality involves an individual manifesting a vibratory force within the whole of Life. That vibration may be viewed as a musical note. That note has validity and identifies that individual from all others. Each note is completely unique. However, that note exists within a symphony of other notes, and all of the notes together have certain effects, collaborative effects, producing what has been termed previously as "consensus reality."

You have asked the question at other times, "If a tree falls when no human being is present to hear its fall, does it make a sound?" And we say, in answer to that question, that it does not make a sound for a human being, but it does make a sound for all of the other living beings affected by the fall of the tree. Certainly, within the Planetary Consciousness, the fall of the tree is heard. Therefore, consider that reality is not simply that of an individual, although the individual may choose to selectively focus upon his/her own sense of reality. Your reality involves the lesser beings that your form encompasses, and it also involves the greater beings of which you are but a tiny part.

CREATING YOUR OWN REALITY

DIANE: There is a current thought held by some people that we create our own reality. Is this a truth? And if so, in what manner do we create it?

MONITOR: Human beings have all too often failed to emphasize the importance of their inner life as much as their outer life. Ultimately it proves to be of great value because each Life essence experiencing the human form outgrows that form and moves on. The reality is that what Life essence experiences corresponds more to the inner life of the human than to the outer life. It becomes very important, then, for you to be aware of the vibrations, qualities and purposes that are being activated inside of your beings, and, indeed, within your hearts, because these expressions of force determine your future.

Indeed, you create your reality. But you are not alone in creating your reality, for other beings around you, and certainly the Planetary Being and the Being of the Solar System, have enormous influence in creating your reality. Often human beings act out the thoughts, desires, and impulses of the Planetary Being. The creation of reality is a shared function for any Life form. And the same statement holds true for the Life essence that declines to enter form, and which flows throughout the universe in what you term "Spirit" expression.

DREAMS AND REALITY

GAEL: I have a question regarding dreams and the nature of reality. Is it possible, in your dream state, to actually meet with other spirits, not just as a symbol representing something, but as the real person you are dreaming about?

MONITOR: Indeed. Understand that such encounters with other individuals, who are not symbolic reflections of your own being, involve the action of your Subconscious Selves. For example, if your Female Self visited, let us say, a deceased uncle living now within the astral plane, you would find the memory of that experience within your Female Self. If she chooses to share that experience with you, the conscious mind, you would have that experience in a dream. If she chooses not to share it with you, then you, the conscious mind, will have no memory of it. Yet, that experience will have occurred for your Female Self. Many important experiences take place with aspects of your subconscious mind during sleep involving contact with other individuals.

GAEL: Is it possible to program a meeting with another person in the dream state?

MONITOR: It is possible, provided that one of your Subconscious Selves is willing to follow through with your wishes. If it is, then it will do so. If you wish to retain memory of that experience, ask your Subconscious Selves to give you the memory.

PRIORITIES

DOUG: As a human, how do I determine the balance between physical reality and spiritual reality in my daily life? Considering the changes that you say are coming, how do I place my priorities? Is there a guideline for placing priorities?

MONITOR: Indeed, the guideline has expressed in various ways. One concise, clear manner of expression is, "Seek the Kingdom of God first, and the rest shall be added." We say that you find God in your creative Life expression as you meet and overcome your fears. We have previously described planet Earth as offering an opportunity for Souls to meet that which they most wish to avoid, which means that the main objective for most human beings is to encounter and overcome fears. Where you find fears, meet them and overcome them. By so doing, you may be well assured that you are on the path of spiritual growth. As you grow, within your own plan, you will be of greater assistance to other beings and to the Planetary Being. And as you are of greater assistance, you receive support commensurate to your value in assisting others.

The human being that hides, seeking to survive times of Earth changes, places himself in a position of frailty. He becomes quite vulnerable because he retreats from his fears and exists within a shell of fear that cuts him off from vital communications. The person who meets and overcomes his fears opens shells of fear, dissolves them, and emerges into a radiant society of compassionate beings. Each one has the choice of fear or Love.

Lesson 10
June 12, 1991

MANNER OF PRESENTATION

MONITOR: We welcome you as Monitor. We realize that, in talking about the nature of reality, you have a number of conceptions to which you refer as we talk. In our last discussion, we attempted to bring to your minds those conceptions that arise when we talk about how you experience reality. We mentioned the human senses, and immediately within your minds there arose conceptions of how the human senses work. Once that occurred, we described other possibilities so that you could use them to broaden your considerations.

We will continue to use this mode as we proceed through this particular subject. We do it this way because, if we gave you a lecture on the nature of reality, most of you would go to sleep. You *would*, because certain parts of your minds would be stressed by what we had to say, and those parts of you would prefer to retreat. You would find yourselves essentially closed off, at least in parts of your being. So we prefer to work in a slightly different manner, pacing the introduction of new concepts with the rhythms of your beings.

When we presented information about the etheric body, we were aware that some of you had already grasped concepts of the etheric body, some of you were open, and some of you were treating what you had previously learned about the etheric body as dogma. We will continue to talk about the etheric body and the other bodies that you inhabit as human beings, attempting to encourage a little greater openness of thinking.

Notice that we're *not* saying that you have closed minds, but that *parts* of your minds at times tend to close. Now it's interesting, isn't it, to consider that happening to you, and we frankly reveal that it happens to us as well. All beings with a mental body have that experience.

One of the reasons for Life projecting into the lower vibratory forms of the astral, etheric, and physical planes is that it provides new ways for those with mental bodies to experience and learn. So we thought you might be interested to hear that all beings in Earth with mental bodies will at times close down and not be receptive to learning.

We often find that you, in your conception of us, consider us to be open *all* of the time for learning, and that some of you consider us to be virtually omniscient. We assure you that neither assumption is true. We have a certain perspective to offer you, and yet you, in the act of experiencing, offer certain perspectives to us. So we stress the relationship that exists here as a relationship of *peers*. We appreciate your sharing of experiences and viewpoints, which may differ from those that we express.

ETHERIC PERCEPTION

We have said that the etheric body is the vehicle for your so-called "physical" sensory perceptions, that your physical senses do not truly perceive, and that you have had a misconception concerning this. The bias in this misconception has been that physical matter exists, and that physical organs perceive. We say not so, that the *etheric body* is the vehicle of perception.

Consider your senses. Do you hear etheric sound? Do you feel etheric matter and radiation? Do you see the structure of the etheric body and the etheric forms of all of nature around you? If you answer "Yes" to one or more of these questions, we say, "Yes, you do have some useful knowledge of the etheric body and the etheric world." If you cannot answer "Yes" to any of those questions, we say that you are operating with knowledge that you have read, based on the experience of others. In this area of exploration, you should be cautious with the reports that others have made about their experiences and should devote greater priority to having your own sensory experiences of the etheric body and its world.

It really is not that far off for you; it is quite close. You live in it without noticing that you notice it. An appropriate analogy is that the last thing a fish notices is *water*.

We encourage you to practice hearing, feeling, and seeing etheric reality. As you gain that capability, you attain a more secure grasp of reality on that level. As it is, you maintain a misconception that you perceive reality when you have so-called "physical" perceptions. In doing this, you see only the *shadow* of the reality and so are easily misled by distorted perceptions.

A significant change will take place in the *vibratory quality* of the planet, resulting in a significant increase in the number of human beings who perceive etheric reality. That change indicates the trend. Wouldn't you like to be leaders of the trend? We certainly encourage you.

SENSES

We would like to make a few statements about senses. When you consider your senses of hearing, feeling, and sight from a broader perspective, and no longer limit them to being "physical" senses, you open to the possibility that you may use these senses on etheric, astral, and mental levels and beyond.

When your Life essence was invested for the first time in a human form, your senses were intended to play a vital role in your fulfillment of that form and your release from it. Your senses have never been limited; they remain quite open. Yet the level of reality that they perceive depends on how you have energized your form by expressing your Life essence in it. As the levels of kundalini evolve within your body and change its vibratory qualities, your senses open to a broader sphere of perception.

Senses are involved in all levels of form. When Life enters a form for experience, it enters into an *enclosure*. The enclosure is made of some type of matter. The enclosure serves to limit the Life's experience and to channel its experience in certain ways. The enclosure of form serves the purpose of giving that Life essence a unique perspective. The Life essence encased in a form experiences Life from a unique vibratory condition.

If you consider the Life essence as having a vibratory quality based on its past evolution, it brings that vibratory quality into its individual enclosure, the form. The form itself has a vibratory quality that has been invested in it by the Divine force of Life assuming the structure of matter. And so within that condition you have two vibratory forces producing a third vibratory force, which is called "consciousness evolving from form."

The evolving consciousness needs a way to understand, from its unique perspective, what Life is, both inside and outside that enclosure. It needs a way to experience "inside" and "outside" conditions. The senses provide that means. By use of the senses, the indwelling Life essence may experience *its vibratory qualities* inside and outside the enclosing form.

We speak now of the senses in a way that may be somewhat obscure, but will have value in your future explorations.

The sense of *hearing* provides the indwelling Life essence with awareness of the <u>direction</u> and <u>placement</u> of other Life forms.

The sense of *feeling* provides a sense of vibratory conditions inside the form and outside the form, a sense of <u>quality</u> and <u>value</u> expressed by Life beyond that form.

The sense of *sight* provides the indwelling Life essence with an inner mode of projection – which you term "visualization" or "imagination" – for experiencing vibratory conditions inside its form. And beyond the form, sight provides a sense of <u>proportion</u>, placing that form within a configuration of forms.

We make these statements about the senses generically, on all levels of form. Our statements do *not* apply to Life that exists beyond form.

The senses, therefore, assist the indwelling Life essence to experience all of the vibratory conditions that unfold during its experience of that form. When the Life essence nears the point of fulfillment, the senses naturally open, energized by an inner vibratory state, to bring awareness of the higher levels of reality. So we emphasize the use of your senses, especially those of sight, feeling, and hearing. The senses of *taste* and *smell*, which you experience as human and elemental creatures, are extensions of the sense of *feeling*. In the astral plane, people who have separated themselves enough from embodiment in human form often fail to have noses and mouths, because they have no need of them.

NONPHYSICAL SENSING

Consider the changes that may take place when an indwelling Life essence fulfills the human form. The senses of that being, especially the senses of hearing, feeling, and sight, become augmented. He/she becomes aware of realities beyond the reality of the physical. He/she perceives the etheric and realizes that the physical is but an artifact. He/she begins to experience the astral world, where a great deal of further development will take place.

The astral plane has several levels that represent vibrational groupings. When a being extends awareness sufficiently into the mental plane, it finds in the mental plane, as well, a series of levels based on vibrational groupings. When a being extends awareness into the causal plane, it does so through its structure already present there, the Soul. The Soul perceives many levels in the causal plane. And as it nears fulfillment, the Soul develops sensory awareness of those levels of reality beyond the causal plane. The senses, therefore, represent an important thread of development, as the indwelling Life essence experiences plane after plane. The senses represent the ways in which you experience reality. They deserve considerable attention.

You may free your mind from limiting conceptions, from limiting beliefs that shutter your senses. As you open your beliefs and are receptive to learning through your senses, you may be able to change the patterns of electrical activity in your brains and nervous systems. Here we speak of *etheric* brains and nervous systems.

As you make those changes, you will find your awareness opening to the etheric, astral, and even mental planes. Then you will be able to grasp a sufficiently comprehensive sense of reality that you may make much wiser decisions regarding how you live.

As you develop that awareness, you will gain a greater sense of compassion, for how could you withhold it, as you perceive the interrelatedness of all Life and know that you are part of all of Life and all of Life is part of you? You gain wisdom as you become able to trace the intricacies of the working of karmic processes, and as you know how your thoughts, words, and deeds reverberate throughout Planetary Consciousness, Solar System Consciousness, Galactic Consciousness, and Universal Consciousness. Those vibratory effects know no barrier.

It sounds like you are on "Universal Candid Camera," and in fact that *is* the case. All that you do is recorded in vibratory patterns, and those patterns may be accessed. The Life forms operating in etheric and higher planes utilize Akashic substance as you utilize a library. Its utilization represents most of what you term "memory" and a portion of what you term "intuition."

As you expand awareness, the only true limitations you face are those in your own habit patterns, conceptions, and beliefs. We believe we have stirred the pot enough at this point, and now, with that foundation, let's consider questions or sharing of experiences.

ENERGETIC RESPONSES TO CHANNELING MONITOR

LINDA: We have been observing our physical feelings as the channeling takes place. From my experience the first four or five times I was here, I got this energy throughout my whole body, a really hot flash, and was dripping perspiration. And then last week, when you first started, it was all I could do to stay awake. You may have answered part of that question in the first part of your talk about the brain being stressed, yet I wonder what happens at these times. My feeling is that there is something else happening to the vibrations of our bodies while you are talking to us.

MONITOR: We appreciate the question, because it enables us to make your experience more relevant to the subject matter at hand. Your experience still labels your sensory experiences as "physical." Notice how much of a habit it is. We wish to do our part to help you change that habit.

The presence that we bring is an energy field, not an energy field of one single entity or Life essence, but an energy field of many. That field is composed of a carefully selected group of beings who are selected partly because of their vibratory capabilities. When we enter, we bring a very rich and varied vibratory force that cannot help but stimulate your own developmental processes. The types of stimulation might be described briefly as stimulation towards accelerated growth in your chakra system and etheric body. That, in itself, produces experiences of heat and, in a few minor instances, of cold. You may also experience sensations of pressure, flow, or tingling throughout your bodies. You may also experience moments of illumination, as though you were seeing a very rapid flash of Light. In those instances, the Light that you see is not from us, but from *you*. It represents a Light that originates from within your form as it is stimulated by our energy field.

MONITOR'S VIEW OF US

We come to you, seeing you as clusters of aggregated consciousness. On one level, we relate to your etheric bodies. But within your etheric bodies, what do we see? We see something that resembles a cosmic anthill. We see a multitude of tiny beings rushing around in a highly ordered structure. In their accumulations, they have various levels of control, a veritable hierarchy within the Body Consciousness. We are aware of all of that, to an alarming degree. We are also aware that, nestled in the etheric body are your chakras and the Thread of Life that connects them.

The chakra system of your bodies blends all levels of these realities together and brings them to your indwelling Life essence. Through your chakra system and that Thread of Life – the "sutratma" – you are connected with your Soul. Through that connection your Soul experiences what it gains from your living.

In your astral and mental bodies, as in the chakras and Thread of Life, we see clusterings of consciousness that resemble broccoli, because from our perspective, you have clusterings linked together through connecting threads which connect to the central Thread of Life. Each of these points of "broccoli" is sentient with mind, a spark of Divine Will, and a functional relationship to the entire structure.

Where do we find the conscious mind, the Surface Mind, the Outer Self? We find it existing as a single point of "broccoli" amid those clusters. And so we have to be very careful to retain a consistent vibratory relationship with that tiny broccoli point of mind.

Now we are *not* talking down to you, unless you happen to dislike broccoli. We are trying to share with you a perspective and help you understand some of our maneuvers in communicating with you.

IMPORTANCE OF BEFRIENDING OUR SUBCONSCIOUS MIND

Most of the energetic effects, which you experience in your Outer Self, are generated through your subconscious mind. The Outer Self has insufficient capacity to conduct much Life energy, so most of the effect of our presence occurs through your subconscious mind, which has many aspects to it. When we spoke earlier of "parts" of your mind shutting down or closing off to concepts we present, we observe certain broccoli points closing down and shutting off. If there are sufficient numbers of those in certain clusters of your subconscious mind, your Outer Self is shut off and closed down temporarily.

You, as a structure of consciousness, are multi-level. You experience most of that multi-dimensionality through your subconscious mind. You are wise to meet your subconscious mind and become friends with it. You literally exist in its hands and much of the time serve its purposes, particularly as it needs to experience certain conditions in order to learn.

Your subconscious mind serves as a vehicle of experience for your Soul. Your Soul serves as a vehicle of experience for its Monad, and the Monad serves as a vehicle of experience for a Cosmic Identity. And thus all are connected.

Each one of your senses represents a direct link of consciousness with a Cosmic Identity and with the Creator of All. How would you become aware of the Creator except through your senses?

Does this make sense? We slipped a pun over on you! Did this answer your question concerning experience of heat?

LINDA: Yes.

ARZANI: If I fall asleep while you're speaking, does what you're saying affect me somehow?

MONITOR: Indeed. It affects you through the medium of your subconscious mind, at least those portions that remain open for the experience. Those aspects of your subconscious mind that close off to shut us out are responsible for your falling asleep. They restrict the flow of vitality to you, the Outer Self, or, as you say, they pull your plug.

Less restricted beings, such as we, often experience the closing off of other forms who experience greater restriction. Yet one manifestation of Life is no better than another, from our perspective. We see in your forms the same Life essence that gleams in ours, that gleams in the Planetary Consciousness, the Solar Consciousness, the Galactic Consciousness, and the Universal Consciousness.

We, of course, desire to assist that precious consciousness to achieve fulfillment in its selected type of experience. Yet as we approach and seek to assist, we experience a certain degree of frustration when you close off. We must have patience, when those we seek to assist close off and hide from us.

OUT OF BODY EXPERIENCE

DONNA: I realized, when you were talking, that the time that I really could observe my etheric body the most was during an out-of-body experience. Though the situation occurred at a traumatic time in my life, I recognized afterwards that during that time I could see, or the part of me that wasn't the body could see. I could hear what was going on around me, and I was able to think during that time. So all of those qualities went with me when I left the physical body. I could observe the etheric body better than I can when all parts of me are all together in the physical body. Is that correct?

MONITOR: Quite correct. It is analogous to removing a fish from water, then returning it to water, which allows the fish to discern the difference in its environment. And so you have sleep and so-called physical death.

In the process of dying, you withdraw from the physical form by withdrawing your etheric form from it. When your etheric body dissociates from your physical body, the physical body begins to dissolve.

Now, all of etheric structure is not removed from that so-called physical body. Otherwise, if your etheric body were to withdraw *all* etheric energy, there would be absolutely no physical body, and you would disappear from physical sight. You have perhaps heard of instances where advanced human beings – those you term "Masters" – appear and disappear through physical form. They do so through utilization of their etheric bodies, using the creative power of mind to empower the etheric body to change its vibratory quality, entering in one instant into full physical form, and in another instant leaving it totally.

CONSCIOUS DYING

JULIE: Monitor, is there a way that we could ask for and experience a *conscious* death, being aware of what is happening as we go through the period of transition? Can we be aware of that process consciously?

MONITOR: Indeed. As you physically die, you may remain aware. In fact, it offers one of the challenges, or lessons, placed before every human being.

At this time, a majority of dying persons fade into a type of sleep, where the Outer Self, as one little broccoli point, closes. Then the subconscious mind continues the process with its awareness, which may be limited or unlimited, depending on its degree of evolution.

An Outer Self, who has sufficiently related to its subconscious mind, can remain aware and open throughout the process of transition. That type of Outer Self is what we consider an "amplified" Outer Self. It allows itself to be an aware *vehicle* for the greater portions of its mind, or being.

An Outer Self who seeks to retain its own paradoxical pseudo-identity cannot sustain itself during the process of transition. But an Outer Self who relates to its wholeness of being may remain conscious and thereby greatly speed the learning of the entire being.

We have spoken to you about developing a *continuity of consciousness*, and we have spoken to you in terms of practicing development of that skill through what is sometimes called the "little death" of nightly sleep. That method remains much more accessible to you than transition from the so-called "physical" form. Through practice, develop continuity of consciousness as you move into, through, and out of sleep, and the skills you gain there will assist you in remaining conscious during the process of dying.

CONTINUITY OF CONSCIOUSNESS

HELEN: How do you know whether or not you have continuity of consciousness as you go into sleep?

MONITOR: Well, we no longer sleep.

HELEN: Oh, I meant "we."

MONITOR: You mean you as a human being?

HELEN: Right.

MONITOR: You retain memory. If you were viewing your mind as a tape recorder, does your tape recorder continue functioning during the time of sleep?

HELEN: Partially.

MONITOR: It does, partially. You may find great value in your expansion of that capability. As you stretch your capability as Outer Self, you recognize how well it relates to your subconscious mind. If your Outer Self can relax in the care of your subconscious mind, it naturally allows its awareness to flow into the subconscious mind. Then the awareness of the subconscious mind flows into the Outer Self. That offers one definition of dream experience.

As you do that with greater facility, you find that you become aware of transitional movements, as though you were moving through nonphysical space. As you move in such a manner, you find that the space you traverse is organized differently than what you are used to. If you are open to accept that organization of space, you may retain continuity of consciousness. If you reject that space, you lose continuity of consciousness.

APPEARANCES OF MOTHER MARY

HELEN: This question has to do with your discussing the ability of a Master to change his/her etheric body into a body that we can see with the physical eye. This was not the way you put it, but is this the way the children – for instance, in Medjugorje or Garanbandal – are able to see Mother

Mary? And why is it that only some can see her, and some cannot, when she appears?

MONITOR: We describe it in a different way. We describe the children's perception of Mother Mary, in those types of visitations, as a direct mental and astral communication from the Mother. She projects to the children in such a manner that the children can accept and not be frightened.

You have asked at times why Mother Mary appears for the most part to children. Our answer is that they are more open and less fixated in perceptual habits. They do not have as much resistance to her projection as do most adults.

Anyone in this room may be open to such experiences with Mother Mary or other enlightened beings. You will find that the most enlightened beings are extremely busy, because they devote their efforts to the evolution of all the consciousness of the planet and beyond. In their busyness, they have gained capabilities that enable them to move with great facility and be quite capable of appearing to you.

What you need to develop, in order to have such a meeting, is *openness,* relinquishing those habits of perception that limit your ability to have such a meeting. Often we find that human beings pray to meet their God, or pray to meet their Christ or their Buddha, and actually have the meeting, but do not realize it on the level of the Outer Self, and even in certain segments of the subconscious mind.

OPEN PERCEPTION

JULIE: What habits, that stand in the way, do we need to let go of?

MONITOR: Habits that maintain a fixed perception. The prime example we have talked about is the habit of considering that you have physical perceptions. It is more than just a semantic distinction, because when you consider "physical," it consists of more than a word. It involves a related system of concepts. Those concepts arise partly from the structure of your language, and partly from what is taught to you by your families and cultures.

You grew up thinking that you are physical beings who are isolated, completely separate from each other and from Life outside your physical skins. You develop, from that configuration of beliefs, other beliefs that further complicate your illusion of isolation. You develop fear reactions that you will be hurt by forces beyond your perception. As that and other complications develop in your thinking and feeling mechanisms, you limit your ability to be open.

Does this answer your question?

JULIE: That helps, yes. Thank you.

TOOLS FOR EXPLORATION
Exercise 5

OPENING NONPHYSICAL PERCEPTION

1. In a quiet place, collect your thoughts and pay attention to each of your senses in turn. As you focus on each sense, deliberately <u>dis</u>identify from "physical only" labeling of that sense.

2. Pay attention to your sense of **sight** by noticing what you can see around you. Notice *shapes* and affirm out loud, "*I* see physical and MORE than physical reality." Notice areas of *light and dark* and affirm out loud, "*You* see physical and MORE than physical reality." Notice *colors* and affirm out loud, "*We* see physical and MORE than physical reality." Repeat this cycle at least three times. How do you feel? What do you notice in yourself? Write down your observations

3. Pay attention to your sense of **hearing** by noticing what you can hear around you. Notice *soft and loud* sounds and affirm out loud, "*I* hear physical and MORE than physical reality." Notice *dissonant sounds* and affirm out loud, "*You* hear physical and MORE than physical reality." Notice *melodious sounds* and affirm out loud, "*We* hear physical and MORE than physical reality." Repeat this cycle at least three times. How do you feel? What do you notice in yourself? Write down your observations.

4. Pay attention to your sense of **feeling** by noticing what you can feel around you. Notice *shapes* that you feel with your hands and affirm out loud, "*I* feel physical and MORE than physical reality." Notice *textures* that you feel with your hands and affirm out loud, "*You* feel physical and MORE than physical reality." Notice *heat and cold sensations* that you feel with your hands and affirm out loud, "*We* feel physical and MORE than physical reality." Repeat this cycle at least three times. How do you feel? What do you notice in yourself? Write down your observations.

5. Pay attention to your sense of **taste** by noticing what you can taste from foods or other objects that you can safely taste in your immediate vicinity. Notice *sweet sensations* and affirm out loud, "*I* taste physical and MORE than physical reality." Notice *sour sensations* and affirm out loud, "*You* taste physical and MORE than physical reality." Notice *salty sensations* and affirm out loud, "*We* taste physical and MORE than physical reality."

Repeat this cycle at least three times. How do you feel? What do you notice in yourself? Write down your observations.

6. Pay attention to your sense of **smell** by noticing what you can smell around you. Notice *sweet odors* and affirm out loud, "*I* smell physical and MORE than physical reality." Notice *acrid odors* and affirm out loud, "*You* smell physical and MORE than physical reality." Notice *musty odors* and affirm out loud, "*We* smell physical and MORE than physical reality." Repeat this cycle at least three times. How do you feel? What do you notice in yourself? Write down your observations.

7. When you have completed the above steps, what have you learned? Do you feel more open to MORE than physical perceptions?

SLEEP, THE "LITTLE DEATH"

LINDA: You talked about the "little death" of sleep and about being open to be whatever you need to be to make contact with the subconscious mind. Is it possible that we can have an experience of a "little death" and not know that we died?

MONITOR: Absolutely. That is the norm among humanity today.

LINDA: Okay.

MONITOR: Most human beings, at this time, ignore the time of sleep. Their memory ends as they go to sleep and begins when they awaken. What lies in between seems a blank. That condition may be greatly altered, for as a human being retains continuity of consciousness through the time of sleep, he/she experiences an expansion out of the etheric body, and beyond the astral body, into the mental plane, which is a prime need at this time for humanity to experience.

Humanity needs to develop sufficient mental capability to remain organized and consistent in its experience of the astral plane. The astral plane is quite fluid in character and may easily disorient the human mind unprepared to handle it. It is like releasing a fish into a swiftly flowing stream so that the fish does not maintain its position, but is swept downstream. The human mind is in the process of developing sufficient mental capability to remain oriented in its experience of the astral plane.

DIFFERENT PLANES OF EXISTENCE IN DREAMS

Some dream experiences reflect mental plane experiences, and some reflect astral plane experiences. Other dream experiences reflect etheric plane experiences. How do you tell the difference between them?

Mental dream experiences have great clarity and a sense of peaceful orderliness, not a vague or cloudy quality. All details remain clear and consistent.

Astral dream experiences are characterized by a cloudy quality in which forms shift and situations change. In astral experience, many people have enough mental capability to experience segments of enactments, "dramas" presented for the benefit of the subconscious and conscious minds. In the astral plane, many "drama" presentations are experienced. Those presentations are made coherent largely through the efforts of a Teacher who has sufficient mental capability to use that type of presentation as a means of instruction. The dramatic instruction is aimed primarily at the subconscious mind.

We assure you that those Teachers, who are often our colleagues, would be delighted to use that dramatic presentation as instruction for the Outer Self.

Dreams of etheric experience appear quite peculiar to human beings because they seem like a reversal of form. In etheric experiences, from your point of view, you encounter reversals of inside and outside, left and right, up and down, and sometimes reversals of light and dark and coloration. This type of experience normally disorients the Outer Self, yet the subconscious mind is accustomed to it.

If you, the Outer Self, are willing to ride along with your subconscious mind and trust it, you will be taken through such experiences. After a sufficient exposure, you will grow accustomed to the etheric perspective. Etheric dream experiences have a quality similar to mental dream experiences, but with a distinctly different quality associated with etheric expression.

LINDA: Does that mean that an etheric dream is like an out-of-body experience?

MONITOR: To the Outer Self, all of these experiences appear to be out-of-body, because of the Outer Self's concept of the physical body, which is illusory. In fact, these experiences are *not* out-of-body, because they are sensed by the same senses that the Outer Self uses. Those senses express through each of the bodies. In the etheric plane, your senses function through your etheric body. In the astral plane, they work through your astral body. And so forth, in the mental plane. So your perceptions may extend beyond the physical body, but are not truly out-of-body.

CARTOON ANIMATION DREAMS

CLAUDIA: When you're in the dream states that we're talking about, and you experience animation in the dream, which one of those three states would that be in, mental, etheric, or astral?

MONITOR: Could you describe what you mean by "animation"?

CLAUDIA: Could anyone help me out?

MONITOR: Are you talking about the process that you know as "cartoon animation?"

CLAUDIA: Yes.

MONITOR: Such experiences are used as a form of mental instruction in the astral plane. In the period of time that animation has been available in the physical plane, the Outer Self, if it's having difficulty accepting a mental projection, experiences it as animation. In the experience of that Outer Self and now, in some cases, aspects of the subconscious mind, animation represents an *in-between* acceptance of reality. That level of mind functions *in-between* its customary habit of perceiving and a full mental mode of perceiving. So animation represents the mind's way of accepting what it cannot fully accept through mental perception. Does this assist you?

CLAUDIA: Thank you.

JULIE: I think that's about all these etheric bodies can handle tonight.

MONITOR: Realize that when you bravely set forth upon this subject, "The Nature of Reality," you knew you were due for troubles.

JULIE: We are stretching!

MONITOR: You knew that strange winds would fill your sails, and that you would be carried off course into alien waters. And so we thank you for journeying with us.

We encourage you again to use your senses in unlimited ways. Consider: How many ways can you see? How many ways can you hear? How many ways can you feel? As you explore those ways, you greatly gain in wisdom. If you become wiser than we are, we will be happy to be your students. We thank you. Now we depart.

Lesson 11
June 19, 1991

MONITOR: We welcome you again as Monitor.

GROUP: Welcome, Monitor.

EXPERIMENTS IN ETHERIC PERCEPTION

MONITOR: We hope that you are taking the opportunity to experiment a little bit with your perceptions of reality. Would any of you wish to share your experiments? As you relate your experiences, you may receive special benefit from our perspective, as we comment on your experience.

ARZANI: I was shocked when you first told us that the senses were primarily of the etheric body. Then I was meditating yesterday and realized that all the experiences that I was having in meditation were all etheric senses. What I was seeing, what I was hearing, what I was feeling, really did have nothing to do with what was happening physically. It wasn't as shocking to me when I saw it in that perspective.

MONITOR: This offers a good example of what we term "discernment," which allows you to perceive more accurately. If you, like most human beings, consider your experience as "physical," you are *not* able to discern etheric experience. In other words, you confuse the two modes of experience and actually mislabel most of your experience.

That might seem a matter of low priority, since some of you have read books describing various energy levels, and you are quite open to accept that as a possibility. But this habit of mislabeling *etheric* experience as *physical* experience provides a major obstacle to your growth. When you truly discern etheric experience, you bring a greater accuracy to your perceptive mechanisms, those ways in which your brains and nervous systems process your sensory perceptions.

Understand that your perceptive mechanisms are greatly affected by your ideas, your conceptions of reality. As a rather absurd example, a person who has the idea that sunlight is green actually affects his perception of sunlight. He will not recognize the variations of sunlight that you recognize as the other colors or the blended totality of colors that form sunlight. If you wish to discern reality more accurately, it is important to distinguish between etheric experience and physical experience.

LOIS: Monitor, last time you said that you would encourage us to practice hearing, feeling, and seeing etheric reality. I would appreciate further clarification of that for myself as to what etheric reality is. Perhaps you can give us some examples of practicing hearing, feeling, and seeing in that reality.

[Following the Lesson, Lois reported the following experience: "After I asked Monitor my question, as Monitor started to respond, immediately everything blurred as I was focused on Harvey. He and the chair seemed to be merging together, and then I saw a white border around his head, the edge of the chair, the side of the bookcase and the picture in the background on the wall. It seems to me that there was a moment of feeling concerned that Harvey was going away, as he seemed to merge with the chair."]

MONITOR: Very good. We find that it is easiest for some people to perceive etheric reality in terms of sight, yet for others the sense of hearing provides the best access, and for even others, the sense of touch. For you, Lois, we recommend the sense of touch as your best means of access to perceiving etheric reality. As you practice etheric touch, you will find that etheric seeing and hearing follow.

ETHERIC TOUCH

Each person should use that sense that, for them, is *most* conducive for etheric perception. For you, Lois, etheric touch may be gained quite easily. As you practice it by holding your hands a distance of 6–8 inches away from, let's say, your leg, you will find that you can sense etheric touch, as you allow your hands to move roughly an inch closer and then farther away from the original position. As your hands move, you sense etheric touch.

Consider how you learn *physical* touch, or how to touch physical reality. You use your hands to touch a variety of physical objects. You touch smooth, sharp, jagged, rough-textured objects, learning how to tell one quality from another. Learning etheric touch works the same way. Practicing gives you a variety of etheric sensations that you find are quite similar to physical sensations.

TOOLS FOR EXPLORATION
Exercise 6

LEARNING ETHERIC TOUCH

In a relaxed seated position, place your hands palm down on your thighs, left hand on left thigh, right hand on right thigh. Notice the familiar sensations of physical touch. Write down the sensations you notice.

1. Lift your hands to a position six to eight (6-8) inches distance above your thighs. Notice the change in sensations. Write below the sensations you notice in your hands and thighs.

    Left hand: Right hand:

    Left thigh: Right thigh:

2. Slowly move your hands alternately closer and farther from your thighs, ranging as close as a distance of four (4) inches and as far as eight (8) inches. Write down the sensations you notice.

3. Find the position where the sensations feel most intense for each hand. Use a measuring tape or ruler to measure the distance between your palm and your thigh at that position. Write down each distance.

    Left hand to thigh =   Right hand to thigh =

4. Consider the possibility that you are actually feeling etheric touch. If that seems difficult to accept, list the possible physical emanations you might be noticing. Is it heat? Is it electricity? Is it magnetism? Look up references that can tell you if you might be feeling any of these physical emanations.

5. If you *can* accept the possibility that you are experiencing etheric touch, you may identify these sensations as *dense* etheric body touch. In effect, you are touching the dense etheric skin of your palm against the dense etheric skin of your thigh at the distance you measured.

6. If you wish to continue the exercise, lift your hands to a position twelve to fourteen (12-14) inches above your thighs. Notice the

change in sensations. Write down the sensations you notice in your hands and thighs.

Left hand: Right hand:

Left thigh: Right thigh:

7. Slowly move your hands alternately closer and farther from your thighs, ranging as close as a distance of ten (10) inches and as far as sixteen (16) inches. Write down the sensations you notice.

8. Find the position where the sensations feel most intense for each hand. Use a measuring tape or ruler to measure the distance between your palm and your thigh at that position. Write down each distance.

Left hand to thigh =   Right hand to thigh =

9. These sensations you may identify as *fine* etheric body touch. You are touching the fine etheric skin of your palm against the fine etheric skin of your thigh. Similar exercises involving the senses of touch and sight have revealed the physical body enclosed within a *dense* etheric body, which is in turn enclosed within a *fine* etheric body.

10. This exercise may be repeated effectively to build your capability for recognizing etheric touch. Other parts of your body can be scanned with your hands. If you wish, you can extend the scanning technique to someone else's body.

11. In doing this exercise, I have learned:

MONITOR: In the initial phase of developing etheric touch, you discover that etheric touch seems to be limited to only a few sensations, such as warmth, tingling, and a sense of current similar to electrical current. Yet as you continue practicing, you will find that etheric touch has a much greater variety of sensations to offer.

When you do physical touching, you place your physical skin against the surface of an object. In etheric touching, you place your etheric skin against the etheric skin of the object. You note one major difference from physical touching: your etheric skin can easily penetrate the etheric surface of the object. With physical skin and surface, you do not experience penetration, but compression.

As you place your hand against the arm of your chair and apply pressure, your physical hand does not penetrate the arm of the chair significantly. Instead, you feel compression on the skin of your hand. But with etheric touch, your etheric skin has no difficulty penetrating the etheric surface of the arm of the chair. With etheric touch, you may feel the textures and qualities of the etheric object throughout its form. Therefore you begin to realize that etheric reality does, in some respects, differ from physical reality.

We liken this comparison to the analogy we've used before, that physical reality exists as a shadow of etheric reality. Physical reality is more limited than etheric reality in some respects. In time, your mathematicians and physicists will develop a set of mathematical relationships that describe the relationship between physical and etheric structures. Etheric structure will be found to have added dimension.

LOSS OF PHYSICAL SENSES

JULIE: Monitor, what happens when you have a physical loss, like loss of sight, loss of hearing? What happens on the etheric level?

MONITOR: In most cases such as that, we find that the guiding consciousness of the individual has introduced the condition of sensory loss to assist development of the subconscious mind. Remember that we defined the subconscious mind as that part of the personality that continues from body to body, lifetime to lifetime. When the subconscious mind becomes too caught up in physical reality, much as a person watching a horror movie becomes caught up in the reality of the movie and forgets where he truly is, the subconscious mind may become stuck in limited perception. The High Self initiates the condition of blindness or deafness or numbness in order to assist the subconscious mind to detach itself from its obsession. Other causative conditions may also occur, but we believe this describes the most common occurrences.

AMPUTATION

ARZANI: If there's an amputation of the physical body, does it still exist in the etheric body?

MONITOR: Exactly. The etheric body may not be amputated by physical means. The physical body, of course, may be amputated by physical means, but the etheric body remains intact. An analogy, which might help you understand this, involves a person who intends to speak a complete sentence, but is interrupted and speaks only part of the sentence. The rest of the sentence remains in the form of an energy potential that could be manifested, but is not.

The karmic pattern of an individual may require loss of a body part by amputation. That experience is often regarded as a major warning to that individual. The loss of an arm represents the loss of capability for action, activity, or service for that person. Yet even when the arm is amputated and lost on a physical level, that person still feels the arm as present. The person feels the etheric arm or, you might say, feels the etheric touch sensations of the etheric arm.

MARLENE: Monitor, in a case like that, what would the High Self be trying to tell the person if his arm was amputated? If it was a loss of capability of service, what would it be trying to tell him? Was the person not serving when he should have been serving, or perhaps serving too much?

MONITOR: The High Self, in the case of an amputation of an arm, would be enforcing what had previously been warned. The warning would have been given primarily to the subconscious mind of the person, for the subconscious mind has a greater need for learning. The Outer Self, in such cases, is often made a shocked spectator.

The subconscious mind receives frequent communications from the High Self and knows better, while the Outer Self may have only a dim glimmer of the High Self's message. When an arm is lost in such a situation, the subconscious mind is forcibly reminded that it has ignored guidance and warnings, and has persisted in misdirection or misuse of its activities. Such lessons may vary, for it may be that the person has engaged in inappropriate activity, or has not served when service was called for, or has been compelled to service beyond the point of balance.

CHAKRA STIMULATION BY SOUL

LINDA: I have a question regarding an experience I had in July of 1985, when I felt that a healing of my heart chakra was happening. In that experience, I felt like I was in Christ Consciousness. I could see molecules of the air in rainbow prisms, like watching the order of the Universe. What reality is that?

MONITOR: A fine reality . . .

LINDA: Of course!

MONITOR: . . . which others wish to share. In that specific instance, your chakra system was receiving stimulation from your Soul. Stimulation was received and moderated through your High Self. It was intended to create a definite point of departure, a landmark experience to assist your subconscious mind, in both Male and Female aspects, to make a change of direction. It was a pre-arranged signal for your subconscious mind.

For you, the Outer Self, it was a spectacular experience, one that gave a sense of bliss, yet raised doubts about your stability, which is a normal reaction in such circumstances. Your perceptions during that experience were a combination of etheric, astral, and mental planes.

What you described, as seeing prismatic effects of molecules of the air, was primarily etheric sight of the action of *prana* in the atmosphere. The etheric body is the prime vehicle for the conduction of prana. Your etheric body, and any person's etheric body, receives its supply of prana from the atmosphere of Earth. You were seeing the prana in the atmosphere.

Your experience moved you into a dramatic shift of perception, which was not only your perception of the world, but also your perception of yourself. Through the action of your Soul, you experienced for a brief time that connectedness, that unity of being which is the natural state of the Soul.

As you and others seek to harmonize and allow Soul awareness to infuse your consciousness, that type of awareness becomes more common. When it does, this planet will truly attain peace, for each individual will be intimately aware of how their thoughts, feelings, and actions affect all of Life. Does this give you enough information?

LINDA: Yes, this is great information. Thank you very much.

SUFFERING

JULIE: Monitor, I'd like to ask a question. First, I would like to share two different views regarding suffering as an experience of our reality. The first one is from the book, *The Seat of the Soul,* by Gary Zukav, which says, "Pain by itself is merely pain, but the experience of pain, coupled with an understanding that the pain serves a worthy purpose, is suffering. Suffering is meaningful. Suffering can be endured because there is a reason for it that is worth the effort. What is more worthy of your pain than the evolution of your Soul?"

And then, here is another excerpt on suffering from *The Science of Mind* text by Ernest Holmes, which has a section called "The World Has Learned All It Should Through Suffering":

> The Science of Mind and Spirit make a tremendous claim when it states that an individual should be free from the bondage of sickness, poverty, and unhappiness. It does, however, carefully set forth the conditions under which freedom operates and the laws governing life, stating in no uncertain terms that unless man understands these conditions and obeys these laws, he will not receive full benefit from its teaching. The world is beginning to realize that it has learned all it should through suffering and pain. Surely there can be no intelligence in the universe that wishes man to be sick, suffer pain, be unhappy and end in oblivion. Surely if God or the Universal Intelligence is imbued with goodness, then it could not ordain that man should ultimately be other than a perfect expression of life.

My question is about your view of suffering, and if you have anything to add to, or differ from, what is shared in these two quotations.

MONITOR: Well, we can answer the question and ask you to "suffer" the answer.

JULIE: I may be sorry I asked!

MONITOR: Suffering is an experience of form by the Life force dwelling within it. Suffering may be regarded in various ways, as these apt selections demonstrate.

The first selection *[Zukav]* refers to suffering as a means to achievement of a purpose. As a person seeks a goal, he/she may be willing to suffer to achieve that goal. Such suffering is intentional, consciously chosen, and an important development of consciousness in that it enables the personality to undertake those challenging experiences which lead to Soul development. If the personality is willing to undertake difficult challenges, it *facilitates* the Soul's experience.

As you consider the personality as a *vehicle* for the Soul, you realize that the personality at times must encounter pain and change. Some parts of the personality are more accepting and flexible, while other parts are more rigid and resistive to change. As has been noted, resistance creates pain.

The second selection *[Holmes]* refers to the development of a free state or attitude concerning the need for pain. It represents a viewpoint that recommends *acceptance* of Life. With acceptance, the personality experiences change with minimal pain. When suffering is encountered by an accepting personality, it minimizes suffering and *maximizes* the value of the experience.

At this stage of human development, pain and suffering are common experiences for humanity. Seeking freedom from inner resistance represents a very wise choice for a person, because this age presents continual and accelerated change. Such change involves a change in the consciousness of the Planetary Being, wherein each person, as a constituent of Planetary Consciousness, also changes. If a person can accept change with a minimum of resistance, he/she can minimize suffering.

ETHERIC BLOCKAGES

ARZANI: I have two questions about health. I saw a healer the other day who told me that she didn't see any blockages in my body at all, and yet after using the Chinese system of pulse diagnosis of different organs, she said that my pulses were all very weak. I've always associated weakness in the pulses with a blockage of some kind. I don't understand how I could be unblocked and yet weak. Could you comment on this?

MONITOR: We surmise that her comments were based on a limited terminology. The pulses, that you refer to, represent the physical circulatory system, which primarily reflects the bloodstream as it responds to the flow and quality of energy throughout the etheric body. The term "blockage" may be used in several contexts, so its meaning may vary considerably, depending on the context referred to.

In review of your etheric body, we say that your etheric body is moderately energized. In comparison, the etheric body of a Spiritual Master is highly energized. You might therefore say that the etheric energy level of your body is relatively more blocked than that of a Master. You might consider how well your etheric body accepts Life force, or prana, how well it absorbs, circulates, and then eliminates it, radiating it away from itself.

Blockages may occur in any of those processes. Blockages may also occur in the *structure* of the etheric body. For example, you might have a blockage in the energy circuitry between two chakras, or a blockage in one of the circuits known as "meridians."

In your case, we say that your etheric body will be brought to a higher level of *absorption* of prana and gain in ability to circulate and distribute that prana throughout the etheric structure, and then eliminate it. As that improvement occurs, your diagnostic pulse will become more pronounced, because your physical body will be more greatly charged with what you term "vitality." Does this make sense to you?

ARZANI: Is there anything I need to do, or is that just happening anyway?

MONITOR: It will happen quite naturally. If you wish specific guidance, you may ask for what is sometimes termed a "Doctor Teacher" to instruct you.

NARCOLEPSY

ARZANI: I spoke to a woman today who had narcolepsy, and I wonder what that really is about, from your point of view.

MONITOR: We find narcolepsy as a condition of the subconscious mind where one aspect of the subconscious mind neglects its responsibilities to the physical body, allowing it to fall into a devitalized state. In the etheric body, this action occurs primarily in the brain, brain stem, and cerebellum. When medical science is more capable of reading the activity of these areas of the brain, it will find that there is a distinct shift of electrical impulses in the rear portion of the brain. The cause, however, remains primarily within one aspect, or Self, of the subconscious mind.

In the woman indicated, it is likely that her Male Self has been accustomed in previous lifetimes to leaving the physical form, which may have been appropriate if that physical form was held in the care of the Female Self. In this lifetime, that is *not* the arrangement, so the Male Self is remiss and needs teaching.

The Outer Self of that individual may ask her Male Self to remain in position and *not* depart. In some cases, such a request will be honored, and the condition will cease. In other cases, the request might not be honored, and the condition would persist. If she contacts her High Self and asks for instruction of the errant Self, the condition will be corrected.

ARZANI: Thank you very much.

COHERENT INTENTION

JERRY: Monitor, I've been given a phrase and am developing a process connected with it. The more I work with it, the more it seems to expand in meaning. I would be interested in your observations about the phrase, "I maintain a conscious awareness of my high value intention."

MONITOR: You find, do you not, that the phrase "high value intention" has a certain charge for you?

JERRY: Absolutely.

MONITOR: The nature of this charge represents an effect of *coherence*, in which the intentions of the Outer Self, subconscious mind, and superconscious mind are in harmony, where their energies are coherently focused and expressed. In analogy, you find that the value of a ray of light is increased when the light is directed through a laser and made coherent. Does this have meaning for you?

JERRY: Yes, it does. That particular thing also seems to be the base point of a pyramid, and I believe the pyramid itself – the three sides of the trinity of the pyramid – includes the conscious, the subconscious, and the superconscious minds.

MONITOR: Indeed. As all three levels of mind unite in intention, the qualities of each level of mind synthesize, producing a state of Oneness of Being. When mind, at any level, achieves coherent intention, it becomes illuminated by the action of Spirit.

JERRY: Does adding the word "congruence" cause that meaning to expand further?

MONITOR: We see "congruence" as a term of similar meaning to "coherence," yet the term "coherence" has greater meaning in terms of scientific development of the laser.

JERRY: Does "coherence" equate to creating a synergistic result from the forces brought into coherence?

MONITOR: In viewing mind as a field of energy, we appreciate the consideration that the predominant function of mind is *to organize*. We view the different levels of mind as different *organizing fields* of energy. If the subconscious mind utilizes one type of organization and the superconscious mind utilizes a distinctly different type of organization, a diminished energetic exchange occurs between them. This exchange may be perceived as radiation or flow.

If the two levels of mind have similar organizing fields, the exchange of energy between them increases dramatically. And if they have exactly the same organization, they achieve a state of Oneness through coupling.

We make reference to the laser because as science proceeds, many technological applications will evolve and people in general will understand more about the action of coherent light. It will become an important metaphor to develop humanity's understanding of the actions of mind. Therefore we refer to the laser and the concept of coherence.

JERRY: Thank you very much. I am now able to evolve the relationship of that phrase into business terminology, which is what I was looking to do. "Coherence" is the key word.

LUCIFERIAN LIGHT AND TEMPTATION

JULIE: Anyone else have a question? I have one more example from the book, *The Seat of the Soul*. It talks about the experience of temptation in our reality, and it says that it has to do with the "Luciferian Light" energy: "Temptation is the Universe's compassionate way of allowing us to run through what would be a harmful negative karmic dynamic, if you were to allow it to become physically manifest." Could you shed any more light on the experience of temptation and the "Luciferian Light?"

MONITOR: We will attempt to be brief. We see "Luciferian Light" more as a principle, the principle of separation that has contributed to the evolution of form. The whole point of Life essence inhabiting a form involves the achievement of a definite and unique perspective of reality. Each form enables its indwelling Life to create qualities of consciousness. For example, as you perceive a rainbow, in some way the rainbow enters your mind and your manifested energy field. You absorb and become the rainbow, and thereby develop rainbow qualities in your consciousness. When your consciousness moves out of your physical body at death, it retains the qualities of the rainbow and all other experiences you have had.

"Temptation" refers to the activation of desires and relates most strongly to your astral body. As you observe your minds seeking to apply a spiritual principle in daily living, you find that your desires often present distractions from that task. When the temptation attempts to pull you off course, you have opportunity to develop certain abilities, certain strengths, by maintaining your course. You use the guidance of principle and resist temptation, thereby developing qualities of consciousness that you would not otherwise develop. This is perhaps another way of stating what the selection has stated, that temptation is a gift of Higher Consciousness.

AUTHENTIC AND EXTERNAL POWER

JERRY: In the previously mentioned book, The Seat of the Soul, Gary Zukav makes a distinction, as well as a correlation, between what he calls "external power" and "authentic power." Can you describe how they relate to the coherence theory you previously discussed?

MONITOR: We relate the term "authentic power" to the personality allowing its Soul expression. Because the Soul acts as the true energizer of the personality, the personality's ability to express its Soul generates the highest power that the personality is capable of generating.

The term "external power" relates to the various types of power that originate in the various aspects of the personality and in interrelationships among personalities. Examples include the power of money, or the power of persuasion, or the power of sexual attraction. In final analysis, all external powers merely reflect internal powers. They reflect the energy of the indwelling Soul who seeks expression through the personality. Does this address your question?

JERRY: Absolutely. Thank you very much.

ENERGY EXPRESSION THROUGH KARMIC PLAN

MARLENE: Is that the only way available in physical form, or is that one of the best ways to express energy through the personality? Are there better ways? If you have sexual energy and don't really have a way to deal with it, would yoga be a good way to express it through the personality? Do you understand what I'm trying to say?

MONITOR: We address your question in terms of the karmic plan of growth for an individual personality. One expression of energy may be more appropriate for one personality than for another. For one person, the expression of Soul energy through sexual attraction may meet the exact need at the moment. But for another person, it may be quite inappropriate. The current karmic lesson determines the appropriateness of expression.

Personalities are creative beings. As they allow their creativity to manifest, they express more of their Soul. The energy of creativity truly expresses the energy of the Soul and even higher forms of Life than the Soul.

SLEEP STATE EXPERIMENT

MONITOR: We would like to give you an interesting project, if you choose to participate. We invite you, as you enter sleep, to ask that we join you during your sleep state. If you do this, we will be present with you. We do not have the ability to assist you to remember your experience. That is up to you. But we will do our part to participate with you in an experiment. As you are willing to share your experiences in this forum, we will be pleased to comment on them from our perspective.

JERRY: Do you have a recommended method for us to use to evoke our remembrance of that activity upon awakening?

MONITOR: As you recognize that memory involves your subconscious mind, you realize the necessity for gaining its cooperation. We recommend that you ask your subconscious mind to assist you to remember and to assist you to be as aware as possible of your experience with us as you enter the state of sleep. Is this clear?

JERRY: As a bell!

MARLENE: Is there something I can say that will make my Inner Selves, or some part of me, feel safe in asking you to join me in my sleep?

MONITOR: We believe that you sense the fear of your lower subconscious mind, or what we term the "Mental Judge Self," who is easily threatened by a change of conditions. We ask that you listen first to what your Judge Self says to you concerning its fear. Ask it, "What do you fear?" and listen. Your listening demonstrates your respect for it. You do not, however, have to agree with what it wants to happen. After you have listened, your Mental Judge Self will feel more safe and be more inclined to cooperate with your request, because you have been considerate of its needs.

MARLENE: Thank you.

MONITOR: We thank you all once again, and now we leave you.

TOOLS FOR EXPLORATION
Exercise 7

CONNECTING WITH MONITOR IN SLEEP

1. Consider the possibility that you can ask Monitor to be with you when you sleep. Do you want to experiment with this possibility? Some persons might find it fascinating, while other persons might find it frightening. Explore your feelings and write down your decision.

2. If you decide *not* to undertake the experiment, write down your reasons and do not follow the later steps.

3. If you are *willing* to undertake the experiment, write down your reasons.

4. As you go to bed and *before* you go to sleep, write on a notepad or journal, "I ask all of my Selves to assist me in asking for Monitor to be with us during this time of sleep, in helping me be aware during sleep, and in helping me remember tonight's dreams."

5. On awakening, pay first attention to recalling your dreams. If dream recall is lacking or vague, use this request, "I ask all of my Selves to help me recall last night's dreams. I give thanks for your help."

6. Write notes about any dreams you recall, whether or not you immediately recognize Monitor's presence in the dreams.

7. Note the *qualities* evident in the dreams, such as love, fear, wisdom, ignorance, etc.

REQUEST FOR PRAYER TO MODERATE MAGMA FLOW

E.C.: We would like to interrupt. We speak as E.C. We would like to ask your assistance in a simple action of prayer wherein you ask for Divine action to moderate the flow of magma beneath the Pacific tectonic plate, in order that volcanic eruptions may be moderated. Is this clear? We ask that you do this now.

We express our appreciation for your assistance. Through you, energies may be manifest that spiritual forces may not manifest alone. We appreciate your cooperation.

JULIE: *[Julie makes certain she has written down the prayer properly.]* There was something else that I didn't get on the end of that statement.

E.C.: Ask that the flow of magma be moderated through Divine action. That will suffice. We thank you.

Lesson 12
June 26, 1991

MONITOR: We hope that you have questions and experiences to share after we give a brief word of preface. We have deliberately avoided being overly complex in our description of reality, and we would like to share with you now how we have managed to do that.

TIME AND SPACE EXPERIENCES

We have avoided, as you have also avoided, asking about concepts of time and space, because you have been pulled through a knothole by other sources who have stretched your concepts of time and space into something approximately more accurate than they were.

Time and space are experiences of the energy and structure of the universe dependent on the consciousness of the particular form that Life inhabits. As you live in the form of human beings, your Life essence is quite unlimited. Yet because your Life essence currently inhabits a human form, your experience of time and space is defined by that form. If your Life essence inhabited the form of a devic being, you would have a distinctly different experience of time and space. If you inhabited the form of the Planetary Being, or Logos, you would have the experience of time and space appropriate to that form.

In consideration of these statements, realize that in each one of you lies the vibratory consciousness which may connect you with virtually any major aspect of Life in the universe. Each one of you has originated as a Life essence in other portions of the universe, has traveled to this place, and will travel on. If you knew how to do it, you could gain access to many other states of consciousness than the consciousness of a human being. Consider, however, that you find a distinct value in exploring your "human being" consciousness. It offers you a unique perspective. It presents an opportunity that your Higher Consciousness has deliberately chosen.

Your consciousness has much to offer. If you explore it, you gain ability to explore levels of experience certain to fulfill you. You may know your Higher Consciousness, or your Soul consciousness, as well as you know your personality. We do not advocate abandoning your personality in favor of some nebulous Soul. We recommend that you fully realize your own being in *this* form.

Further, you benefit from recognizing your perceptions of etheric experience and distinguishing them from physical experience. We have suggested to you that you do *not* truly have "physical" senses, that your concept of "physical" being represents the reality of a shadow, that more substantial perception is found in the etheric plane, and that your senses function etherically.

We've indicated that your senses may function on many planes, but they will not so function if you do not fully explore them. So we advocate exploration of your own being as you find it and de-emphasize elaborate descriptions about the reality of the universe. We believe this preface puts a perspective on the topic, and we are now ready for any who would like to share experiences, viewpoints, or ask questions.

PRAYER FOR MAGMA FLOW MODERATION

MARLENE: Monitor, at the end of the last Lesson, when we were asked to pray that the magma flow moderately under the Pacific tectonic plate, some of us were wondering how much of an impact our prayer had.

MONITOR: We're glad you asked that. We sometimes forget to respond to your questions about the effects of prayer.

The situation within the planet is intensifying on several fronts. The elemental Life forms in the molten magma underlying the continental plates of the planet's crust are being deliberately stirred up by the Spiritual Hierarchy. The elementals also have a plan of evolution, and the Hierarchy now stimulates them in an orderly fashion toward greater growth. As they become stimulated, the magma moves and achieves greater velocity in its flowing. Several areas of the world are affected because the magma seeks to penetrate thin or punctured areas in the crust. It also creates a pressure against, and movement of, tectonic plates.

The situation, which you prayed for, has been moderated. You may have noticed that volcanic eruptions in the Pacific Ocean area have not increased significantly, but rather have maintained current levels of activity.

Volcanic activity will continue for several reasons. Therefore, we encourage you to continue your prayers. As you pray, you activate forces beyond your conscious awareness. Those forces, which are part of your deeper being, create significant effects.

Of course, you are not the only group being asked to pray for these events. The accumulated effect of several groups praying provides a significant contribution to the evolution of the planet. We thank you for your contributions to prayer and ask you to continue them. Did this answer your question?

MARLENE: Yes, thank you.

ELEMENTAL CONSCIOUSNESS

LINDA: Monitor, would you define, more specifically and clearly, the "elemental consciousness of the body?"

MONITOR: Elemental consciousness represents a Life-line, an evolutionary line whereby Life evolves in the forms of mineral, vegetable, animal, and human kingdoms and beyond. The elemental consciousness in your etheric and physical bodies consists of consciousness that evolved from the mineral to the vegetable to the animal kingdoms and then achieved expression in the human kingdom. As it evolves, it animates atoms, molecules, and minor and major aspects of the biological structure of the physical body. It is active primarily in the etheric body, and its vitality animates the physical body. The Body Self amounts to an accumulation of billions of small Life forms.

You may consider a single cell in your body as a Life form inhabited by a Life essence as valid as your Life essence. Because its form is small in comparison to yours, you may have the tendency to consider it as of lesser importance, but we assure you it is not. Its importance equals yours. That elemental consciousness makes its own contribution, and if it was not present, you would not have your etheric and physical bodies to occupy, and you would lack opportunity to experience this planet in the way you now enjoy.

Elemental consciousness evolves beyond human form as well. It functions in the human subconscious mind until it evolves beyond it. Its process of growth encompasses a large number of etheric and physical embodiments. Ultimately, elemental consciousness achieves mastery and evolves beyond human form. Does this answer your question?

LINDA: Yes, thank you.

MULTIPLE REALITIES

SUSIE: It's my understanding that we all share a common reality, which we perceive as our physical environment. Each of us also simultaneously experiences our own individual space/time locations, and we also sense that we are part of a larger cosmic reality. Are these the only three realities that we have in the three-dimensional plane?

MONITOR: No.

SUSIE: How many are there?

MONITOR: We may not adequately number them, but indicate this for your consideration. We previously mentioned the elemental consciousness of a cell. That living entity of a cell has its own individual reality, yet is part of the accumulative collective reality of all of the other elemental Life forms in your body, so your body has a reality as a collective form.

As your Life essence inhabits the body, it brings with it other energies and awarenesses that also have their realities. Taken altogether, you, as a human being, have approximately 800–plus realities to experience. Numbers, in this instance, are not very significant. What is more significant is that you may realize that one individual is contained within a larger individual. For example, the living cell in your body is contained within the reality of your body. Your body is contained within the reality of your personality. Your personality, in turn, is contained within your Soul, the Soul within its Monad, and so forth.

The nature of reality involves an individual manifesting a vibratory force within the whole of Life. That vibration may be viewed as a musical note. That vibratory note validly identifies that individual from all others. Each note is completely unique. However, it exists in a symphony of other notes, and all of the notes together have certain collaborative effects, producing what is termed "consensus reality."

You have asked the question at other times, "If a tree falls when no human being is present to hear its fall, does it make a sound?" We say, in answer to that question, that it does not make a sound for a human being, but it does make a sound for all other living beings affected by the fall of the tree. Certainly, within Planetary Consciousness, the fall of the tree is heard.

So, consider that reality involves not just an isolated individual, although the individual may choose to selectively focus on his/her own isolated sense of reality. Reality involves the lesser beings, which your body includes, and also the greater beings of which you are but a tiny part. Does this address your question?

SUSIE: Yes, it does. Thank you.

CONJOINT CREATION OF REALITY

DIANE: It says in the *Bible*, "As you thinketh in your heart, so shall it be." There is a current thought held by some people that we create our own reality. Is this a truth? And if so, in what manner do we create it?

MONITOR: Much of what we said in the previous discussion applies in response to this question.

"As a person thinketh in his heart" refers to the importance of the *inner* Life, which human beings have all too often failed to emphasize as much as their outer Life. Your inner Life proves to be of great value, because ultimately your Life essence in human form outgrows that form and moves on. The reality, which your Life essence experiences, corresponds more to the *inner* Life of the human than to the *outer* Life. It becomes very important for you to be aware of the vibrations, qualities, and purposes activated in your being, and indeed in your heart, because these expressions of force determine your future.

You indeed *create* your reality. But you are not the only creator of your reality, for the other beings around you, certainly the Planetary Being and the Being of the Solar System, have enormous influence in creating your reality. Often human beings act out the thoughts, desires, and impulses of the Planetary Being.

The creation of reality, for any Life form, is shared by many beings, both great and small. This statement holds true for the Life essence who declines to enter form and, instead, flows throughout the universe as what you term "Spirit."

Now, have we confused you, or have we caused some gain in understanding?

DIANE: That helped. Thank you.

PLANETARY BEING AS ADOLESCENT

ARZANI: Monitor, regarding your last answer, could you tell us what state the Planetary Being is in, that we are reflecting?

MONITOR: The Planetary Being of Earth is a consciousness that you may at this time approach mainly through "imagination," which is quite appropriate because what you term "imagination" represents a vital aspect of the Planetary Being.

Imagination represents the creative dreaming, constructive aspect that now most easily allows you to access awareness of the Planetary Being. It allows that which is your potential to manifest.

The Planetary Being of Earth is now undergoing turbulent change. Otherwise, disturbances in magma, and the present states of conflict within humanity and the devic kingdom would not be taking place.

The Planetary Being is engaged in a process of growth, just as much as you are engaged in a process of growth. It measures its growth in comparison with that of other Planetary Beings in this solar system, and with the Solar Being, or Solar Logos.

We may describe the state of progression of your Planetary Being now as that of an adolescent who is experiencing emergence of elements of consciousness that have not been previously recognized and which ultimately need to be synthesized and integrated. The Planetary Being is undergoing increasing stress, as aspects of its form are being stretched beyond normal capacities due to the expression of other aspects.

The Planetary Being now seeks a greater degree of self-expression and attempts to define its individuality within the bounds permitted it by the Solar Logos. Specific help is given to it from its counterparts in the planets, Venus and Saturn, who provide the greater amount of assistance at this time.

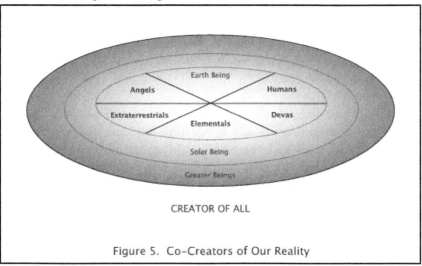

Figure 5. Co-Creators of Our Reality

Figure 5. Co-Creators of Our Reality

You may recognize the state of the Planetary Being as you comprehend the state of humanity, which forms a center of activity—a Self—within the personality of the Planetary Being. Other centers of activity also exist, of which human beings are not particularly aware. Therefore you will be somewhat frustrated in your attempt to imagine the complete essence of the Planetary Being. At this time you are only aware of part of its structure and part of its essence.

Because you exist as cells in the body of the Planetary Being, you often experience that Being as "God" because your powers of discernment are now limited. It is difficult for you to tell the difference between the quality of this individual Planetary Being and that of other, even greater, Beings.

Consider that you approach awareness of the Universal Creator through awareness of your own Soul and through awareness of your own Planetary Being. If you dedicate yourselves to benefit your Planetary Being, you open yourselves to greater expression of your Soul and thus achieve fulfillment of the human form. Does this address your question adequately?

ARZANI: Beyond!

AWARENESS ENHANCED BY MONITOR

JULIE: I want to report my experience with the experiential exercise you suggested during our last Lesson. I have asked, on a number of evenings, to have you, Monitor, be with me during sleep. And then on Sunday I had an experience in a building in a little place near Cornville of, for me, very heightened awareness. An experience of hearing, feeling, perceiving, and I wondered if that was any connection at all with having asked for assistance, or if it was something else?

MONITOR: Indeed, it was part of our encounter with you. Let us point out that it is extremely easy for us to be with you, once you ask us. Once we are with you—and we have been with several of you when you have asked—we are present with your energy field, with your consciousness.

When we visit you, part of your consciousness is pleased, but part is often displeased. Part of your consciousness is willing to receive our assistance, yet part of your consciousness wishes we would go away. We're speaking of several of you and of mankind, in particular.

We are very careful not to intrude where we are not welcome. When you, the Outer Self, ask us to be with you — especially during sleep — we *are* there. We have no difficulty achieving that. But when we are present with you, you have Inner Selves who have their own distinct reactions to our presence. Now Julie, in your case, your Mental Judge Self was not at all pleased.

JULIE: That's nothing new!

MONITOR: And we spent time, during several nights, working with your various Selves until your Judge Self saw some value in our companionship. We believe that your Mental Judge Self has truly grown because of the sharing. You have noted that change as expanded awareness, which resulted primarily from your Mental Judge easing control. Does this make sense to you?

JULIE: Yes, very much, thank you. I appreciate the assistance.

MONITOR: We encourage each one present to ask for our companionship. We are pleased to share it. This assists us in our purpose of assisting the evolution of humanity. We benefit, as you benefit.

DREAM INSTRUCTION BY FEMALE SELF

LINDA: Monitor, I'm another one who asked to meet you in my slumber, and also asked to remember. Yet I *don't* remember that we were together, but I did have a dream one night that I would like to tell you about.

MONITOR: Please do.

LINDA: I had a dream about my former husband and his present wife. I went to him and told him I wanted to be friends with him and his wife, but he was too busy. He had an ocean liner waiting to take him on a day's tour. So I sought out his wife. I went to the home where we used to live. I was angry because I couldn't spend the night there, because he had his wife in my former home in this dream. I told him that I just didn't appreciate her being there. As I was trying to talk to him, a friend of mine from Honeywell that I used to work with, looked at me and said, "Why are you talking to him?" I replied to her, but don't remember what I said. She said she understood. There were three girls by the name of Nancy that she symbolized. Something happened to the other two Nancys, and she was the only one left. That's why she understood that I was talking to my former husband. There's more to it, but those are the main things I wrote down.

MONITOR: Do you wish our impressions?

LINDA: Yes, please.

MONITOR: We have been with you several nights, and this dream was produced mainly by your Female Self, who is seeking to communicate with you, the Outer Self, about some lingering illusions generated by your Mental Judge Self, who in the dream is represented by your former husband. Your Female Self is seeking to help you identify a few remaining illusions that keep you from being fulfilled within your own being.

As you examine the dream in this light, you may begin to identify the illusions. Consider the *lack*. Do you truly lack? The dream reveals your sense of lack in that you could *not* sleep at home. It also reveals a sense of being *rejected* and *displaced*, which involves another illusion that would be well for you to resolve and discard.

Your Female Self provided this type of illumination as an aid to your Male Self. If you wish, you may assist *him* to release these illusions. These are not illusions held by you, the Outer Self, but by him. If you examine the remainder of the dream experience, you will find even more to assist him with. Does this make sense to you?

LINDA: Yes, this is very helpful, and I thank you.

REMEMBERING DREAMS

MONITOR: We thank you for working with us. If you, the Outer Self, do not make sufficient contact with your subconscious mind, you will *not* remember dreams. If you *do* make significant contact with your subconscious mind, you find that it does remember your dreams. Therefore it is possible for a psychic person to learn of dreams that you do not remember consciously.

What more would you like to explore?

DREAM CONTACTS WITH OTHER PERSONS

GAEL: I have a question regarding dreams and the nature of reality. Is it possible, in the dream state, to actually meet with another spirit, not just as a symbol representing something in your dream, but as the actual person you are dreaming about?

MONITOR: Indeed. Such encounters with other individuals, who are not symbolic reflections of your own being, involve the action of your Subconscious Selves. For example, if during a dream, your Female Self visited a deceased uncle living now in the astral plane, you would find the memory of that experience in your Female Self. If she chooses to share that experience with you, the Outer Self, you *would* remember that dream. If she chooses *not* to share it with you, you will have no memory of it. Yet that experience will have occurred.

Many important experiences during sleep take place with aspects of your subconscious mind involving contact with other individuals. We estimate that for you, Gael, approximately 80% of your sleep time is spent in contact with other individuals, and the remainder of time is spent in symbolic experiences. Does this address your question?

GAEL: Yes it does, thank you. Is it possible to program a meeting with another person in the dream state?

MONITOR: It is possible, provided that one of your Subconscious Selves is *willing* to follow through with your wishes. If it is, then it will do so. If you wish to retain memory of that experience, ask your Subconscious Selves to give you the memory.

GAEL: Thank you.

STARSEED TRANSMISSIONS AND PREDICTIONS

DOUG: You've invited the opportunity to compare different perspectives. And one perspective I have been reading has been Ken Carey's *Starseed Transmissions*. It predicts a very different reality occurring for the human race in our generation. My tendency is to react to protect the physical through all these predicted changes, and yet I realize that if the spiritual portion is kept in line, physical reality will probably take care of itself. We experience physical and spiritual realities, but how do we balance them? I'm also interested to hear if you agree with what's been written in *Starseed Transmissions* about the "Second Coming?"

MONITOR: We agree with the viewpoint expressed in Ken Carey's books in general, but differ in some respects. We find there a tendency to want specific answers for questions to which the Hierarchy will not allow specific answers at this time. We find, therefore, that the information provided to the subconscious mind of Ken Carey is at times elaborated on by his subconscious mind. Having acknowledged this, we do say that he is an extraordinarily clear channel and that the vast majority of what he describes as events to come in your time are quite valid. In particular, he captures the qualities of consciousness that are now active in the Planetary Being. He presents a viewpoint of great change, which can be quite traumatic to human and devic beings.

This viewpoint we agree with, but emphasize to you that we have a perspective that is *not* unlimited. Our perspective has its limits, and we, as a collective entity, are also subject to karmic law. Because of that, we will *not* provide details of events that the Hierarchy has decided, in its wisdom, should *not* be provided to human beings at this time.

We ask you to understand that the Hierarchy is highly intelligent, highly compassionate, and extremely sensitive to the needs of all Life forms evolving in and visiting the Planetary Being. The Hierarchy's decisions therefore change, as their sense of how the highest good may be achieved changes. Do you have further questions?

BALANCING PHYSICAL AND SPIRITUAL REALITIES

DOUG: How do I determine the balance between physical reality and spiritual reality regarding all these changes that are coming? How do I place my priorities? Is there a guideline for placing priorities?

MONITOR: Indeed, the guideline has been expressed in various ways, yet one concise, clear manner of expression offers, "Seek the Kingdom of God first, and the rest shall be added."

You find God in your creative Life expression as you meet and overcome your fears. We previously described planet Earth as offering an opportunity for Souls to meet that which they most wish to avoid, which means that the main objective for most human beings involves encountering and overcoming *fears*. Therefore, in answer to the question, we say that where you find fears, meet and overcome them, and by so doing you may be well-assured that you follow the path of spiritual growth. As you grow, within your own plan, you offer greater assistance to other beings and to the Planetary Being. And as you are of greater assistance, you *receive* support commensurate to your value in assisting others.

Persons who hide, in seeking to survive Earth changes, place themselves in a position of frailty. They become quite vulnerable, because they retreat from their fears and exist in a shell of fear which cuts them off from vital communications. Persons who meet and overcome their fears open shells of fear, dissolve them, and emerge into a radiant society of compassionate beings. Each one of us faces a choice of fear or Love. How do we choose?

INSTANCE OF CLAIRVOYANCE

SUSIE: Earlier this evening, while Harvey has been speaking, off and on I saw an old Chinese gentleman, and it was an odd experience. Am I hallucinating, or is that really happening?

MONITOR: Our view of your experience is that you are experiencing a Teacher held in common by you and the channel. If you wish, you may seek that Teacher and ask his name through your own channels.

SUSIE: Okay. It was very interesting to watch!

CHANNELING

LINDA: Monitor, I have a question regarding last week when we talked about an experience I had in July 1985. At that time I also channeled. I was somewhat frightened by that channeling, but it provided messages for seven different people in that hospital. I was told to be still, and messages were given through me to these people. It was like it was me, but it wasn't me. Can you give me further explanation of that experience?

MONITOR: Indeed, you were channeling your superconscious mind through your subconscious mind. It was "you," yet more than you, the Outer Self. The messages were given, as intended, to help those in your vicinity, which demonstrated for you that your experience was more than fantasy.

LINDA: Thank you.

MONITOR: We hope that you have come to understand that you may open as a superconscious channel when you are willing to ask for assistance to manifest on that level.

MONITOR & HIERARCHY

ARZANI: In my conception of the hierarchy of beings, including the personality, Soul, Monad, Planetary Being, and Solar Logos, where do you, Monitor, fit in?

MONITOR: We fit in as peons. We work voluntarily to assist humanity and the devic kingdom of Earth to evolve. We consist of individuals not yet fully activated to the point of Monad Consciousness. Some of us are opening that consciousness. The majority of us deal with Soul Consciousness, and approximately one third of us relate comfortably with human and devic consciousness as it is incarnate in this planet. We are not limited to this planet, but our primary assignment is here. Does this answer your question?

ARZANI: Yes, but it brings up another. I've never heard Monad Consciousness defined.

MONAD & SOUL CONSCIOUSNESS

MONITOR: Monad Consciousness is most active on the level of Solar System Consciousness and beyond, to Galactic Consciousness and even higher. Soul Consciousness functions mainly within the focus of Planetary Consciousness. The Monad operates within a larger scope.

ARZANI: When we talk about having a separate Soul from the Soul of the Judge Selves, do our Souls join on some level?

MONITOR: Souls are quite congenial. They are not as involved in the limitations of form as human personalities. Souls are more open to the radiance of Light and Life essence. They easily sense the Oneness of Life and its evolving purposes. Therefore Souls inhabiting one planet may readily accept Souls from another planet. Only on the level of the human personality does fear and limited perception place obstacles in the way of such acceptance. Does this answer your question?

ONENESS

ARZANI: Yes. If Souls experience Oneness, do they exist in the One? I always thought that the Soul was the last step in spiritual growth, and now I hear that there are at least five or six steps beyond. If the Soul experiences Oneness, how can you go past Oneness?

MONITOR: All of Life exists in the One Life, but as Life essence enters a particular form, it accepts the unique perspective of that form. The human perspective is much more limited than the Soul perspective. The Soul is composed of Life essence inhabiting the Soul form, and so is not fully expressive of Universal Oneness.

The Soul realizes the unity of Life with great clarity, yet is *not* fully identified with all of Life. It must grow and expand to the point where the Life essence within the Soul dissolves that form and is absorbed into the Monad form. And eventually the Monad form is, in turn, dissolved and exceeded by the Life essence. Through that process Life essence proceeds back to the point of Creation, and creation becomes an increasing activity of that

Life essence, as it learns to express creatively in all forms and circumstances throughout the universe.

When such Life essence has achieved sufficient integration and expanded its identity to universal scope, it may assist others to do the same. When *all* aspects of Life essence have achieved that, the entire living universe reunites in conscious union with the Creator. All of creation is *never* separated from the Creator, yet must evolve into the *capacity* of the Creator. In doing so, all *achieve* the One.

FOOD AND NOURISHMENT

JULIE: Monitor, I would like to ask something far less lofty than that. How come it's so difficult to find out what's good and what isn't good food for you on the physical level? It seems like some of us struggle with it all our lives, and I'm frankly tired of the struggle. Do you have anything about the physical reality of food that would be helpful?

MONITOR: One person may find food challenging, while another person may not. What is the difference? We suggest that the difference lies in the understanding and capability of the individual's subconscious mind. If a person has a subconscious mind that is experienced and balanced in physical, etheric, and astral maintenance, that person will have great ease with all forms of nourishment. If the subconscious mind is still in the process of learning balance, that person will experience difficulties.

On a practical level, a person such as you, who has difficulty with the subconscious mind in the area of food, may ask your High Self to bring a Teacher to that aspect of your subconscious mind which needs to be educated about food.

Food is more than physical food. Nourishment, considered comprehensively for a human being, consists of physical, etheric, astral, mental, and causal nourishment. If a person is not nourished by the sense of *purpose* of his Soul in the causal plane, he/she will be subject to lacks and distortions. If a person lacks *awareness* of knowledge and wisdom, his mental capacity will be subject to distortions. If a person is imbalanced in astral expression, his *desires* will be relentless in pursuing one object or another, none of which proves fulfilling. If a person is eating a good physical diet, yet is not properly absorbing the Life force, or *prana*, on the etheric level, he/she will experience distortions in vitality.

Consider the wisdom of educating your subconscious mind, because the Outer Self is truly not capable of keeping track of all these levels of nourishment. A deficiency in any one of these levels may lead to deficiencies in the other levels. Your subconscious mind is in training to properly manage all of these aspects, so you are well-advised to ask your High Self to bring Teachers to your Subconscious Selves who need assistance in learning balance in assimilation and elimination. Does this address your question?

JULIE: Yes, it really does.

MONITOR'S APPEARANCE

DIANE: If we were able to perceive you, Monitor, would all of you—all 153 individuals—appear the same, or would you appear different to us?

MONITOR: We would appear as a "family" to you. We are composed of distinctly individual forms, yet all are related by a common Light, or common purpose activated through us, thereby producing a common Light.

DIANE: If I were to see you on the street, Monitor, could you describe yourself in such a way so that I would be able to say, "There's Monitor over there"?

MONITOR: No, we may not do so because we cannot adequately utilize human language to describe nonphysical individuals. To do so would be a waste of time. You already know us in your subconscious and superconscious levels of mind, so all you need do is ask your High Self if we are present.

DIANE: One other aspect. How do we appear to you?

HUMANS APPEAR TO MONITOR AS BROCCOLI

MONITOR: We see you in various ways, depending on which aspect of your forms we focus on. We have greater variability in maneuvering through vibratory forces than you, so we approach you from different angles.

We see you primarily as patterns of Light that have distinctive characteristics. We have described the structure of your subconscious minds as similar to broccoli, because you have clusterings of Selves who join on stems and thereby appear like broccoli. From other viewpoints, you have distinctly different appearances to us, and as we interact with you, we essentially become one with you to the extent that we are capable. That state of attunement allows for maximum communication. Such communication offers more than mental telepathy. It involves a sharing of being which exceeds mental energy and mental bodies.

SEEKING PERSONAL GUIDANCE

MARLENE: Monitor, earlier when you said you guys were volunteers, it sparked a question that I've been thinking about for a while. Do you have suggestions about some type of volunteer service I could do?

MONITOR: Your question has real value, since our answer will apply to each person. In seeking to volunteer your services to others, we ask you to seek the guidance of your High Self as to which avenue of service is most appropriate. Your High Self represents your link with your Soul. Your Soul provides the motive for service, which is based on the Soul's awareness of the unity of all Life.

If you ask your subconscious mind, you might get different answers, because your Subconscious Selves have different desires and backgrounds. So if you ask your High Self, you obtain your highest quality guidance, which takes into account the needs of *all* aspects of your being and other persons who might best benefit from your volunteer effort. Seek your High Self for such guidance. It will benefit you more than if we advise you in terms of specific avenues of service. Do you understand?

MARLENE: Yeah, that's what I thought you were going to say. Thank you.

MONITOR: You already have awareness! *[Group laughter.]*

CONCLUSION

MONITOR: We thank you all for sharing with us. We hope that you have a more friendly approach to the nature of reality.

Consider how you will approach the topic for the coming month, "Origins." Surely that is a topic of extreme breadth. We ask you now to consider the origins you wish to know about. We can assure you that you will be exposed to more than you wish to know!

Chapter 4

Origins

Lesson 13

July 3, 1991

TYPES OF ORIGINS

MONITOR: We are pleased to be with you again, and we welcome newcomers. We launch now into the formidable subject of *Origins* and dare anyone to ask us about the origin of the universe, or your own personal origin. We're trying to threaten you! No, really, we ask you to observe the lines of thought that this topic, *Origins*, leads you to consider. When you consider origins, do you *not* find yourselves thinking in terms of *time*—what came *before* that led to a *later* development?

Yet you can also consider origins in terms of *form*. When you look on the spectrum of evolving Life, you see evolution more clearly in plant and animal Life. Biology studies the evolution of forms and species. The study of *evolving form* offers another approach to origins.

A third approach to considering origins derives from Life itself, which dwells within the form. And that's a very risky area to consider, is it not? You have questions already, so we will proceed with that as a background.

HUMAN MIGRATIONS TO NORTH AMERICA

DONNA: Well, I think this is not in the long distant past, but how long ago did the Indians come to this continent?

MONITOR: First you must consider the definition of the word "Indian." If you are speaking of people from the nation of India, you refer to a time period approximately 4,000 years ago. At that time that nation was not a nation and was not called India.

Such considerations give you an idea that some definitions need to be clarified before we can answer intelligently. We assume that you refer, instead, to those now termed "Native Americans" and their ancestors, their precursors. Is that so?

DONNA: Yes.

MONITOR: In this area of the southwestern United States, we find that they entered from two directions. The earliest entries came from the east, coming from Atlantis, and from the south, coming from Central and South America. Minor incursions have come from the west, but those have not truly settled in this area of the Southwest. Those who came from the west, from the Asian continent, moved across the northern portion of the North American continent and did not truly enter the Southwest.

Ancient civilizations inhabited this Southwest in the early days of Atlantis about 500,000 years BCE. You find it difficult to locate any archaeological evidence of such civilizations, but we assure you that they were present in this area.

Atlanteans circulated throughout the globe, traveling in vehicles of high technological accomplishment—what you term "airships" and "speed trains," traveling through tunnels carved through rock by laser-like devices. Their laser-like devices, however, did *not* work on the principle of electromagnetic light, but on principles of sound affecting etheric structure. Those tunnels were carved with precision and permitted vehicles to move at very rapid speeds, even under oceans.

Atlanteans also had lighter-than-air craft, which enabled them to travel throughout the globe. The southwestern United States was then occupied during a period of colonization, one colony established after another in periodic developments. From those original colonies, people moved outward and formed separate clans, because the clan organization predominated in Atlantis.

After that period of migration and colonization, later incursions came primarily from the south, originating from different civilizations at different times. The earliest incursions derived from the even more ancient civilization of Ibez in the areas known today as portions of Venezuela, Colombia, Ecuador, and Peru. Later civilizations derived from Ibez formed diverse peoples and a variety of societies at different time periods.

Most notable among those were those who were precursors to the Incans whom we identify by the name Og *[pronounced Ohg]* who traveled in advanced technological modes of transportation and were free to settle where they found places that provided suitable conditions for living and natural resources.

Later came the Mayans—to you, a mysterious people who are not yet well understood—who ventured forth and formed the basis for those who you term the "ancient Indians."

What you find archaeologically of ancient Indians in this Southwestern area relates to derivations from Mayan peoples. Their modes of architecture were substantial and contained distinctive features, including circular and semicircular structures and buildings. They have, like their home race, the Mayans, mysteriously appeared and disappeared.

We have sketched this as a general background. Perhaps you would like to ask more specific questions.

ORIGIN OF RACES

DONNA: Could we back up just a bit and talk about how the races evolved? Was there an original family, or were there different races of people in different parts of the world?

MONITOR: An interesting question! The races that you know today are an amalgamation. Part of the amalgamation refers to physical structure, including such items as color of skin, hair, and eyes. Other aspects come from other than physical dimensions. It is necessary to understand this to gain a clear concept of the word "race" as we perceive it.

The races began *before* humanity began. They represent evolutionary forms of different characteristics that originated in places other than the physical plane of planet Earth. Some of these races began in other solar systems, and some of them began in the mental plane of planet Earth. Do you get an idea of what we are talking about?

When humanity was activated in the physical plane of Earth, five basic physical structures were distinguished by characteristics of skin, hair, eyes, etc. But within these five races were 22 other racial structures. So we need to clarify the term "race." Would you prefer to focus on the beginning of the five physical races?

DONNA: I don't know that we're wanting to do that as much as... . I think you have said enough for now until we learn more, so we can consider that in our system of thought. Can we come down to more recent times?

MONITOR: Certainly.

ORIGIN OF HOHOKAM AND ANASAZI PEOPLES

DONNA: Right here in this area were the people called the Hohokam, a different group of people than the Anasazi, the people from Mesa Verde and Chaco Canyon. What was their origin?

MONITOR: They were from the same root stock, from the Mayan peoples. The people to the south, designated as Hohokam, lived in this area at a later time than those who settled to the north, termed Anasazi.

The Anasazi peoples came at an earlier time. They were present in this area at the time of your year "zero." They were an extension of the Mayan peoples that moved away from Mayan homelands because of political differences. They sought to find their own way in new lands, and they had sufficient force to take the lands they wanted.

The Hohokam came later about 400 AD and settled to the south as a new stream of migration. They came as colonists, retaining linkages with their home culture. Does this give you some helpful designation?

DEPARTURE OF HOHOKAM PEOPLE

DONNA: Yes it does. Why did the Hohokam leave here so suddenly, it seems?

MONITOR: We find a combination of factors. First, a general deterioration of their culture. They had attempted to continue the culture they derived from, and as their home culture underwent tremendous changes, they were unable to sustain their original form of culture. Several competing cultural factions formed, and in that competition people lost their original sense of unity. Fragmentation led to competition for resources.

The moral character of many of the people deteriorated as they struggled to survive. At that time weather conditions also deteriorated, producing weather extremes that made the food supply scarce and unreliable. Those people who survived in the original cities moved away from the cities and formed the basis for the later Native Americans.

HOPI PEOPLE

DONNA: Are the Hopi people a distinct group? They seem different than the other groups who are here presently.

MONITOR: They *are* distinct. They came from Og and represent a tradition that preceded Og, that of Lemuria or Mu. So their origin, if it is traced in terms of culture or sacred traditions, goes back to Mu to a specific area west of the Marshall Islands, an area now under ocean. Their people traveled to the east and became engaged with the peoples of Og. Later, as a combined culture of Mu and Og, they journeyed to the north, where they are now situated.

DONNA: All right, now from what you said it sounds like most of the people here in the Southwest had ancestors from the Mayans, and that was from Atlantean origin, while the Hopi came originally from Lemuria? Is that correct?

MONITOR: Correct.

CHACO CANYON

DONNA: Could you tell us about Chaco Canyon? Was that a religious center for the Anasazi?

MONITOR: It was constructed and maintained as a center of religion, but a religion unlike your present religions. The religion of those peoples, which is as yet embodied in the structures found in Chaco Canyon and other places, reflects a type of cosmic fellowship. You must understand that in the early development of Earth, beings who incarnated came from other planets in this solar system and from other solar systems. That type of exchange and intercourse was normal and is still normal today.

DONNA: Are the vibrations still there? So many people seem to have religious experiences when they go to Chaco Canyon.

MONITOR: Indeed. The circular form of the structures honors sacred structures of their distant past that were part of the early Mayan system of structures. Most of the circular Mayan structures have not been archaeologically determined as yet, because most of those structures were built over with rectangular structures as a deliberate act of establishing the primacy of a new religious order.

The circular structures, found in Chaco Canyon and other areas, represent the form of ancient temples, if you will, which were used for communication with beings on higher levels of consciousness. The circular form is more conducive, in the physical and etheric planes, to quality communication with those in the higher planes. The rectangular form may suffice, but is less efficient.

The circular form also portrayed the shape of the spaceships that maintained contact and trade with those peoples. Celebrations in Chaco Canyon were often held at times when the ships from the sky arrived, and then the people would gather. And when the ships departed, the people dispersed to return to their separate living areas.

DONNA: Were these people the ones who made the structures that showed the sun dagger phenomena?

MONITOR: Yes. They had extensive knowledge along certain lines of cosmology. They were indoctrinated in various meanings of forces representing planetary and star emanations. In addition, they were taught about the various peoples from other planets and solar systems who from time to time interacted with them.

DONNA: What happened to the residents around Chaco Canyon at the time they dispersed?

MONITOR: The final dispersal reflected again the deterioration of culture. The visits of the ships had become quite infrequent, and the peoples understood, as they had been taught, that they must develop their own independent system of living. Resistance among the peoples produced conflict and competition for resources. Many people died in that process. Others fled from that area and, in smaller numbers, formed the basis for those you call Native Americans.

KIVAS

HELEN: In the area that the group, known as the Sacred Drama, went to visit in Chaco Canyon, in the circular area that we call the "kiva," is that where they had communication with the spacecraft?

MONITOR: Yes. You will notice that they have a number of circular forms that are known today by the name of "kiva."

SACRED DRAMA GROUP VISIT

HELEN: Could you tell us what was accomplished by our visit there?

MONITOR: Do you mean the visit of that specific group?

HELEN: Yes.

MONITOR: We find a certain degree of healing forces generated, based on a partial integration of diverse energetic conditions. Our answer is somewhat abstract because we describe a level of effect not readily appreciated from the physical perspective.

Consider that in that area a number of diverse Life forms had interacted, often in conflict. Therefore healing of the conflict would offer substantial benefit. This process was initiated, but was of too great a scope to have been totally accomplished by one small group. What was done by that group has been augmented by others, and there are those who have accepted guardianship over that area, who continue healing the old wounds of that area.

KOKOPELLI

DONNA: May I ask a question about some of the rock art up in that area? Most of the rock art shows a legendary figure called Kokopelli, the hunchbacked flute player. Those carved figures are also found at Mesa Verde and many other places. Was Kokopelli a real individual? And why does Kokopelli show up so often?

MONITOR: We find that symbol of Kokopelli more of a legend that had its origin in events in the physical plane. The origin may best be described as the use of sound in the creation of realities, including mental, astral, etheric, and physical realities.

That legend originally designated a specific type of training that was part of the culture. Later, as the culture deteriorated, it was misunderstood, and the figure of Kokopelli was treated as a divine or God figure. The proper understanding of the figure refers to the use of sound properly employed, with the force of mind properly focused, in creativity. The understanding or discipline behind those powers of manifestation may be learned. But in the later culture, it was only viewed as a Divine force, separate from men.

SUN TEMPLES

DONNA: Thank you. May I ask about the sun temples, such as the one up at Mesa Verde? How were the sun temples used by the ancient peoples?

MONITOR: Their original use involved communication with beings of higher consciousness and timing of ceremonial events through astronomical configurations, such as equinoxes, solstices, and positions of sun, moon, Venus, Mars, Jupiter, and Saturn.

TWELVE TRIBES OF ISRAEL

DONNA: May I ask if any of the Twelve Tribes of Israel made it to the New World?

MONITOR: Indeed, we find that they did. They entered in two places. First, in what you now term the Southeast part of the United States, and then in Central America.

DONNA: How did they travel?

MONITOR: They traveled in ships or boats on the waters.

DONNA: Did they make up any part of recognizable groups left in the United States today?

MONITOR: No, they are quite blended.

ATLANTEAN IMMIGRATION TO AMERICAS

DONNA: At Tula, north of Mexico City, is a whole cluster of giant figures called the "Atlantes." Had the Atlantis story come down to the villagers there?

MONITOR: Very definitely, and throughout Central America and South America will be found, and have been found, archaeological objects which support that thesis.

The Atlanteans ventured out in various waves of travel. In the later portions of their civilization, they sent out waves of colonizers and refugees at times when Atlantis was badly shaken, split up, and finally submerged in the greater portion. The traditions of Atlantis were strongly conveyed to areas of Central and South America, as well as to portions of North America.

ORIGINAL ESSENCE

JEAN PAUL: Here's a question about the original essence itself. What would be your guidelines to normal people about how to bring about its conscious emergence and how to refine and develop this original essence of Self in practical terms?

MONITOR: We use a metaphor to answer this question, in which form is seen as a jewel, and Life essence is seen as light. When the Creator created the universe, all of substance in the universe was an expression of the Creator's Light, and it is still. As portions of that Life force, or Life essence, explored expression in form, each form provided a unique facet in the jewel of the universe. The essence of Life may be viewed as the Wholeness of Life shining in a single facet.

Inasmuch as a human being is a form filled with Life essence, a person may best express that essence by its intentional linkage with all of Life.

Most human beings are not yet capable of this. To accomplish this, a person must develop awareness that allows him/her to be sensitive and responsive to all of Life throughout the universe. This is possible! It has not yet been accomplished, but in time it will. Although in that future time, you would not recognize the form as the form of the human being of today.

A person, in opening to universal Life, changes quality as its sponsoring form, the Soul, allows Life essence to flow in more completely to the personality. As the personality opens to that essence, the Soul transforms the personality into a Soul radiance. As that occurs, the Soul is more open to receive additional Life essence from its sponsoring form, the Monad. In turn, the Monad evolves along similar lines.

We do not wish to become too technical in this answer, but wish to give some indication that it is indeed possible for a human being to be sensitive to and responsive to all of Life throughout the universe. Does this answer your question?

JEAN PAUL: Thank you.

EVOLUTION OF PLANETARY BEING OF EARTH

DOUG: Related to the question that was just asked, Ken Carey likens the human race to an embryo and then goes on to suggest that the entire race will be born to something new, a new origin. In his readings he says something very similar to what you say, that we will come to a higher level of consciousness. But he predicts that there will be one event that triggers all of mankind to come simultaneously together, as opposed to individual by individual. I'd like you to comment on that whole premise.

MONITOR: We are pleased to comment on that. Consider what event would produce a true unity, not only of mind but also of heart, of spirit, among the diverse individuals of humanity. That event, we suggest, will be an evolutionary development of the Planetary Being of Earth.

As the Planetary Being achieves sufficient mastery over its existence, its component beings, which include humanity, will be brought to unity. Understand that such an event is *not* likely in the near future. We have suggested that the Planetary Being is in, what you might term, an adolescent stage of development. Large amounts of time will pass before that event occurs. Does this answer your question?

DOUG: Yes, it answers my question.

NATIVE AMERICAN RELATIONSHIP TO PLANETARY BEING

ARZANI: I have a question about the Planetary Being and the Native Americans' relationship to the Planetary Being. It seems that they have a closer relationship. Is that possibly a different function? Could you describe the relationship of the Native Americans and the Planetary Being?

MONITOR: We will attempt an explanation based on oversimplification of factors.

If human beings are components of the Planetary Being, like cells in the body of the Planetary Being, you might note groupings of human beings who would be equivalent to the structure of organs or systems in the body of the Planetary Being. Such groups of human beings are identified by their purpose, just as you identify groups of cells in the human physical body by their common purpose. For example, the cells that perform the function of filtering the bloodstream can be identified by the name "liver."

We find that Native Americans are *not* all of one functional group. They consist of various groups with varied purposes. A more useful designation would identify human, devic, and elemental beings by their common purposes. This is not a detailed explanation, but an attempt to suggest a different approach to that concept.

SUN AS SYMBOL OF CREATOR

DONNA: Do Native Americans believe the sun is a symbol for the Creator?

MONITOR: Most do consider the sun as a symbol of the radiant Creator, the One who creates the manifest universe.

In that symbolism much is conveyed, for a person sees the Creator rise into awareness and, by the radiance of the Creator, is enabled to live. But inevitably the Creator passes from view, and darkness curtails the former way of life. This rhythm, this cycle, is very instructive because it portrays the fundamental cycle of creation, sustenance, and destruction of all levels of form. Only the Life essence, which does *not* inhabit form, is exempt from that cycle.

MOON AS SYMBOL OF CHANGE

HELEN: Along those same lines, how would they view the moon?

MONITOR: The moon is seen in varied ways by groups of Native Americans and by other groups. The moon becomes a symbol of *Life within form*, subject to constant changes of quality, which Light manifests in the form.

This may be viewed in several ways. One way involves the quality of the human being as a child, who changes to the quality of the mature human being, who changes to the quality of the aged human being.

These phases of changing qualities also remind human beings of the changing influences of force or rays of cosmic force which constantly change in their aspects. These forces produce orderly changes in the quality of all Life manifesting in form.

The moon, therefore, represents the changing qualities of Life experiencing form. It does *not* reflect the Creator, but instead reflects the creation.

ORIGIN OF FEAR

JULIE: Monitor, could you give us the origin of fear in human beings or in whatever forms existed before human beings?

MONITOR: Fear has its origins *before* the creation of humanity. Fear, as an astral experience, exists throughout the universe in planets and suns that have Life expression in the astral level. And here we speak of cosmic octaves of force, as well as lower octaves of force.

With human beings, fear is found in the structures of both physical and astral bodies. The astral body carries unresolved fear from one physical lifetime to the other. The physical body of a subsequent lifetime is impacted by the fear activated in the astral body. Thus you may have a physical experience of fear that originated in other lifetimes and other experiences in the astral plane, independent of physical lifetimes.

HELEN: Would they necessarily be from the Earth, or could they be from another planet brought here by that astral body?

MONITOR: They could be from another planet, as well as from an astral body created in planet Earth. Either is possible.

CLEARING FEAR

HELEN: Do you have a magic way for us to clear ourselves of fear once and for all?

MONITOR: Certainly. The magic is hard work!

HELEN: That doesn't sound too magical.

MONITOR: It depends on your understanding of magic. From our perspective, magic reflects a capability that is exercised with competence to manifest realities.

DESIRE

JEAN PAUL: Would you consider desire to be an emotion or a mental pattern? And would you talk about integration of desire patterns as the human being evolves.

MONITOR: We find the term "desire" to be descriptive of force patterns in the astral and physical bodies primarily, yet also including patterns in the lower mental plane. Desire patterns therefore may be transmitted from experiences in other planets and other solar systems, and then activated in planet Earth.

Desire patterns involve configurations of force based on a focus of consciousness, and so a person finds a variety of such configurations, some of which are quite familiar, and some unfamiliar. A person may experience desire patterns created in other lifetimes, or created in nonphysical experiences in the astral and lower mental planes of Earth. A person may also experience desire patterns brought from other planets and solar systems, conveyed by Soul and Monad.

AVERAGE NUMBER OF PHYSICAL LIFETIMES

HELEN: I would like to ask what the average number of lifetimes is on Earth before we learn all the lessons? What would you say the average number of lifetimes is?

MONITOR: Let us consult our statistical department to see what the latest average is.

JULIE: You have computers?

MONITOR: As we consider the two waves of beings inhabiting the forms of humanity, and averaging them together, we find the average to be 1,660 lifetimes.

JULIE: Where is Helen?

HELEN: Lifetime Number 10, thank you!

MONITOR: Be not discouraged, evolution is quite mechanical. If you enter at one end, you most assuredly come out the other.

JULIE: Yay!

HELEN: We have your word on that?

MONITOR: Indeed.

INNER GUIDANCE VERSUS CULTURAL STUDY

ARZANI: This is a continuation of my question about the Native Americans and the Planetary Being. If different groups of beings have different functions in the Planetary Being, is there any purpose, for example, for someone in my group to study Native American culture to learn their cultural expression, or a Buddhist culture, or some other culture. Or would it be more beneficial for me to move through my own roots towards helping the Planetary Being?

MONITOR: We find that you would be, as a single individual, more advised to follow your own individual path, since you are engaged in seeking and receiving guidance from your High Self and Soul. This type of guidance proves most effective, far more effective than studying other paths.

The study of other paths does have value because it opens your conscious and subconscious minds to greater possibilities. So we would not advise you to ignore what other cultures, such as the Native American and Buddhist cultures, have accomplished. Yet we do encourage you to find your own path, and let your intuitive guidance direct you to those aspects of knowledge you need to gain, and to those skills you need to learn.

ARZANI: Is it true that my subconscious mind has experienced life in those other cultural expressions before, and perhaps that some of my interest in them is generated by past lives?

MONITOR: That is so.

CONCLUSION

MONITOR: As you think about our exchange this night, consider different approaches to the question of origins. Consider which aspect has been most meaningful to you and then compile questions or present viewpoints or other materials that you feel would yield greater understanding.

We thank you for joining us.

GROUP: We thank you, Monitor.

MONITOR: And now we leave.

Lesson 14
July 10, 1991

MONITOR: We welcome you all as Monitor. We are pleased to be here with you again. We have provided you with some interesting and stimulating information concerning origins, and hope that you are motivated now to study some of these areas more closely. We remind you that we have asked you to consider *three* types of origins.

The first type is *origin through time*, what you consider causative events. We have also asked you to consider the *origin of form*, or the process of change or transformation of form. And we have asked you to consider the *origin of Life itself*, the dweller inside the form.

We would say at the outset—since we are aware of your prior discussion—that we will be pleased to help you take a journey in consciousness, and we will leave that to a later time this evening. Now we would like for you to proceed, if you would. What questions or comments would you like to share?

TWO WAVES OF EMBODIED SOULS

HELEN: Last week we asked about the average number of physical lifetimes, and in consulting your statistical department you mentioned that you considered the two waves of beings inhabiting the forms of humanity to get your average. Would you explain what these two waves were?

MONITOR: Certainly. The first wave are those Souls who were involved in physical embodiment and present in planet Earth *prior to* the Maldekian immigration. This first wave of Souls were those who came to Earth and embodied only in the mental and astral planes. They participated in the first plan of evolution of human or, shall we say, pre-human Life forms in this planet. They had a separate plan of evolution, participating in the lessons that Earth offers.

They were, in many instances, severely impacted when the Maldekian immigrants were brought to Earth. The resultant change in vibratory conditions necessitated a change in the plan of evolution for those Souls involved in the first wave. As the Spiritual Hierarchy evolved a second plan of evolution and put it into effect, the first wave of Souls proceeded within the second plan, and many are still involved in completing their plan of evolution, seeking spiritual mastery.

The second wave of Souls refers to those who entered *after* the Maldekian immigration. Most of those Souls entered with the intent to assist the first wave Souls who became handicapped as a result of severe changes, and to assist the Planetary Being of Earth in its evolution.

We wish you to understand that no planet stands isolated. Each planet is part of a family of Beings. When one planet has difficulties, other planets assist. This is true also of stars, even though your commonly held concept at this time regards planets and stars as inanimate. We assure you that nothing could be further from the truth.

If you wish, you may at times sense the living qualities of the consciousness of your planet and realize that you are part of its Being, and it is part of a greater Being, which you may visually refer to as the sun, the star Sol. Your sun is part of an even greater Being. And so all parts of the universe are alive and intimately connected.

Does this answer your question concerning the waves?

HELEN: Yes. Thank you very much.

MALDEK AND ITS BEINGS

LOIS: Monitor, I'm not familiar with "Maldekian beings." Would you elaborate on that, please?

MONITOR: In this solar system a nonphysical planet orbits between Mars and Jupiter. This planet we refer to by the name "Maldek." It had a specialized type of evolutionary plan that allowed it to evolve more rapidly than evolution occurs in Earth. During its evolution, problems developed that created a crisis. Energies were expressed that caused the etheric and physical forms of that planet to disintegrate. The force holding together those forms was temporarily overcome, and so you have now the physically visible fragments of that planet, which you know as the "asteroid belt."

We assure you that the planet Maldek continues in its astral, mental, and causal forms, but because of the destructive force manifested, the bulk of its population was removed from that planet. Most of its beings were transferred to Earth, and in Earth they became immigrants, survivors of a catastrophe that they themselves inadvertently caused.

When Earth received these immigrants, the primary development of Earth at that time occurred in the astral plane. Some of the immigrants were brought to the astral plane in a state of shock, and as they began to recover, they were most unhappy with their experiences and their new environment, which offered a distinct contrast to their native environment. The Maldekian immigrants therefore continued their conflict and had to be contained within what is now known as the "lower levels of the astral plane." The containment was necessary to protect the Maldekian beings and other beings who already inhabited Earth.

These Maldekian beings have been, in part, integrated into the second plan of evolution, to which we previously referred. They entered into that plan, which led to the creation of physical humanity, and they are known today in the personality of the human being as the "Shadow Self" or the "Judge Selves."

They have a part in the evolutionary plan of humanity, and when a single human being achieves spiritual mastery and earns freedom, their Judge Selves do also. And the Maldekian personality, who had been a component of the human personality, then is freed to return to the astral and mental planes where it may assist others of its kind to gain freedom. Like all evolutionary processes, this process takes place over long periods of time, from an Outer Self viewpoint, yet the plan is working quite well. Does this answer your question?

LOIS: It does. I appreciate it very much.

MONITOR: You'll notice that we presented information about origins in our answer. This particular information has *not* been given at earlier times to humanity, except to select groups, because the earlier stages of development of the human personality would have been too threatened by this knowledge. And even in this time, such knowledge must be used carefully.

Many persons feel quite threatened at the thought that their personality contains a being from another planet. From our perspective, *all* beings in planet Earth have cosmic origins. To us, this situation seems no different than the case where one child, whose family is impacted by a disaster, goes to live temporarily in the home of a neighboring family. One family helps another, which is the way of Universal Being. And so, within a large perspective, this is how we view the situation.

We encourage you to become friends with your Judge Selves, because they have endured major difficulties and losses in their history and are deserving of your assistance. The Judge Selves may learn from you how to be friends. And when they become your friends, you have their great support to aid you in your spiritual growth.

We will entertain another question before embarking on a journey.

CHACO CANYON EXTRATERRESTRIAL CONTACT

DONNA: Monitor, let me thank you for the material on the Native Americans in the Southwest area and tell you how excited I am with the information.

MONITOR: You are very welcome.

DONNA: I would like to speak again of the Mayans that came to Chaco Canyon. Can you tell me how they contacted the "space brothers?"

MONITOR: They used a form of mental telepathy. The technology that you have today for communications, such as radio, was not needed in that time. They utilized simple methods of sound to allow one or more persons to focus their minds on those with whom they wished to communicate. The slow beating of a drum and such simple, repetitive sounds allowed them to accomplish that type of communication.

DONNA: What was their purpose of communicating with the "space brothers?"

MONITOR: They realized that they had gained much from the "space brothers" in gifts and trade. They realized that the space beings were quite wise and could provide considerable assistance.

You must realize that the destruction of the continent of Atlantis had imprinted many of the peoples among the Mayan culture. During that time of destruction, space beings played valuable roles in assisting with the rescue of people and certain technological objects and helping in other ways. The Mayans were well aware of the potential benefits of retaining a relationship with space beings.

Does that address your question?

DONNA: Yes, that answers that question. Why did they stop coming to Chaco Canyon?

MONITOR: Whom do you mean?

DONNA: The "space brothers."

MONITOR: They ceased coming due to the deterioration of the consciousness of those peoples. That deterioration may be described as an increase in the amount of fear, which led some persons to seek control over others for exploitation and self-aggrandizement. Not all of those people in that area were affected in such a way, but a significant shift occurred in the consciousness of the peoples. The space beings then, quite appropriately, recognized that assistance they might give to the peoples would most likely lead to conflict and abuse. So they withheld their presence.

ORIGIN OF SOUL AND JUDGE SELVES

LOIS: I would like to know about the origin of the Soul, and whether that was always connected with the evolutionary process of the Judge Selves?

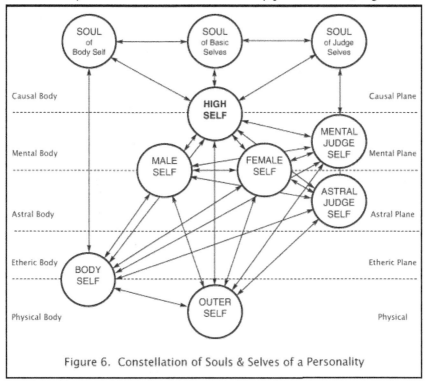

Figure 6. Constellation of Souls & Selves of a Personality

Figure 6 Constellation of Souls and Selves of a Personality

MONITOR: We will attempt to answer this rather complex question in simple terms.

Consider the Souls who were part of the first wave of Soul embodiments in Earth. The Soul lives in the causal plane and projects part of its being into the mental plane and then into the astral plane. It invests itself in a series of experiences in planet Earth. When the Maldekian immigrants came to Earth, their discordant, conflicting vibrations caused widespread changes in the astral plane and even in the lower levels of the mental plane. The causal plane was not affected.

Maldekian beings consisted of Souls from Maldek who came to live in the causal plane with the Souls of the first wave of Souls embodied in Earth. The Maldekian personality consisted of a Soul, situated in the causal plane, and its personality projections in the mental and astral planes. The Maldekian *mental* personality components were situated in the mental plane, and its *astral* personality components were located in the astral plane of Earth. The astral Maldekians were most uncomfortable and disconcerted. The mental Maldekians were, for the most part, able to adjust.

When the Spiritual Hierarchy evolved a second plan of evolution and put it into effect, they arranged for the creation of the "human personality." The human personality was initially formed by an Earth-based Soul animating a two-member team of Male and Female Selves. Then that personality was expanded by an attachment of an astral Maldekian. This attachment allowed the astral Maldekian to enter the second plan of evolution wherein they evolved within the human personality, lifetime after lifetime. And with the attachment of the astral Maldekian, its mental counterpart, a mental Maldekian, also was included in the evolving human personality. We regard the included astral Maldekian as the "Astral Judge Self" and the included mental Maldekian as the "Mental Judge Self."

The astral and mental Maldekians have contact with all other elements in the personality, yet still maintain connection with their Maldekian Soul. The Male and Female Selves maintain connections with their Earth-based Soul. So you may consider that each human personality has a primary connection to an Earth-based Soul and a secondary connection, through two Judge Selves, to their Maldekian Soul.

The primary Soul connection through the Basic Selves provides the principal growth of the personality. The secondary Soul connection comprises what you might call a "hitchhiker," which enables the astral and mental Maldekians to evolve beyond their previous limits and achieve freedom from the bondage of fear and doubt.

You, as a human personality, are best served by relating to your Earth-based Soul as a primary connection. But you may also assist your growth by helping your Judge Selves in activating their Maldekian Soul connection.

When persons consider Souls, they often desire to have one Soul exclusively, as if they owned it. This desire reflects the insecurity of part of the personality, not all of it. Such insecurity most often comes from the Judge Selves.

Souls are radiant beings like Gods to the human personality. And so, having connection to not only one, but *two* Souls offers a great advantage. The Earth-based Soul of the human personality relates in a very harmonious manner with the Soul of its Maldekian partner. Souls in the causal plane are not troubled by the types of conflicts, fears, and divisions that occur among human personalities. Souls represent a tremendous resource and the true fulfillment of human evolution.

Over the reaches of time, as the second plan of evolution proceeds, tremendous benefits will accrue to the Planetary Being of Earth and the Planetary Being of Maldek. The Maldekian Souls, who have completed the plan of joint evolution, will be freed to return to their home planet. Great benefits will derive from the joint plan of evolution for these planets and the entire solar system. So we encourage you to consider the long-range view of evolution in these matters.

Did this address your question?

LOIS: Yes. Thank you very much.

EXPERIENTIAL EXERCISE: JOURNEY TO YOUR SOUL

MONITOR: Are you ready now for a journey?

GROUP: Yes!

MONITOR: Then we suggest that you relax and, if you feel comfortable doing so, close your eyes. See yourselves as each one a pinpoint of Light. Your Light shines brightly, and around you lies a dim world. And for this time you are not attached to that world. You are freed from it. Feel the sense of freedom. Feel the lightness of your being. Look above you and see before you a pathway of Light, a Light that is Loving, a Light that feels like home. Know that you are free, protected, and safe.

You may, if you wish, ascend in that pathway of Light and come to a place of brightness, of Love. Be there now. In this place you are within the presence of your Soul. Time, as you have known it, does not apply here. You are in an eternal moment. You are in the presence of Light that is free. Allow your minds to relax. Feel comfortable and at ease. Allow yourselves to be as open as if you were held in a mother's arms. Feel the Love. The being you are in *is* Love.

Allow yourselves to fill with Love and be aware that wisdom is permeating your being. You do not need to know of it, for you are not ready. Simply trust. Know that it exists now within your being. *[Long pause]*

And now bid farewell. Allow yourselves to descend the path of Light. And as you descend, retain what you have been given in Love and wisdom. Retain that Light within your being as you return, in full awareness, to awareness of your physical bodies. Allow your bodies to absorb the Light you have brought with you. Breathe more deeply and absorb. And when you feel comfortable, open your eyes.

Allow yourselves to remember your experience. Now we would be happy to entertain any who wish to share their experience. We will comment, if it seems appropriate. Who wishes to share?

TOOLS FOR EXPLORATION
Exercise 8

JOURNEY TO YOUR SOUL

1. Relax and close your eyes. See yourself as a pinpoint of Light in a dim world. You are not attached to that world. You are temporarily freed from it. Feel your sense of freedom. Feel the lightness of your being.

2. Look above you and see a pathway of Light, a Loving Light that feels like home. Know that you are free, protected, and safe.

3. If you wish, you can ascend in that pathway of Light. As you do so, you come to a place of brightness, of Love. Be there now.

4. In this place you are within the presence of your Soul. Time, as you know it, does not apply here. You are in an eternal moment. You are in the presence of Light that is free. Allow your mind to relax. Feel comfortable and at ease.

5. Allow yourself to be open in a place of pure Love. Feel the Love. The being you are in *is* Love.

6. Allow yourself to fill with Love. Be aware that wisdom permeates your being. You don't need to know it all. Just relax and trust the Loving presence of your Soul.

    [Long pause]

7. And now bid farewell. Allow yourself to descend the pathway of Light. As you descend, retain what you have been given in Love and wisdom. Retain the Light within your being as you return, in full awareness, to awareness of your physical body.

8. Allow your physical body to absorb the Light and Love that you have brought with you. Breathe more deeply and absorb.

9. When you feel comfortable, open your eyes, and continue deeper breathing. Remember your experience.

10. Write down notes of your experience.

11. As you review your notes, notice the *qualities* that you observed in the possible presence of your Soul. Write down those qualities.

12. Remember when, in your life, you have experienced those qualities before. Write notes about such times. They represent other occasions when you made contact with your Soul or other Souls.

HELEN: I will try. It was a most glorious experience of completeness, of Love and Light, of a great emotion of joy that was almost more than I can express!

MONITOR: We thank you for sharing and comment that your experience of your Soul goes beyond your mind's ability to grasp. Your minds are growing, and they are accustomed mainly to other levels of reality. You are preoccupied with physical experience and learning about astral and mental experience, but you do not have the mechanisms yet in your minds to grasp truly your experience in the causal plane, where your Soul resides. So Helen's report of a glorious sense of joy represents the human appreciation of Soul contact.

We ask you, over the next several days or weeks, to notice new forms of understanding, new insights, new intuitions that originate from your experience this evening. You were infused not only with Love and joy, but also with *wisdom*. That wisdom will work its way within your mind. The wisdom that each of you acquired will work its way through your minds and find expression through time. Are there other sharings or comments?

LOIS: When we first started, I felt my face going into a wonderful smile. I hadn't felt that I'd experienced anything yet, but just immediately felt that way and felt wonderful. And then I had the sense of a lot of activity at the top of my head and around *in* the top of my head. I didn't have much visual imagery, but more of feeling, a really good feeling. When I came back, I was very, very, very warm as we were bringing wisdom back.

MONITOR: Thank you for sharing. The activity at the top of your head reminds you of that energetic flow of Life which connects you always with your Soul, that stream called the "sutratma."

Even though you may have had difficulty sensing events in the causal plane, in time as you evolve, your sensory mechanisms will also evolve. In time you will merge with that Loving, wise presence that you call your Soul. And when you merge, you will find your senses fully capable of functioning in the causal plane. And perhaps as you felt this evening, you will feel a grand sense of returning home.

Let us point out, to put the matter in perspective, that Soul *is* the "home" for a human personality. The Monad is the "home" for the Soul. And so there are higher levels of existence than the Soul. We decline describing much about them, because it has little practical value for you. Yet we indicate that all Life in the universe is intimately related in the exact sense that you use the word to describe your physical relations with your family.

During their evolution, Souls travel throughout the universe. They are created by their parent Monad in a given solar system. They evolve by learning to use the characteristics of being that are present in that solar system. When they are sufficiently matured and accomplished, they begin their journey throughout the universe, moving from solar system to solar system.

The Souls, whom you have met this evening, are here in planet Earth only for a time. They *invest* themselves. They learn what they have come to learn. They contribute what they have come to contribute to the evolution of the Planetary Being, then they move on.

We wish you, as human personalities, to realize that each of you is intimately connected to *cosmic* origins. When your personalities are sufficiently developed, you are able to read the memories that your Soul wishes to share with you and thereby gain awareness of your Soul's experiences in other planets and solar systems.

We thank you for asking us to provide a "tour" for you. We suggest that we repeat this type of experience, for we can provide other tours. And we assure you that they will be interesting for those who are open to receive them. Now do you have questions or comments?

JULIE: May we ask other questions about the experience we just had, or move along to some other questions? Or does it matter?

MONITOR: We are open. What do you wish?

DEALING WITH MENTAL DISTRACTION

DOUG: Monitor, thank you for that journey. While I was on my journey, I noticed that several Light streams were happening through my heart center, and in the meantime my mind was chattering. And while it was a very pleasant experience, I somehow feel as though I cheated myself out of an even grander experience. Can you suggest methods for calming the chattering mind, the "monkey brain?"

MONITOR: What you ask is a difficult task to accomplish. The human mind is in the process of evolution within the mind of the Planetary Being, within the mind of the Solar Being, within the mind of greater Beings. One level of mind communicates with another.

The aspect of mind that, as you say, was chattering during your experience represents what we call the mind of "intellect," which is based primarily on physical experience. You may, for example, consider your physical scientists and the type of training that their minds receive. They are trained to observe physical phenomena and analyze it in various ways. Most of the ideas, introduced to those scientists who are open, come from the *intuitive* mind, which is needed to guide the intellectual mind. When the intellectual mind encounters experiences beyond physical phenomena, it feels insecure and seeks to satisfy or comfort itself in the only way it knows how, by performing its intellectual functions. You perceive those functions as "chatter."

Throughout the history of various spiritual disciplines, the quieting of the intellectual mind requires persistence and a prolonged, disciplined approach. For example, the experience of so-called "mindless meditation" refers to the personality seeking to still the intellect and allow the intellect time to learn how to be comfortable in nonphysical awareness. These disciplines take time to be effective, especially when the intellectual mind does not realize it is fearful. So we cannot give you a simple answer to the question of how to help the intellect be quiet. You may work with it over time through meditation of stillness.

Does this answer your question?

DOUG: It does. And I thank you again for the origin of the experience.

MONITOR: You are welcome.

DOUG: And I encourage more "tours"!

MONITOR: We are pleased that you have introduced this subject of guided experiences, for we find that you may learn, in such fashion, lessons that you may not as easily learn through the exchange of words. So we are pleased with the process.

SELECTION OF BIRTH FAMILY

LOIS: I have a question about the origins of physical life. I've heard it said that we choose the family we come into at birth, and I'd be interested in knowing why one would choose to arrive in a situation of being born out of wedlock and then placed into an orphanage and eventually into an adoptive parents' home?

MONITOR: In this specific case, we may say that the choice of the vehicle of birth and subsequent placements in homes occurs by choice of your High Self seeking to provide your Male Self with awareness that he had not completely grasped.

Your Male Self had previous experiences of a similar nature. These experiences were introduced by the High Self in order to allow the Male Self to experience the consequences that he had caused in others. This represents a situation where the Self who has been the victimizer becomes the victim, which we assure you is a very popular aspect of the curriculum.

The Selves of the personality need to learn how to express power with the motive of wise Love, and thus many steps of learning are required. If you consider this one lifetime's experience as just one step that leads inevitably to glorification and freedom, you gain the benefit of a helpful perspective. We encourage you and all others to see your life experiences as one step in a greater pattern.

Now, because your minds are focused in intellect, you immediately have the tendency to ask, "What is the pattern?" and "Where am I in this progression of lifetimes and lessons?" And we, of course, refer you to ask those questions of your own High Selves.

HIGH SELVES

We will comment briefly on the role of your High Selves. They are more accessible to you than your Souls. The High Self occupies an intermediate level of consciousness between the level of your personality consciousness and the level of your Soul consciousness.

The High Self is appropriately termed your "guide," your "teacher," and, if you will, your "baby-sitter." The High Self is the aspect of higher consciousness most challenged to keep you out of mischief. Your High Self, therefore, is well informed as to what is taking place in all aspects of your personality. Your High Self seeks to develop *all* aspects and sometimes gives priority to the needs of one aspect over the others.

The High Self is wise and quite capable of evaluating all human conditions. Your High Self, however, is not always fully sensitized to the level of *suffering* that any of the personality Selves may experience. The High Self may note the suffering, but not always fully comprehend the degree of the suffering.

The High Self does not intend to be insensitive or uncaring. On the opposite, it is immensely sensitive and caring. This particular difficulty in perception is due to the distance of its consciousness from the Selves' consciousness. So we find great value in encouraging the aspects of the personality to communicate with the High Self.

We encourage you to inform your High Self whenever you feel that you are suffering too intensely. Your High Self will appreciate the information and, if it so deems, will make appropriate adjustments in your life experience. Such adjustments involve what has been termed "Divine Grace." In this aspect, Grace operates to ease suffering. The High Self has many options and resources available to ease your suffering.

ORIGIN OF SUFFERING

Since we are talking about suffering, we will comment that the evolution of the Planetary Being of Earth involves suffering. The Planetary Being is approaching a time of testing and, hopefully, successful initiation which will lead to great advancements for all human and other beings in the planet. Yet, in this time, suffering constitutes part of the experience of the Planetary Being and so of its component beings, including humanity.

Suffering is *not* imposed as punishment by higher levels of consciousness on lower levels of consciousness. The origin of suffering lies in the growth of the Life essence in the form. As Life essence senses that it is *other than* the form it occupies, it begins to suffer. This suffering represents its sense of deprivation from the freedom it knew prior to entering the world of form. Suffering has great value because it motivates that Life essence to seek expression *beyond* the form to express itself more fully, and to fulfill itself *in* the form and so be free of it.

We are talking about the pattern of *crucifixion,* which you know historically and which is still a vital part of the evolution of humanity and the Planetary Being. The experience of crucifixion may be met most constructively by *acceptance* of the suffering. Acceptance yields rapid learning of lessons and release from suffering, whereas denial and rationalization of suffering simply prolong it.

As you accept the crucifixion that you experience in various aspects of your being, you act in accord with the best interests of the Planetary Being. You, as a unit of Life in the Planetary Being, assist that Planetary Being to accept *its* suffering. Once suffering is accepted, on any level of form, the Life essence dwelling within that form may then act to relieve the suffering and achieve freedom.

You might say that the origin of some of your suffering lies in your own karmic lessons, but the origin of other aspects of your suffering lie beyond your own being in the actions of the Planetary Being. As you seek freedom, you perform a service for yourself and the Planetary Being.

We believe that this is enough for tonight.

JULIE: We thank you, Monitor.

MONITOR: We thank you all! We encourage you again to bring questions about origins and share other sources of information. Such exchanges allow for better assimilation of what we have to share. And so we thank you for your cooperation.

GROUP: Thank you.

MONITOR: We leave you now.

Lesson 15
July 17, 1991

MONITOR: We welcome you once again. We are interested if you have observed any fallout from your journey last week.

DOUG: I slept all weekend!

ENERGETIC REORGANIZATION

MONITOR: That is quite a fall! We will comment, as we promised, for those of you who noticed effects from last week's journey.

Doug, the energies, which you transacted during that experience, provided some re-circuiting of your structure, necessitating "time out" for you to be successfully restructured. We believe that you will find the restructuring greatly to your benefit. During the journey to the Soul, part of your circuitry was open, and part was blocked. Re-circuiting was done in the area of blockage, so you will perhaps find a different response the next time you undertake such a journey.

JULIE: A few of us had a common experience during the trip—Paul, Lois, Luckie, Helen, Julie, and Linda. When you asked us to feel as safe as if we were in our mother's arms, a number of us experienced some fear. I felt as though a hammer had smashed the mirror. Everything just went. So everyone, collectively, would like to know what that was about?

MONITOR'S MISTAKE

MONITOR: That was our miscalculation. We assumed that you would have a peaceful experience with the suggestion of being cradled in your mother's arms. We neglected to take into account that part of your "mother" memory pool relates to traumas, and so we apologize. Yet you may find that a certain benefit comes from that experience because it does reveal to you what is, as yet, unresolved. We encourage you to seek within yourself that connection with the true Mother of all, who allows you to feel safe when cradled in such arms.

Any journey to paradise brings surprises. The Soul may be viewed as "paradise." When a statement is made about establishing or restoring paradise on Earth, the only feasible way that can be accomplished, in our opinion, is through establishing Soul consciousness in the human, devic, and elemental kingdoms.

JULIE: That's helpful. Thank you. Luckie had an associated question.

GROWTH OF "MOTHER" EARTH

LUCKIE: I am interested in your reference to trauma and the mother experience, and also your views on "Mother Earth" and our environmental problems at this time.

MONITOR: You ask a tall question. The term "mother," for human beings, brings memories of one's own biological mother or psychological mother. The question you ask relates to Earth as "mother." Indeed it *is*. Consider the function of mother. Mother provides the form which Life essence occupies. Thus Earth *is* mother. Thus matter *is* mother.

The Earth, in its full consciousness, is at present in a state of struggle. It encompasses portions of consciousness that are quite clear and coherent, and portions that are quite confused. The state of consciousness of your encompassing Planetary Being reflects itself in humanity and other kingdoms. The present state of the physical environment is only one area of concern. It has its parallels in etheric and astral environments. From the viewpoint of the Spiritual Hierarchy, what occurs in the *astral* environment is perhaps more important than what is happening in etheric and physical environments.

ASTRAL GROWTH

The astral environment consists of the accumulation of astral energies emanated by all beings functioning with astral bodies. From the Hierarchy's viewpoint, the confusion of emotions, desires, attitudes, and expectations present in the collective astral field needs to be resolved before the confusion and pollution in etheric and physical levels may be resolved.

As you resolve difficulties within your emotions, you aid the Planetary Being. As you resolve difficulties with desires and expectations, you extend the effect of your accomplishment beyond your own astral field. Your accomplishment creates a vibratory event that extends beyond you into the astral field of the planet. As more beings, such as you, gain mastery over astral expression, the planet greatly benefits.

While astral confusion reigns, in both senses of the term, you will have disturbances in etheric and physical realms. The expression of volcanoes, earthquakes, devastating winds, and droughts manifest an extension of the astral confusion in the planet.

We believe we've been perhaps depressing enough to encourage other questions!

EMOTIONS AND NEEDS

LUCKIE: I would like to know some guidelines about how to work on my astral body.

MONITOR: You ask for guidelines to work on the astral body in accomplishing eventual mastery. In order to successfully and effectively work with your emotions, you must first *recognize* them as they occur. Once you recognize them, you may allow appropriate expression, since emotional energies *require* expression. They are like the wind that must blow. When it ceases blowing, it is because its need for expression has been met. Astral energies, and emotions in particular, express a facet of need that Life essence experiences in form.

When understood, emotions lead you to understand the underlying *need* that must be met in order to function satisfactorily. The emotion of fear must be recognized and heeded, then it leads to a greater understanding of its underlying *need*. If fear is disregarded, it persists and reappears repeatedly until it is heeded as a warning signal. When you learn to recognize fear as a warning signal and *meet the need* it indicates, you gain considerable freedom of expression, because fear inhibits the expression of other emotions.

We will abridge our comments on this subject because it is a broad subject, and we suggest that you schedule the topic of "emotions" for one of the coming months.

CHACO CANYON ROCK ART

DONNA: May I ask a few quick questions on Native Americans again? I'm trying to fill in some of the information I don't know.

MONITOR: Please do.

DONNA: All right. Let's go back to Chaco Canyon. Is there any place in the rock art that portrays the "space brothers?"

MONITOR: Indeed, there are several figures that portray extraterrestrials. However, they are not always clearly distinguished. The older figures were used with clear understanding, but later generations utilized some of the features of the old figures in new ways with a different understanding. If distinction can be made as to the older figures, it may be possible to distinguish those figures that designate the beings from space.

Their general configuration is that of a humanoid or semi-humanoid form within a circle, either a partial or a full circle. The figures in the partial circle resemble what in your time would be considered a space helmet—which is not at all what was originally designated. The original designation of the partial circle was that of an energy field around the individual. The figures within a full circle are completely contained, and the circle represents their response to the whole of Life, which is evident in those beings who were great beings of Light and teachers to those peoples.

HUMAN SACRIFICE AT CHACO CANYON

DONNA: Thank you. Was human sacrifice ever carried out at Chaco, as it was with the Maya of the Yucatan?

MONITOR: Only in the last days of deterioration of that culture. It was in those times that the peoples dispersed.

Human sacrifice is a symbolic act, which represents in some cultures a very positive meaning, yet in that instance represented an attempt to control people through fear.

CASA GRANDE PUEBLO

DONNA: For what purpose was the Casa Grande pueblo built for the Hohokam?

MONITOR: We find a combination of purposes. First, it was utilized as a temple, a sacred place that was raised above all other structures. It was built in the square or rectangular pattern, which reflects a later element of civilization in Mayan culture. It is therefore associated with those later times.

The structure was also used as a place of justice where disputes were resolved in a process that incorporated Divine guidance. The structure, in its temple function, contains references to the various positions of planets, stars, sun, and moon, which were part of the knowledge of the Mayan people. Does that address your question?

DONNA: Yes, it does, and thank you.

SEDONA AS DIMENSIONAL GATEWAY

ARZANI: In following up on the archaeological type of questions, could you explain to us the significance of Sedona? Is it a communications place between two realities? Is it a doorway?

MONITOR: We assume you mean the physical location. The area now called "Sedona" has been, since the early times of the planet, a gateway between planes of expression. It has enabled beings from the mental plane and the high astral plane to materialize into the etheric and physical planes without following the process of biological birth. It has also enabled them to depart without the process of normal human death.

As a gateway, it has had a limited population. In our perception, it functions as the fourth chakra of the planet and so functions on a planetary level. The physical structure of the area is not itself the fourth chakra, but the *beings*, who mainly exist on a nonphysical basis in the area, function as the chakra. Human beings entering that area are subject to the radiatory effects of those beings and what they perform for the planet. Do you have more questions?

ARZANI: I don't think so. I know I had an experience of healing there. It always seems like it would be very easy to die there where the separation between form and non-form is more blurred.

MONITOR: Indeed it is. In past civilizations it has been used as a place of birth into, and death from, the human physical form. It is also quite active on the etheric level, and so you have many beings, who exist in the etheric level and not in the physical, engaging in numerous activities there.

DONNA: Are they all positive activities?

MONITOR: Not all, but most are.

HELEN: Is that area also, as we suspect, a base for UFOs?

MONITOR: Indeed, it has been for a long time, in your sense of time, almost from the beginning of the cultivation of Life within this planet. And the reason for this involves its ability as a gateway.

ARZANI: Thank you.

MONITOR: You will notice that civilizations, such as those found in Chaco Canyon and Casa Grande, were *not* found in the Sedona area, That arrangement was purposeful. The Hierarchy did not, and still does not wish, to have a large populace in that area because it creates a form of slight interference with the functioning of those beings who comprise the chakra activity.

ARZANI: Montezuma's Castle and Montezuma's Well are just outside of that area.

MONITOR: Indeed, you will find them around the periphery, but not in that specific area.

MODERN AND ANCIENT RELIGIONS

DONNA: Are the modern revealed religions superior in any way to the ancient nature religions?

MONITOR: Only in some aspects, as the more recent religions many times involve greater use of mind. They become more abstracted from the concrete perceptions that characterize the nature religions. They are not superior, but in some ways inferior to the nature religions in terms of motives. For, in mankind's present development, the average human being uses mind so little that he/she may easily be manipulated by those who are more clever and who utilize a religious structure to enslave.

SPIRITUAL ABUSE

JERRY: That discussion brings up to me the term of "spiritual abuse" as being about the most prevalent form of abuse on the planet right now. Could you elaborate on that term as it relates to modern day religions and the attempt by everybody to be in unity in a limited, rather than unlimited, fashion?

MONITOR: "Spiritual abuse" offers a fortuitous term, in our viewpoint, since it characterizes most of the religions of humanity. We describe it as promising, with one hand, connection with the Creator, yet with the other hand, blocking that connection through various devices. We find, throughout the history of humanity, pure initial motives of those who make spiritual breakthroughs and act as inspirational and spiritual teachers. Yet within one, two, or three generations, that original pure impulse becomes distorted and subject to the fears and desires for control of the followers. Therefore "spiritual abuse" may be described as offering promise of spiritual connection in order to gain an individual's commitment, then using that commitment to enslave the individual in one form or another. Does this address your point?

CHALLENGE OF RELATIONSHIPS

JERRY: Yes. Taking it a step further, out of the church and into the family, or into a relationship, the active commitment to relationship, in many cases, seems to inhibit a person from freely expressing all that they can be, particularly with children and parents.

MONITOR: This presents a valid observation in our view. In a relationship, individuals play out patterns that the Planetary Being plays out. The levels of ignorance, miscommunication, and fear in the relationship represent in the microcosm what occurs in the macrocosm. Understand that this involves a process of growth, and that human relationships give opportunity for each individual to gain greater self-awareness and, through that awareness, greater capability for living free of fear.

Fear will be present in any human relationship in these times and in times to come. Fear needs to be recognized and handled appropriately. Fear distorts personal relationships from their full potential and also distorts religious institutions from their full potential. Eventually, as small groups of people gain sufficient awareness and capability to free themselves from fear reactions—not fear itself, but a prolonged chronic reaction to fear—it will be possible to have relationships and spiritual institutions that truly serve and fulfill the promise they make.

JERRY: Okay, if you have two people who are willing to make a commitment to each other to evolve a synergistic relationship for spiritual empowerment, what would be the most appropriate techniques or methods to accomplish that?

MONITOR: We would have to speak for a week on that subject.

JERRY: That may be a monthly topic.

MONITOR: Indeed, that is an excellent suggestion!

SELF-SUFFICIENT RELATIONSHIPS

JERRY: Is there any short introduction to that you'd like to share, as food for thought—seeds for future questions?

MONITOR: Any relationship between human beings benefits when each person becomes self-sufficient in its supply of Life force and nourishment from its source, the Soul, and beyond the Soul, the Creator.

When two individuals enter into relationship and neither is self-sufficient in that sense, each struggles with fear and the illusions produced by fear. Their relationship involves continual struggle, which in the final analysis, is productive, yet not always pleasant. When one individual in a relationship is self-sufficient and the other is not, the one who is not struggles greatly, sensing needs within itself that have *not* been met, but which it senses that the other *has* met. If the one, who has the need and is not self-sufficient, accepts the challenge of the struggle, he/she grows, and the relationship may truly mature from a spiritual basis.

When two individuals, who have achieved self-sufficiency, join, they are more capable of fulfilling the promises of relationship. They are more capable of understanding, caring, loving, sacrificing, and radiating the Light of essential Life to themselves and to the other. Such a relationship is capable of tremendous growth, and such growth will not nearly be the struggle of the other relationships that lack self-sufficiency. Relationship struggles are moderated by the qualities of understanding, caring, and loving. A self-sufficient relationship offers a more interesting and pleasant journey.

JERRY: Thank you very much. Good seeds!

DREAM ABOUT SOLAR PLEXUS CHAKRA

HELEN: I would like to bring up a dream, if I might. I don't know whether it has anything to do with origins, and I'm not sure it has anything to do with the experiential trip we took last week, but it has happened since then, and it's very short.

I'm with a group of friends, and we're discussing some subject. I don't know what it was. One friend, whom I'll call BJ, suddenly, upon some kind of a command or suggestion, started to become *smaller*. She gradually became smaller until she was about the length of my little finger, moving across the carpet. In the dream it didn't seem particularly humorous, but afterwards I thought it was quite humorous. Then suddenly, because of a command that was given or whatever, she started to become larger and larger until she resumed her original size. The only sense I could make of it, in trying to analyze it, was the ability of expanding in some way in consciousness. Would you please give me your thoughts on this?

MONITOR: We find that dream experience has several levels of meaning. The level of meaning that you have indicated, of expansion of consciousness, could be one. However, we find the most significant level, in terms of what was occurring in your being, is the action of the third chakra located in the solar plexus. It is in that chakra that you, and all other human beings, experience their *perception of size*.

The sense originating in that chakra is sight, sight on the physical and other levels. With sight, a person has opportunity to gain a sense of proportion, among other considerations. So this chakra is involved whenever a person undergoes the experience of shrinking or expanding. In your case, there has been such an activity in your solar plexus chakra, and we believe that activity determines the primary import of this dream.

On a practical level, you may explore the concept that sight originates in that chakra, and that your sense of proportion of beings, events, and environment is perceived through that chakra. In daily terms, you may at times make—how do you say it?—"a mountain out of a molehill," if you are affected by fear in that chakra. Or, you may make the mountain into a molehill, if you exercise courage, faith, and trust through that chakra. It is a quality of perception that you can learn to consciously control, for the most part. Do you understand this?

HELEN: Yes, thank you very much. It helps a lot.

DETERIORATION OF EYESIGHT

JULIE: Speaking about sight, what happens to our sight as we become older and hopefully wiser? One would think that we would gain wisdom as we grow older, and yet our eyesight seems to deteriorate and get blurry. What's the origin of our sight beginning to fail? I would think it would get better as we get older.

MONITOR: Deteriorating eyesight is not part of the original plan for human beings, but what you could best describe as an accumulated habit. It began when a person experienced sufficient stress to create disharmonies in his etheric body. The greater portion of this stress came from *astral* confusion. His physical vehicle then developed characteristics of aging, which were *not* part of the original plan, since the human body was designed to sustain itself as long as the indwelling Life needed it. Does that not make sense?

Accumulations of stress changed the habitual functions of the body. Of course, we're speaking of the etheric body. That habit was then promulgated through generations, and may be overridden, in these times, by a person's strenuous effort or a special intervention of the Hierarchy, which does occur, but rarely.

The deterioration of sight, as with other senses, *does* serve a purpose for the person who is aging to the point of obsolescence. It encourages the person to realize that its Life essence is independent of that form. The loss of *outer* sight encourages *inner* sight. It prepares the person for transition from the vehicle.

MENTAL DETERIORATION

JERRY: Regarding Alzheimer's disease, it came to me that it is the closest an adult gets to returning as a child with no past, no future, but just being in the moment. Is that, in fact, a form of intense preparation for transition?

MONITOR: That type of incapacitation of certain mental functions provides opportunity for an individual to live in the moment as a child and thereby fulfill desires that have not been met when intellect has dominated.

"FALL" FROM GRACE

JULIE: I'd like to bring up Doug's question, which I thought was very interesting. He mentioned that both Ken Carey and Emmanuel, talking about what we call the "fall from grace," suggest that the "fall" was caused by our consciousness becoming fascinated with form. Would you comment on your view of that?

MONITOR: Yes, it is fascinating to us as well. The term "fall from grace" is interpreted as a negative event, when it is *not* negative at all, in our perception.

If you view the entry of Life essence into form as a process of growth that contributes to the evolution of Oneness of all Life, Oneness with its Creator, you see that the indwelling Life inevitably becomes fascinated with form and identifies with a form and forgets its origin and destiny.

In the history of this planet during the first wave of Souls, the indwelling Souls occupying mental and astral forms were less likely to become lost. Yet, they *did*. They became fascinated with the forms evolving in the lower astral plane, those forms which you term "elemental" evolution. The first wave Souls experienced those elemental forms and sometimes became lost in them, so fascinated with the qualities of mineral, vegetable, or animal Life that they forgot *who* they were. And so you have the origin of *death*, which is death of the form only. Death provides a way out when the indwelling Life has forgotten how to gracefully exit the form.

HIGH SELVES AS SOLAR ANGELS

In the second wave of Souls entering Earth, confusion was accentuated, and the Hierarchy needed to invest greater effort in maintaining clear communication with those Souls dwelling in forms in the various planes. Here, in the human kingdom, you were given the gift, the very gracious gift, of the Solar Angels who became your guides, or what you term your "Higher Selves." They assisted in mediating between the consciousness of the human being and the consciousness of its Soul. This great act of service by the Solar Angels inspires all of Life in this planet, for it is *not* a frequent occurrence throughout the universe.

And so, in your present form, you have evolved what you call a "personality" which consists of various components. Some of those components are quite comfortable in the form and seek nothing outside of it. Other components feel quite uncomfortable in the form and seek escape.

In some cases, they do not know what they would escape *to*, yet they desire escape as though from prison. In other cases, they understand that they would escape into a greater freedom and repeated opportunities to return to form until they have gained mastery of it.

Still other components in your personality actively seek mastery of the form, which is the only way that they may be truly released.

Grace is evident in all phases of this process, should the indwelling Life seek it, for the Creator has ever provided direct communication and direct assistance to all of Life, no matter in what form or in what state. Thus the implication of the phrase, "fall from grace," which indicates a separation of Life essence from its Creator, is quite misleading. There never has been, nor, we may safely predict, will there ever be any such separation.

LUCIFERIAN PRINCIPLE OF SEPARATION

HELEN: What about the separation that Lucifer was reportedly in charge of?

MONITOR: Lucifer, as one of the Cosmic Identities, acted in a creative manner and activated what you term the "principle of separation," which was the choice presented to a Life essence that entailed its choosing to unite with or separate from the whole. Its separation occurred only in its own mind and what its mind manifested, which is, of course, how forms were manifested.

The world of forms exists in the world of mind. The principle of separation works through the world of mind, creating what appears to be a real separation to the individual choosing separation. In truth, no separation of Life essence occurs. It remains whole. Life remains a whole, undivided fabric incorporating all individual Life essences embodied in form.

The principle of separation, when properly understood, creates all of the opportunities and possibilities present in the world of forms. It allows Life essence the opportunity to experience the unique perspectives of many forms in order to gain awareness and capabilities that enable it to free itself from form and rejoin the wholeness, the Oneness of Life essence.

When the principle of separation expresses itself down to the level of what we refer to as "germ consciousness," it reverses direction and oscillates upward, creating unity. In its return path, it separates the individual from its sense of separation, thus promoting the experience of connection, relationship, and unification with Life essence in other forms. Thus the Luciferian principle is not something to be feared, but a principle to be understood and properly utilized. Does this address your question?

HELEN: Yes, thank you. I believe that would be part of what they call the "illusion"?

MONITOR: Indeed, illusion exists only in mind.

SOUL AND CELLULAR MEMORY

JERRY: How would you distinguish between "Soul memory" and "cellular memory?"

MONITOR: "Soul memory" refers to the Soul as a unit of consciousness remembering its experiences and the experiences of other Souls to which it has access.

"Cellular memory" represents a function of the etheric energy contained within the structure of a cell that is part of the etheric body. A portion of that etheric energy records the experience of all units of consciousness, from the very smallest to the very greatest. Cellular memory, literally taken, refers to the memory of those cells. We believe you refer to it in the sense of a human being experiencing cellular memory? Do you not?

JERRY: Yes. What about the ancestral perspective?

MONITOR: Cellular memory, because it is involved with the etheric body that continues a pattern from lifetime to lifetime, gives access to the memory of one's ancestors and also one's past lives in the physical and other planes as well. Gaining access to such memory requires training in the skill of attunement for working with astral and etheric energies, which combined, provide the coding for means of access to the memories.

DEVELOPMENT OF THE CHANNEL

ARZANI: This is just a curiosity. Monitor, I was wondering if you were familiar with the other entities who speak through the channel, Harvey.

MONITOR: Yes, we are.

ARZANI: Could you explain how? Like with Michael, for example.

MONITOR: We have direct being-to-being communication with other sources of teaching through this channel, and with many other channels as well. What do you wish to know?

ARZANI: I noticed that you are now doing the life readings instead of Michael. I was wondering what the dynamic was.

MONITOR: The dynamic is simply that we, at this point in the channel's growth, offer means of development that are needed at this time. Michael is not displaced and will be present when needed. We are simply concerned with the development of the channel.

SPIRITUAL HIERARCHY

LUCKIE: Could you give us the origin of the Hierarchy?

MONITOR: The Hierarchy has its origin in the Maker, the Creator. From there, the Hierarchy extends to Creation and is found in the Cosmic Identities. From the Cosmic Identities, the Hierarchy moves into the realm of form. In the realm of form, the Hierarchy may most easily be identified, in human terms, with those kinds of stellar structures that you perceive as galaxies, sub-galaxies, solar systems, stars or suns, planets, planes, and rays of influence.

Within the category of Planetary Hierarchy, you have various lines of evolution that have their hierarchies. The concept of "hierarchy" permeates the human being down to sub-atomic entities. The Hierarchy exists on *all* levels of form, expressing intelligent stimulus to the evolution of Life essence through one form after another, until it is freed from form.

Perhaps you have not considered "Hierarchy" to that degree. If you consider the Hierarchy of Earth, you would say that Hierarchy began through assistance from distant stars and neighboring planets. At that point the Hierarchy was primarily organized around beings who came from Venus. As the evolutionary plan progressed, many of those beings returned to their home planet, and their positions have been filled by beings who have evolved through Earth.

The Hierarchy of Earth consists of all kingdoms of Life working together in harmony. They have groupings that reflect the greater impulses of the planet and other planets of the solar system and beyond.

No Hierarchy at any level of form is ever disconnected from the totality of Hierarchies, for all of them represent the constant flow of guidance from the Creator to all of Life essence journeying through form.

JULIE: Is there anything else that needs to be said before we close?

ETHERIC "WEATHER" PATTERNS

MONITOR: We won't offer you a journey tonight as we did last time, but you may consider that for the next meeting. The reason for this is due to the energy level of the channel and several present in the room.

Those of you who have noticed an increased sense of stress or fatigue may be pleased to note that it is not simply your individual condition that you experience, but part of what you term "weather patterns" in the etheric structure of the planet.

When major changes occur beneath the crust of the planet, the etheric structure of the planet and all of its beings share that effect. Major movements are taking place in the magma structure, leading to what you term "Earth changes" in the form of volcanic and seismic activity. Such movement is now underway, and events are set into motion with which you will become familiar as time proceeds.

Along with these changes are very important changes that occur as elemental beings in the magma are graduated or released from the forms they have occupied. These elemental beings have earned the right to freedom. With their release comes a change in the structure of the magma.

We wish you to know this so that you will have an example of what lies, at least partially, at the origin of Earth changes.

We thank you for being with us again, and we look forward to our next time together.

Lesson 16
July 24, 1991

MONITOR: We welcome you as Monitor.

GROUP: Welcome, Monitor.

MONITOR: We hope that you have gained some new viewpoints concerning the origins we have discussed. We're quite interested in what aspects you would like to explore this evening.

JULIE: We'd also like to request another experiential exercise, whenever you feel that it's the wisest timing.

MONITOR: An experiential trip?

JULIE: Yes.

MONITOR: Very good. What is your preference?

JULIE: About when we do it?

MONITOR: When or where would you like to go?

DOUG: I'm personally open to visiting the Soul again. That fascinates me and feels very safe.

JULIE: Any other ideas about that, or does that feel comfortable to everyone?

ELAINE: How about if we go to our source of origin?

JULIE: Our "source of origin" and our "Soul" have been brought up as possibilities.

EXPERIENTIAL EXERCISE FOR SOUL ORIGIN

MONITOR: We believe that it may be possible for you, at the time of our choosing, to visit your Soul and then activate your Soul's memory. We believe that this would work for most of those present.

JULIE: Thank you.

MONITOR: We will tell you when the time arrives.

SOUL AND SUFFERING

ARZANI: I have a question about the Soul, based on the reading I've been doing in *The Seat of the Soul* by Gary Zukav. He says something that doesn't agree with my understanding of the Soul, so I'd like to read it and then hear your interpretation.

MONITOR: We would be pleased to do so.

ARZANI: "Spiritual psychology will bring to light those situations that would shatter the spirit if seen clearly. Brutality, for example, shatters the human spirit. The soul cannot tolerate brutality. It cannot tolerate abundances of pain and irrationality. It cannot tolerate being lied to. Consider that on our planet. It cannot tolerate non-forgiveness. It cannot tolerate jealousies and hatreds. These are contaminants, poisons, for it."

I never felt that the Soul could be hurt in any way, unless it's incarnated, the incarnated part, but I never felt the Soul could be intolerant.

MONITOR: From our perspective, the Soul is *not* hurt by such experiences. It always *gains*. The vehicle that the Soul uses to gain such experiences can, of course, be hurt, as all of you know.

His use of the term "tolerate" is perhaps misleading from our perspective. The Soul endures and utilizes all of its experiences. It does not "tolerate" such experiences. The word "tolerate" implies that the Soul suffers, which we do *not* agree with.

The Soul, who resides in the causal plane, represents a high level of form compared to the form of human beings. It is able to learn and develop its capabilities by embodying in the form of a human being. By the way, it is not limited to embodying just as a human being in this planet.

The Soul uses *all* of its experiences to gain what it needs. Its range of experience is extremely extensive when compared to human lifetimes. The Soul has usually experienced a number of star systems or solar systems before it comes to Earth to embody. So the brutalities, stresses, and suffering of its embodiment *affects* it, but does not cause the Soul itself to *suffer*.

We have spoken of the Soul as being like a God to its personality. The personality would not exist if it were not for the active creativity of the Soul. When a person raises his/her awareness, moving it through and beyond the human form, his/her Soul starts to infuse the person with more of *its* awareness and energizing presence. And it fills the person with its own motives.

Those persons, in your history and in the present time, who attempt to bring about a practical unity among humanity and all creatures inhabiting this planet, act on the impulses of the Souls who sponsor them.

In the causal plane, Souls relate with each other in great harmony, even though they may be from very different parts of the universe. True, they do have their *challenges*, which would not be easily understood by personalities. As human beings view it, the Soul is able to exercise enormous powers, including what seems to be infinite sensitivity, compassion, and Love. The Soul attempts to manifest its quality of being in the Planetary Being and its vehicle, the human being, as both a means to aid the Soul in its growth and a means to aid the Planetary Being in its growth.

MONAD AND SOUL ORIGINS

MONITOR: Would you like to hear of the origin of the Soul?

GROUP: Yes.

MONITOR: Well, we'll tell you sometime. How about now?

HELEN: Yes!

MONITOR: When the Creator—which is perhaps the best approximate term we can use—created the manifest universe, the universe first took shape in the form of a swirling mass of Life essence. As that swirling mass evolved, portions of it developed an ability to distinguish itself from the rest of the mass. And the first major step of the manifested universe was the formation of what we have termed twelve "Cosmic Identities."

From the human viewpoint, these Cosmic Identities are very difficult to consider. Their existence is, in one sense, far removed from the dimension of human existence, and yet the active Life of the Cosmic Identities permeates all of the universe and human beings in the process. You best know them as *principles*, similar perhaps to your principles of physics. Yet to truly understand them as principles, you must first assume that all of existence is alive; it consists of consciousness.

As the twelve Cosmic Principles or Identities formed, they began to exhibit their own unique qualities and movements. Some of the twelve desired unity as a way to return to the unity of the Creator from whom they had been born. But some of the Cosmic Identities preferred to *reject* unity, and in the resulting conflict, many levels of reality, or dimensions, were created. The unity that could not be achieved willingly in the level of Cosmic Identities was then pursued in realities less cosmic in scope. We will not mention all of these levels, but suffice it to say that the Soul level consisted of Life essence entering into forms which have derived, in both form and essence, from the twelve Cosmic Identities.

Souls were created because unity of the Cosmic Identities could not be achieved in the next higher level, that of the Monad. The vehicle of the Soul was created and energized through Monads. One Monad creates, sustains, and ultimately absorbs a large number of Souls.

The Monad gives its Souls incentive to explore their expression of individuality through the facets of form and has also motivated its Souls to seek unity.

But when Life essence inhabits any form, including that of the Soul, it must first become *aware* of its form. It must gain *mastery* of its form, and then *relate* to other Life forms in creating harmony or unity through voluntary means.

Souls have their origins in a high level of the universe, and they have permeated the universe. Some are involved in the process of creating *other* forms through which they may grow, while others have assumed more of a caretaking role.

For human beings, awareness of the Soul constitutes a major accomplishment. It represents the epitome of spiritual mastery as a human being. A person who achieves spiritual mastery is freed from human form and subsumed in his/her Soul. Souls have integrated masculine and feminine energy expressions, so the human being must achieve a similar mastery in human form before it can be subsumed by its Soul.

Well, we are wandering a bit away from origins, but we wish to give you a perspective to consider. Perhaps you have more questions or comments?

ELAINE: It is correct to assume the term "Oversoul" as the Monad? Is that one and the same?

MONITOR: That term has been used by some human teachers and through some channels. We accept that definition because the Monad, in effect, is the "Oversoul" of the Soul.

REASSURING JUDGE SELF

LINDA: Speaking of masculine and feminine energy I'm working with Julie with that in a class, and I got stuck the other day in dialoging with my Male Self. I felt that maybe I was trying too hard or just wasn't patient enough. I'd like to know what suggestion you may have, so that I can definitely know I've made a contact with that, and if I have the right energy going for that.

MONITOR: We find that your experience was inhibited by your Mental Judge Self, who has been threatened by the concept of you gaining greater access to your Subconscious Selves and especially your Male Self. We encourage you to reassure your Mental Judge Self that it will not be harmed by this process, that you do value its contribution, and then proceed to contact your Male Self.

As you have repeated meetings with your Male Self, you will identify his distinctive energies, his patterns of thought and feeling. Indeed, you will find that he has a most distinctive sense of humor!

DREAM ABOUT A CAT

LOIS: Monitor, some time ago you had asked us to ask you to join us when we went to sleep, and I had an experience. I awakened during the night and, before returning to sleep, asked you to join me. This is the dream that I had. My cat was vocally expressing pain, physically putting her head and specifically one ear down on the floor and pushing along the floor as she walked. I caught on that she was hurt. There was a bit of blood. This awareness seemed to come slowly to me. I moved to catch her and pick her up. She turned and headed back in the same direction before I caught her. The whole side of her face that was injured was enlarged and dark. The ear opening was larger and dark, matted with blood. She let me pick her up.

MONITOR: We believe that this does refer to your cat as a type of warning or advisement for you to take care of her. This was given to you by your Female Self. As you heeded the warning, your cat was kept from such difficulties.

EXPERIENCE WITH MONITOR

LINDA: I've been inviting you, Monitor, to come in. I have checked with my Subconscious to remember my dreams, but I don't remember. Yet at times when I'm working around the house, I feel the presence of Monitor during the daytime. Is this happening, or am I just imagining it?

MONITOR: This is happening. There are quite a number of us, so we get around.

LINDA: Thank you.

MONITOR: We want you to understand that we do have a sense of responsibility for those who share with us, and so we look in from time to time and do what we can to assist with your growth.

ANASAZI AND HOHOKAM

DONNA: May I ask a few questions on the Native Americans again? I really appreciate the material that you've given me on this, Monitor. If the ancient Anasazi and Hohokam were both of Mayan extraction, could they communicate with one another in the same language?

MONITOR: Indeed, they did. Although some groups became more isolated and developed dialects, the basic root language remained the same.

DONNA: Where did the Hohokam go when they left this area?

MONITOR: They moved into the region of the Colorado River and migrated south.

DONNA: Are the present Native Americans in this area, the Pimas and Papagos, descendants of the Hohokam?

MONITOR: For the most part, yes. They are also partially the result of other groups of Native Americans who passed through the area. But their prime stock derives from those called the Hohokam.

ATLANTEAN RUINS NEAR BIMINI

DONNA: Thank you. My husband, John, went with Dr. David Zink and some of the A.R.E. crew to Bimini to view the ancient ruins there. Can remains of Atlantis be seen in Bimini?

MONITOR: Yes, in terms of structures. There are a number of structures in that area and in other portions of the Atlantic, but those in the vicinity of the island of Bimini are sometimes visible from the air. Because of difficulties with considerable currents of water in that area, the sands often shift and make identification and precise location of such structures difficult to obtain. This is a site where major installations from Atlantis will be found and ultimately definitely identified as Atlantis. We project that process as occurring over the next forty years.

ATLANTEAN IMMIGRATIONS

DONNA: Did some of the Atlanteans go to Britain, and some to Egypt?

MONITOR: Britain was part of Atlantis. It was a high mountainous area with plains, and so some of the people went to that area.

During the major times of the city-states of Atlantis, the area that is now the British Isles was used only in part, since it was not accessible or favorable to most of the people.

DONNA: Egypt?

MONITOR: Immigration took place to Egypt at different times, because Egypt was an ancient civilization begun even before Atlantis. The times of the major immigrations from Atlantis to Egypt occurred approximately 120,000 years BCE, 52,000 years BCE, and 10,500 years BCE. At that point the Atlantean continent, for the most part, sank beneath the waves. You may find, in Egypt, evidence of Atlantean dwelling.

ELEMENTAL KINGDOM

ELAINE: Monitor, would you expand on the origin of the beings known as "centaurs?" Were they physical or mythological? What they have become, or who has followed them? How have they reincarnated? How have they evolved?

MONITOR: You ask a major set of questions.

ELAINE: I'm sorry.

MONITOR: We will attempt a more simple answer, and then if you desire to pursue it, please do so.

In the early days of astral expression, when Souls embodied primarily in the astral and mental planes of Earth, evolution of the elemental kingdom was begun. The elemental kingdom, consisting of the forms that you know today as mineral, vegetable, and animal—which evolve into the human body—began *first* in the astral plane. Their evolution began with very simple forms. Similar to the concept of your biologists, simple one-celled forms were the originating forms.

To gain a new perspective on this, consider that in those times the Soul, as a radiant being with a boundary, manifested in the mental plane as a radiant form with a boundary, similar to what you term a "bubble," but a *radiant* bubble. When the mental form projected itself, on behalf of the Soul, into the astral plane, its astral form also manifested as a radiant bubble. From that point of origin, it is only natural that the beginning forms were in the form of radiant bubbles, or one-celled creatures. The amoeba, as you know it today in the dense physical plane, had its origin in the astral plane.

As forms evolved, largely with the impetus given by the devic kingdom assigned to such tasks, a time came when experimentation was initiated by the Hierarchy to find suitable forms for expression of the next stage of growth beyond that of the animal kingdom. In that time, approximately sixteen million years BCE, forms were created which blended the forms of animal and what later became "human." In that time, beings were created as centaurs and other forms which you know today through mythology. Human beings, who spoke of such creatures, spoke either from memories of their own or memories of the race as it evolved.

Those who were centaurs have *not* embodied in any distinct pattern in your world today. They have moved on. While you have considered the Native Americans as descendants of centaurs, we find that this is not so. Anyone in this room may be the descendant of a centaur or a satyr.

Consider the evolution of form. It is plastic to the indwelling Life. As the indwelling Life essence experiences that form, its creativity shapes it. Over time, the shaping process evolves a more suitable vehicle for the indwelling Life essence.

From the viewpoint of the Soul, the human form is quite primitive, but appropriate for the planet at this stage of development. The higher forms throughout the universe are radiant beings with boundaries. The more highly evolved the being, the greater the radiance and boundary. Does this address your question?

ELAINE: Yes, thank you very much.

DEVIC BEINGS AND ATLANTIS

MARY: You talked about part of Atlantis being England. Does that also include Ireland and the rest of the British Isles?

MONITOR: Yes.

MARY: That's very interesting. The tales of the Druids and the "little people" can all be traced back to Atlantean times?

MONITOR: To those times and before. The "little people," as spoken of in their folklore, refer actually to lower forms of devic beings and not to human beings at all. The people, who perceived such beings and at times had relationships with them, could only describe them to others in terms of human form, but we assure you they do not have human forms. They have devic forms.

MARY: When we talk about Atlantis, there have been recent scientific discoveries and predictions that Atlantis, or at least part of it, is going to rise in 1992. Is this true?

RISING OF ATLANTIS

MONITOR: We find some basis for these statements, yet the process of rising is quite gradual until significant changes occur in the flow of magma beneath the Atlantic Plate. At this time, the major upward magma currents occur in the Middle East and the Pacific Plate. As those currents express themselves, pressures and stresses will be distributed among the various plates, and an uplift will be experienced in the Atlantic in a much more accelerated rate than what has been evident. But we do *not* claim 1992 as the year for the appearance of Atlantis. In retrospect, from the historians' future viewpoint, Atlantis will have been identified much earlier by those who had eyes to see.

You must understand that, with the present structure of academic institutions, true innovation is discouraged, and the perspectives that are encouraged are quite conservative. Any major archaeologist or geologist who claimed that Atlantis was rising would soon be discredited and penalized. So it is to the future historian to give credit where credit is due.

HAWAIIAN MENEHUNES AND LEPRECHAUNS

BOB: Would the Hawaiian menehune also be a devic type similar to the leprechaun or the creatures in the mythology of that part of the world?

MONITOR: Quite so. The menehune are still quite active as devas of the lower forms, as are the devas that have been identified as the "wee folk" in the British Isles. They are active throughout the entire planet and even in this area of the desert.

BIO-CONNECTION

ELAINE: Does the evolution of the Soul, which occurs in individuals, affect the evolution of the Earth to bring about a volcano or an earthquake when a major pattern of change occurs?

MONITOR: Yes. All Life forms and Life essence within the boundaries of the planet affect each other. The action of one affects all, and the action of all affects one.

We find a direct correlation between the presence of volcanoes and the experiences of Life in all kingdoms of form. A volcano represents a major advancement for those elemental and devic beings who have evolved in the magma below the crust. As they achieve higher growth, they are permitted release from the realm that has been their home into a new realm on the surface of the planet.

ELAINE: And the earthquakes. How would they be affected?

MONITOR: Earthquakes are caused by various factors, the major factor being the movement of magma. The Spiritual Hierarchy assumes responsibility for seismic and volcanic events. They carefully manage such events and are quite capable of doing so. You must understand, however, that they seek to benefit all forms of Life in this planet and not simply the human form.

BIRDS AND DINOSAURS

DONNA: Do birds antedate the dinosaur age, or are they, as some believe, descendants of the dinosaurs?

MONITOR: We find they are descendants of the dinosaurs.

Other flying creatures existed, but they would have been considered variations of dinosaurs. What your biologists identify as the progression from single-cell to multi-cell to fish to amphibians to land-based dinosaurs, we find quite accurate. What they do not yet understand is that most of that evolution took place in the astral plane and later in the etheric plane. Their physical manifestation occurred quite late in the process, as did the Earth that you walk upon. Evolution of biological forms took place over a shorter period of time than if it occurred only in the dense physical plane.

EVOLUTION OF EARTH

LOIS: Monitor, some time ago, when we began talking about origins, you talked about how all Life, whether it seemed inanimate to us or not, was indeed alive. You talked about the magma, about elemental beings changing and evolving. How does our Earth evolve? What is it evolving into?

MONITOR: The Earth Being consists of many units or, if you prefer, cells. Remember that each unit of form represents a temporary encasement for Life essence. That temporary encasement allows the Life essence opportunity to grow for its own purposes and to contribute through its participation in Planetary Consciousness. Thus, Planetary Consciousness evolves through each form as Life essence inhabits and outgrows it. Forms are created as incubators, wherein evolving Life essence is protected and productively focused. When Life essence fulfills its form, the form is destroyed, removing the vibratory qualities of that Life essence.

The evolution of the Planetary Being functions in a similar way. It moves as a gigantic collective consciousness into many different permutations of form, becoming more and more capable and absorbing greater vibratory qualities from the greater form which sponsors it, the Solar Logos. When the Planetary Being fulfills its form, that form is destroyed. It is transformed into a radiant form on a higher level of existence. Therefore the evolution of planet Earth will produce a radiant Being who may join with other planets in the solar system who will eventually merge. As they merge in stages, the entire solar system transforms. And when the Solar Logos has fulfilled its form, it, too, moves into a higher level of radiance. This pattern remains consistent from universal levels down to the microscopic level of subatomic particles.

JULIE: Mary has a question.

MONITOR: Could we interject first?

JULIE: Sure.

EXPERIENTIAL EXERCISE FOR SOUL ORIGIN

MONITOR: This would be an opportune time for you to have your trip.

JULIE: Okay.

MONITOR: Are you willing?

JULIE: Is everybody willing?

GROUP: Yes.

MONITOR: Let us call it a guided tour. We suggest that you become comfortable. Allow your body sufficient circulation and close your eyes. Breathe more deeply, more fulfillingly. We promise you that we will not deliver you this time into the arms of your mothers or fathers. We have learned our lesson!

JULIE: Thank you very much.

MONITOR: Relax and begin now to feel in your hearts a definite radiance. Let that radiance expand throughout your physical bodies and throughout all your bodies. Realize that your Life essence indwelling in this physical form is Light. [*Pause*] Now sense the radiance in your head. [*Pause*] Know that the mind that occupies your body is radiant Light. Sense the Light rising in that pathway above the top of your head. Follow the Light as it rises. [*Pause*] Feel the Oneness that marks the presence of your Soul. This Soul is not separate from you, it *is* you. Feel the presence. [*Pause*] Observe images given to you, sensations given to you, of the *home* of your Soul. It is *your* home. [*Pause*] And now relax. Once again, be aware of your physical thoughts. If you wish, you may remain, as much as possible, in the presence of your Soul. Then, open your eyes and maintain awareness of your Soul. [*Pause*] Seek now to remember what you sensed, what you observed. [*Pause*] Are there one or two who wish to share their experience. We will be pleased to comment, if it is appropriate.

TOOLS FOR EXPLORATION
Exercise 9

JOURNEY TO YOUR SOUL'S PLACE OF ORIGIN

1. Relax and close your eyes. Feel in your heart a definite radiance. Let that radiance expand throughout your physical and higher bodies. Realize that your Life essence, which dwells within your physical form, is Light.

2. Sense the radiance in your head. Know that the mind which occupies your body is radiant Light. Sense the Light rising in a pathway above the top of your head. Feel a Loving Light that feels like home. Know that you are free, protected, and safe.

3. If you wish, you may follow that Light as it rises. Feel the Oneness and Love that marks the presence of your Soul. This Soul is not separate from you; it *is* you.

4. In this place, observe the images and sensations given to you of the *home* of your Soul. It is *your* home. Be aware of what you see, feel, and hear. *[Long pause]*

5. Allow your mind to relax. Feel comfortable and at ease. Once again, be aware of your physical thoughts, yet remain in the presence of your Soul. Allow your physical body to absorb the Light and Love. Breathe more deeply and absorb.

6. When you feel comfortable, open your eyes and continue deeper breathing. Remember your experience.

7. Write down notes of your experience. Note the qualities you perceive.

SIZE OF SOUL

ELAINE: I felt expanded. I felt huge. I saw my existence in a field of gold and a color that I can't describe, which is like a combination of gray and blue and purple. I felt much bigger than I could ever possibly imagine. I still feel that way now.

MONITOR: Indeed, your comment on size is quite relevant from our view, since Souls operate on a vibratory level equivalent to that of the Planetary Being. You might say that the size of the Soul can be considered as equivalent to the size of the Planetary Being.

Who else would like to share?

MARY: I had a similar sensation of much expansion and a deep purple kind of atmosphere. I expanded all over.

MONITOR: Indeed, when you consider the relationship of what you perceive as size of the Soul compared to the size of the Planetary Being, the Soul is in contact with all places in the planet. However, it must embody in order to have the specific vibratory experiences obtainable only through form within the planet.

HELEN: It was very similar to the first time that we took a trip. It was mostly a feeling of tremendous joy and bliss. I don't know a high-enough term to express a complete joy.

MONITOR: Indeed, that represents a natural experience of the Soul.

HELEN: It was beautiful, and I want to say, "Thank you."

MONITOR: We appreciate that.

PAST LIFE MEETING WITH SOUL

DONNA: I went up hand-over-hand on a beam of Light, and I got to a very warm and comfortable spot. When you said there was a place where I could go to meet my Soul, I went to one of the ancient sun temples. Now presently, I meet the Sun each day. Do I go there to meet my Soul?

MONITOR: That is quite advisable for you. We find that the place of which you speak has meaning for you in terms of past lives. It represents a time when your human personality was in contact with its Soul.

COLORS ASSOCIATED WITH SOUL

JULIE: I can still feel activity in my heart center. It's hard to describe the feeling. Pressure, movement. When we went up, I experienced incredible Light. Bright, just bright, bright Light. Then I went to a place where the background was deep purple-blue velvet with plays of all kinds of Light. It's like I was in a Light show, just all kinds of incredible Light and sometimes geometric designs. It was a lovely feeling, very colorful.

MONITOR: Quite so. You will find that what you experience is the infusion of Soul awareness into your human form. You have, for example, mentioned colors. Those colors may best be understood as colors that are equivalents, in human perception, to the colors which the Soul perceives.

Each level of form has its own range of perception and perceives vibrations differently as the rate of vibration of the form changes. The colors that the Soul perceives, human beings are generally unable to perceive. Yet the Soul's vibratory influence is passed through to the human being, and so the human being experiences colors appropriate to its range of perception.

Did you have any observation of the home of your Soul?

BOB: I also experienced a lot of activity in the heart. It was almost like a bubble pulling out my shirt. I saw colors that were blue and white and purple. It was a strange color, and the brightness seemed like one concentrated area of Light. I couldn't distinguish any shapes. They were all fuzzy, not in clear focus.

MONITOR: Seek to repeat this experience. If you call on us, we will be present to assist you. As you repeat the experience, you become aware of more, which is difficult to describe in human words. We encourage you to notice *qualities* that you experience in the state of Soul contact. The qualities of your experience will be expressed to you in terms of your senses. Many of the qualities you will experience as tactile sensations because you lack visual equivalents. So we encourage you to explore in that way.

We enjoy sharing with you these guided tours. Personal experience remains the best teacher. Do we have more questions or comments?

DONNA: Is it possible to go to an ancient place or to another time or a different civilization in another time?

MONITOR: Indeed it is, and we would enjoy providing that experience to you, perhaps on the next occasion.

JULIE: Everyone feel complete? Any more questions?

MONITOR: Does Lois's cat have your tongue?

JULIE: I think so. Bob.

PREDICTION OF SEISMIC EVENTS

BOB: Going back to an earlier subject, seismic activity, can we expect, in this location, significant seismic activity in the near future?

MONITOR: Indeed, seismic activity is accelerating. We have specifically noted that, at this time, areas under and around the Pacific Plate are experiencing accelerated activity, both seismic and volcanic, because the movement of magma under the plate is quite definite. This particular current will continue, with some initial force being presented to the seams in the plates and where plates abut each other.

This activity will predominate for a time in the Northern Hemisphere and then become quite severe in the Southern Hemisphere. As that cycle fulfills itself, the activity will shift to the Atlantic Plate.

While all of this is taking place, the magma flow in the Mideast will gradually continue to accelerate. Throughout most portions of the planet, seismic and volcanic activity will steadily increase. In time, this cycle will be fulfilled, and the magma flows will have accomplished their purpose. Then the world crust will become more stable and calm.

Understand that this is a time of significant change, a time of testing and breaking out of old forms. Much of this initiatory activity takes place in the elemental and devic kingdoms. Their processes of transformation provide testing for human beings. The Spiritual Hierarchy maximizes the benefits of these changes for *all* beings.

Any further questions or comments?

EXPLOSION OF KNOWLEDGE

BOB: The traditional academic world is experiencing an explosion of knowledge. Is this considered to be good and part of evolution, or is this something not all that significant in the scheme of things?

MONITOR: The explosion of knowledge, or communicated ideas and information, represents humanity's gradual acquisition of the powers of mind. In the distant past of humanity, the powers of mind were quite minimal. The Hierarchy furnished a great deal of guidance, a beneficent intelligence, to humanity. In these times, humanity has evolved to the point where it gains the powers of mind. The increased quantities of communicated knowledge reflect that condition. The knowledge itself may, in large part, become outmoded, but the capability of mind of humanity will continue to evolve. Its evolution moves from instinctive mind to intellectual mind, which now predominates, to intuitional mind, which will dominate.

ELEMENTAL COMMUNICATION

LOIS: Monitor, as I thought of your response to my dream, I have another question. I find it difficult for me to understand my cat and relate to her in a caring, loving way to which she is receptive. Can you give me some guidance?

MONITOR: Consult with your Body Self, who constitutes the accumulated elemental consciousness of your body, which has its own form of intelligence and ability to communicate easily with the equivalent intelligence of your cat.

Incidentally, that is just your point of view. Your cat considers you as *hers*. [*Laughter*]

From a practical point of view, you will find that, as you communicate with your Body Self, you will be guided into its awareness of the Body Self of the cat. Then you will find awarenesses coming to you. You will sense a vibrational adjustment that will make the relationship between you and the cat more compatible.

EXPLORING YOUR BODY CONSCIOUSNESS

We encourage all of you to explore your own Body Self. As you go to sleep, put your attention into the sensations of your body. Feel sensations with acuity. As you pay attention to them repeatedly, you gain awareness of many activities taking place within your body, including activities that are for your health and activities that are not. As you become self-aware through these means, you may be able to better maintain your health, if you choose to. So we encourage you to explore in that direction.

Our next meeting will focus on the topic of "Dreams." We ask you to bring your dreams to present and discuss. We will have much to share, and we hope you will also. We thank you once again, and we leave you.

Lesson 17
July 31, 1991

MONITOR: We welcome you as Monitor.

GROUP: Good evening, Monitor.

MONITOR: We will continue the subject of origins, but also begin with dreams since dreams provide an excellent way for you to learn about yourselves and your world. Where would you like to begin?

CROP CIRCLES

ARZANI: I'd like to know if you could shed some light on the crop circles that are appearing in the British Isles.

MONITOR: How bright a light do you wish?

ARZANI: As much as I can take!

MONITOR: To have a more complete understanding of crop circles, we suggest that you consider the perspective that Life on this planet has always enjoyed an interchange with Life from other planets and solar systems.

Crop circles offer a demonstration of benign and helpful energies applied to growing plants in a field, creating designs that demonstrate a higher form of intelligence at work.

Crop circles give scientists evidence that invites those who are willing to be open to consider possibilities beyond what their present science can now generate. The designs are formed by devices, not necessarily the flying craft that contain beings, but usually by smaller devices, what you call "probes."

Some of the configurations appearing in the more elaborate designs are intended to awaken memories in human beings who have been in other planets and star systems. We do not mean that a human being has been out of the periphery of Earth, but that the Life essence contained in the Soul of the human being has been in such distant places. Crop circles act as stimuli to those people, causing the awakening of memories and generally exerting a benign influence.

If you have noticed, discussion of extraterrestrials has generated a great deal of fear among the general populace of the planet. The presentation of information about extraterrestrials has been carefully paced by the Hierarchy, allowing people to release their fears gradually. The greatest obstacle to a friendly interchange between Earth people and people from other planets consists of the *fear* generated by many Earth people. Therefore, a number of activities have been allowed by the Spiritual Hierarchy to enable people to release their fears. Does this address your question?

ARZANI: Yes. Thank you very much.

MONITOR: The energies used in generating crop circles are *not* physical energies; they are etheric. If identified by your scientific instruments, the atomic structure of portions of the plants has been altered etherically. It may be identified on the physical level as a distinct change. We believe that even advanced scientists cannot produce such effects using physical energies.

DREAM ABOUT TEACHING

DONNA: I have a dream. Are you ready for dreams?

MONITOR: We're ready for dreams!

DONNA: I was back teaching high school chemistry. I thought I was not covering enough material or teaching well enough for thorough understanding. I decided I must combine theory and practice. First I would introduce the theory of a mole of material and then have the students use the balance to measure out a mole's worth of several different compounds. Is this also the method of teaching *Explorations*?

MONITOR: Exactly. We find that your dream is instructive and originates with your Male Self who desires to remind you of his capability not only for learning, but also for teaching. As a favor to him, we would say that he *does* encourage you to engage in teaching situations that give him a great sense of satisfaction.

DREAM ABOUT RELATIONSHIPS

LINDA: I had this dream the night before I spoke from the pulpit last Saturday. It was night, and I was outside with my friends, Karen and Dottie. We were walking down the streets as some type of festivities was going on. The street was dark except for a corner streetlight shining on the corner house of the block. Karen was sitting in a parked car alongside the house. We stopped by my house. As we walked in the door, Dick, my former husband, was sitting in the middle of the room. As I started to say something to him, he told me shut up or he would shut me up. Somehow I knew he had been drinking with Karen's husband. It was rather strange that he spoke to me in that rough manner. He was not really that way, even while drinking in real life. I walked down the hallway, and my children, all grown, were in one bedroom, some of them sleeping. As I stood there, my oldest daughter came climbing through the window.

The next thing I knew, my friends and I and my youngest daughter were on a porch on a two-story apartment building, leaning against the bars watching the festivities going on below us. We decided to go down and join the festivities. We came down to the main floor and crossed the lawns to get to the sidewalk on the other side. My daughter asked me about this guy I had met recently who had walked me home and wanted a kiss goodnight. She questioned why I had said, "No." We got to the other side, lined up on the sidewalk, all four of us, and started dancing in a straight line, all doing the same dance in unison. Can you give me further understanding?

MONITOR: We find this dream presents the viewpoint primarily of your Female Self, representing how she is affected by your Mental Judge Self. We find that you are just gaining acquaintance with your Female and Male Selves and your Judge Selves. This dream is intended as instruction.

Much of the dream is symbolic. Part of it is experience. The sense of going down the street with your friends was part of an experience.

The symbolic portions present the perspectives that your Female Self has experienced through earlier portions of your lifetime. The harshness of your former husband reflects her perspective of the harshness of the Mental Judge Self.

Your experiences with your home represent your mode of living, from the Female Self's perspective. She has been active in the astral plane and in times past when she was bored with the activities that you, the Self, were engaged in, she would leave and pursue her own desires.

Ask her what she is truly interested in and assist her to focus on what she needs to learn. She is inclined to move away from areas she wishes to avoid, and so needs reassurance.

Knowing these things then, we ask that you re-examine the dream experience. Note the qualities of the early portion, moving down the dark street, which represents her astral movement with friends. Note the presence of an observer, one who is watching and, in a sense, protecting, which is a common practice in travel through the mid to lower levels of the astral plane. We believe we've given you enough to go on.

DREAMS ABOUT DOG AND CHIROPRACTOR

ARZANI: I had two dreams, Monitor, that seemed to give me answers. I would like to know if they were true answers.

One dream was that my dog had both ears infected, and I took him to the vet, who said that his right ear was okay now. But on looking at it now in real life, it doesn't look like it's okay, so I have a question about that one.

The second dream was that I was talking to Harvey about my chiropractor. Harvey said that he had just done a life reading on him, and that my chiropractor had never had a life on Earth before this lifetime. I want to ask you whether I should trust these dreams, or whether they are my imagination?

MONITOR: We suggest that you view these dreams not as direct guidance, but as symbolic displays.

The dream about your dog's ears is *not* valid guidance, as we find that some infection remains in the right ear as well as the left. You may view that dream as wish-fulfillment, which gives you comfort to know that your dog is healed.

The second dream is also *not* literal guidance, but suggests an expression of quality that you sense in your chiropractor, which seems pristine, pure, and unsullied by repeated Earth experiences. What you sense in that regard is truly the expression of his Soul quality, not the quality of his subconscious or conscious levels of mind. Does that assist you?

DREAM GUIDANCE

ARZANI: Yes. Without asking you every time I have a dream, is there a way to tell when it is valid guidance and symbology for me?

MONITOR: Yes, we suggest for you, and for all others, that when you attempt to determine the validity of specific guidance from a dream experience, attune to your High Self and ask it if the dream guidance is true. On some occasions you will receive clear indication of the validity of the information. On other occasions you may be given information from your High Self that indicates that the information is valid, but perhaps not your specific interpretation.

In the two dreams we just addressed, we find that there is validity in the message, but not in the specific interpretation you attempted. Your High Self will have the opportunity to encourage a different viewpoint, which may be quite productive.

Consider the dilemma of your subconscious mind attempting to give you guidance or advice. If you do not recognize it is present, you are unlikely to listen to the advice, even though it permeates much of your dream experience. If you do realize that your subconscious mind is present, but that you know very little about it, then you can easily misinterpret what it attempts to communicate.

So we recommend that you become well acquainted with the various aspects of your subconscious mind. One aspect is normally quite distinctly different from another. When you gain ability to progress from generalizations to specific knowledge of these aspects, you gain much greater ability to interpret your dream experiences.

We also encourage you to ask—either during a dream, if you are capable of "lucid dreaming," or on remembering a dream—which aspect of your subconscious mind has given you the dream.

Your dreams come primarily from your subconscious mind, from one aspect or another. If you know *who* produces the dream, you will be much more capable of gaining the benefit of the message. If you have an anonymous message, often you find difficulty in correctly interpreting it. If you have a specific message from a specific Self in your subconscious mind, you find it much easier to interpret correctly.

DISINCARNATE MOTHER IN ASTRAL PLANE

PATTIE: My mother passed away a few months ago to the other side, and sometimes when I'm thinking about her I feel as though she's never left, as we were very close. Are you able to tell me anything at all about my mother?

MONITOR: When you use the word "left," you imply movement from the place where you are to a distant place. We challenge you to consider that the movement of a person, who leaves the physical body and moves into the astral plane of existence, does not move a great distance. The astral plane co-exists in the same matrix with the physical plane and the other planes. All are present at the same *place*. So there is no significant distance between you and your mother.

The other significant illusion of distance comes with fear, in this case, primarily the fear of loss. Fear creates a shell in the energy field of the person who generates the fear. That shell is created of astral substance. In this way a barrier is created between the astral perception of the person in the physical body and the astral perception of the person in the astral body. Fear can create an illusion of distance when there is no distance. So release of fear becomes the best way to experience continuous connection with those who have departed the physical body. We assure you that, in their experience, they have not gone away from you at all, they have simply moved into a different vibration.

What we refer to as "planes" are distinct levels of vibration. Within the astral plane exist several layers like bands of vibrations. Each layer is experienced as a world in itself. When you, in your subconscious mind, leave your physical body at night, you go principally to the astral plane. Where you visit in that plane depends largely on the vibration of your subconscious mind.

You may visit those who have left the physical body and those who have yet to enter the physical body. You realize, in your subconscious mind, that most of the beings in this planet, who enter physical human bodies, live normally in the bands or levels of the astral plane.

You may also visit the mental plane, which more human beings are becoming capable of doing. In the mental plane you function on a higher vibratory level and are capable of learning at a much more rapid rate than if you were learning in the astral plane.

Pattie, in terms of your mother, we find her existing in the fourth level of the astral plane, still at times resting, yet at other times meeting with family and friends, acquaintances from many lifetimes. We find that she does not feel *any* sense of distance from you and is quite alert to your moods and needs. We find that she is still working to free herself of false understandings that limited her when she was in the body physical. Therefore her learning progresses. Does this address your question?

PATTIE: Yes it does. Thank you.

NIGHTMARE AND OPENING REPRESSED TRAUMA

JULIE: I have a question, Monitor, and it pertains to a time during our seminar last weekend. We asked for help in remembering dreams. So we all did that, and I asked for assistance in dream work. And on Friday night I had the worst nightmare I have ever experienced in my life and woke up in great distress. I've asked my High Self about that and found that both Male and Female Selves are helping me remember repressed memories of pain of which I still have no conscious memory. How can I assist myself in opening up that memory to be healed?

MONITOR: We find that the significant development of your Inner Selves concerns the merging of what have been two feminine aspects into a single Female Self. As that has occurred, you find greater readiness to accept the childhood trauma represented by the dream.

The other significant aspect has been the willingness of your Mental Judge Self to release the memory. He has been primarily responsible for the sequestering of that memory. Your Mental Judge Self has considered that the memory would be too traumatic for the two Female Selves to process, yet now his understanding has grown and he is more trusting of their ability.

JULIE: Thank you. The other thing that was very strange to me was that we had meditation each morning at 7:30 in the morning, and I was so exhausted from not resting well that on Sunday morning I slept. I said, "I won't get up for meditation." As I was waking up, however, I heard monks chanting and thought to myself, "Oh, I've missed meditation. They're using the meditation tape, and I hear it." I was lying in bed thinking, "Well, I'll just get up slowly." I listened to the chanting, and it felt beautiful and wonderful. I got up leisurely, took a shower, and thought, "Maybe I'll get over in time for breakfast." When I got over there, meditation had *not* begun, and there was no tape on. No tape had been played. And I just wonder what happened.

MONITOR: We find that it was a gift from your High Self, utilizing a symbol to honor a request that you had made—if you recall the previous evening—that you would awaken in time for participating and guiding the meditation. The request was honored in a pleasant way.

JULIE: Thank you very much. It feels very valid.

NATIVE AMERICANS

DONNA: I have some Native American questions when we're ready. Are you ready, Monitor?

MONITOR: We are quite ready for Native Americans in all forms!

DONNA: All right, good. Did any ancient people come to this country by way of the Bering Strait, as the scientific community believes they all did?

MONITOR: We find that approximately 10% came from that direction. They came from certain areas along the coast of what you now term Siberia. In addition, peoples lived there as remnants of an advanced civilization that had existed in the area known today as Alaska. These combinations of peoples stayed in the northern portion of the North American continent. They did *not* migrate to the south. They did trade with peoples to the south who came from the Mayan civilization.

DONNA: Who lived in this area before the Mayans and the Lemurians came?

MONITOR: We must clarify that, before Mayans came to this area, there were those from Og, that portion of South America. Before them, those who came from Atlantis, and before them, those who came from Lemuria at various times.

Lemuria existed over a long period of time and generated several diverse civilizations and diverse forms of peoples. In the early times of Lemuria, the

Spiritual Hierarchy advanced the elemental beings from an animal octave of consciousness into what became the human octave of consciousness.

Lemuria contained a great blending of beings from other planets and star systems and of various colonies from various star systems. These star beings, as Souls embodying in Earth, provided means of cultivating and educating the elemental beings into what became the human kingdom.

From Lemuria, therefore, numerous immigrations of peoples came into what you term the United States and Southwestern United States. At times the area of the Southwest submerged beneath the ocean. Lemurians were here *before* the oceans and in between oceans. So we're speaking of a long period of time as you count it. Does this address your question?

UNDISCOVERED RUINS

DONNA: Yes it does. Are there any undiscovered temples or pyramids in the state?

MONITOR: Many that are not recognized as constructed by human beings, but were. The length of time has been sufficiently great to erode the stone structures so that they appear to be native and not artificial. We find clusterings of these structures throughout the state in different portions.

The oldest of the structures exists in the area known as the land of "Four Corners." These structures antedate the civilization we previously discussed concerning the Anasazi and the civilization found in Chaco Canyon.

Within the area of Springerville have been found the remnants of one of intermediate peoples, not the most ancient. But in that area there are also structures, contained partly in caves and partly underground, structures from much more ancient times when Lemurian beings came into that area and lived.

In general, the prevalence of civilizations in early times of humanity's history is much more extensive than your scientists presently recognize. They have tended to ignore evidence that has been presented, but in time the evidence will be convincing.

LIFTING AND CUTTING STONE BY SOUND

DONNA: May I ask one more? Was sound used to raise the blocks during the building of the Great Pyramid of Giza?

MONITOR: We will hold our sound while the pyramid is built! *[Tape is turned.]*

Sound was used, not only to lift the stones, but also to cut them precisely. We find that the powers of sound, as they have been used by ancient civilizations such as those in Egypt and other places, have been amazing in comparison with your present technology. These forces of sound have been carefully protected from discovery by human beings during the past ten thousand years. Humanity during this time has explored the extremes of individual expression, and the danger was too great that an individual opening the potential of mind would gain access to the powers of sound and use them for destruction of others.

This information regarding the use of the powers of sound will be released gradually and only to those who demonstrate their ability to work harmoniously in groups. Those who work harmoniously in groups demonstrate greater Soul awareness and Soul activation. Only they may be trusted with the gradual release of such information.

Regarding the Great Pyramids in Egypt, that one known as the Pyramid of Cheops was added onto in the time of Cheops. Other structures exist within it, covered by what has been added later. In time this, too, will be discovered.

INNER EARTH

HELEN: Monitor, would you please discuss the Inner Earth and the possibility of cities and civilizations within the Earth?

MONITOR: Essentially Life is a radiatory force. It enters into a form of lower vibration in order to experience what that form offers, yet the indwelling Life continues to radiate. This is true not only of human beings, of atoms, but also of planets.

Within planet Earth is radiant Life. Surrounding the radiant Life are various planes of manifestation. In physical manifestation, the form of the Earth is that of a shell, not quite spherical in shape. In terms of physical matter, the shell has cooled. Beneath the shell lies molten matter called "magma." Below the magma lies a shift of dimension from physical to etheric, and then within the etheric, astral and mental and causal dimensions exist.

If you were capable of viewing it, you would see the Planetary Being shining as a star. And if you looked at the dimmer periphery of the star, you would see a series of shells. The physical crust of the planet represents one of those shells.

Within the Earth dwell great numbers of beings of various kinds. Human beings have been oriented to live on the crust and currently consider the crust the only habitable place. This assumption is quite narrow, for it does not include the possibility of existence in etheric, astral, mental, or causal planes.

Much of the evolving Life force of the elemental kingdom begins in what you term the "elements," but not strictly within physical elements. We also find evolving elemental Life forms in etheric elements. Some of them you recognize from the physical perspective. For example, you may recognize the Life essence in a crystal, even though you perceive the physical structure of the crystal primarily. If you are open to perceive other levels, you may perceive it as being more active in etheric and mental levels, with little activity in the astral level.

Within the astral body of the planet, much activity is taking place that is stimulated from Great Beings beyond this planet and beyond the solar system. This stimulation constitutes part of the plan of growth. Human beings are buffeted by this stimulation, causing them to become more aware of their astral existence in terms of emotions, desires, attitudes, and expectations based on desires. The astral plane then stimulates the etheric plane, causing considerable agitation and growth in the Life forms that have been quite comfortable in the etheric plane.

This situation applies directly to the growth of elementals who have been quite comfortable existing in the magma beneath the crust of the physical planet. These elementals have been stimulated to such a degree that they are passing their tests and being initiated into higher levels of etheric force.

You wonder why we describe them in such detail. We do so because these elemental forms move from the magma up into the atmosphere of the physical planet, and in so doing pass through the human place of habitation. As they encounter you, they become involved with your etheric and astral forms, causing you at times to experience extremes of fatigue or excitation. Many times their emotions are quite undeveloped, so their emotions affect your astral bodies, giving you strong emotions, often those of fear and anger, which you have difficulty accounting for.

Your role in this elemental encounter involves helping to process those emotions and the etheric energy interchange so that these elemental beings may complete their transition into the etheric element of air, and there evolve another civilization which will be quite necessary for future changes in your planet, changes which will affect the entire physical aspect.

There are a number of civilizations within the Inner Earth. We have attempted only to give you a brief sketch because most of the civilizations are difficult for you to comprehend. We say in passing that there are highly evolved beings and Life forms in the center of the planet close to the core of the Planetary Being. Does this answer your question?

HELEN: Yes. But even those highly evolved ones are not physical, right?

MONITOR: Indeed. They have no need to be physical. They are learning and expressing in service what they have learned in other forms, principally in the astral and etheric planes. The highest-evolved exist in the mental and causal planes, and they render service to the etheric and astral planes, attempting to help their little brothers and sisters evolve.

BEINGS IN HOLY MOUNTAINS

ARZANI: I've heard that there are nonphysical entities that live in what we call "holy mountains." For example, Mt. Shasta in California and Black Mountain in Carefree. I've heard that Black Mountain has been turned off. That there are beings living in these mountains who turn on and off the energy, modulating the energy of the planet in that way.

MONITOR: We find this statement to be generally accurate. We modify the statement that the beings turn energy on or off. They *modulate* the expression of the energy in accord with planetary conditions.

The beings that exist in such locations have a different reference than physical. If they are working in the mental plane, as the highest of such beings are—that and the causal plane—they have quite a different sense of space than if you view that same space from the aspect of the physical plane. To them, the mass of a mountain on a physical level, gives them a relatively quiet place in which to work in the astral and etheric planes. Physical mass of a mountain does not affect the mental or causal planes, but does create a stable condition for the transfer of energy from causal and mental planes to astral and etheric planes. Therefore mountains are frequently used, as are large bodies of water.

SHAMBALLA

HELEN: Would this hold true also for Shamballa in the Himalayas?

MONITOR: Shamballa exists within the higher elements of the etheric plane and represents a special location that has been specifically energized for those who have come from beyond the planet in certain lines of duty or opportunity. Those known as the "Kumaras" from planet Venus historically have resided there. And so, a specific focus of activity within the Spiritual Hierarchy has been associated with Shamballa.

Shamballa has been described as existing in one geographic location simply as an aid for human beings to consider the possibility that an advanced society, with all the complexities of a city, could exist in a place that appears to be, from the physical viewpoint, barren desert. We say that Shamballa is not fixed to a given physical location.

EASTER ISLAND

DONNA: May I ask a question about Easter Island? Why is that such an enigma? And are the monoliths produced there done as recently as the scientists believe?

MONITOR: We find that the monoliths on Easter Island depict a race of beings who existed in that area approximately 75,000 years BCE. They were a combination of beings from another solar system and human beings.

Again, etheric technology was utilized to process the cutting of stones. That particular group of people—who may be referred to by the name of "Astri"—were located at several points in that vicinity of the planet. Easter Island represents one point that has remained above the ocean. Several points have sunk. Some points existed in the area known as Peru and Chile.

That civilization represented one of the diverse civilizations characteristic of that broad area now known as "Mu." Mu was used for many experiments in working out the possibilities of physical form. Consider the value to the Life essence of experiencing diverse forms, with each form offering new perspectives and new potentialities.

For the scientists of your time to consider the diversity of forms that existed in Mu would be too extraordinary for them to feel secure. Their concept of the evolution of the human body has been carefully handled because it offers a way for human beings to find a sense of security. They find, in the evolution of their form as presented by the scientists, a sense of placement in the field of Life. The identity structure of human beings has been quite fragile in some respects, and so the Spiritual Hierarchy carefully releases new aspects of knowledge so that the security of human beings will be jarred, but not destroyed.

DONNA: Thank you, Monitor.

MONITOR: What is at stake in such progress of knowledge is the gradual development of mental capability among human beings, where they yearn to develop the powers of mind and pay more attention to mind and what it opens to them, rather than the distractions of emotions and desires.

COMMUNICATION WITH BASIC SELVES

LINDA: Could you verify, in working with my Basic Selves, that I am truly in touch with George, the two Nancys, and Omar. As I continue to dialogue with them, when I get stuck I ask my High Self to help me, and nothing happens. What can I do to further the dialogue?

MONITOR: When your dialogue becomes difficult, realize that it is because of fear. The next question is "Who is afraid?" As you ask that question, your High Self sees that you receive the answer. Then you may address that Self who is most fearful. As the fear is recognized and dissipated, the ability to dialogue will again emerge. We find that your contact with those Selves is valid, yet just beginning, and you have much to share, much to look forward to.

WUPATKI RUINS

ARZANI: Today Doug and Dianna and I went to Wupatki Ruins. They had some unexplained structures there. One was a circular structure that they called the "ball court." The archaeologists know it's not a kiva. They think maybe the people danced there or played some kind of game. And the other is a blowhole, which is a geological structure where air actually comes out from vents deep in the earth. It seems to me there's more to it than that. Could you elaborate on those structures?

MONITOR: We find that the circular structure was a ceremonial center related, as we have stated previously, to contact with beings on higher planes, including extraterrestrials. The structure was used for various purposes at various times. It was considered essentially both a sacred and a social place. As contact with the higher beings diminished in frequency, it became more social than sacred.

The blowhole represents a natural phenomenon of winds entering and leaving the earth, which provided a symbolic value for those people. Various interpretations were placed on the movement of air, and it still has value from that viewpoint. It may be viewed as the movement of Life to dwell in the form, or as the exit of Life from the form. And its cyclic motion, which occurs daily, offers a rhythm which people may recognize and relate the actions of their own lives with the actions of greater beings, especially the Planetary Being.

ARZANI: Like the inhalation and the exhalation of the Planetary Being?

MONITOR: Indeed, that offers the dominant explanation.

ILLUMINATI

DONNA: Is the current scandal of the Bank of Credit and Commerce International (BCCI) the one long predicted by intuitives as the work of the Illuminati?

MONITOR: Indeed, and it is only the beginning of exposure. The degree of corruption caused by those called the "Illuminati" is only barely being exposed and not yet truly exposed by the media. Those in the governments involved recognize the presence of the Illuminati—or the international group of financiers—yet it is only a small part of what has been and is currently taking place.

When the Spiritual Hierarchy deliberately destabilizes the world economy, many persons will defect from posts where they have held information in confidence because of what they have received in compensation. As the world economy tumbles, many such individuals will be discharged and thus motivated to reveal what they know. This will be part of the necessary restructuring of the world economy.

If you consider that your economy is based mainly on the control of corrupt forces—those who seek to control others because of their own fears—you will welcome the restructuring which will release the corruption, as though your physical body were releasing infection.

EXPERIENTIAL EXERCISE FOR PERCEIVING PLANET EARTH

We would like to introduce you to another "tour" which will take just a brief amount of time. So if you would, become comfortable. Breathe more deeply, close your eyes, and feel the comfortable protection of surrounding Light. We act in accord with your Higher Selves and suggest that the Light now completely surrounds you and maintains your safety, that you are guided into a greater awareness.

As you feel the energy move your awareness, begin to perceive the entire planet from a height far above, high within the atmosphere. Perceive the planet glowing. At the center of the planet, see a shining, beautiful star. As you adjust to the brightness of the star, perceive shells around the star. *[Pause.]*

Consider that you are perceiving more of the natural energy state of your planet. Gain, if you would, an appreciation for the radiance, the Life essence of the planet in which you share. *[Pause.]*

And then, within the Light, return to your focus of awareness in your physical body and retain memory, as much as possible, of what you have experienced. When you open your eyes, some of you may wish to share your experience, and we will be pleased to comment. Who will share?

TOOLS FOR EXPLORATION
Exercise 10

PERCEIVING OUR PLANETARY BEING

1. Relax and close your eyes. Breathe more deeply and feel the comfortable protection of surrounding Light. Your High Self now guides you to greater awareness.

2. As you feel the energy move your awareness, perceive the entire planet from a height far above, high within the atmosphere. Perceive the planet glowing.

3. At the center of the planet, see a shining, beautiful star. Write down a description of the star.

4. As you adjust to the brightness of the star, perceive shells around the planet. Write down a description of the shells.

5. Consider that you are perceiving more of the natural energy state of the planet. If you wish, feel appreciation for the radiant Life essence of the planet. Feel how you share Life essence with all other Life forms in the planet. Write down what you sense and feel.

6. Within the Light, return your awareness to your physical body and remember what you have experienced. Breathe more deeply and absorb the Light and Love of the planet. When you feel comfortable, open your eyes, and continue deeper breathing.

7. Write down notes of your experience.

DOUG: I will, Monitor. When you first asked us to rise above the Earth, I couldn't bring the Earth into central focus. It was as if I was glancing at the Earth out of the left side of my body. The only way I could truly appreciate what you were saying was to bring it into my heart, and then it became central. I saw the shell, not around the Earth, but I saw the Light as my heart center and the shell as my body rather than as you suggested. If you'd like to comment on that, I'd love to listen.

MONITOR: Indeed, we find that your heart, as you know, is more open than the centers in your head which affect your experience of mind. And so you perceived through your heart in the manner of a telescope that gives you the image of a reflection, not the direct image. That offers an adequate approach.

As your fear patterns are recognized and released, especially those of the Mental Judge Self within you, the centers in your head will also open and share in the radiance. It is simply a matter of working consistently toward freedom from fear. We thank you for sharing. Who else will share?

HELEN: I was able to move above and view the Earth from that perspective and see it as you directed, as a star, bright and brilliant, a beautiful star. I thought it was a lovely experience.

MONITOR: Very good. We thank you for sharing. Who else will share?

LINDA: I felt like I was in outer space and tried to see the Earth. I saw a far, distant star swirling, but couldn't get it focused in a ball. I couldn't get to the Light in the center, either through my head or heart.

MONITOR: Very good. We are pleased that you share such experiences because it does assist others to understand more of the mechanism of perception.

In this exercise we enlisted the service of your High Selves, who in turn chose at least one of your Basic Selves, Male or Female, to move from the physical perspective into a perspective as high as they could achieve, which functions within the higher astral or lower mental planes.

In terms of metaphor, it was as though that Self acted as a remote camera viewing the phenomena of the Planetary Being directly from their perspective and giving you the information, the experience. Of course, you, the Outer Self, had the experience pass through your "perceptual filters. Certain vibratory patterns, which your extended Self provided, were beyond the capability of your filters to process.

You may think of this type of experience as similar to sending a space probe to another planet. Sometimes the processing of its images is quite difficult to achieve.

In this type of experience, you have the opportunity to identify areas where your filters limit perception. They function quite effectively for your normal Outer Self perception, but do limit your reception of the perceptions of your subconscious mind as they are transmitted to you, the Outer Self.

Moving away from technical considerations, we ask you to remember this experience and, if you wish to seek it again, ask your High Self to provide the experience for you. This will assist you in gaining a new and more valid perspective of your Planetary Being.

GROUP: Thank you.

MONITOR: We thank you for being with us tonight.

Chapter 5

Dreams

Lesson 18

August 7, 1991

MONITOR: We welcome you as Monitor once again. What would you like to know about dreams? Dreams and the act of dreaming? The topic could involve years of sharing. What would you like to ask?

DREAM ABOUT RELATIONSHIP

CYNTHIA: I've been having a lot of dreams lately—very cyclic dreams on a regular basis about my first husband to whom I haven't been married for a number of years. And they've included a lot of nightmares about his past psychosis and that kind of thing. When I made my decision to come this evening, last night I had a dream that I asked you about it, and in that dream you had said that the relationship was a "virus." I would like a comment on that.

MONITOR: We invite you to consider what you understand a "virus" to be.

CYNTHIA: Something that can snuggle into your body and make you sick. Antibiotics don't cure it. There's always the question about how one gets rid of a virus. It just has to work its way through. There are viruses that just burrow into your spinal system, like herpes, and you're told it's never curable. So that's my understanding of virus.

MONITOR: Very fine. We offer this approach, that a virus involves a hidden invasion from outside your being into your being. If you do not know that it comes from outside, you believe that what you experience comes from your own reactions. What we find within you can be described as an astral cord of fear established by your ex–husband to you, which is and has been compromising your energy. It may be simply taken care of.

The symbol in the dream of asking us for information was symbolic of you asking your own High Self, who gave you the information. It did not come directly from us. Does this assist you?

CYNTHIA: Yes. It makes a lot of sense. If I visualize that astral cord of fear being cut, would that help?

MONITOR: We suggest a procedure involving a prayer which your friend, Arzani, knows.

CYNTHIA: All right. My life has gotten very happy except for these nightmares at night. There is and was a great deal of fear involved in that relationship, so I'll be happy to get rid of it.

MONITOR: We find that your ex–husband is still quite disturbed. He has not yet realized how he creates his own difficulties. He reaches to you as a source of support. He does not have a negative intent.

Removing the cord will help free him from fear. We suggest that in the healing prayer, after the cord is severed, you include a request that beings of Light assist him and help him gain freedom from his despair.

CYNTHIA: I pray for him quite a bit. I wondered if it was me still reaching out to him, but it's him reaching out to me?

MONITOR: We find his action reaching out for a source of support. Your nightmares reflect the fear present in your Subconscious Self, knowing that the cord represents an intrusion that is against the will of your Subconscious Self.

Your nightmares have been attempts at communication from two aspects of your Subconscious Self who seek to inform you about the problem. If you had sufficient memory of the nightmares, you would likely find some symbol of the cord of fear, which is a tube composed of the energy of fear connecting your astral body and his.

Often nightmares represent attempts at communication *to* the Outer Self *from* Subconscious Selves. Some nightmares may be quite repetitive. If so, that offers a clear indication that you, the Outer Self, are *not* receiving the message clearly. What can you do in such circumstances? We suggest that you learn to communicate directly with your Subconscious Selves. Then you may have substantive and clear communication that will resolve any need for nightmares.

CYNTHIA: Thank you very much. That helped me quite a bit.

RECURRENT DREAMS

NANCY: I have, for years, had a recurrent dream, probably related to the need to urinate, in which I am trying to get up from a prone position. Also I may be trying to drive some kind of vehicle and can't get up to see where the vehicle is going. In the last year or so I have managed, either with or without any dream, to fall out of bed. I saw a program on "20–20" that considered talking in your sleep, or this kind of action, as a classic nightmare and sleep disorder. I wonder if that is the situation that I'm in.

MONITOR: We find the basis for your repetitive dream is a communication from your Male Self, who feels quite inadequate despite his appearances to the contrary. He conveys his sense of inadequacy for being able to steer the vehicle of the personality. His influence has been considerable, in your experience, yet he does not truly feel adequate.

Falling out of bed represents a more recent symbol, which is similar to the earlier symbol of being unable to steer the vehicle. Both circumstances reflect a sense of lack of control, of helplessness. We find that he is, in an indirect way, stating his position and asking for help.

Help in this instance may most effectively be given through assistance of the High Self. Your Male Self has not truly been willing to receive its guidance, but over a period of time is becoming more motivated to receive the help of the High Self. If you wish to assist him, before sleep ask your High Self, whether you believe in it or not, to assist your Male Self. That is all you need do. Do you understand us?

NANCY: I think so. Thank you.

HELEN: Along that same line, I have recurring dreams of having parked the car somewhere and can't find it. I think it has something to do with the body, but I don't quite know why I lose it all the time.

MONITOR: We find that this is a concern of your Male Self regarding your Female Self who does not hesitate, when you go to sleep, to leave the vicinity of the etheric body and go to places she favors in the astral plane. Your Male Self is concerned because, when she leaves, he often needs to stay to protect and monitor the regenerative processes in the body. He is truly not pinned down, but resents the imbalance where he feels that she imposes upon him and his sense of responsibility.

If you wish to change the situation, ask your Female Self to talk with the Male Self and work out a more satisfactory arrangement. If that cannot be accomplished, due to reluctance on the part of the Female Self, you may call in your High Self, who will be quite capable of assisting in the achievement of an agreement. Does that address your question?

HELEN: Yes, I think so. Does the Male Self resent having to stay and do these duties because primarily they are her responsibility and he has other things to do? Is that the idea?

MONITOR: Very much so.

HELEN: Okay. Thank you very much. I'll talk to them.

DREAM ABOUT COMPLETING RELATIONSHIP

LOIS: I had two dreams this week. My first dream is about a woman named Sarah who was my spiritual teacher and friend. I severed my connection with her, at least physically. But I have infrequent, sad dreams about her. The dream I had this week was that I was in a well-lit part of the house, and Sarah and her man were there, loving and having fun together. I went into a dark, dirty area and was sweeping it. She and the man came in, and began to complain about the dust from my sweeping. Actually, there was a lot being stirred up. I refused to stop. I told them that they didn't want to be in that area of the house until I went there and began cleaning. Sarah said, "Okay." When it was apparent that I didn't intend to stop, she was going away, and I felt so sad. I turned and looked at her looking the last look back at me. I ran to her and hugged her. I told her that I didn't want her to leave and that I didn't understand why I was always so opposed to her. We cried in each other's arms, and she said, "I want to go, but I want to stay and watch you." She wanted to watch my life and watch me grow. And I woke up crying.

MONITOR: We find this is an instructive dream, presented from the viewpoint of your High Self. Your High Self is advising you to assist your Female Self in completing her relationship with the one called Sarah, or more precisely, with Sarah's Female Self. Your two Female Selves have been united in prior lifetimes and enjoy a close, affectionate relationship. Your Male Selves have been often opposed to each other.

In the karmic path of this lifetime, you have chosen a different direction than she has taken, which is wise. Yet your Female Self has left unfinished business, or an unclean house, which you are now being invited by your High Self to clean. You are being invited to complete the, not termination, but respite, from continuation of your relationship with Sarah's Female Self. The sadness comes from your Female Self's sadness.

Your Male Self sees the wisdom of changing your path from Sarah's path. He assists your Female Self in doing this, but she has been reluctant to completely release her connection. She must do so, according to your High Self, for the highest good to be accomplished. Do you understand?

LOIS: Yes. I'm not quite sure what more I can do. Is this work that I would do inside myself to suspend the relationship, since I have physically terminated it?

MONITOR: We suggest that you talk with your Female Self, ascertain her viewpoint about this matter, and help her to realize the benefit of a temporary termination, a respite in the relationship. Assure her that the relationship will continue when it is again appropriate. If she has difficulty accepting this, ask your High Self to assist her. Is this clear?

LOIS: Yes. Thank you, Monitor.

PRECOGNITIVE DREAM

DONNA: This is a dream I had as a child of seven or eight. Back on the farm in Michigan, I was down at a gate in front of an extensive garden with a large, palatial home in the background. As I watched closely, first one and then a second uniformed servant rushed around by the house. I waited and waited, but never did see who lived in the house. Fifty years later, my husband and I moved into a company house in Africa. I had taken a morning walk, but when I returned to the gate the security guard wasn't there. I could have called for him, but instead leaned against the gate and gazed up through the terraced garden to my beautiful new home. I thought, "People who go by must wonder who lives in this house." As I watched, first one and then the second uniformed servant rushed around near the house. Instantly I recognized the fulfillment of my dream.

Two questions. First, was this a precognitive dream? And second, was my life's pattern determined to that extent when I was so young?

MONITOR: The answer to the first question is "Yes." The dream was given to you in childhood by your High Self, who had determined a plan for your lifetime. We would not use the word "predetermined" because it implies that your will, operating on the level of the Outer Self and Subconscious Selves, was pre–ordained. This was not the case.

The entire object of the Life essence dwelling in the human form involves giving that Life essence opportunities to use its will and experience the consequences of its choices. The Life essence in the human personality expresses through the Outer Self, exercises will, and through Subconscious Selves, each of which exercises will. Their use of will operates within guidelines established by the High Self, who has the dominant will, or access to the powers that control the personality.

The High Self seeks to provide those experiences that most aid the Soulof the personality in gaining what it needs. The High Self exercises great wisdom, sensitivity, and care in establishing plans for a given lifetime. It has in mind the patterns of past lifetimes and also the patterns of future lifetimes. The High Self has access to many time streams and may experience all of them simultaneously.

Subconscious Selves have access to a smaller number of time streams. The Outer Self is limited normally to one time stream. The access to time streams gives the level of mind involved the opportunity to explore upstream or downstream—what you view as "past" or "future."

In this situation, your High Self created a plan and placed within your Subconscious Selves and Outer Self the image of the house so that you would recognize it when you arrived at that point in time. You, the Outer Self, finally recognized the house, yet your Subconscious Selves recognized it much earlier. Your Subconscious Selves utilized the image of the house as a means of making their own decisions, which were the decisions that you made, in conjunction with your mate, that led you to that place.

An additional layer of meaning derives from the dream in the sense that, when you were a child and had the dream, the palatial house and the servants gave you a sense of assurance that your needs would be met, that your life would be abundant, and that your need for order would be satisfied. Does this address your questions?

DONNA: Yes, but I guess I completely missed the message because I thought that it was really like the nursery rhymes or the stories I was reading. I thought that the King and the Queen lived in the house. It never occurred to me, at that time, that any part of the dream referred to me.

MONITOR: This type of confusion occurs on the part of the Outer Self of virtually every person. The Outer Self faces the difficulty of taking information from beyond its scope and interpreting it correctly. This constitutes one of the difficulties involved in the process of receiving clear guidance or channeling accurate information. So it represents a central issue, and you may at some future time consider the entire subject of guidance.

DONNA: Thank you, Monitor. That was great!

MONITOR: We further comment on your dream that the interpretation you made as a child, of the King and Queen living in the palatial residence, was useful. What you did not realize was that the King and Queen are symbols of power or empowerment, which applies to your own being. As you realize that the power of the King and Queen lies within your being, you become more capable of fulfilling your role and meeting the challenges of your karmic plan. You have had a tendency to place power outside of yourself. We suggest that you utilize this symbol and visualize the King and Queen in the house of your own being.

DONNA: Thank you, Monitor. I'll try.

DREAM ABOUT CHAKRAS AND ETHERIC ENERGY

BOB: Last month I had a dream on the 12th of July. In this dream I was in a house or apartment. Some lady came in. My impression was that she was going to provide some service, give a massage or something like that. About that time my wife left the room, going up some stairs. As she left, she pointed out an object nearby, an art object. It was about three feet long and had a lot of energy, so much that I could very easily touch and feel this energy. It was like the energy you feel around your body, except much stronger. I was so excited about it that I went up to tell my wife, who apparently had gone to sleep. I wanted to show her. I also wanted to share it with the kids. I felt like everybody could see and share this. I would like to know what the meaning of that object was.

MONITOR: We find that, in this dream, the symbol of the residence represents a symbol of the form in which you live. It has a lower area and an upper area, which symbolizes the lower and higher vibratory aspects of your being. More specifically, the object of power represents increased availability of energy in portions of your etheric body. Because you have been working to open certain chakras, your etheric energy supply—particularly that which enters through the back side of the heart chakra—now exhibits greater supply. The energizing, which you have been receiving, has made you more sensitive to etheric perception through *feeling* and *seeing*. In time, you will also experience etheric *hearing*.

In the dream, the agent responsible for most of this is your Female Self, who is represented by the lady who came into your being to assist or heal. Massage, as a symbol, represents the use of the sense of *touch*, which has been the most advanced sense in your sensory perception of etheric energy. Your sense of *sight* has lagged behind, and your sense of *hearing* has not yet been actualized.

With your discovery of the energetic object, you went upstairs, where your wife symbolizes the feminine aspects of your being, beyond that of your Female Self. In this sense, the feminine represents the qualities of *acceptance* or absorption of nourishment. This experience displays your attempt to *assimilate* etheric energizing in your astral and mental bodies, which are considered higher vibratory levels than the etheric. Does this address your dream?

BOB: Yes, thank you very much.

VIEW OF GOD AS PUNISHER

JULIE: I'd like to slip in an "origins" question that was asked by a friend who is not here with us. She asks, "Where did the concept of God as a punishing, domineering authority figure come from? How did that concept begin?"

MONITOR: That point of view began as a larger number of human beings gained some contact with their Judge Selves. Essentially this concept represents the view of God held by the collective Judge Selves of humanity. To understand why this development occurred requires considerable explanation, and if you wish to go into that, we will comply.

JULIE: We'll do that at another time. I think this will do for now. Thank you.

MONITOR: We further comment that the view of God as a punisher or a punishing parent reflects the relatively childlike state of the Judge Self in comparison to the Male and Female Selves. A Judge Self finds itself more isolated from experience than the Male and Female Selves. It views the High Self with suspicion and mistrust. It fears for its very existence and is suspicious of all attempts in the human personality to express powers which it itself has not expressed.

It has known Love in ages long ago, but has spent a long time dwelling in relative darkness. So it fears Light, and it fears Love. Its concept of God as Creator has become quite distorted. Its experience of loss has led it to resent greater powers that may be blamed for its loss.

CORPUS CALLOSUM

BOB: The other morning I woke up and became aware of a dream that had just completed. It occurred to me that the feeling of becoming aware of the dream is very much like when you become aware of creative thinking. Are these processes similar?

MONITOR: We find these processes quite similar, and in time, brain wave research will reveal just that. The mechanism of the corpus callosum, which links right and left brain hemisphere functions, generates part of that sensation which you noted. The corpus callosum acts to integrate left and right brain functions, and when it is functioning well, it provides a sense of harmony, a sense of relatedness. These qualities are commonly felt in acts of creativity, especially where a sense of illumination or inspiration occurs. Commonly, when a person has a dream generated by the High Self, he/she experiences such sensations. This reflects the quality of energy or consciousness of the High Self and of the Soul, both of which are immensely creative.

JULIE: Would that same feeling be involved when we experience a true connection of masculine–feminine qualities?

MONITOR: Indeed, because that does correlate, in large part, with left and right brain functions.
Brain wave research is beginning to study the phenomenon of channeling and finds similar results to what we have described.

ARZANI: Regarding the corpus callosum, I know someone with severe epilepsy who had her corpus callosum severed to prevent seizures. Does that mean that it would be impossible for her Male and Female Basic Selves to communicate?

MONITOR: No, but more difficult for her to correlate sensations associated with them, because such sensations are transmitted through the mechanism of the senses which are normally correlated in centers of the brain acting in reflex from activities in the interplay of the sympathetic ganglia and the spinal cord. Therefore she would have difficulty correlating sensations involving left and right brain hemisphere reflexes. Because her mind is not limited to the condition of the brain, she would still be quite capable of integrating Male and Female Selves.

ARZANI: Would that be done more in the etheric body than the physical?

MONITOR: It is always done in the etheric body, because the physical body is only an extension or shadow of the etheric body. The etheric body has no division in the corpus callosum.

This can be confusing to human beings who are indoctrinated to the reality of the physical body. This is why, in prior Lessons, we have suggested that you consider that your senses function on the level of the etheric body, not the physical body.

Once you begin to identify experiences of your senses functioning *etherically*, you find it easier to conceive the reality of the etheric body. Until you achieve such a point of conception, you are hampered by the distracting thought of the reality of the physical body.

We have indicated that, in time, this idea of the physical body will become obsolete. The reality of the etheric body will be increasingly recognized. When it is scientifically identified, measured, and studied, a great transformation will occur in the attitude of the general public.

ETHERIC EFFECT ON HAIR

LINDA: I have a question about energy, I think. Once a month I get my hair colored. The last three or four months, I've had a real problem with the color staying. My hairdresser asked me, "What is it you're doing that's different in the last three or four months?" "Nothing that I can think of." And then I realized that I've been coming here since April and also asking Monitor to come in when I'm asleep to work with me and my Selves. On those nights, I wake up in the middle of the night, and my head is really wet from perspiration from the energy of whatever's been going on. I would like to know, and my hairdresser would also like to know, if this energy has been turning my hair purple.

MONITOR: The difference in the energy experienced by your body has made a distinct difference in this regard. We describe the difference as your body absorbing more energy on several levels. In doing so, the cells, molecules, and atoms of your body are changing vibration. Your body therefore has a greater need for enhanced elimination to rid itself of cells that are outmoded in vibration. Your skin, which is one of the means of elimination as sweat carries waste products out of the pores, becomes more sensitized to the chemical components used in the hair dye.

LINDA: Thank you. I appreciate the answer.

MONITOR: If you ask us what you should do about it, we would refer you back to your hairdresser.

LINDA: I was going to ask, but I was afraid you would say that. *[Laughter]*

PHYSICAL AND ETHERIC BODIES

LOIS: I want to go back to the discussion of the etheric body. With the things that we humans are doing on this Earth at this time, and the possibility of the destruction of the physical form as we know it, is there any plan in the future that we might continue on this Earth in etheric bodies, giving up our physical form?

MONITOR: You inhabit the physical form only because of certain vibratory conditions that were necessary for human development and the development of several other Life forms. The physical vibration constitutes an artifact. It has no fundamental basis in vibratory principle.

To place this in terms of a musical analogy, the physical vibration exists only as an undertone, a lower harmonic of the etheric. It, the physical, has no true basis, on its own, for existing. The Life force is not transmitted through the physical, but through the etheric. The physical exists as merely an artifact, a shadow, a projection.

Therefore, changes in planetary environmental conditions will indeed do away with the physical form. But that will be a *glorious* occurrence. It will remove the basis for much confusion. All of us look forward to that time.

When human beings realize the form that they truly occupy, they will be much more open to perceive other Life forms with whom they need to establish harmonious relationships. The growth of consciousness in the Planetary Being will then be greatly facilitated.

Let us use this analogy. If you fell in a mud puddle and lost consciousness, you would awake covered with mud. With the force of the blow on your brain, you would not remember prior existence. You would conceive of yourself as a being of mud, which is quite confusing to all the other human beings who are *not* covered with mud. And because your eyes and ears are covered with mud, you are not able to recognize or communicate with them, even though they desire to assist you out of your condition. When they seek to touch you and remove the mud, you become frightened and drive them off out of fear. We believe this is an appropriate analogy for the condition of a human being in physical form. Do you understand us?

LOIS: Yes, that's a very hopeful thought. Thank you.

DREAM ABOUT SUBCONSCIOUS SELVES

HELEN: I have a dream I'd like to share. We had moved, and I'd been wandering around a beautiful church building. I'd admired a huge beautiful statue of Mother Mary on the side of the building. It's white, trimmed in blue, with places for candles and flowers. This is actually like a part of the architecture, built into the side of the church. I say that it's nice to be a part of a new church and watch the improvements being added as it grows. I look inside one door, and it seems to be a large confessional. I hear a priest say, "Anyone else?" A boy asks if it's too late for him to go, and the priest answers, "Never for you, George. Come on in." I go back outside and ask my oldest daughter if she would like to go to confession. She says, "No."

I had been brooding about a Latin class that was supposed to be in progress, but wasn't. I couldn't find the teacher. She's an old cosmetology teacher of mine. While I was waiting, I had also been holding on my lap my younger daughter, who is only about three or four years old in the dream, and talking to her about things at the church. There was a doll–like elemental figure in the flower garden. Now as I looked at it, it was gone. Someone said it had gone inside. I said, "Someone should be watching it. It shouldn't be allowed to wander off on its own." Next I'm sitting outside on a high ledge, edged in flat rock, still waiting for the Latin class. Someone grabs me and says, "Hi, gorgeous. Where have you been all my life?" It's Harry Young, an old boyfriend from way back, cleanly shaven and looking very young. I say how wonderful it is to see him. I ask what's new in his life, what's he doing here, etc. He moves away and sits alone for a moment until I tell him to come back and tell me. He does, and says he just signed up for a new job serving meals on a ship on the West Coast. I say he should have asked me to join him first. I would have said, "Yes." That's it.

MONITOR: We find that this is a dream from your High Self indicating some changes with your Male and Female and Judge Selves. The figure of Mary in the church represents a symbol of devotion, which is directed to the High Self, Soul, and the Creator, or God. There are aspects in the dream that readily relate to that path of devotion, and those that do not, at the moment, relate to it.

The figure in the garden represents your Astral Judge Self who is beginning to enter into that devotion, where it has previously avoided any contact. This represents distinct progress.

The figure of the man, Harry Young, represents both your Male Self and the activity of your entire personality. He has moved into a type of service upon the water, the ocean, which in this instance represents emotions. He represents, in some ways, an option in your life that you have perhaps wished you had taken. His name is Young, and he looked young.

This sense of having missed an opportunity and then having the opportunity reappear is part of the renewal which takes place in both conscious and subconscious levels of mind when it seeks contact with the Divine. In many situations, people lose hope because they experience lost opportunities. As one focuses upon one's own Divinity and connection with Divinity in all of Life, one finds that nothing is ever lost. Opportunities appear when they are for the highest good to appear.

Remember that the conscious and subconscious levels of mind require choices in order to grow. In order to grow into a state of Oneness with Divinity, they must make many choices. Some of their choices seem acts of obedience and others seem acts of rebellion. They learn from each choice and, through consequent experiences of pleasure and pain, evaluate the wisdom of their choices.

In this dream you have a building sense of devotion, yet you have the aspect of your oldest daughter, who chooses not to enter the structure. Because she does not enter into the structure does not mean that she is excluded or excluding. It simply is not the appropriate time for her. This aspect of the dream, we find, applies to your concerns about her at the present time, while other aspects of the dream are symbols of some of your past experiences.

Do you wish any more illumination of the dream that we might supply?

HELEN: The age of the younger daughter, of three or four, being nurtured more or less on my knee, what significance does that have?

MONITOR: This relates to your memories. Consider what was occurring in your life when that daughter was that age. Consider your relationship with God at that time. Consider your integration or lack of integration as a personality at that time.

DREAM WORK

MONITOR: And let us advise all of you, who seek to have us interpret all dreams and all aspects of all dreams, that we will sometimes turn part of the job back to you, which is quite appropriate for us to do.

In approaching conclusion for this evening, we give you notice that during this month of discussing dreams and dream experiences, we will endeavor to share with you ways to interpret your experiences in the dream state. We invite you to apply those ideas we share in interpreting dreams that you have in the coming weeks. We assist you to develop your capability for utilizing the richness of your dream experiences. So, note the types of symbols discussed, the types of interpretations given.

This evening we have emphasized the role of Subconscious Selves in the structure of dreams, which is a subject that has *not* been sufficiently addressed in dream research.

Another level of interpretation, regarding the structure of the human personality as it applies to dreams, might be dream interpretation as it applies to the Body Consciousness, or Body Self. You have an entire range of experience within the consciousness of your bodies.

Often, your dreams are used to communicate to you, the Outer Self, a state or condition within your physiology. You might consider dreams from that aspect, as well as other aspects.

We invite you, if you have studied dreams from the viewpoint of various authorities, to bring statements from those authorities to our future meetings on this topic. Share different viewpoints and create greater wealth of understanding. We hope that we have provided some stimulation for you. You have stimulated us, we assure you. We thank you now, and we leave you.

TOOLS FOR EXPLORATION
Exercise 11

IDENTIFY SELVES IN YOUR DREAMS

1. Make notes of your dreams on a regular basis. While reviewing your notes about a dream, consider the following questions.

2. Write down the descriptive actions, emotions, and attitudes of the major characters in the dream. As you review what you have written, which of the dream characters exhibits *traits* that you can connect with your Inner Selves?

    Traits Matching Inner Self

    Dream character 1:

    Dream character 2:

    Dream character 3:

3. If you perceive a clear connection between a dream character and one of your Inner Selves, write the *plot* of the dream—the action or transformation that takes place in the dream, or how a character changes or does not change.

    Dream character Inner Self Action or transformation

4. If step 3 makes sense to you, considering what you know about your Inner Selves, you might have interpreted the dream successfully as a status report of *interaction among Selves.*

5. If that interpretation does *not* seem productive, consider the dream as a status report about the *dynamics of one Self.*

6. Taking into consideration the dynamics (action or transformation) of the entire dream, who is the single Self it best describes?

7. What does the dream tell you about that Self?

    What is its situation? (conflict, harmony, etc.)

    What are its reactions? (fleeing, fighting, searching, loving, finding, etc.)

    What are its emotions? (fear, anger, guilt, love, joy, etc.)

    What are its options? (hide, confront, accept, reject, etc.)

    What are its intentions?

How do you, the Outer Self, feel about the Self as it is portrayed in the dream?

8. How can you assist that Self to improve?

9. Now talk with that Self via inner dialogue. Ask it how it feels about your interpretation of the dream. Write what it says.

10. Ask that Self how it wants you to help it improve. Write what it says.

11. Commit yourself to provide at least one specific act of assistance to that Self. Write down that commitment for assistance, including when you will do it.

Lesson 19
August 14, 1991

MONITOR: We welcome you as Monitor.

GROUP: Good evening, Monitor.

BIRD TRIBES

JULIE: I would like to start with one quick question from a friend who asks, "Since you are a group of entities, are you also known as the "Bird Tribes?"

MONITOR: We have been identified with the Bird Tribes on occasion, and our activity relates sometimes to the activities attributed to the Bird Tribes. Yet we at times function in areas beyond their function. So we are not totally synonymous with the Bird Tribes, yet are quite supportive of them and they supportive of us, since we overlap in purposes.

DREAM ABOUT ILLUSION OF FEMALE SELF

ARZANI: I wrote down a dream that I think has a message for me about some misconceptions I have about my spiritual growth. I want to ask you about it.

I dreamt I was visiting my friend Mary Jo's new house. I was there alone, sitting in the kitchen. The kitchen, we had always felt, would be a very sunny room because it had a southern window, but this kitchen wasn't sunny. I went into the living room, which we thought wasn't going to be a sunny room because it had windows that looked onto a wall, but that room was very sunny for some reason. So I was sitting in the living room, and it was light there. Then Mary Jo came in, and I explained that I was showing her house to my husband, Doug. She didn't react especially to the fact that I had entered her house when she wasn't there. I told Doug I thought it was a nice house, about the same price as ours—although it really was $20,000 more, and I knew that. He was impressed, and I didn't correct his impression. I liked her house because it was new. It had a lot less space than ours and no backyard, but I liked the high ceilings and the new kitchen, new appliances, and the large windows. And then Mary Jo told me that the builder had gone bankrupt before completing the development, and she hoped that the unbuilt homes would sell. The first thing I thought of was that her monthly fee for the pool and everything would be higher, and I wondered if she knew that, but I didn't think to say it to her.

That's the dream. I wonder, being that it's about a house, whether I'm concentrating maybe on the wrong chakras, with the Light being in a different place than I expected it.

MONITOR: We find that this dream is submitted by your High Self to illuminate a discrepancy of understanding or value on the part of your Female Self. In the dream, she is motivated to enter a house of a friend—not her own house—and finds greater value in the house of the friend than she does in her own house. This discrepancy in values is important to note, for we find within your Female Self a tendency to de–value her own home, which includes the physical body, the physical home, and the home relationship. She sometimes prefers something better. As the saying goes, "The grass is greener on the other side of the fence."

This represents in the Female Self a tendency to not accept what she already has manifested. She seeks to find something greater, which causes her to give away her power to illusions. This makes her vulnerable to the Mental Judge Self, who may then lead her more readily into illusions of expectation.

Once she accepts an illusion of expectation, she is subject to the illusion of lack or loss. So we note her sense of values as involving a discrepancy, because it weakens her and is more based on illusion than truth.

In the dream we see the discrepancy reflected. She expects the Light to be in the kitchen, but it is found in the living room. She discusses other items that she has knowledge of, but does not express accurately, such as the accurate price of the friend's home.

In the dream you have the symbol of the builder going bankrupt, which is a statement that the basis for construction of her viewpoint is faulty and bankrupt because it is based on illusion. We believe this is the main point we would comment upon.

DREAM ABOUT COMMUNICATION WITH A TREE

MARY: I have two experiences I wanted to get some feedback on. They both occurred as I was waking up. In one, I woke up and was talking to the spirit in the tree that I'm going to cut down—don't ask me how. Essentially the conversation was about the fact that the tree needed to come down, what would happen, and how I would protect the area for the spirit. And the other dream this morning was seeing a face that was an alien face, and then experiencing like a turning over, as if the capsule or the ship they were in was turning over. There was fire, and people were being hurt. That was both of those experiences. I wonder what they relate to.

MONITOR: We find the first experience being a communication to you from your Female Self, informing you of your communication with the tree. Is the tree an actual tree?

MARY: Yes.

MONITOR: Even though it is a physical reality to you, it also represents a symbol. The symbol might be discussed in various ways, but we note the meaning of the good gardener pruning the vines that they might be more abundant.

The tree represents elements in your life where you have used the creative force of Life to create. The symbol of cutting the tree down represents a need to establish new priorities for your creative endeavors and to cut down or cut back those that are not truly productive. Your Female Self wants you, the Outer Self, to take this kind of productive step. Often human beings find it difficult to make priority decisions, yet priority decisions are extremely important in making progress on the spiritual path.

DREAM ABOUT STRESSED OUTERSPACIAL MALE SELF

MONITOR: The second incident is projected from your Male Self, who, in his outerspacial aspect, is in communication with outerspacial beings and is part of a plan integrated through the plans of the Spiritual Hierarchy to assist this planet on the part of those who are here from your Soul's star of origin. Your Male Self maintains that connection within your personality and functions during your sleep time to perform actions which implement that plan.

His message to you, through that dream experience, is that difficulties have occurred in that plan involving unexpected opposition from another group of star beings. If you understand that beings from many star systems are present in your solar system and are concerned with actions in planet Earth, you will realize that some of them have conflicting or competing interests. Your Male Self does not require you to understand such things, but informs you that he is stressed as he does his part to assist those beings from your home star system in a time of difficulty. Do you understand us?

MARY: Yes. Is there anything I can do to help?

MONITOR: You may, if you wish, pray, asking for Divine assistance for your Male Self and those whom he assists. That will be sufficient.

DREAM ABOUT STRESSED FEMALE SELF

HELEN: I had a dream I'd like to share. I had asked this after an evening of working, I believe, with my Soul. Before sleep, we were to ask for a dream from our Soul. The dream is: I am somewhere where a meeting was to take place. Instead, two to four men are playing instruments. They take a break. I say to someone that this is not what I came for. I gave up a Sunday evening, and we're not learning anything. We decide to leave. Sissy—an old friend of mine who has since passed to the other side—meets someone on the way out and decides to dance with him. I have trouble finding my way out. I think I lose a shoe, but someone says, "You have both shoes on." I look down and see that I do.

I get outside and can't find my car. A dog comes up to me. I feel his teeth with my hand and know they are sharp, but he doesn't bite me. He has a leash on, and I think he must have gotten away from someone. He seems to be better in knowing that someone is guiding him. He pulls a lot and doesn't know where he wants to go. I finally let him go. I had seen some suspicious-looking characters around before, and I felt the dog was a safety device against them.

I come to some buildings and go in. I keep turning into more rooms without doors to the outside. I find some children. A little girl tells me that she will help me find my way to a street. She leads me in and out of more rooms. They are shabby and messy, and we pass people from time to time. I can see water through the windows like swimming pools and/or natural lakes, but we can't find a door leading outside to get to them. Earlier, before I left, I said I didn't have a purse, and I had my car keys in my pocket. None of this was a nice experience.

MONITOR: We find that this is a dream from your Female Self, making you aware that your Male Self has been, in her view, overly rigid in his maintenance of responsibilities. She has a preference for music and dance, creative actions that bring a certain degree of vitality into your personality and body. She feels that she is having to act in ways which at times threaten the Male Self, but which have value. In the dream, the meeting where learning was supposed to occur, did not occur. Instead there was music. The music was not recognized as a positive experience, yet your friend began to dance on leaving the meeting.

The lack of a car or vehicle refers to the state of the physical body. If you review which of your inner Selves is primarily responsible for the care of your physical body, you will find that some change of assignment has occurred over a period of years where your Male Self and Female Self have sometimes exchanged areas of responsibility in caring for the physical body.

The dog represents potential fear for the physical body deteriorating or "going to the dogs." The dog shows teeth but does not bite, which indicates that this dream is providing a message of warning, indicating that the responsibilities for the care of the physical body need to be clarified as they are presently distributed between Male and Female Selves. The dog, which represents the Body Consciousness, the elemental consciousness of the physical body, wishes to be guided. Who guides the dog in the dream? In this instance, the Female Self, which is proper at this time.

The entry into the rundown house reflects the fears of deteriorating structure within the body. The view of water through the windows reflects the fear of negative emotions, which can result if responsibilities are not clarified in the near future. The loss of the shoe reflects the loss of half of the understanding. It reflects the Female Self's viewpoint that half of the understanding has been lost by the Male Self. Now, realize that the Male Self may not share this perspective.

We find that you have been more receptive, in general, to the communication of your Male Self than to the communication of your Female Self. She has given you this dream in order to reflect her viewpoint and gain your assistance in asking the High Self to clarify the responsibilities of Male and Female Selves, especially that concerning the physical body. Is this sufficient?

HELEN: Originally I had the understanding that the physical body was completely the responsibility of the Female Self, and that the Male Self only has responsibility for the chakras. Could you tell me how that has changed?

MONITOR: That changed approximately three years ago.

HELEN: And now?

MONITOR: What the High Self introduced at that time was an action of cooperation between Male and Female Selves.

HELEN: For all the responsibilities?

MONITOR: They may learn cooperation by sharing an area of responsibility. An exchange was arranged whereby the Female Self, who had been previously too flighty and undependable, would take over a function that required consistent responsible action. In her view, she has met her challenge. In the Male Self's view, he finds drawbacks in her performance. We emphasize that you will do well to ask your High Self to clarify their respective responsibilities.

PHYSICAL MANIFESTATION OF DREAMS

DOUG: I'd like to ask a couple of questions on dynamics of dreaming. The first one I have relates to the time between having a dream and having it manifest in reality. If something is resolved in a dream, how long before we can expect it to happen physically?

MONITOR: The time between the dream action of resolution and its manifestation varies from person to person and from different levels of energy manifestation. One person may have sufficient ability to manifest almost immediately changes that occur in the physical, emotional, and mental life of that person. Another person may take months or, in some cases, even years to achieve equivalent manifestation.

The manifestation of a *mental* change is most likely to occur quite soon after the dream event. *Emotional* change takes longer, and *physical* change even longer yet. We find no general way to estimate the timing, except as these factors are taken into consideration.

As an instructive project, a person might consider noting the length of time it takes for such resolutions in a dream to manifest. Such a study would be quite useful. Some people have the ability to see the connection between their inner and outer lives. Having that perspective contributes greatly to what we have termed "continuity of consciousness." When you have continuity of consciousness, you learn more rapidly because you are able to recognize the linkage between inner cause and outer effect. If you lack continuity of consciousness, you take longer to learn, because the linkage of cause and effect may not be clear to you. If a person studies the timing of their rate of manifestation on mental, emotional, and physical levels, he/she will benefit greatly. We thank you for raising the question.

INTERPRETATION OF DREAM SYMBOLS

DOUG: Several books have been written which generalize the symbols of dreams, and we've run across a couple tonight where a house represents the body and a car can also represent the body, and water displays emotion. I'm wondering if you could give comment to that generalization of symbols in dreams, whether it makes sense to buy into somebody else's symbols or not.

MONITOR: When a person is learning to interpret the symbology of dreams, knowledge of general symbol meanings has value. Knowing the general meaning of symbols allows a person to understand the probable subject of the dream. Once a person gains proficiency in symbol interpretation by general meaning, then it is important to become much more specific in interpretation of personal meanings.

In the dream you cited, the house was seen as a symbol of the physical body. That offered an appropriate personal meaning. If a person does not know if that particular symbol in their dream means the physical body, he/she could explore several other possible meanings.

If a person has the capability of asking which Inner Self communicated the message in the dream, the person may ask that Self specifically what a particular symbol means. This type of skill represents an advanced level of dream interpretation, saves much time, and avoids the risk of unfocused or misleading interpretations. Did this address your question?

DOUG: Yes. Thank you.

DREAM ABOUT PURIFICATION BY DIVINE FIRE

LOIS: I had a dream this week that I went through some kind of process that I can't remember. At the end of the process I was set on fire, and I became a cone of fire, inverted with small end to a group and large end upward. It was very beautiful, with colors of red and gold and orange, and it didn't hurt. I wasn't at all frightened. I wonder what that dream meant.

MONITOR: We find that the symbol in your dream of being set on fire represents a type of purification by the energy of what is termed "Divine Mind" or "manas." The cone shape reveals the influence that is greater at the top of your form and lesser at the bottom. This type of purification represents purification of the atomic structure of your etheric and astral bodies. The purifying agent is the Divine Fire of Mind, which manifests first in your causal body, then enters through your mental body to your astral and etheric bodies. Your physical body is purified as well, as the etheric body completes the process.

The dream burning is a very positive step in your development and signals your release from limitations, especially in the astral body, which you have carried from previous lifetimes. You may consider that type of physical karma of burning has been completed.

In general terms, as applied to people in general, fire experienced in such a form represents most often the ending of a cycle. The fire, which is broader at the base and narrower at the top, may well represent the beginning of a cycle that is initiated by the spark of Divine Mind in order that karmic patterns may be appropriately initiated, recognized, and resolved. Does this address your dream sufficiently?

LOIS: Yes, thank you very much.

GEOPHYSICAL ALIGNMENT DURING SLEEP

LOIS: Does it make any difference which way you sleep in the energy field of the planet?

MONITOR: We believe you are referring to geophysical alignment of the physical body during sleep. Is that so?

LOIS: Yes.

MONITOR: The alignment of the physical body does make a difference, not only during sleep but also during other states of consciousness as well. The most harmonious relationship that the human body may have with the energy fields of the present world is that of facing east. If one is standing, sitting, or lying down, the head would be to the east for greatest experiences of harmony.

When the head is oriented to the west, one will have an increasing tendency to experience memories and emotions connected with past actions.

Facing to the east represents a more open attitude, both in completing actions of the past and accepting actions occurring in the present.

With the head facing north, a person experiences a greater affiliation with the forces of mind as they reflect Spirit.

As the head faces south, a person experiences the forces of the physical body and emotions as they reflect Spirit.

The geophysical alignment of the physical body represents a significant factor and should be researched. Brain wave studies and studies of other physiological factors may reveal significant differences in different geophysical alignments of the body. Does this address your question?

LOIS: Yes, it does.

DREAM ABOUT JUDGE SELF ANXIETY

DONNA: I have a dream. It seems like I was giving a dinner party. The first part went off okay, and there were scads of people there. Then something seemed to go wrong. Some of the food wasn't put out because it wasn't ready. Others went out to bring back ingredients. Finally the young people were singing and the older gang was drinking, and it didn't seem like anyone would get the rest of their dinner. I was having an anxiety attack and was thankful to be awake.

MONITOR: We find that this dream is from your Mental Judge Self, who fears that the other elements of the personality would not learn their lessons. Your Mental Judge Self has developed the role of attempting to pace the other Selves in their rate of learning, which is *not* an appropriate role. You are well advised to ask your High Self to instruct and assist your Judge Self to learn how to perform more useful functions.

To generalize from this dream, most anxiety dreams reveal the fears of a Judge Self. Anxiety dreams may also reveal the fears of the Outer Self and of Basic Selves.

When you analyze your dream, determine what the major threat appears to be. If you are on good speaking terms with your Mental Judge Self, you may ask it that question directly. What in the dream represents the threat to the Mental Judge Self? If you are not on such good terms with it, then you must fish for the answer. You may find that your High Self will offer true assistance.

When you have dreams of anxiety, fear, and panic, you would do well to understand that you are being given the gift of assistance in releasing your fears. Nightmares may seem quite disturbing to you, but recognize them as gifts from your Higher Consciousness. Nightmares and disturbing dreams help you identify your fears and release them.

The Outer Self often believes that it is free of fears and then has a nightmare. This process of dream revelation helps the Outer Self recognize the fears held by Subconscious Selves. If the Outer Self is able to communicate readily with those Selves, the fear may be resolved quickly through cooperative action of the elements of the personality. If the Outer Self does not have that capability, more time and effort are required to recognize the precise fear being revealed. Remember that the release of fear exists as a high priority in the growth of all human beings.

DREAMS ARE THERAPEUTIC

DONNA: Are you saying that a dream is therapeutic, even if it is not remembered or understood?

MONITOR: Indeed. Human beings do not remember most of their dreams. We find that they remember only about *one to five percent* of their dreams, at the most. Only those persons, who have built that faculty which we call "continuity of consciousness," have ability to remember most of their dreams.

DREAM PREPARATION FOR CHANNELING

JOYCE: I have a question about a sleep experience. For years I've been having some interruption of my sleeping by a voice trying to speak through me. It began when I was taking a channeling class and missed the first class on protection. I was able to keep it under control by receiving Divine Light on a regular basis, but did not have it removed. I wanted to remove it because it was waking me up. The voice would usually wait until I was about ready to awaken and then speak through me. Sometimes it gave messages. Sometimes the voice would come through just as a noise, but the words would come into my head. And one time I had an extraterrestrial tell me that was where it was coming from. But it was something I did *not* want. Lately I've been sleeping with a candle every night, and that has prevented it from happening. I wonder if I have to continue using the candle, or is there anything else I can do?

MONITOR: We find that you are *not* truly subject to abuse by an outside force. What you are experiencing comes through your Male Self, who is *not* trying to abuse you but trying to help you fulfill your accomplishment of the role of channel.

If you ask your Male Self to desist in this practice—which is quite well-motivated—we believe that he will desist. From his perspective, he is trying to pass on to you information from higher sources. This is what he believes you have asked for.

In your attempt to learn channeling, you were not taught about Inner Selves. When a person who learns to channel does not know the Inner Selves, he/she may often become confused, because Inner Selves form a necessary linkage in the chain of channeled communication. If a person recognizes their role and appreciates their assistance, the quality of reception distinctly improves. Often, when the quality of reception is not sufficiently high, Inner Selves are frequently responsible, because they feel neglected by the Outer Self. Do you understand us?

JOYCE: Yes, I do understand. I have the choice of either asking the Male Self to cease and desist, or asking it to refrain from waking me up and set up another time to listen to the messages?

MONITOR: We suggest that you first thank your Male Self for diligently helping you. His efforts deserve your recognition. Then you may make an agreement with him for another time during your waking state for the communication to take place. You will have no further trouble being awakened for that reason.

JOYCE: Would it have to be a specific time of day?

MONITOR: Whatever is necessary to gain your Male Self's agreement. He is not difficult to deal with.

JOYCE: He chooses to speak through me that way, as opposed to putting pictures or words in my head?

MONITOR: He understood that your desire was to be a channel for higher teachings. Being a channel, in his interpretation, involves speaking, not simply receiving.

JOYCE: Okay. Thank you.

MALE SELF USES SLEEPING BODY

NANCY: During the past week I had requested to remember to write down dreams. I have not had any narrative dreams, maybe a flash, like a snapshot. Last night, around 5 AM, I discovered that my telephone was off the hook. The handset was on the floor. The base of the instrument was on the nightstand next to my bed. But I had no conscious memory whatsoever having anything to do with that telephone.

MONITOR: That experience was motivated primarily by your Male Self, who does not always have an appropriate concept of how you, the Outer Self, should be treated. We find that he is growing somewhat anxious, fearing that he may not complete his lessons for this lifetime. In his anxiousness, he has been appropriating use of your body while you, the Outer Self, lie dormant. This is *not* appropriate. He exceeds his proper boundaries. We recommend that you ask the High Self or Higher Power—whichever you recognize—to instruct him to observe proper boundaries. Do you understand?

NANCY: I think so.

DREAM ABOUT SEXUAL CHOICES

LEAH: I have a dream in which my husband, my brother, and I were near a river. I noticed that my dog was being very well behaved, which was surprising to me and very comforting. He was not on a leash. We all kept talking, and then I looked down and noticed, a short time later, that the dog was gone. When I called him, he came and seemed disturbed. I noticed that he smelled of skunk. I confirmed this with my husband and decided that I would take him down to the river to wash him off. When I got to the river it was no longer my dog, it was my cat. I decided that he did not need to be washed off. Being a cat, he wouldn't appreciate it.

The next scene is that I am in the river, and the river is moving very fast. I felt I needed to get to the edge very soon, for farther down the stream was something that was very disturbing to me, possibly people or something. I had my cat with me in the river, and it was difficult for me to get to the edge. Sometimes, more often than I wanted, the cat's head was under the water. That was very disturbing to me, but I found that I needed to allow that to happen in order to get to the edge on time. I remembered thinking that my husband and brother were on the shore, not far away, but they did not know that I was in distress. The dream ended with me getting to shore and telling them about my experience.

MONITOR: We find this dream to be motivated by your High Self, who wishes you to become more aware of the effects of some of your decisions and actions. Once you become aware of what causes the actions, which you do *not* enjoy, you will be more capable of making wise choices and avoiding unpleasant consequences.

The dog represents the action of the first chakra, which represents affection and also sexuality. The actions of the dog reflect concerns that these energies have been, are, or will be, moving beyond control.

The image of the dog changes to that of the cat, which represents the energies of the third chakra. When the energies of the dog, or first chakra, are brought under control, the energies of the third chakra tend to over-control. The cat then is loath to experience the water, which represents the energies of emotions.

A number of emotions form the basis for the tendency to over-control. The cat and you, the Outer Self, are drawn into the river and swept along, which represents a loss of control in the flow of life experience. Much of that experience represents emotional experience. The net effect is cleansing, but it distresses you, the Outer Self, and the cat (your third chakra) where stress accumulates in your body.

The smell of the skunk represents the negative consequences of the dog's actions. The negative consequences must be cleansed. We assure you that, in the dream, the cleansing does take place, but it has not been pleasant because you, the Outer Self, have not fully been aware of the relationship between your choice and the results of those choices.

As you examine your experiences, in the use of the energies of the first chakra, you will realize how you have reacted. On many occasions, you have reacted with the tendency to over-control, which is *not* the best reaction, but perhaps the best that you have been able to manage with the degree of awareness you have utilized.

As you gain greater self–awareness, your capabilities for control will become more effective and balanced, enabling you to experience greater freedom and greater creativity in your life expression. Do you understand?

LEAH: I think so. Thank you.

JULIE: It looks as though our time has about run out. Do you have any closing ideas for us, Monitor?

EXPERIMENT IN DREAM COMMUNICATION WITH SUBCONSCIOUS SELVES

MONITOR: We invite you to dream, asking a particular Inner Self to supply the dream. Consider this as a means of communication with that Inner Self. For example, if you ask your Male Self to communicate with you through a dream, your Male Self will use that dream to convey what he feels is important to communicate to you. You may consider any of your Inner Selves in this manner. In fact, if you wish to be ambitious, you might use this method to gain communications from *all* your Inner Selves that you know. We even encourage you to ask for a dream communication from your Body Self.

As you do this, in sharing dreams during our future meetings, we will appreciate your sharing your experiences with each other and with us, indicating which Self you asked for communication. We will, of course, be happy to elaborate on what occurred.

TOOLS FOR EXPLORATION
Exercise 12

ASKING A SELF FOR A DREAM

1. Consider the status of your Inner Selves. Select a Self who relates well with you. Write down that Self's name.

2. Ask your High Self to fill your personality with the Golden Light of Grace, especially the Self with whom you wish to communicate.

3. Mentally ask that Self to communicate with you through a dream that night.

4. Recall your dreaming the next morning and write notes about it.

5. If you have little or no dream recall, continue the exercise by writing on your dream note pad each night before bed, "I appreciate the assistance given by all Inner Selves in helping me achieve complete, accurate recall of my dream this night." Continue until you have dream recall.

6. In reviewing your dream notes, does a dream appear to be related to that Self?

7. If it does, what is that Self saying to you? What is the message of the dream? Write the answers that come to you.

8. Through inner dialogue, ask that Self how it feels about your interpretation of the dream message. Write its response.

9. Ask the Self, "Did I receive your complete message? If not, what do you want me to know that I missed in the dream?" Write its response.

10. Thank the Self for communicating with you.

PRAYER FOR MODERATION OF MAGMA FLOW

MONITOR: We also note that, at this time in the planet, stresses are beginning to accumulate in portions of the Pacific plate, especially those related to the Western Coast of South and Central America. We ask you to include this situation in your prayers, this evening and in the following week, asking that magma pressures be moderated. Do you understand?

JULIE: Yes, would you repeat, "portions of the Pacific plate along the coast of South America and…".

GROUP: Central America.

JULIE: Central and South America, the West Coast.

MONITOR: We thank you very much for your assistance and willingness to share your experiences and your learning. We very much appreciate the effort you are making. We thank you, and we leave.

GROUP: Thank you, Monitor. *[Group prays for Central and South America.]*

Lesson 20
August 21, 1991

MONITOR: We welcome you as Monitor. What do you wish?

JULIE: Well, we're ready with some questions, more about dreams.

MONITOR: You've been quite busy, haven't you?

JULIE: Yes, we have.

MONITOR: We know, because we have been with most of you through this time.

JULIE: We appreciate it. We do. Who would like to begin?

EFFECTIVE VISUALIZATION

ARZANI: I have two questions, Monitor, one from my lovely husband, Doug—who couldn't be here tonight—and one from myself. I'll start with

Doug's. He wanted to know if there was any difference in effect if, for example, you were to visualize love in your heart as part of a visualization exercise, or have that experience in a dream, or in a meditation, or in a hypnotic trance. Would the state of mind make a difference on what effect that experience had on your Soul and personality?

MONITOR: It would, indeed, make a difference when you consider the motivator of that state. When a person consciously visualizes the opening of the heart center, the motivator is primarily the Outer Self. When it happens in a hypnotic state, the motivator is primarily the hypnotist, who could be another person. In the case of hypnosis, the hypnotist motivates one of the Basic Selves, who then brings about the opening of the heart center.

In sleep, the opening of the heart center may be motivated by one of the Basic Selves, the High Self, or the Soul. In some instances, which are few in occurrence, the opening of the heart center may be motivated by a Teacher, another being who acts through the High Self of the person experiencing the opening.

As to the effectiveness of the heart center opening, it depends upon the cooperation of the Male or Female Self. It depends upon which of those Selves has been assigned responsibility for caring for the chakras. Does this answer your question?

ARZANI: It does answer it the way I put it, but Doug had not asked it with an example of opening the heart. He didn't give an example. So if it were just a dream, for example, with imagery that wasn't particularly related to a chakra, how does it work?

MONITOR: If, for example, the experience being sought is that of a physical condition—let us say, the warming of a foot—then it depends on the Basic Self assigned to care for the physical body. If the experience sought is that of a past life memory, then it depends on the Basic Self assigned responsibility for memory.

DREAM INFLUENCES ON COUPLES

ARZANI: Thank you. I hope that answers it for Doug. It certainly does for me. My other question is one that came up last week. What is the influence of sleeping as a couple, sleeping with another person? Does that affect the dream state?

MONITOR: Indeed it does, because the proximity of the astral and mental bodies of the couple make it quite likely that one body's condition affects the condition of the other. This does not mean, necessarily, that the two share the same dream. This happens quite rarely and depends on a very fine attunement of the mental bodies of both.

However, if one member of the couple experiences emotional distress in the dream state, that distress is most likely transmitted to the partner. Such distress is most likely transmitted by the astral body of one affecting the astral body of the other. Conversely, the experience of peace or enlightenment, which affects one partner, affects the other. The distress of one partner experiencing a dream of distress, where they find themselves threatened by some circumstance, is most likely transmitted to the other partner, but with a different format in which the partner observes someone in distress. In that circumstance, the partner may be motivated to assist or flee, but they most likely will not, themselves, be the focus of distress.

DREAMING FOR OTHERS

ARZANI: Is it possible to have a dream for another person?

MONITOR: Indeed, it is possible, and in some societies this has been raised to an art form. It constitutes one of the healing arts. For example, in the ancient temple of Aesculapius [Esklepios] in Greece, some individuals demonstrated ability to bring forth illuminating or Divine dreams. They became dream healers, where they brought forth dreams of diagnosis for ills experienced by others, and also dreams of healing power wherein they acted as channels of Divine energy to heal those with ills.

HEALING DREAMS

ARZANI: I've had dreams where I have healed other people. Some people have told me they had dreams of me coming to heal them, and sometimes both, where I was aware and they were aware.

MONITOR: Indeed. Human beings are quite active during the sleep state, but not in the mode of their Outer Selves. Their Outer Selves are close to one hundred percent dormant during that time in order to meet the needs for body regeneration. Also, most Outer Selves are not very capable of negotiating etheric, astral, and mental realms.

Most of the activity during sleep involves Subconscious Selves—the Male Self, the Female Self, and less frequently, the Judge Selves. They often are motivated to visit other people for various purposes. They are also motivated to pursue various activities, especially in the astral plane.

TEMPLES OF KNOWLEDGE AND WISDOM

JULIE: A number of years ago I had a recurring dream, where I would go to a place called the "Temple of Wisdom." Is that an actual place?

MONITOR: You can find a number of Temple of Wisdoms, which are advanced learning centers situated in the fourth, fifth, sixth and seventh levels of the astral plane and in the mental plane. They provide instruction to those motivated to seek wisdom. They bring about changes in those who seek.

Consider here, in your own being, who is it that seeks the Temple of Wisdom? Is it the Outer Self? We say, "No." The Male and Female Selves of persons find their way to the Temple of Wisdom. Yet most human beings at this time do *not* seek the Temple of Wisdom. They may seek, in the lower levels of the astral plane, the Temple of Knowledge. There are many more Temples of Knowledge. People go there to understand those aspects of Life that appear external in their experience.

One distinction between the Temple of Knowledge and the Temple of Wisdom is that the Temple of Knowledge imparts knowledge about events *external* to a person, while the Temple of Wisdom focuses intensely on events occurring *within* a person.

The Temple of Knowledge serves a very useful function. It helps many people gain greater understanding of events, which they can observe, and develop a sense of trust in the Teachers, the sources of information. What you have, in the physical plane in the form of educational institutions, represents a dim reflection of what is available in the Temple of Knowledge. It bears an even dimmer relationship to the Temple of Wisdom.

The Temple of Wisdom may be approached only as one is willing to submit to the processes of testing, whereby one demonstrates what one *knows* and what one *does*. Most of what must be demonstrated consists of inner skills, abilities to master the forms one occupies as a Life essence. The Temple of Wisdom focuses intensely upon self-knowledge and self-mastery.

Those who go to the Temple of Knowledge are often fearful of exploring their own selves, while those who go to the Temple of Wisdom may be fearful, but overcome their fear, pursue the testing and, through perseverance, become initiated to the deeper mysteries of inner mastery.

DREAM ABOUT FRUSTRATED FEMALE SELF

DONNA: I have a classroom dream. I was a class member at a college, but not one where I have actually gone. There seemed to be an argument between students and faculty. The students didn't think they were learning anything, and the faculty didn't think the students were taking enough responsibility for their work. I was in several different classrooms, but each time the argument was going on there was no regular class work. I was mildly upset. Can you shed any light on that dream?

MONITOR: We find that this dream reflects the viewpoint of your Female Self, as she relates to the Male Self and Mental Judge Self. She is frustrated at the impasse that has persisted in her relationships with each of them. She is aware of the need to grow. She knows that growth requires learning. Many of the lessons set before her involve relationships. Her primary relationships involve the Male Self, Mental Judge Self, and High Self. She relates to the High Self satisfactorily, but not to the other two Selves. The dream conveys her frustration.

If you, the Outer Self, would assist her, ask your High Self to assist the Male and Mental Judge Selves. In this case, assistance may bring those experiences necessary to motivate each of them to extend themselves in learning and relationship, especially with the Female Self. Does this address your dream?

DONNA: Yes, I think so. Thank you.

DREAMS ABOUT MALE SELF'S LIMITATIONS

BOB: Through the last couple of weeks I've only been blessed with one night of dreams, but that night I had three different scenes and have been unable to get an interpretation that made sense to me.

I was upstairs in a house and had to urinate. I was with a man, but in order to relieve myself I had to go downstairs. I went downstairs into a basement, and the urinal was a large flat rock or stone with only a small hole in the middle. The stone was raised, and I had to stand near the edge and aim for the hole. A young boy was present with me, standing to my left. I got the impression that he was the son of a boss or superior who was with me upstairs. Since there were close quarters, he had to be there. A young man or young boy—I had the sense that he was my youngest son – was on my right. To add further to the situation, I had an erection, which caused me minor embarrassment. It also took me quite a while to accomplish the task. Then I realized this was the second time that I'd been down there to the rock.

Then I was at another location, where a group of people was getting into a boat. But the boat was only a framework made out of pipe. The boat was about ten to twelve feet wide and thirty to forty feet long. Some people were getting into the boat—twenty or so. They were going to ride the boat down a hill, like a slide or a sled, a number of times. When they rode down, they were packed in with snow. That seemed like an unusual circumstance.

Someone on the hill was engaged in sexual intercourse in what's known as the "69 position." One partner suffered because his partner bit off the end of his penis.

The third scene occurred later in the evening or in the morning. I was crossing a set of railroad tracks and was traveling to the west. To my left was a large locomotive driven by someone I knew. It was stationary. I was with some other people, although I don't know who they were. I crossed in front of the locomotive, across the tracks, and noticed there was a red light flashing. I was unconcerned about that. As I crossed the tracks, I realized that I was at the end of a drag strip, at the end that the cars approached. As I was crossing the end of the drag strip, I saw a slow–moving vehicle being used to clear the track. It was a red vehicle that had a lot of damage, sheet metal damage. I also noticed a guardrail at the end of the track. The red vehicle went across the track, even though that was beyond where cars normally stopped. I thought it was unusual to have protection across the track, as opposed to having it open. I attempted to go down to the stands to watch the race. As I was trying to make the decision, someone tried to sell me a car. It wasn't a racecar. One of the features of the car was that it had a lot of space inside. The seat could be laid down, giving it room inside.

MONITOR: We find that this series of dreams represents three statements of the view of your Male Self. In each segment, the Male Self is concerned about restrictions about which he is, as yet, undecided. Your Male Self is beginning to discover that he has been imposing limitations on himself, and that he has the possibility of releasing those limitations. His awareness is only in the beginning stages. Therefore he finds himself acting in ways that encounter self-imposed limitations and he is not yet capable of moving beyond those limitations. Each of the three dream segments express this type of perception.

In the first segment, his concern relates to performance. His limitations are represented by a sense of others observing, which represents the limitation that he has created concerning what other people may think of his performance.

The second segment relates to his sense of limitation about relationships, where the people were contained in a pipe boat. Even though it functioned successfully, he has concerns about being locked or frozen into relationships. He is just becoming aware that it is a self-imposed limit.

In the third segment, we find a restatement of limitations, in this case, dealing with the field of possibilities. The drag strip has its limit, and the guardrail constitutes an inappropriate limit, one that could cause damage.

He is offered the opportunity of a vehicle that has more space than he is used to.

In this explanation, we only touch upon the general features of the dream segments and leave to you more specific applications. Does this assist you?

BOB: Yes, thank you very much.

DREAMS ABOUT DISINCARNATE MOTHER

LOIS: Monitor, my mother left her body in 1980, and we were very close. During her death process I had a fragrance of roses all around me. I know that she must have left with a lot of love. During the years that have passed, I've dreamed of her from time to time. Always in the dreams I have a lot of things to do, and then I'm going to see my mother. I know exactly where she is, but I have all these things to finish. By the time I finish and am going to her, the dream is over.

In the only dream where I saw her, I had finished all my tasks. I came to the edge of a valley and looked down, seeing my mother by a house. She was smiling and very happy. She was with a man. I felt that I heard a voice behind me telling me not to go down and interfere. I'd seen how happy she was, and that was enough. She had a very unhappy life in this embodiment. I was just wondering why I've never had any feeling of the presence of my mother.

MONITOR: First you must understand that her experience is taking place in a different time stream than you experience as an Outer Self. From her perspective, we find no sense of neglecting you or others for whom she cares. She has been active in a positive sense, recuperating from the stresses of the past lifetime in the physical plane and achieving a state more nearly approaching normality in the astral plane. She has been actively involved in re-embodiment and has chosen a path of accelerated learning, which more people are choosing between physical embodiments. Conditions in the Earth at this time are quite conducive to providing opportunities for accelerated learning.

We find that she may still be accessible to you in the astral plane at night. We suggest that she is now physically embodied in Europe, and so you must consider those hours of the night when she would be asleep and freed from the physical body. If you ask your High Self to connect you, it may be easily done within the time limits noted.

TIME STREAMS

JULIE: Monitor, you've mentioned the term "time streams" in our dream segments. Would you elaborate on that term?

MONITOR: The experience of time depends upon the being experiencing time. Within a human being, you have the Outer Self, who is closely derived from the physical body. So the Outer Self is attuned by its body to a certain time stream.

The Male and Female Selves of the same person are not limited to the physical Body. They exist mainly in astral and mental forms. Just as physical and etheric forms affect the attunement of the Outer Self and thereby link it to a time stream, so do the vibratory qualities of the astral and mental bodies of the Male and Female Selves link them through attunement to time streams.

In the astral plane a Self with a low vibratory attunement is limited to the lower levels of the astral plane. The lower levels have many more time streams available than are accessible to the Outer Self in the physical and etheric planes.

The upper levels of the astral plane have an even greater number of time streams available. The mental plane again has a dramatic increase in the number of time streams available to those attuned to the mental plane.

Time remains largely a mystery to the Outer Self because it has such a limited experience with time, compared to all the possibilities experienced by Subconscious and Superconscious Selves.

The experience of time is linked to the form in which the Life essence dwells. The form has a vibratory quality that establishes a certain range of conditions. These conditions result from the interaction of Life in that form with the whole of Life. Therefore, each form has a unique attunement, which is why a Life essence seeks to dwell within it.

Time, viewed from the aspect of a form, constitutes a personal experience. An Outer Self has a personal experience of time. Other Outer Selves, who vibrate in the same octave, tend to share similar personal experiences of time. Thus, you find an overlap among personal experiences of time. This overlap may be referred to as a "time stream."

The sense of time of one Outer Self may affect the sense of time of another Outer Self. What we are talking about here are vibratory conditions in consciousness. We are not referring to purely psychological conditions.

The forms of lower vibration have a limited access to time streams, and forms of higher vibration have virtually unlimited access to time streams. Those occupying forms of high vibration have freedom of movement through what the Outer Self defines as "time-space" which is virtually unimaginable to the Outer Self. You know of reports where Spiritual Masters have been physically present in two places at the same time. They gain this capability because they function primarily in the level of the mental plane. They have developed their mental body to the point where it predominates in vibratory force over their astral, etheric, and physical bodies.

Perhaps you have heard too much about time? *[Laughter.]*

DREAM FROM HIGH SELF

HELEN: I had a lot of dreams in the past week because I asked for them from my High Self and the Male and Female Selves. I can condense it to one dream from the High Self and one from the Male Self for you, if that will be all right.

MONITOR: Proceed.

HELEN: The first one I requested from the High Self particularly. I asked her to help me understand what the responsibilities of my Male and Female Selves were, and how I might assist them. I got two dreams, but the first one puzzles me.

We're going to move. Either my father or husband, I wasn't sure which, found a house in the same neighborhood. He didn't ask the price. I hadn't seen it from inside, and didn't know if it had enough bedrooms. Carol, my youngest daughter—about age six or eight in the dream—comes home from school with black bugs in her hair. I pick them out and brush her hair. They fall to the floor, and then I step on them. She hadn't been doing too well before she went to school, but seemed fine now.

I figure the house should be about the same amount as our present house, since it's in the same neighborhood. I'm hoping that if it doesn't have as many bedrooms, that one is extra–large to accommodate two double beds. Diane and Carol could each have a double, and if Gail came home or they had company stay over, there would be room.

So, then the dream that I received last, from the Male Basic Self . . .

MONITOR: Could we deal with this dream first?

HELEN: Fine.

MONITOR: We find that, in the dream from your High Self, you are experiencing a sense of dismay or discomfort in not being fully consulted or informed about the characteristics of the new house. This illustrates the High Self's observation that your Male Self sometimes does not communicate information fully to the Female Self.

We observe that the Male Self is at times offended by the actions of the Female Self. He still does not fully appreciate her nature. Her devic qualities still disconcert him. She sometimes appears undependable, in his viewpoint. He considers her behavior as either neglect of him or willful withholding of information from him, and so he returns the action to her, not out of spite, but as a means of making her aware of the effect of her actions on him.

Moving into a new house represents a new type of living together, or relationship, which is possible and may be accomplished if the two work together. The qualities of the house represent, in symbolic form, the qualities of relationship between your Male and Female Selves. If you examine those aspects, we believe that you will gain useful insights. We will not attempt to go into them. Does that assist you with the dream?

HELEN: Yes. I'm trying to get to the place where I can understand these myself, and it's puzzling me as to how you come up with that kind of answer.

CONTACTING HIGH SELF THROUGH NON-DOMINANT HANDWRITING

MONITOR: We suggest that you continue searching, and as you seek to interpret a dream, especially one from the High Self, ask your High Self to assist you in the interpretation. If you have difficulty letting the information come through, utilize your left hand, with a pen, to act as a channel for your High Self to express its interpretation. At times you have a tendency to over–control and thereby block the flow. If you utilize your left hand, you may find yourself maintaining a more appropriate level of control.

HELEN: All right. Thank you. The part of that dream where the young child is sent to school, I interpreted that as the possibility that the Female Self has been sent to school. Is that correct?

MONITOR: Indeed. She has been attending school, in this case, beginning the Temple of Wisdom. She has come to the point of committing herself to growth, which requires that she become more diligent in listening, which she finds to be a challenge. As she continues her studies, she will experience significant breakthroughs in her own concept of herself and what she may contribute to the personality in service. At this point her service is limited because her self-concept is limited. This is typical of devic consciousness, which must act itself out to the point of frustration before it is able to exceed what it has been.

HELEN: Thanks very much. That's very helpful. I don't know whether I should go on with the other dream.

JULIE: Why don't we see if there are others, and then we'll come back to Helen. Is that okay for you? Anybody else have a question?

PAST LIFE AND PRESENT LIFE PROBLEM-SOLVING

LUCKIE: How are we to determine the difference between past life and present problem solving in our dreams?

MONITOR: The Outer Self is confronted with this dilemma more as it opens up its arena of awareness. The Outer Self depends upon the Subconscious Selves, specifically one or both of the Basic Selves, for the function of memory. The Outer Self itself has very limited memory. Its memory is essentially the memory of the Body Self. If it were limited solely to that type of memory, it would live only in the moment and have no thought for past or future. However, the personality is so designed that the Outer Self relies upon the Subconscious Selves for performing the functions of memory. In your case, the Male Self maintains primary functions of memory. If you, the Outer Self, seek a memory, you mentally place a request. Your Male Self answers that request and provides the memory you seek.

The difference between the memory of this embodiment and the memory of a prior embodiment may best be discerned by the quality it expresses. Here we resort to a metaphor. If you watch a motion picture made in 1991, you recognize it by the quality of its color, rhythm, subject matter, and how it treats the subject matter. If you watch a movie made in 1945, you recognize it by its color—which you term "black and white"—and by its rhythm, which is distinctly different from the rhythm of the movie made in 1991. You may also recognize differences in its subject matter, and how that subject matter is treated.

Taking this metaphor and applying it to memory, you notice the difference in qualities distinctly present in memories of the present lifetime and memories of past lifetimes. You learn to mark these distinctions through practice. If you practice asking your Male Self for past life memories, you will soon be able to make distinctions. You need to do this in a waking state first, so that you are able to fully appreciate the experience. Once you are trained in marking those distinctions, you can recognize the different memories projected in dreams. Do you understand us?

LUCKIE: I think so. It may take some time to assimilate, but it sounds very interesting. Thank you.

MONITOR: The average human being can learn to make these distinctions within three months.

DREAM ABOUT FEMALE SELF WANTING THE TEMPLE OF WISDOM

LUCKIE: I will try. I have one dream of my own. I was in a new house that I had built. It was very large with Mexican tile floors and many rooms. The rooms had no furniture or pictures. I didn't think that I would ever build a house this large and thought to myself that it was on a very busy street with lots of noise. An elementary school was across the street and a college next door. I thought to myself that I had an opportunity to go to either school and learn, which was a very interesting idea.

In the second segment, I found myself on television with Diane Sawyer. We were installing a toilet seat. I couldn't quite figure out why I was there. Evidently it was in her house, because in the next segment we were standing in front of a very large clothes closet that was totally empty, with a table and a vase in front of the door.

In the third segment, I found myself in a supermarket, pushing a basket behind an old man. When he came to a metal detector, the baking pans in his basket kept him from going past. When he asked the checker what happened, she said, "I don't know. This has never happened before." I was aware that there was a thunderstorm outside, and I woke up very tired. Can you give me some insight into this?

MONITOR: These dreams are presented by your Female Self. She wishes to open you to greater possibilities, which are represented in the increased type of housing in the first segment. The way to accomplish greater possibilities occurs through education. Your choices for education relate to what we said earlier concerning the Temple of Knowledge or the Temple of Wisdom.

The elementary school represents the Temple of Knowledge; the college represents the Temple of Wisdom. You have choices. The choices reside with your Female Self and Male Self. She is concerned about the need to grow and feels uncertain about the Male Self's commitment to grow. Her concern is based upon her impending choice of entering the Temple of Wisdom, which she has not done up to this time.

The second dream segment presents an image of her as Diane Sawyer. You may analyze the name for connotations. The action was one of improving means for making eliminations. As the Female Self faces her choice of where to pursue education, she has concerns and fears. Some of these she projects upon the Male Self, giving away her power to him. She does this through her illusions. She fears that he will not decide to enter the Temple of Wisdom with her, and that if she does pursue that course, she and he will be drawn further apart. We find this fear to be without substance, yet it is a fear that she needs to eliminate—hence the work of improving the toilet seat.

The third segment concerning the market reflects her fear for the Male Self, who is represented by the old man who experiences difficulty. In summary, we find that your Female Self needs assistance in recognizing her fears and getting free of them. Do you understand us?

LUCKIE: Yes, thank you.

DREAM ABOUT BODY CONSCIOUSNESS

LOIS: Last week at the end of the Lesson, Monitor, you mentioned to us about asking for a Body Self dream. I asked Monitor for that kind of dream and had a short dream. First, I have to say that my husband died a long time ago, and this dream took place in my mother-in-law's home. I unlocked the door. A lot of locks were on the door, but only one was locked. I stepped out on the porch and looked across the street. Then I had a "fear of danger" feeling. I turned around, and the door was locked. I saw only a very tiny key in a very tiny lock. I put the key in and prayed that the little key wouldn't break. It opened right up. I went inside and could feel danger coming toward my back. I got inside and shut the door, and a car came into the driveway. And so I was inside, the door was locked, and I stood in the middle of the room. I thought, "I'll have to be very quiet. Maybe they won't know I'm here." That was the end of my dream.

MONITOR: We congratulate you on receiving a dream from your Body Self. In general, dreams from Body Self present many physical symbols. The Body Self thinks in such terms. Its consciousness is evolving through the elemental kingdom and is most familiar with physical reality, or, if you wish, etheric reality which you perceive physically.

Dreams from your other Selves use physical symbols as well, yet you will find differences. The dream of a devic Basic Self has drama and contrast, which you do not find in a dream by the Body Self. Dreams by the Body Self are also likely to concern themselves with threats, because the Body Self is used to facing threats. Much of its organization is based upon meeting threats and overcoming them. You may relate Body Self to the evolution of Life through the mineral, vegetable, and animal kingdoms. It most often represents an animal viewpoint.

In this dream the house is symbolic of the body, which the elemental consciousness maintains. The threat came from outside, which is significant to note. In some instances, this could relate to the threat of external stress, sources of infection or injury to the body. The Body Self is alert to such threats. In this dream the threat was external and, for the time being, was met.

The central action of the dream involved working the mechanism of the locks. The key was tiny because your Outer Self has, as yet, limited ability to communicate intelligently with your Body Self. Yet the tiny key *did* work. The lock was opened, and you were safe inside.

BODY CONSCIOUSNESS DREAMS

MONITOR: Other themes of Body Self dreams relate to a threat from the inside. If the image of a house occurred, the threat could exist within the house. The source of such threat might be internal toxicity, either from what is ingested or what is not properly assimilated or eliminated by the body. Other themes are possible, yet they are not likely to be presented in your initial acquaintance with your Body Self in dreams. Once an Outer Self establishes a deeper relationship with its Body Self, the themes become more varied and of deeper meaning. This reaction is similar to that of an animal, which at first places limited trust in a human being. Only when a human being has proven trustworthy, does it make itself more vulnerable.

We encourage you to experiment in dream communication with your Body Self. You may also communicate with it in terms of guided imagery and visualization, which allows for two–way communication. If you treat your Body Self as a stupid animal to be commanded, then, although it may sometimes obey the command, it will eventually rebel.

The Body Self of human beings has been elevated in vibratory quality to the point where it is moving toward its own emancipation. As the personality makes progress and advances beyond its need for human form, the Body Self that has been developed within the human form will also progress.

This type of progression, in a slightly different format, took place earlier in Earth's history at the time of the ancient civilization of Mu, leading to the present human form. Another graduating class of elemental consciousnesses will evolve into higher form—which, by the way, will *not* be particularly human. Did this address your dream sufficiently?

LOIS: Yes it did. Thank you, Monitor.

VIEWS OF CHANGE

MONITOR: We encourage you to consider these aspects of your own consciousness. As you become aware that you are a meeting place of various aspects of Life, you can learn about and appreciate those aspects. If you remain closed in fear, you find yourselves missing many opportunities.

Planetary Consciousness is advancing. As it advances, all beings in Earth are transformed. Rapid change is now the rule. If you consider this change as a struggle, your resistance intensifies the struggle. If you view this change as a desirable transformation, such as that of birth into or death from form, you reap many benefits.

We assure you that vast numbers of Souls desire to be in physical embodiment in these times because of vibratory opportunities. When you experience your aches and pains, your limitations and frustrations, please keep this in mind.

MURDER OF THAI MONKS

ARZANI: I want to know if you had something you could tell us about the murder of the Thai monks near Phoenix. It's heavy on my heart. I can't understand why that happened.

MONITOR: We are limited in what we may say, because permission has not been sought from those involved, yet we are free to say that an Oriental gang was involved, whose motives were fear of betrayal of confidence. The confidence concerned trafficking of drugs. We assure you that those in the monastery were quite innocent of such activity. The fear, on the part of the gang, called for their destruction, and their karmic pattern provided the opportunity. We assure you that, as Souls, they did not lose; they gained.

ARZANI: Thank you very much.

JULIE: Those are all the questions for now, Monitor. Thank you.

ASK DEVAS FOR RAIN

MONITOR: We thank you all for wading through some deep water tonight.

We encourage you all to use your powers of persuasion to call upon the devas of the air to bring rain to your area. You have noticed that your weather has been unnaturally dry. This occurs because of an accumulation of toxic energies arising from various industries in the vicinity and from the nuclear plant. Therefore, this pattern will tend to repeat unless it is counteracted by means of such persuasion as each of you may exercise.

We thank you once again. Continue your work with dreams. We encourage you to apply some of what we have shared concerning dream experiences. Ask various Selves within you to provide you with a dream. Once you have a dream, but do not fully understand its meaning, ask that Self for further clarification. You will find such experiences greatly rewarding. We thank you once again, and we leave you now.

Lesson 21
August 28, 1991

MONITOR: We welcome you as Monitor.

GROUP: We welcome you, Monitor.

MEMORY OF DREAMS

MONITOR: The act of switching on the tape recorders is somewhat similar to what you, as Outer Selves, accomplish when you remember your dreams. The tape in the recorder records patterns of experience. You, as the Outer Self, create a contact with your Subconscious Selves that enables you to access the experience that occurs during your sleep.

It is important that you consciously *initiate* memory of dreams. That shows your Subconscious Selves that you are interested in activities beyond the relatively narrow limits of the Outer Self. Your Subconscious Selves then become encouraged that you, the child of the personality, are becoming interested in adult matters.

Consider the hundreds of lifetimes of experience that have given your Subconscious Self wisdom and a wide range of abilities. A Subconscious Self has access to etheric, astral, and mental levels of experience. It is able to negotiate many dimensions that you, the Outer Self, are not able to negotiate.

Consider the perspective of your Subconscious Self, who is busy learning and growing, working on behalf of the High Self and Soul. Your Subconscious Self receives many communications from many different kinds of beings. It has a large number of concerns that are seldom, if ever, shared with you, the Outer Self. From that perspective, you may gain a greater appreciation of why it is important for you to remember your dreams.

CHANGES IN PSYCHOLOGY

At this stage in human development, most human beings consider themselves as Outer Selves and little else. That represents the pragmatic daily experience of most human beings.

With the beginning of psychology as a science, the first glimmerings of credibility were attached to the existence of more than the Outer Self. Most of psychology, to the present, has been based on the limited viewpoint of the Outer Self. When Freud, Jung, Assagioli, and others have written their concepts of psychology, they have all written them from the viewpoint of the Outer Self.

The time has arrived now when psychologists will begin to present the viewpoints of Subconscious and Superconscious Selves. Channeling offers one way to accomplish this. A study of dreams offers another. A study of mystical or transpersonal states of consciousness provides yet another. If you had our perspective of human evolution, you would appreciate the importance of this step in the evolution of psychology.

The world view, held by most world leaders, remains quite limited and based on the viewpoint of the Outer Self. It views reality almost entirely as a physical reality. Political leaders give lip service to talk of spirituality, yet too few of them have spiritual experiences that open their Outer Selves.

The contribution of psychology, in opening a greater perspective than that of the Outer Self, will affect all other areas of human endeavor. Eventually, political leaders will possess conscious experience of dream states and states of consciousness beyond what is now considered normal. The trend of human evolution is definitely in that direction. A political leader, who is capable of knowing himself or herself in depth, will have much greater impact than the relative shallowness of political leaders today.

In some ancient cultures, political leaders *did* pay great attention to dreams and visions, to oracles and prophets. Today most do not, but tomorrow they will pay attention and understand even more than those in the past understood, because the political leaders of tomorrow will have greater self-knowledge based upon experiences with their Subconscious and Superconscious levels of mind.

We wish to make these comments to place the topic of dreams into perspective. We hope that you will entertain some of these thoughts. As you consider them of importance, you energize these thought forms, and they begin to manifest.

Now we will climb off our soapbox to deal with questions and comments. What do you wish?

DREAM ABOUT VALUING THE BODY

ARZANI: I think you were hanging around this morning. I had a very strange dream experience. I was in Paradise Valley Mall, a shopping center right by my house, and there was a room right in the middle where people walked. It was a special room that no one else had access to. I was led into the room, and there were three objects there that I could buy. I can only remember one of them—two of them might have been clothing—but one of them was a cylinder–shaped pump, green in color, about four feet high and two feet in diameter. It had two hoses coming off of it, and it cost $14.50. It had a price tag on it. I was feeling cheap and didn't know how much I valued it.

Then I woke up and wrote it down, and as I was writing it I was told things. One of them was that this was my body that I was being offered to buy. I was rationalizing that I didn't need it, that I didn't need to spend the $14.50 because I didn't need to buy it. Then a woman was there, who cuts my hair, and I was trying to help her understand what was and wasn't important. We were trying to decide whether it was important to buy these things or not.

Then I went back to sleep and got the exact same scene again, right back in that room with the three objects. Again I had the opportunity to buy them. Then I felt that the pump was a heat pump and that buying it was a chance of a lifetime, and that this was the truth behind the form. These things came to me when I wrote it down the second time. I also got these other insights. The secret room was the truth behind the form of Life. They said it was like the real person who did the dancing in "Flashdance." It was comparable to that metaphor. I knew who the real dancer was. And I was being helped to analyze it while I was writing. I was also told that it was connected with my function as a therapist and the care of my body, that it was like buying my chakras and buying devas—which I never associated with my chakras. I don't know what any of this means, but I wrote it down as they told it. I had the sense that somebody was trying really hard to get the interpretation through to me by giving it to me twice and giving me those words. Was it you?

MONITOR: We participated with your High Self, since you had requested us to be present. The message might be stated in these terms as well as what you have received. We *do* value what you have received, because as you receive the meanings and place them into symbol and word form, you gain by developing your capacity for interpretation and understanding.

What we add is clarification that your various Subconscious Selves and you, the Outer Self, all have different ways of approaching the physical body.

Consequently, the approach of your personality is somewhat fragmented in that regard.

Your Female Self often wishes to flee and abandon the body. Your Male Self often considers the processes of mind more important than the body. The Mental Judge Self often wishes to secure the body, so that it, the Mental Judge Self, may be secured. No wonder the Outer Self is confused about the body.

The message of the dream was that the body is a form which serves as a pump, or conduit, for Divine Love. The message is that simple.

The location of the secret room was in a shopping mall that invited you to buy, or not to buy, the message. The price [$14.50] reflected the energy states of your chakras with the Life force created through the first chakra, raised to the fourth chakra, and expressed through the fifth chakra.

This energy condition is correlated with your ability to use your body as a pump for Divine Love. That function has a direct bearing, not only on your personal life and relationships, but also on your work as therapist and teacher.

The significant point is that you, the Outer Self, need to take a clear stand in valuing your body. Only in that way will you be able to unite the fragmented viewpoints of your Subconscious Selves concerning the body. As you campaign for that value, if you choose to do so, you can create an alignment among your Subconscious Selves. When that alignment is achieved, you will see the tangible results in your body. What you achieve will be far more than what you have achieved to date in terms of physical health. Do you understand this?

ARZANI: So the Basic Selves can be brought to an acceptance of the body through the effort of the Outer Self, or do I need to work with them in getting them to agree?

MONITOR: You, the Outer Self, need to take a clear position concerning the value of the physical body. Once you have done that, you may seek to gain the agreement of the Subconscious Selves with that position. You will need to approach each one in the way that is most effective for each.

PROMOTING SELF INTEGRATION

JULIE: Monitor, in our meditation, we prayed for raising the consciousness of all beings in our Planetary Being. Then, in your opening, you mentioned how few of our leaders and how few of our people really know of anything beyond the Outer Self. Do you have any guidance for this group as to how we can best help in spreading this?

MONITOR: You may be most effective by testing these concepts in your own lives. As you find them to be of value, you add your Life force to them. An analogy for this process involves a slide projector, where one person projects an image of a greater awareness of the mind of humanity. If only one person projects that image, very few perceive it. If 100 people project the same image, many more notice. As the number projecting escalates, soon it becomes accepted. It becomes the norm. Does this answer your question?

JULIE: It does, thank you.

LOVE TRANSMITTED TO ELEMENTALS AND DEVAS

MONITOR: We would like to make one further comment to Arzani, which will have value for all others.

When a person truly values and loves their body, they transmit that love to those lives who compose the body. What are those lives?

You can perceive the tissue, and you know of the cells, molecules, and atoms that compose your body. Your science, as yet, does not recognize that all of matter is alive. It is alive through the contribution of the elemental lives who inhabit the forms of atoms, molecules, cells, and tissues of the body. Yet you must also consider those beings, those lives who create the form itself. These are the devas, another line of evolution of consciousness which interweaves with the human line.

As a human being loves his/her body, that love is transmitted both to elemental and devic lives. Love, therefore, is transmitted in many directions and dimensions.

Human beings have had the unfortunate concept that the human body is limited, or negative, or evil. That concept is based on fears and judgments that are far more limiting than the human body ever could be.

When you love your body, your love is transmitted to the lives composing your body, and that love flows in all of the directions taken by those lives. So consider that loving your body is not a selfish, closed act. It is an act of generosity that is invaluable in affecting the consciousness of those lives who form and sustain your body. When you consider that your body is part of the consciousness of the Planetary Being of Earth, you can use your body as a means of communicating your love to the Planetary Consciousness.

We've climbed on our soapbox again. It must be the stars!

DREAM ABOUT RELATIONSHIP TRANSFORMATION

BOB: I had a dream last week that I would like some insight into. In my dream someone needs to die so that my wife, Diane, doesn't have to. A replacement male adult has volunteered to be killed in her place. I come to bed expecting this replacement to have died. He is still alive, lying between Diane and myself in the bed. Our bed is pointed toward the east. A male comes in and puts a blanket over the head of this person that is to die. He then shoots the person in such a way that it may look like a suicide. I go to the bathroom while the shot person gets up and walks to the left side of the bed. Some blood is spilled, which I help to clean up. He is still covered by the blanket. Finally he dies. He voluntarily does this, by agreement, so that Diane doesn't have to. The death is necessary, and everybody concerned understands that. I don't like the sloppy manner in which the killing has taken place, but I realize that it's necessary.

MONITOR: We find that this dream is presented by your High Self to prepare both Subconscious Selves and you, the Outer Self, for the death of the old or former relationship in your marriage. The death is a positive action that frees your relationship to be creative. It frees you from past patterns.

This essentially represents a sacrifice, which is the act of making your relationship holy. The person, who becomes the sacrifice, gives up the form. Life is released from that form to be creative to a far greater degree than if it had remained in that form. In this way, the relationship becomes transformed.

Your High Self was preparing you to participate in the process and not resist it. Do you understand?

BOB: Yes, thank you very much. I really appreciate that.

DREAM ABOUT INTEGRATION OF MALE AND FEMALE SELVES

LOIS: I asked my High Self for a dream this week that would help me move on with my life to do whatever work I'm supposed to do, or just to have a deeper understanding. Last week I talked to you about a recurring dream, and my High Self gave me the recurring dream again. In this version of it, I was driving in a car with my daughter and her children. I asked them to stop and let me out, as I wanted to see my mother before she laid down for her nap. I wanted to take her out to dinner that night, since that was my last day there. My daughter and the people in the car were very agreeable to that. They stopped and let me out.

As I walked by mother's house, I noticed my daughter's dry wash was on the clothesline. I took the wash down and decided to carry it with me and fold it at my mother's house. There were many pairs of my youngest granddaughter's little socks, and I thought, "Oh, mama's gonna be so surprised when she sees the socks and hears about her great–grandchild." In the backyard I had to go through a fence and garden. The neighbor man was sitting in his garden, and many beautiful flowers were blooming and growing wild every which way. Some were tall, and some were close to the ground. I complimented him on the beauty of the garden, and he responded, "It is like a jungle." I told him I liked that wild look. He was sitting reading his paper as I stepped through and wound in and out of the flowers. As I stepped out onto the path, the old man said, "Well, they got that guy out of there and stopped another Hanoi war. I'll bet they had to pay him." I said, "I don't care who they have to pay, as long as they stop a war." As I turned to go to my mother's house, the alarm went off and I woke up.

MONITOR: We find the dream to be presented by your High Self, as you requested. In music, the repetition of the same note adds emphasis, does it not?

LOIS: That's true.

MONITOR: This dream is presented in that concept. You have been exploring the status of your mother, and as you explore it, you understand and accept more of yourself. As you accept yourself in greater depth, you naturally come to the point of accepting the Divinity in yourself.

Many times, to a human being today, Divinity is not apparent on the surface, but may be found inside, at the core of the personality. In this dream, your mother represents what you are becoming within the image or influence of Divine Mother.

You find the clothes, washed and cleaned by your daughter. The clothes represent the way you present yourself in daily life. Your daughter represents perhaps a younger aspect of yourself. The clothes represent your attitudes and behaviors, which enable you to survive and prevail in the world. The socks of your granddaughter represent new understanding, for feet that are as yet small, but will surely grow.

The growth of all of the Feminine Selves, in this dream, is part of the realization of Divine Mother.

The man with the garden represents your Male Self, who has been productive. He is sometimes overly concerned with order and meeting the expectations of others. Yet, in the dream, you reassure him that the order he has produced is quite acceptable to you. The "you" of the dream also represents the position of your Female Self. There you see a productive meeting of Male and Female Selves, which represents an important action in your life at this time. As your Male and Female Selves voluntarily unite in activity and more and more in values, you find even greater productivity and creativity in your life. All of this is viewed with favor by Divine Mother.

Consider this approach. Does this address your dream?

LOIS: Very much. Thank you, Monitor.

DREAM ABOUT NEEDS OF FEMALE SELF

DONNA: I have a dream, Monitor, of which I'm afraid I know the meaning. *[Group laughter.]* I asked for a dream from my Female Self. I seemed to be living alone at the time, and a couple of men came along and asked if they could do anything for me. I thought I should give them a drink for being so nice. I decided against hard liquor—which I had in my cabinet—and looked around for some beer. But I found only one can, so I made up some frozen cranberry juice and gave it to them. I told them that my gardener was working for a cousin. As I had nothing for him to do, so I had nothing for them either. Later I heard a bell and decided it was the first bell for school. I had trouble finding anything to wear. Another gal was there—maybe a roommate. She quickly dressed and was off. I was hurrying around, but still wasn't ready to go. I thought I would be late. Would you care to comment on that?

MONITOR: We find that this dream presents the views of your Female Self, where she finds herself sometimes isolated from the Male Self. Her self–image causes her to be timid in relating to the Male Self, with the net result that your Male Self tends to dominate your life, with the Female Self wishing that she could be more prominent.

She needs encouragement from you and the High Self. She doubts, at times, that she is worthy of more. In the dream, the roommate is prepared, goes out into the world, and integrates with the world. But your Female Self is not truly motivated to overcome her fear to do the same.

We recommend that you ask your High Self to assist her. The High Self may explain things to her and answer her doubts regarding her own self-worth.

She projects her self-doubts outward and often limits herself by considering that what she has to offer would not be valued by others or that she might act inappropriately. In these ways, your Female Self defeats her own cause. She *does* need assistance.

You, the Outer Self, can draw her out. In written form, ask her about herself, how she feels about herself, and what she would truly like to do. What are her treasured goals? Then, having her respond in writing, you may study the information and determine how you might reassure her through your own efforts.

With your assistance and the assistance of the High Self, she will be able to learn. She will be able to respond to the signal of the bell calling her to learn and demonstrate what she has learned. Does this address your dream?

DONNA: Yes, I think it does. Thank you.

DREAM ABOUT SUBCONSCIOUS FEAR AND ANGER

MARY: I had a dream that my son, as a small child, and I were driving to my parents' house. As we approached the house, we saw a number of fire trucks. They had the street blocked off in the neighborhood. It was clear that we weren't going to be allowed to go any further, and there was no information as to exactly where the problem was. We could go no further. First, I had a tremendous sense of fear and panic. I asked the firemen some questions, and then I became resigned to the fact that I would know nothing more about my parents' safety or what was going on. It was necessary for me to give it up to a higher power and just hold my parents in Light, knowing that everything was okay. And we drove off. It was a very short dream, but it was extremely vivid.

MONITOR: We find that this dream was presented by your High Self. It represents emotional patterns active in yourself and reflected, to some degree, in your son. These patterns are not necessarily evident on the surface of your daily life, but exist below the surface in your Subconscious Selves, specifically in your Mental Judge Self and Female Self. Your Mental Judge Self is fearful and, instead of resolving its fears projects them throughout the personality. Your Female Self has been most susceptible to those fears and has accepted them as her own.

Part of the fear reaction is anger, which in the dream is represented by the fire. In the dream the fire is being tended, but still remains a threat. The fact that, in the dream, your dream self cannot find out what is happening perpetuates the fear. As the fear is perpetuated, so is the anger, the fire.

This is a dream of warning to look within yourself in order to ascertain self-knowledge about what you are fearful of and what you are angry about, especially in relationship to your son. As you do this, you gain conscious ability to help your Female Self release the fears, which we find are not truly realistic. They are the production of the Mental Judge Self, who is not qualified to evaluate relationships.

You may assist your Female Self in freeing herself from the illusions created by the Mental Judge SelfEven though the illusions are false, her reactions of fear and anger are quite real and dynamic. Your High Self has given you this dream as a warning, calling you to take action. Do you understand us?

MARY: Well, in part. I have to say I'm mystified. I must really be in extreme denial about it, because I don't have a real clear sense of what the source of the anger and fear is.

MONITOR: We find that you consciously do not know at this time. You must search within your emotions, not your thoughts. Your emotions will reveal the pattern.

DREAM ABOUT POWER STRUGGLE

JERRY: I have two things: one is a dream, and one is an unrelated question that came to me to specifically ask tonight. I'd like to do the dream first, and then I'll present the question.

I had a dream about three weeks ago, up in Minnesota, as part of a workshop where a dream was requested. It seemed very powerful and simple to me when I first got it and is now growing in meaning. As a young child— maybe eight or nine years old—I was on a loading dock with a truck backed up to it. A big rectangular load rested on a flatbed truck covered with a green tarp and neatly tied off with rope. I got on the back passenger side of the truck and hung on to the side of the rope. My oldest brother—I have three brothers—got on top of it, and we started to leave the loading dock. My dad came off the loading dock at the last minute, got on the end of the truck, and held onto it. He looked at me. As we pulled away, my brother was up on top of the truck, and my dad and I were leaning. He was around the end. And it came to me that he was mean and ugly. That was my experience of him most of my life. The phrase came a number of times, and I realized that I could sever him in an instant from that truck. He knew it also and had a fearful look on his face. We had a stalemate, yet even though I could, I couldn't. Then he switched from the back of the truck up over the top and turned around in front of me, hanging off a rope in front of me. I still got the phrase, "mean and ugly," "mean and ugly." He had a look of arrogance and contempt. He knew I could have knocked him off, but he also knew that he was so powerful that I couldn't. That was the dream.

The next day, from that dream, I realized that was what went on all my life with him, and that was one of the reasons I do not trust people. I have a reluctance to trust people. I had three older brothers and a mother, and they never came between me and my father, no matter what. So I developed an inability to trust people. I had to do everything myself.

MONITOR: We find this dream is presented by your High Self, who is seeking to bring illumination to your Male Self and ultimately to your Mental Judge Self.

The truck represents continuation of the pattern that has been carried down through your family for some generations. What, in your dream, was described as "mean and ugly" represents the pattern in the family. That pattern is caused, in our point of view, by domination of the Mental Judge Self. The Mental Judge causes the Male Self to be over reactive in one form or another. The expression of that pattern varies from member to member in your family. Some are aggressive; some are passive.

The pattern in the dream that you recognized, within your father, is that of the aggressive expression of this pattern. As you examine your own life, you will find these patterns playing out.

Your High Self is attempting to assist you, the Outer Self, in breaking free of the pattern. The dream indicates that you have not yet broken free of it. You have not, from our point of view, because your Male Self and Mental Judge Self continue the pattern.

If you will query your Male Self and ask him to express his feelings and position relative to your father, you will assist him in gaining greater objectivity concerning his own position. He has been vulnerable to the Mental Judge Self, who has been quite insecure.

Much of your life has been devoted to exploration of the uses of power. You have explored power used for the sake of power, and power used in the extreme positions of victim and victimizer. And you have diligently explored the use of power expressing Love and wisdom. Each of these experiences of power is intended, not only to benefit you, the Outer Self, but especially your Male Self and Mental Judge Self.

When you express power motivated by Love and wisdom, you combine the efforts of your Male Self with your Female Self and sometimes with your High Self. When you exercise power without Love or wisdom, you express mainly your Male Self and Mental Judge Self.

As you gain illumination concerning these inner dynamics, you gain ability to change the pattern. The dream states that the pattern has not truly been changed, and so the challenge is presented to you. Do you understand this?

JERRY: I understand everything, except I'm not sure I understand exactly what to do about it, what direction to take in healing it? I'm looking at bringing spirituality through power right now.

MONITOR: We are giving you suggestions concerning how you may relate to your Subconscious Selves in expressing power.

For the human personality, the most spiritual expression of power is that which unites the cooperative efforts of Inner Selves. Spirituality is related to the expression of Oneness and wholeness in the personality.

When a personality expresses the power of only one Self, it tends to be less spiritual. If your personality expresses the power of your Mental Judge Self, which at times it does, it expresses power based upon motives of fear. If it expresses power through the Female Self, it expresses more the motives of Love and compassion, which are more spiritual, yet still less than if you achieve Oneness and wholeness of motive for the use of power within your personality.

At this point you have experienced mixed results, which has been important in helping you, the Outer Self, to understand these dynamics.

Your Male Self remains the strategic focus for illumination. If you assist your Male Self in understanding these dynamics, you will experience a distinct change. Your Male Self must first learn to separate himself from the attacks and urgings of the Mental Judge Self. When your Male Self accomplishes that, you will experience greater consistency in your use of power.

Not until you convert your Mental Judge Self into a positive position in the personality, as one who supports the spiritual use of power, will you truly achieve full spirituality in the use of power. Consider these things, and we suggest that you take action first with your Male Self. Your Mental Judge Self will be too capable of resisting and distracting you from approaching it. Address your Male Self first, and you will gain results.

NON-DOMINANT HAND METHOD OF DREAM INTERPRETATION

HELEN: Monitor, last week you suggested that after a dream I interpret it using my left hand to write, in order to clear the channel and not stop the flow of information that I might be getting. So I asked my High Self to help me understand more clearly where my Male and Female Selves stood now in their responsibilities. I would try to help them in a dream. So I had a couple of dreams, and I did as you requested in using the left hand in interpreting. I'd like to take one dream, tell you how the left hand worked with it, and see what you think of it.

MONITOR: Proceed.

HELEN: All right.

MONITOR: We are quite interested in such experiments.

HELEN: I found it very interesting to do it that way. In the dream I had to get my hair done. I overslept through my appointment time. I tried to call the operator to say that I would be late. There was some difficulty getting the number. Mac, my husband, did someone's hair for them, and they are really pleased. I don't think it looks so great, but they really brag about it. I'm somewhat surprised that they like it so much. Someone is going to do mine that has never done it before. I think of ways to turn my house into a shop. We also talk about a trip somewhere. I clean out a sink with a toilet brush.

So with my left hand, after I wrote the dream, I did this interpretation. Getting the hair done was changing mental attitudes. Mac was taking the place of the Male Self, and I think he is doing a pretty good job in the Female Self's regular job of doing hair or taking over her duties. I don't believe that she is too sure about this. She doesn't agree with it. There's more work to be done with the Female Self's thinking process.

Turning the house into a shop, I feel, is making the body into a place to do business, which means to perform more efficiently. The new experience coming up is a trip. A trip means there is a new experience coming up, probably for the Female Self and what she's learning.

The cleaning I ascribe to the fact that I am in the process of using a castor oil pack, and it's doing the job of cleaning the body. So that's what I got with the left hand.

MONITOR: Congratulations!

HELEN: Thank you.

MONITOR: You have been quite open to the input of your High Self. You have worked diligently to understand what is taking place in your Subconscious Selves, and your ability to receive the guidance of your High Self is apparent. We suggest that you continue this process. You are using your left hand to write the interpretation, where you would normally use your right hand?

HELEN: Yes.

MONITOR: We suggested to you previously that you tend to over-control on the Outer Self level, and thereby close yourself to receiving guidance from your High Self. Your normal mode of writing, with your right hand, represents your normal tendency to over-control. By switching to your left hand, you gain greater access. This strategy has value in many aspects of life. Certainly you have demonstrated its worth in terms of gaining a greater interpretation of your dreams.

HELEN: I could almost feel it working at the time. Using it right away, after I wrote the dream down, it seemed to come so much easier by allowing it to come through the left hand. It was really amazing. I did wonder if I missed anything, however.

MONITOR: One item you missed was that you are being recommended by your High Self to take internal dosage of castor oil drops.

HELEN: I do that.

MONITOR: Then increase the dosage and allow it to work within you.

HELEN: I thank you very much.

CHRISTOPHER COLUMBUS

DONNA: Monitor, I was wondering if you could tell us something about Christopher Columbus. Was he merely a first class adventurer or was he a Master Soul who knew that the Earth was round, and knew beforehand the destiny of the voyage?

MONITOR: Christopher Columbus was not a Master, yet was not a fool either. He had access to information that his intuition said was valid. He was an adventurer, and he did seek to become a wealthy man. His motive was not altruistic.

He did perform a service, but he was not the first to venture from European to American shores. However, he did perform the service at a time that opened those routes to many. A tremendous amount of exploitation followed. That occurred in a time when human individuality was reaching an extreme point of development. The Spiritual Hierarchy, at that time, began to change the trend of evolution for humanity, moving from individual development to the development of group consciousness.

Christopher Columbus represents the individual seeking to profit and daring great risks.

JULIE: Monitor, is the channel up to two more questions?

MONITOR: Definitely.

TIME STREAMS

LOIS: I have a question about time streams. If one individual is working in embodiment in one time stream, and an individual is working in embodiment in another time stream, and if they come together, can they see each other and talk to each other, or are they in different parallel dimensions?

MONITOR: We must differentiate between levels of mind, within the human personality, in answering this question.

The Outer Self of the human being is normally limited to one time stream. If it attunes to its Subconscious Selves, it may get access to several time streams. If it attunes further, to its Superconscious Self, it may have virtually unlimited access to time streams. Yet the Outer Self is a product of the body that it occupies and may not leave that body. Even if the Outer Self makes contact with other beings in time streams accessible on subconscious and superconscious levels, it must always return to its body.

In the subconscious level of mind, the Male and Female Selves have the greatest capability for negotiating time streams. The Judge Selves are usually more limited in this capability because of their fears, which cause them to remain immobile much of the time.

Male and Female Selves frequently encounter other Male and Female Selves as they negotiate different time streams. When they and the other being are in different time streams, they are beyond the reach of their senses. In other words, they do not see or sense each other. When they occupy the same time stream and meet within it, they can sense each other and communicate. Such meetings are commonplace for Subconscious Selves. Does this address your question?

LOIS: Yes, it gives me a lot to think about. Thank you.

BAPTISM

JERRY: I have been requested to participate joyfully in baptizing my nephew's son on Saturday. And today I got the inspiration to pose a question to you. The question is, what are your reflections on baptism from the point of view of the effect on the person being baptized. Please consider the phases of pre–baptism and post–baptism and their relationship to the birth process.

MONITOR: When Life essence dwells in the human form, it must light the fires within that form. Those fires, over a number of lifetimes, cause the human form to raise its vibratory quality.

We use the symbol of fire because wood has a certain vibratory quality. When ignited, its vibratory quality completely changes. Thus it offers a symbol of transformation by fire. Life consists of Divine Fire, and so the human form is gradually raised in vibration to the point where its consciousness more closely approximates the consciousness of its sponsoring Soul. And when the Soul activates that form, progress is rapid.

The act of baptism represents the application of the water of Spirit. Water, in this sense, has several connotations. We will not go into all of them, but select one connotation.

Water represents the rising vibrations of the qualities known as emotions and desires. The energies of the astral plane are often represented by water. When a human being experiences lower, self-centered, self-defeating emotions and desires, the astral body becomes heavy and coarse. The Divine Fire of consciousness raises its quality to the point where emotions and desires are refined.

When they become attuned sufficiently high in vibration, the action of kundalini begins in the physical and etheric forms. As it rises from the base of the spine to the crown of the head, the kundalini action of fire completes the process of refinement of the astral energies in the personality. The act of baptism represents that point of attainment where kundalini rises to the crown chakra, the crown chakra opens, and the blessings of Spirit pour forth for the personality and all in its vicinity.

The Logos of Earth initiated the process of initiation, which represents a consciously applied method, on the part of the Logos, to speed the process of evolution of its constituent Life forms. Through spiritual initiation, the Logos and its representatives in the Spiritual Hierarchy give energetic stimulation to those Life forms who seek Light and Love, who seek the blessings of Spirit.

The higher Life forms energize the lower. The application of these energies brings about accelerated growth. Baptism represents this process, specifically as it relates to the overflowing of the waters of Spirit, which bring a blessing to the form and to the Life dwelling within it. Does this address your question?

JERRY: Beautifully! Thank you very much.

JULIE: That completes our questions for the evening, Monitor. Thank you.

DREAM WORK

MONITOR: As closing comments, we ask you to continue to work with your dreams. Your dreams represent one vital gateway to wisdom, the wisdom of self-knowledge.

Most of your dreams focus on your own dynamics of being and growth. When you have grown sufficiently, your dreams may be used to help others.

In the dream state you may ask your High Self and your Subconscious Selves to bring illumination and healing to others. These powers have been used by various people and have been institutionalized in various civilizations. One example, in your written history, is represented by the Temples of Aesculapius *[Esklepios]*, where dreams were used to heal the body, emotions, and mind. The dreamer asked for Divine Help, and it was believed by many that help would be given. Therefore it was, because their belief opened the pathway.

Consider what you might accomplish as agents of the Divine You may at times accomplish more in your dreams than when you are awake.

We thank you, and we will see you next time to discuss relationships. We leave you now.

TOOLS FOR EXPLORATION
Exercise 13

ASKING A SELF FOR HEALING OF OTHERS

1. Consider a person or situation that, in your opinion, needs healing or blessing. Write that person's name or a brief description of that situation.

2. Select a Self who relates well with you. Write that Self's name.

3. Ask your High Self to fill your personality with the Golden Light of Grace, especially the Self with whom you wish to communicate.

4. Mentally ask that Self: "I believe that *(person's name or the situation needing help)* has need of healing and blessing for the highest good of all. Will you link with higher consciousness tonight to bring healing and blessing to *(person's name or the situation needing help)*?"

5. Write the Self's response.

6. If the Self agrees to help, ask: "Will you share the healing and blessing experience with me in a dream tonight?"

7. Write the Self's response.

8. Recall your dreaming the next morning and write notes about it.

9. If possible, identify a dream that seems to relate to the requested healing and blessing experience.

10. Mentally ask the Self if that dream does portray the healing/blessing experience.

11. Write its response.

12. Ask the Self what else it wants you to know about that experience. Write its response.

13. Thank the Self for its cooperation.

Glossary of Terms

Adic plane – According to Monitor, the highest plane of existence composed of the least dense matter of the seven planes of existence in the universe. Adic energies, often regarded as **universal forces**, come into the human energy system through the **sutratma** and **chakras,** but awareness of the adic plane usually lies beyond human ability.

Akashic records – Permanent vibratory records of every thought, emotion, and action are maintained in a nonphysical matter and energy termed "akasha" by ancient Sanskrit texts. These records can be read and interpreted by trained persons, yielding specific information about history, past lives, etc.

Angels – A nonphysical species that inhabit the universe. In some ways similar to **devas,** angels are characterized by their continuous sensitivity and responsiveness to Divine Will and Divine Love. Monitor says that angels can best be understood as one fire with many flames.

Antahkarana – A Sanskrit term for the personality's energetic response to the Life force offered by Soul. Monitor says that a person's wise and Loving choices, attitudes and actions construct a positive energetic sheath around the sutratma, the stream of Life force that Soul supplies to the personality. The antahkarana facilitates a personality's reception of what Soul offers. A spiritually advanced person develops a full antahkarana that harmonizes with Soul intentions and radiance and facilitates the transmission of Soul energy and order into the personality. A less advanced person experiences greater shock and resistance at the impact of Soul energy and order attempting to enter the personality.

Astral body – A subtle energy human body that expresses emotions, desires, attitudes and expectations. Monitor views human beings as multidimensional, existing on several planes of existence simultaneously. A person's astral body exists in an environment called the **astral plane**, which is the astral body of planet Earth.

Astral plane – A subtle energy environment strongly associated with feelings and characterized by a fluid, watery appearance, where the substance of solid objects moves about in tiny currents, yet maintains general shape. Its substance can be shaped by the insistent force of will and the imaging power of mind. The astral plane has at least seven "levels" of distinct variety. The **first level** is the densest, a dark, viscous, oppressive "hellish" environment dominated by intense negative emotions such as fear, rage, lust, and greed. Its inhabitants have little freedom due to the intensity of their desires and emotions. They are usually found in groups expressing a dominant desire or emotion, learning how to control it instead of being controlled by it. The **second level** offers a "limbo-like" misty gray twilight environment in which fear, alienation and loss keep its inhabitants trapped in sad isolation. The **third level** presents a "normal" environment similar to physical existence, where most persons reside in living situations suited to their preferences. Its residents demonstrate some self-mastery over their desires and emotions and enjoy a greater measure of freedom, yet they are still limited by fears, ignorance, prejudice, and lack of thinking ability. The **fourth and higher levels** contain smaller numbers of persons than the three lower levels. Each of the higher levels is attained by those who demonstrate increasing self-mastery and spiritual connection, thus earning greater freedom and harmony. Images of "heaven" describe the sense of divine partnership expressed in these higher levels.

Astrology – Defined by Webster as a method of "predicting events by the stars," astrology studies the qualities associated with the astronomical positions of stars, planets and the Earth's moon and observable events. An astrologer combines art and science in creating an astrological chart for an individual or group as a way of gaining better understanding of their dynamics and predicting significant events for them.

Atlantis – An ancient civilization thought to exist on a continent in the Atlantic Ocean until the continent sank beneath the ocean approximately 12,500 years ago (10,500 BCE). Information about Atlantis has been limited to references in ancient literature, most notably Plato, and to channeled sources, such as Edgar Cayce. Archaeological research has yet to verify its existence. Atlantean culture is said to have achieved high levels of refinement and advanced technology that our present culture is only beginning to attain.

Attunement – 1) The process of attaining harmony in one's own being, which may be accomplished by meditation, prayer, or significant actions. 2) The process of attaining harmony between one person and another person, or between one person and another being or object. The process is considered similar to tuning a musical instrument so that it plays at its highest potential.

Aura – A complex energy field surrounding people, animals, vegetation, and physical objects, that may be visible to some persons and potentially detectable by instruments. Kirlian photography might portray images of the electromagnetic portion of this energy field. Clairvoyants may perceive any of the etheric, astral, mental, and causal bodies as a person's aura.

Avatar – A physical embodiment of a Spiritual Master who "descends" into the physical plane on a mission. The term derives from the Sanskrit word "avatara" which means "to descend." In Hindu tradition, Krishna is considered an avatar of Vishnu. The concept can be extended to consider Jesus as an avatar of the Christ, and so forth.

Awareness – 1) The ability to be cognizant of one's own perceptions, feelings and thoughts. 2) One's sensitivity to oneself, others, and the environment.

Bailey, Alice Ann – A spiritual teacher who produced more than twenty inspiring metaphysical books presenting ideas dictated to her telepathically by the Tibetan Master, Djwal Khul. She was born in 1880 in Manchester, England, and died in New York City in 1949 at age 69. Her books are reprinted by the Lucis Trust, and the Arcane School that she founded continues to offer esoteric training.

Basic Self or Selves – Monitor calls the masculine and feminine aspects of the subconscious human mind the "Male Self" and the "Female Self." These "Selves" evolve through relationship stages over approximately 1,600 physical lifetimes. They exist at first as separate individuals accumulating awareness and skills. They can each occupy separate physical bodies. As they evolve, they are brought together in a single physical body. As they become acquainted, they relate to each other with fear, alienation, and aggression. Gradually, over a span of 100 lifetimes they learn to respect, support, and love each other to achieve increasing intimacy. Eventually they merge energetically in achieving androgyny, a state of fulfilled masculine-feminine unity. The relationship of a person's Basic Selves often determines the quality of that person's interpersonal relationships.

Body Consciousness – The evolving elemental consciousness of the physical/etheric body. It expresses either masculine or feminine qualities during its early stages of evolution through physical and etheric lifetimes. In later stages, it increasingly expresses androgynous qualities of unified masculine and feminine energies. Its intellect is similar to that of a dog, cat, or horse at a pre–verbal level. It responds well to affectionate touch and other signs of physical caring. It consists of a coordinating **Body Self** and thousands of **Somatic Selves** associated with body structures, such as organs, glands, bones, etc.

Body Self – Coordinator of the physical/etheric body. The **Outer Self** may communicate with it mainly through images and feelings, since it is usually pre-verbal and does not understand many words. A Body Self can be encouraged or discouraged by other Selves or circumstances. If encouraged, it can sustain or improve physical health. If discouraged, it can allow health to deteriorate. A person's state of physical health is strongly affected, but not totally determined by their Body Self. The **High Self** might activate karmic conditions, such as genetic weaknesses, injuries, and illnesses, as a way of assisting the growth of certain Selves.

Buddha – 1) The historical man, Siddhartha Gautama, who became enlightened in 563 B.C.E, and whose teachings became the focal point for the Buddhist religion. 2) A title used in reference to one who has reached and maintained a state of **enlightenment.**

Buddhic plane – According to Monitor, the buddhic plane of existence was created from the original matter of the adic plane. **Cosmic Identities** in the **adic plane** created **Monads** in the buddhic plane. The Monads created **Souls** in the **causal plane,** extending the lineage of Life forms toward human beings in the mental, astral, etheric, and physical planes. Buddhic beings in the buddhic plane offer the Golden Light of **Grace** to us in lessening the severity of karmic conditions.

Causal plane – The plane of existence where Souls live in causal bodies. According to Monitor, an Outer Self experiences the causal body of its Soul through the sharing of at least one Subconscious Self making **Soul contact and linkage.** In daily life, altruistic and compassionate ideals, values, and intentions reflect the causal qualities and intentions of our Soul.

Cayce, Edgar – (1877–1945) A clairvoyant and prophet considered America's most authenticated psychic. Over his lifetime he gave more than 14,000 readings dealing with health and past lives. The records of these readings are maintained at the headquarters of the Association for Research & Enlightenment in Virginia Beach, Virginia. His readings dealing with the subject of **Atlantis** and ancient civilizations are considered the most extensive available. The remedies given in his health readings are the subject of extensive research, and have become widely used and commercially available. A considerable number of best selling books have been written about him and his revelations.

Cellular memory – A reference to patterns of activity and behavior which are held in the body cells, and which are apparently encoded both genetically and from experience within the body's lifetime. It is believed these patterns affect not only physical health, but also personal behavior and emotions as well. Monitor says that cellular memory resides with the **Body Self** and **Somatic Selves** of a personality.

Center – 1) A point of power in a person's physical body. 2) Term used to mean finding balance in any situation or condition, i.e., "to center." 3) Point of energetic balance of the Life force within the human body.

Chakra – Sanskrit term which refers to points of energetic activity and exchange within the human body. Seven major chakras are identified that correspond to the body's endocrine gland system. These radiant points are responsible for the reception and distribution of higher energies from the higher planes of existence, affecting physical, emotional, mental, and spiritual activities and behaviors. Chakras maintain a balance of inflow and outflow of Life energies for each body of a personality. According to Monitor, the sacral and solar plexus chakras are locations where fearful **Astral and Mental Judge Selves** normally hide.

Christ – 1) The Divine Presence that infused the Spiritual Master known as **Jesus,** Jeshua, or Yeshua, whose teachings became the Christian religion. 2) A highly evolved being who works for the benefit of the spiritual evolution of all species, i.e., a "Christed Being," 3) The "Office of the Christ" which represents a position of high and vast responsibility in leadership of the **Spiritual**

Hierarchy of Earth. 4) A level of highly advanced collective consciousness sometimes referred to as "Christ Consciousness."

Clairaudience – The psychic ability to perceive, through the sense of hearing, sounds that originate in nonphysical **planes of existence,** inaudible to ordinary physical hearing. Associated with development of the **throat chakra.**

Clairsentience – The psychic ability to perceive, through the sense of feeling or "knowing," sensations that originate in nonphysical planes of existence. Associated with the development of the **heart chakra.**

Clairvoyance – The psychic ability of an Outer Self to perceive, through the sense of sight, images in nonphysical planes of existence or images beyond normal physical sight. Associated with development of the **solar plexus chakra.** According to Monitor, the Outer Self gains this ability through rapport with one or more Subconscious Selves or an energetic infusion from the High Self.

Consciousness – 1) The totality of an individual's perceptions, awarenesses, thoughts, senses, and motivations for activity and behavior in any and all planes of existence. 2) The collective perceptions, awarenesses, thoughts, senses, and motivations of beings and matter.

Conscious Self – This term derives from psychology, which recognizes the distinction between "conscious" and "unconscious" levels of mind. However, the term "Conscious Self" implies that the rest of the personality is *not* "conscious" or intentional. Monitor prefers to call it the **Outer Self** since its attention is normally focused in the "outer" world of the physical plane.

Cosmos – A reference to the whole of manifested essence, including all planes of existence; the universe and its functioning in its entirety.

Cosmic Identities – Cosmic entities who live in the adic plane of existence. Monitor describes twelve Cosmic Identities who evolved at the beginning of Creation of the universe. They animate **Monads** and begin the "cosmic tree" of Life, which eventually branches to human and other beings.

Devas – A nonphysical species whose purpose is the creation, expression, and maintenance of Life forms in all the planes of the "world of forms." Their level of development varies from Divine to primitive. So-called "nature spirits" include devas. The term originates from Sanskrit and means "shining ones."

While similar to angels in some respects, devas value their individuality and make decisions based on esthetic impulses. Consequently, their appearance frequently changes.

Devic – Pertaining to **Devas.** 1) The qualities or forces of creation, maintenance, and destruction that derive from devas. Includes such elusive forces as wind. 2) Describes the difficult-to-contain qualities, attitudes and activities of devas. Often used to identify creative, including sometimes impractical but expressive, activities.

Dharma – Buddhist and Hindu term from Sanskrit that: 1) in general, refers to the supreme operating function of the universe or cosmos, the underlying dynamic pattern and force which manifests the universe; and 2) individually, refers to one's activities for evolving beyond personal **karma,** the manner and principles within which one lives one's life, and specifically in relation to the teachings of Siddhartha Gautama, the **Buddha.**

Divinity – Reference to the high **planes of existence** and Beings who motivate evolution in and out of the world of forms. Evolution leads Life from unity to diversity of forms and functions, and then returns to unity enhanced.

Earth changes – Major geological and meteorological changes, both natural and human-caused, in planet Earth that change ecological and human conditions. Such changes may affect the continuation or extinction of species. Many prophets have warned of imminent catastrophic changes, such as global warming, magnetic and geophysical pole reversals caused by human activities, such as global war, unregulated pollutions, and destructive selfishness that ignores overpopulation, financial imbalance, or technological irresponsibility. Earth changes also offer opportunities to uplift society and correct the damages that have been inflicted on Earth's natural systems, plus the potential raising of human existence and consciousness into higher dimensions.

Earth plane – The physical three-dimensional world that people perceive as a plane of existence among other non-physical planes of existence.

Ego – 1) A term derived from the work of Sigmund Freud to refer to the self and to ways of behaving and thinking realistically. 2) In psychology, an aspect of conscious and subconscious levels of mind affecting rational thought and activity with regard to one's own being. 3) In popular metaphysics, "ego" refers to the aspect of a personality that resists transcendence. Monitor defines "ego" as the fearful aspects of the **Outer Self** and **Subconscious Selves** who resist growth and evolution.

Elementals – 1) Nonphysical beings who live in and help develop Life qualities in the mineral, vegetable, animal, and human kingdoms. Monitor describes the elementals of a flower as "tenants" and the supervising deva of the flower as the "landlord." A balance is needed between elementals and **devas** to sustain the planetary bodies of Earth through coordination of the four energetic elements of fire, water, earth, and air. 2) Qualities associated with sustenance of Earth, such as "elemental" or "primitive" energies. Humans need to radiate Love to elementals and devas in furthering their evolution.

Enlightenment – 1) The highest state of awareness and being for a human, an indescribable mystical condition in which one directly experiences the unity and oneness of all that exists, seen and unseen, in the universe, including **God,** the Creator. 2) A series of partial enlightenments lead gradually to full enlightenment. Monitor describes this as a sequence of enlightenments occurring to the various Selves of a personality until the bodies and consciousness of the personality are uplifted into higher states of being.

Entity – An individualized being on any manifested level of existence, i.e., a spirit entity, a human entity, a Divine entity.

Etheric Body – An individual body of a person or some other being in the **etheric plane.** A person's etheric body can exist without a corresponding physical body when a person lives in the **interlife** between physical lifetimes. When a person enters physical embodiment, their etheric body becomes the template for creating a new physical body. The etheric body interpenetrates and surrounds the physical body. The etheric body acts as the dynamic principle, and the physical body reacts to it. Sometimes called the "vital body."

Etheric Plane – The level of matter in the universe nearest to the physical plane. It interpenetrates and surrounds physical matter, giving it vitality, whether organic or inorganic. The collective etheric body of Earth contains all individual etheric bodies. In turn, the planetary etheric body is contained by solar, galactic, and universal etheric bodies. Monitor regards the etheric body as the "real" body and the physical body as a lower energetic expression of the etheric body.

Evolution – The process of growth and refinement toward eventual cosmic divinity and return to **God,** the Creator.

Female Self – The major feminine Subconscious Self of a personality. According to Monitor, Male and Female Selves are manifested in the **mental plane** by a Soul entering embodiment in Earth. These **Basic Selves** develop individual characteristics and capabilities over approximately 1,600 physical lifetimes until they voluntarily unite with each other, and then with their **Soul.** See: **Basic Self/Selves,** also **Male Self.**

Feminine energy – In terms of duality, the energy that is characteristically attractive, nurturing, and receptive, acting as one half of creative force. The **yin** force of Chinese Taoist concepts. Monitor describes this energy configuration as moving from the periphery to the center of forms. See **Masculine energy.**

Freedom – Monitor defines freedom as having access to many options. We gain freedom when we gain access to more options than we previously had. Often we limit our access to options, such as asking for Grace, because of confusion caused by maya, glamours, and illusions that we maintain out of ignorance.

Glamour – Monitor describes a glamour as a distortion in the **astral body** of a person, a group of people, and the evolving **Planetary Being.** Only humans create glamours, beginning with glamours of separation and progressing to glamours of self-pity. These astral distortions, often based on fears, not only complicate a person's reactions but also pollute the collective astral bodies of groups and the astral body of the Planetary Being. Glamours derive from **illusions** (misperceptions and misinterpretations occurring in the mental body) and block a person's true perception like a fog. Glamours occur as distorted or unrealistic desires, emotions, attitudes, and expectations. However, not all of these astral expressions are glamourized. Glamour also contributes to **maya.** Spiritual growth requires that individuals and collective humanity destroy the glamours they have created, and so free the Planetary Being from glamour. In the footsteps of Djwal Khul, Monitor presents a method for glamour-clearing through use of Soul Light.

God – Monitor usually refers to God, the Creator of all Life, in and out of the world of forms. They say that most of the illuminating and mystical experiences recorded in history are experiences of Soul contact and linkage, not contact and linkage with God, the Creator. However, linking with our **Soul** brings us closer to contact with God.

Grace – Monitor refers frequently to Grace as a resource that we can call on. They describe it as a response to our requests and prayers from highly evolved Beings in the **buddhic plane,** given to ease the stress of karmic consequences. According to Monitor, the Law of Grace represents a higher law or principle than the Law of **Karma.** Applying Grace helps us learn our karmic lessons faster and with less stress.

High Self – According to Monitor, the High Self of a personality is usually a Solar Angel who volunteers to help an embodied Soul in development of a personality until it matures and voluntarily unites with its Soul. The Solar Angel comes from its home in our sun and is free to return there when its job in Earth is done. One Solar Angel may act as High Self for a number of personalities. Monitor recommends that the **Outer Self** frequently ask the High Self for assistance and guidance.

Holism – Term from the Greek word "holos," meaning whole, complete, total, all-encompassing. The concept that every energetic manifestation in the universe participates in every other energetic manifestation, so that any action or change affects the entire universe.

Holistic – A position arising from **holism,** in which concepts and activities are carried out in acknowledgment that everything is ultimately connected, that every action affects the whole, and that energy is never lost but only changed. Used particularly to identify approaches to health and healing which reflect that attitude, including alternative medical treatments that recognize the natural connections between body, mind, and spirit, such as homeopathic, herbal, environmental, energy medicine, bio-electric & magnetic therapies, acupuncture, ayurvedic medicine, and methods that explore the energetic causes of disease or malfunction.

I Ching – Pronounced "ee-jing." An ancient Chinese system of divination that identifies patterns, forces, and causes active in the Life process. A book that now has many translations, it is used as a divination instrument for clarifying and giving guidelines for wise behavior in the context of a situation that is explored by asking specific questions about it. While in deep concentration about the inquiry, either three coins or fifty sticks are thrown down, and their falling positions are considered as indications harmonious with the universe. The positions form combinations of both static and changing **yin** and **yang** "trigrams" and "hexagrams" that designate specific information. One of the more highly evolved behavior divination systems. Among recommended translations are those by Carol K. Anthony, and R. L. Wing.

Illumination – A reference to nonphysical Light or force transmitted from higher to lower planes of existence. Similar to the term **Enlightened** when used generally. In the Monitor model, the **Light** of the **Soul** is requested to fill the chakras and bodies of a personality as a means of creating attunement or linkage with the Soul. The Golden Light of **Grace** is also requested as a source of comfort and assistance to fearful Selves, especially **Judge Selves.**

Illusion – Monitor describes illusions as misperceptions and misinterpretations of experience by a personality or Self as expressed by their thought forms in the **mental body.** The primary illusion of "separation" – which occurs to Selves in the process of individuation – leads to clusters of illusions, false, inaccurate, and incomplete ideas and concepts of self and the world, which, in turn, foster **glamours** in the astral body. Spiritual growth requires that we clear our individual illusions, group illusions, and collective illusions of humanity. That clearance process reduces our experience of **maya.**

Incarnation – Monitor defines incarnation as the entire process of a **Soul** entering into a series of physical embodiments or lifetimes. The process of incarnation begins when a Soul animates the Basic Selves of a personality and ends when the **Basic Selves** unify with each other and then with the Soul. An incarnation includes approximately 1,600 physical embodiments.

Initiate – A person who commits him/herself in service to assist the Spiritual Hierarchy in their illumined work for the benefit of all Life, and who is tested through ceremony and service and found capable by the Hierarchy in an on-going process of initiation. Most persons have not made this commitment.

Intention – Webster defines intention as "a determination to act in a specified way." In Monitor's model, it refers to the application of a Self's will in making choices that apply the understanding that the Self has attained in recognizing and working with Divine principles or laws in order to create an outcome. A personality whose Selves express diverse intentions can be described as "incoherent." A personality whose Selves express the same or similar intentions can be described as "coherent."

Intuition – A "knowing" that arises from other than linear intellectual process, sometimes referred to as a "gut feeling." Associated with development of the heart chakra. Monitor relates the development of intuitive abilities to opening reliable lines of communication between the **Outer Self** and the **High Self** through the cooperation of at least one Subconscious Self.

Involution – The process of downward, infolding development; the reverse of the upward, forward, outward process of **evolution**. In Monitor's model, a person's or Self's inability to overcome fear creates motivation for pursuing involution. An involutional person or Self seeks to control others in lieu of resolving their own fears. Historical examples can be found in Adolph Hitler, Saddam Hussein, and others.

Judging – The act of labeling someone or something as "bad" or "wrong" and creating feelings of blame, condemnation, etc. Judging is based on black-or-white thinking associated with the adrenal "fight or flight" response to stress. Judging includes labels that are variations of "bad" or "wrong," such as "unworthy," incapable," "unlovable," etc.

Judge Self/Judge Selves – A term from the Monitor teachings that refers to two subconscious aspects of the personality. According to Monitor, the Judge Selves, one in our mental body (**Mental Judge Self**) and one in our astral body (**Astral Judge Self**), are actually aspects of another devic species of being who were brought to Earth as refugees in an effort to heal the trauma which had severely damaged them when their home planet, Maldek, disrupted on physical and etheric levels. A Maldekian personality has its own Soul that relates in harmony with the Soul of our Basic Selves. The Maldekian Soul can be a major resource for us, but first we are challenged to bring healing to both Judge Selves. Because of trauma, the Judge Selves isolate themselves and mistrust other beings. In their fearful isolation, they can abuse other Selves in the personality and other persons until the Outer Self helps them desensitize their fears. Once they begin to emerge from their fears and isolation, they can become powerful allies and speed the spiritual evolutionary process for the personality.

Jung, Carl – (1875–1961) Swiss psychiatrist whose own extraordinary mystical experiences and belief in **reincarnation** contributed to his break with the Freudian view, followed by his pursuance of fields which include what Jung himself called the "collective unconscious," "archetypes," and study of dreams, visions and various psychic, mystical experiences, the **I Ching** and synchronicity. Jungian psychology is now considered one of the two main branches of psychological practice. His prolific writings fill more than twenty published volumes.

Kabbalah – The mystic form of classical Judaism, handed down by secret oral tradition. It appears to have been influenced by Gnosticism, and its earliest form is found in the tradition of the Merkabah mystics (100 BCE–1,000 AD). Merkabah means "God's Throne-Chariot" and refers to the chariot of Ezekiel's vision. Classical Kabbalah was born in the thirteenth century in Provence, France, and developed most extensively by medieval Jews in Spain. Also spelled Quabbalah, Quaballah, Kabala, Cabbala.

Karma – A Sanskrit term meaning "deed" or "demonstration." Its use in the Western world originated from Hindu and Buddhist traditions in reference to the law of cause and effect, reaping what a person has sown. When applied to **reincarnation,** karma refers to the effects of our Subconscious Selves' past deeds on our present and future lifetimes. Monitor describes karma as an automatic response of the universe to correct our course in evolution. When we get "off course," the universe provides experiences that motivate us to improve our **intentions** and actions, bringing them into closer harmony with universal **laws.** As karma applies to our personalities and their Selves, it brings both positive and negative experiences, all of which are designed by our High Self to promote spiritual growth. By making wise, Loving choices that benefit all of Life, our Selves attain Soul linkage and illumination, which leads to unification of personality with Soul. A person can complete karmic lessons and achieve an "akarmic" state of living, operating in accord with universal laws.

Karmic lesson – A step in learning presented to an **Outer Self** or **Subconscious Self** by the **High Self** of the personality. Each lesson provides an opportunity for a Self to demonstrate its understanding, values, and intentions. As Selves evolve from selfish to universally altruistic intentions, their karmic lessons invite them to develop sensitivity and responsiveness to the needs of all Life, including the needs of their **Soul.**

Kundalini/Kundaline force – A Sanskrit term meaning "snake," or "serpent power," arising from the Hindu tradition which refers to the powerful psycho-spiritual energy which resides within the human body. It is likened to liquid fire or liquid Light, and remains in a dormant state until, through the cycles of reincarnation, an individual grows spiritually and "awakens" the kundaline forces that rise from the lower chakras to the crown chakra, producing transcendence and ecstasy of enlightenment. According to Monitor, kundaline forces activate when the Male and Female Selves consistently express Love and caring for each other, causing their masculine and feminine energies to blend in the etheric body and thus produce the androgynous kundalini force. The kundaline force rises through the interwoven energetic channels of the **Sutratma** and **Antahkarana** called the ida, pingala and sushumna.

Karmic plan – Monitor says that the High Self of the personality guides the learning of the **Outer Self** and **Subconscious Selves** by proving them with graduated choices. As each Self makes choices, it demonstrates what it has learned. The High Self's plan is not "set in concrete," but remains creative and responsive to the progress of Selves and the entire personality.

Karmic relationship – A relationship can be considered karmic because it provides opportunities for each personality and Self to make wise, Loving decisions. While many persons have come to believe that they "have karma" with another person, Monitor says that a relationship does not involve "debts" or "obligations" to another person or Self, but rather "opportunities" for learning how to be more wise and Loving. Difficulties that arise in a relationship signal a need for one or both persons to learn greater sensitivity and develop greater relationship skills on conscious and subconscious levels.

Kundalini/kundaline – A Sanskrit term meaning "snake" or "serpent power" arising from the Hindu tradition that refers to the powerful psycho-spiritual energy that resides within the human body. It is likened to liquid fire or liquid Light and remains in a dormant state until, through the cycles of **reincarnation,** an individual grows spiritually and "awakens" the kundaline forces which rise from the **root chakra** upward through the body until, reaching the upper chakras, produce transcendence of personality and the ecstasy of **enlightenment.** According to Monitor, kundaline forces activate when **Basic Selves** begin the process of energetic merging and produce androgynous force in the three kundaline channels: the ida, pingala, and sushumna.

Laws – In reference to spiritual development, the universal, cosmic principles that create and sustain ordered, dynamic evolution in the world of forms. Also refers to conceptual traditions, such as the "Law of **Reincarnation,**" or the "Law of **Karma.**"

Lemuria – A legendary lost continent and ancient civilization, first brought to our attention in the nineteenth century by some scientists in response to a need to explain Darwin's theory of evolution through a common ancestor, and then through mystical and psychic sources such as Madame Blavatsky, Rudolf Steiner, and Edgar Cayce. Lemuria is thought to have existed prior to the civilization of Atlantis in the Indian and Pacific ocean areas of the southern hemisphere. There is a tradition that the survivors of the sinking of the Lemurian continent evolved into the Atlanteans. See: **Mu.**

Ley lines – Properly referred to as "leys," these natural currents of etheric energy create alignments and patterns that connect various sacred sites such as stone circles, holy wells, churches, temples, and other locations of spiritual or magical importance. Their existence was first proposed in the mid-1920s by Alfred Watkins, an Englishman. Controversy exists as to whether they are actual energy configurations within the earth, or simple man-made alignments. Although they are believed to exist all over the world, the study of leys has been primarily in Britain as a part of what are called the "earth mysteries." Monitor regards ley lines as planetary "acupuncture meridians." Where they intersect, they often form vortices. See **Vortex/vortices.**

Life – Monitor says that every form in the **world of forms** expresses Life, the ongoing Presence of **God,** the Creator, and that non-individualized Life expresses beyond the world of forms as "Spirit." Monitor agrees with the beliefs of most indigenous peoples that all matter and energy are alive at varying levels of consciousness. Because of the universality of consciousness, a person can impress intentions on physical objects and energies to influence their qualities and actions, as shown by scientifically documented instances of psychokinesis.

Light – 1) May refer to the appearance of Divinity within spiritual and religious traditions, and therefore the source of the terms **enlightenment** and **illumination**. Describes perception within a visionary or higher state of consciousness in which nonphysical Light, or Divine Light, is experienced, i.e., to "be in the Light." 2) In science, physical light. In Monitor's usage, physical light has a lowercase L, while nonphysical Light has an uppercase L.

Love – Monitor describes Love as a universal force that enhances the individuation of Life essence and matter in all the **planes of existence** and draws all toward unity in the **adic plane.** Monitor identifies this universal Love with a capital "L" and distinguishes it from the personal, emotional, and often selfish love that characterizes many human relationships. Monitor says that this solar system focuses on development of Love-Wisdom (Love integrated with Wisdom), the second ray of Divinity. Consequently, our capacity for love needs to develop into a capacity for Love exercised with wisdom.

Lucid dreaming – When a dreamer (Outer Self) dreams and is sufficiently aware to act with intention to change events in a dream. This is considered a useful way to apply problem solving, creativity, and assistance to one's health, relationships and life condition. Advanced degrees of dream lucidity can be achieved with practice.

Maldek – According to Monitor, Maldek is a nonphysical planet that exists in the orbit where the asteroid belt is now located between the orbits of Mars and Jupiter. Asteroids compose the physical matter remaining from an unintentional disruption of the physical and etheric aspects of Maldek by combined actions of its native inhabitants. Since the disruption severely traumatized its native inhabitants (Maldekians), the Spiritual Hierarchy transported them to Earth and devised a plan that incorporates those beings into the composite structure of human personalities. In the human personality, Maldekians are called the Astral and Mental **Judge Selves.** This evolutionary plan provides ways for restoring and continuing the evolution of Maldekian beings so they can eventually reunite them with their Souls. Monitor also indicates that the Maldekians will someday return to Maldek where they will be given opportunity to rebuild its etheric and physical aspects.

Maldekians – Beings native to Maldek. Monitor describes the Maldekian personality as a Soul with devic qualities who animated a mental Self in the mental plane of Maldek, and together they animated an astral Self in the astral plane. This three-level personality was transported to Earth to continue its evolution as part of the composite makeup of the human personality.

Male Self – The masculine Subconscious Self of a personality. According to Monitor, Male and Female Selves are manifested in the **mental plane** by a Soul entering embodiment in Earth. These **Basic Selves** develop individual characteristics and capabilities, and evolve over approximately 1,600 physical lifetimes until they voluntarily unite with each other, and then with their **Soul.** See **Basic Self/Selves,** also **Female Self.**

Mantra – From the Sanskrit, *man,* meaning "mind," and *tra,* meaning "to deliver," as used in Hinduism and Buddhism. 1) A reference to certain syllables or sounds that carry in their tones basic vibratory patterns of cosmic law, and so represent cosmic forces. 2) The use of certain of these sounds or names in a meditative process in which the sound is repeated until it uplifts the meditators into more spiritual states of awareness. 3) In other religions, such as Christianity, Judaism, and Islam, the names of God are considered to be powerful mantras and are used in prayer and chanting in a similar fashion.

Masculine energy – In terms of duality, the energy that is characteristically active, radiatory, penetrating, and initiating; one half of creative force. The **Yang** force in Chinese Taoist concepts. Monitor describes this energy configuration as moving from the center to and beyond the periphery of forms. See **Feminine energy.**

Master – 1) In spiritual life, a person who attains **enlightenment** or **illumination** and then leads others toward that same goal. Generally, it refers to an individual who gains profound understanding and wisdom, and on spiritual and mundane levels performs Loving service for the benefit of others. 2) In Christianity, a specific reference to **Jesus Christ** or **Yeshua**. In Theosophical tradition, a reference to illuminated beings such as Koot Humi, Morya, Djwal Khul, Babaji, Sananda, etc. A Master's clear perception of reality is made available to others through their creation of **Master Thought Forms** in the higher levels of the mental plane.

Master Thought Forms – When a Master achieves profound understanding of spiritual law and reality, he/she creates and sustains a thought form composed of organized mental substance that another person can encounter and read. Like a skilled mountain climber, a Master ascends in understanding and leaves behind a trail for others to follow. When a spiritual seeker finds and reads a Master thought form, he/she experiences not only greater insight, but also energetic stimulation.

Mastery – *The achievement of a person who* accepts profound partnership with Soul and higher Beings and assists in the spiritual evolution of other beings. Masters join the Spiritual Hierarchy of Earth in promoting the spiritual evolution of humanity and other kingdoms of Life as part of the spiritual evolution of the Planetary Being of Earth.

Matter – The basic structure of forms on all the planes of existence. Monitor says that the physical plane reflects the structure of higher planes, and that physical atoms and subatomic particles are derived from etheric atoms and subatomic structures. Throughout the universe, matter is created by the "mother" principle of Divinity, which offers forms for Life essence to experience. Thus, matter is seen as animate or "alive."

Maya – A Hindu term from the early *Vedas*, which means "powerful trickery." Monitor describes maya as a belief, common to humanity, that **physical plane** existence constitutes the only true existence and that any nonphysical existence is somehow less real or valid. Maya suggests the separation of a personality or Self from all other Life, and makes it difficult for a personality or Self to perceive its true nature. Since maya is composed of a combination of **illusions** and **glamours,** the practice of glamour- and illusion-clearing also clears maya, freeing our perceptions from distortion.

Meditation – 1) In spiritual traditions, a disciplined practice intended to uplift a person's consciousness into a high state, and ultimately into a state of **enlightenment** or union with the Divine. Many forms of meditative practice exist to quiet internal mind chatter, some of which use sound, mantras, or music, some requiring strict disciplines to "still the mind," some using visionary suggestions or guidance, some using contemplation of an object to focus and quiet the mind. All have potential to achieve high mystical states of consciousness and linkage with Soul. 2) In mundane use, it characterizes the focus of intellect on a subject to achieve a desired understanding.

Mental plane – Created as an extension of the causal plane, we experience the mental plane as the realm of ideas, concepts, knowledge, and understanding. As our mental body develops, we evolve from instinct to intellect to intuition to illumination, as our mental body attains the capacity for attunement to successive higher levels of the mental plane. We comprehend greater expressions of "truth" as our mental bodies become able to interface with thought forms created by various **Masters** (Master thought forms).

Metaphysics – A Greek term meaning "beyond physics," it is the field of philosophical and spiritual topics that deals with the nature of reality and spiritual evolution in physical and more than physical realms.

Monad – According to Monitor, **Cosmic Identities** in the **adic plane** create Monads in the **buddhic plane.** Monads, in turn, create **Souls** in the **causal plane** and assist Souls in achieving the maturation of the human personalities that they create in the lower planes of existence.

Mu – According to Monitor, the ancient City of Gold in the Gobi spawned the derivative civilization of Mu, situated in the western portion of what is now the Pacific Ocean. Later Mu evolved into **Lemuria.** Mu is the name given to this lost continent by Colonel James Churchward in 1870, when he claimed to have seen secret clay tablets hidden in India that recorded its history. See **Lemuria.**

Mystic – A person who experiences profound, expanded perception and senses the Oneness of All. Mysticism refers to a form of spirituality, religious or non-religious, which is specifically a direct perception of unification with the Oneness of All. Although various approaches to mysticism exist, all commonly include: 1) a unifying perception of the One, the Divinity in all reality, 2) direct experience of spiritual ecstasy and bliss, and 3) awareness of the sacredness of all Life. Boundaries between subject and object disappear for the mystic; one perceives being one with all that exists, as opposed to having only heightened appreciation or understanding.

Nature – Forces and forms indigenous to the Earth, including the mineral, plant and animal species, the four elements of fire, water, air and earth, as well as planetary forces, such as geological and meteorological conditions, earthquakes, volcanic eruptions, winds, storms, and cyclic forces such as tides and seasons.

Negative energy – The use of energy in a manner that is destructive or inhibiting, as opposed to creative and growth-promoting

New Age – An ambiguous term applied to the spiritual and social movement that encompasses a broad range of interests including both eastern and western religions, philosophy, health, psychology and parapsychology, metaphysics, the psychic, the occult, and esoteric or arcane traditions.

Non-judgmental – To remain free of judging oneself and/or others and thereby avoid emotions such as anger or envy. The ability to be non-judgmental is often associated with development of the heart chakra. See **Judging.**

Outer Self – The term used by Monitor to refer to the *interface* of all aspects of the personality who have lived before and the new physical body, the aspect focused primarily on the outer events of physical life. The Outer Self generally refers to what is commonly called "the conscious mind." However, that term implies that other aspects of the personality are not conscious. The term, Outer Self, removes that implication.

Out-of-body experience – In parapsychology, often referred to as OOBE or OBE, a condition in which the Outer Self gains awareness and perception outside the physical body, and beyond the normal range of senses. In an OBE, an Outer Self may move without the restrictions of physical matter and see their physical body from a distance. This experience occurs most commonly as a result of severe trauma to the body; however, it also occurs spontaneously to some persons without apparent cause. In some shamanic traditions, a person can develop the skill to do so at will. It is often the initial stage of what is called a "near death experience," or NDE.

Parapsychology – "Para" means "beyond" in Greek, and refers to the branch of psychology concerned with matters that go beyond its ordinary boundaries. Parapsychology dates back to the late nineteenth century with the formation of the Society for Psychical Research in London, "psychical" being the term commonly used in Britain. It is involved with the study of psi phenomena such as extrasensory perception and psychokinesis; however, its practice has expanded to include any paranormal experience or phenomena.

Past lives – A reference to prior lifetimes, prior physical embodiments, in a process of reincarnation. According to Monitor, the **High Self, Basic Selves, Judge Selves, and Body Self** aspects of the personality experienced those prior lifetimes. The **Outer Self** of a new lifetime can gain access to past life memories from the Selves who retain them. Monitor recommends that the Outer Self ask the High Self to guide the past life recall process.

Past life connection – The connection between two or more people who have had relationships in past lives. This produces responses of either positive or negative feelings and behavior for which there is no apparent cause in present circumstances.

Physical plane – The usual focus of awareness of the **Outer Self,** which comprises only a very small part of the universe. In Monitor's view, the physical plane is created as a dense projection or "shadow" of the **etheric plane.** The etheric plane is seen as active, and the physical plane as passive, so the etheric plane vitalizes the physical. **Subconscious Selves** and the **High Self** do not normally perceive the physical experience of the Outer Self, but can extend their sensitivity to that level when needed.

Planes of existence – The seven levels of matter that coexist in a dynamic relationship. According to Monitor, the Creator created the adic plane of the universe, where Cosmic Identities live. Their impulse toward individualization led to their creation of the buddhic plane where Monads live. Their impulse toward individualization produced the mental, astral, etheric, and physical planes where humans, elementals, and less-evolved devas live.

Planetary Being – According to Monitor, the living, evolving Being of a planet. Monitor describes the Planetary Being of Earth as functioning at an "adolescent" level of maturity and therefore needing the assistance of other Planetary Beings and the Solar Logos. The concept of planetary consciousness is found in most indigenous cultures. Additionally, a modern scientific hypothesis was put forward by James Lovelock in the early 1970s called the "Gaia hypothesis" (the name referring to Gaia, the ancient Greek Earth Mother goddess), which proposed that the Earth is a self-regulating organism. In Monitor's view, humanity plays an important role in developing the rational mind of Earth.

Polarization – The separation of energies and qualities into polar opposites that reside in the lower planes of existence. As personalities and Selves encounter the polarities, they are challenged to develop sufficient awareness and capability to synthesize their own understanding and qualities of unified consciousness.

Positive energy – The use of energy in a manner that is creative and growth-promoting, as opposed to destructive or inhibiting.

Prana – A Sanskrit term that refers to the enlivening universal Life force expressed in the lower planes and absorbed by our bodies and chakras. Monitor views prana as etheric force. See **Etheric Plane**.

Precognition – Intuitively perceived knowledge of future events. Precognition is one of the most frequently reported extrasensory experiences. It occurs in dreams, visions, thoughts that flash into the Outer Self's awareness, and in **clairsentient** "knowing." Monitor describes precognition as occurring through transmission of probable future events from the **High Self** or **Subconscious Self** to the **Outer Self.** Transmissions from the High Self are more reliable than transmissions from Subconscious Selves.

Protection – In spiritual or paranormal activities, the use of various techniques to protect one from potentially harmful energies and influences on all planes of existence. Techniques include prayer, visualization, and placement of sacred objects charged with protective intention, such as amulets, crystals, and icons.

Psychic – A person with ability to acquire information through extrasensory perception on demand. Although anyone can develop some psychic ability with training and practice, most psychics are generally either born with the ability or acquire it through some life-threatening or traumatic experience that triggers the ability. A psychic may or may not be spiritually motivated or advanced.

Rays of Divinity – In the series of books by Alice Ann Bailey, the Tibetan Teacher describes the seven rays of Divinity as the major spiritual evolutionary forces impacting our personal and collective growth. Monitor adds details and perspective to that concept.

Reading – Psychic information, provided by someone with extrasensory abilities, intended to assist the person for whom the reading is given.

Sanskrit – The classical ancient literary language used in the Hindu spiritual writings, the *Vedas*. Sanskrit is believed to carry in its sounds a direct relationship to qualities related to the object or function to which the word is referring. Also spelled Sanscrit.

Self – Webster defines self as "the identity, character of any person or thing." According to Monitor, a Self represents an avenue of expression of Life essence. A personality is seen as a jewel with at least seven major facets, the seven Selves. See also the **High Self, Male Self, Female Self, Judge Selves (Astral and Mental), Body Self,** and **Outer Self.**

Self Integration – A system that allows the Outer Self opportunity to meet and befriend Subconscious Selves, High Self, and Soul, using techniques of inner dialogue, guided imagery, and dramatization for direct communication.

Shaman – A person trained in nonphysical perception and healing abilities in the tradition of an indigenous culture, such as Native American. A shaman can be a male or female who undergoes an individual process of transformation and spiritual initiation. The shamanic path emphasizes individual growth, as compared to the path of priesthood, which emphasizes spiritual instruction in a group.

Sol – Name from ancient Rome for its Sun God, given to the sun that is seen as responsible for the creation and evolution of our solar system. Monitor views the sun as a highly evolved Being. The guiding aspect of the Solar Being is called the Solar Logos. According to Monitor, High Selves are Solar Angels, angels who volunteer to come to Earth and take on the task of acting as guardian angels for the evolution of individual personalities.

Somatic Selves – The elemental consciousness that controls the functions of portions of a person's physical and etheric bodies, such as organs, glands, and limbs. A Somatic Self of, for example, a liver or a foot may be receptive or rejecting of healing processes. The Outer Self can establish a friendship with a resistant Somatic Self to facilitate health and healing. Monitor says that Somatic Selves eventually evolve into Body Selves in control of the entire forms of physical and etheric bodies. A Somatic Self may cooperate or disagree with its Body Self. See **Body Self.**

Soul – The higher Life form that creates and sustains the human personality in Earth. Created by a **Monad,** a Soul occupies a causal body and travels among solar systems for its development and for giving assistance to other Life forms. The life cycle of a Soul encompasses many eons and culminates when a Soul matures and willingly merges with its Monad in a demonstration of unity. In Earth and other planets, a Soul has the option of observing or participating in the evolution of Life. A participating Soul harmoniously links with other Souls in animating elemental and human lives. One Soul can animate a number of personalities, mineral forms, plants, and animals. As humans tap their Soul awareness, they naturally seek universal benefit for all Life forms.

Soul activation – As a personality matures, its **Basic Selves** attain Soul contact and linkage in a voluntary partnership of personality and Soul, which allows activation of the Soul's purposes and goals through the agency of the personality. This type of Soul-motivated service brings expressions of Love and Wisdom into the lower planes of the planet.

Soul contact – A temporary energetic connection between the mental body of a Basic Self and the causal body of its Soul. Male and Female **Basic Selves** evolve to the point when the **High Self** provides them with sporadic energetic infusions to create a series of brief moments of Soul contact for each of them separately. Each Soul contact triggers paradoxical reactions in the Basic Self of ecstasy and crisis. Soul contacts often provide the Outer Self with "mystical" experiences of the higher order active in the lives of Souls. See **Soul linkage.**

Soul family – The term that Monitor applies to all personalities sustained by a single Soul. Monitor says that the concept of "twin Souls" offered an initial, but oversimplified explanation of the capacity of a Soul to animate simultaneously up to 150 personalities. Those personalities are linked by their Soul and affect one another's awareness and growth.

Soul group – A group of Souls bonded together by a common purpose or function. When a mature personality attains Soul linkage, the Soul activates its purposes through the personality and interfaces it with other personalities in the Soul group for Soul-coordinated accomplishment of projects of universal benefit.

Soul illumination – The brightening, uplifting effect produced by the systematic incorporation of the causal radiance of a Soul into the mental, astral, etheric, and physical bodies of a personality. The causal radiance of the Soul simplifies the lower bodies and creates the subtle radiance associated with spiritual **Masters** and exceptional historic persons such as Jesus and Buddha.

Soul linkage – A lasting energetic connection between the mental body of a **Basic Self** and the causal body of its Soul. Repeated **Soul contacts** produce refinement in the Basic Self which allow it to sustain Soul contact for prolonged periods of time and attain Soul linkage. When attained, Soul linkage permits more rapid transformation of the entire personality and leads to a productive time of dedicated service and discipleship with **Masters.**

Soul mate – A person who has been in love in previous lifetimes with another person. Monitor prefers the term "previous mate" as a more appropriate term for this type of relationship. Because two persons have shared love in one lifetime does not mean that their love relationship in the present will be mature and fulfilling, as the term "soul mate" implies.

Spirit – 1) Life essence that lives outside the world of forms. As "Spirit," this Life essence chooses to remain universal and not individuate in a form. It interacts with Life essence in the world of forms, often in inspirational ways. 2) The inner spark of Divinity in each person, mineral, vegetable, animal, and object within the world of forms.

Spirit guide – A nonphysical person or other being who offers protection and guidance to a person in a physical body. Most often, spirit guides are members of a person's **Spiritual Family.**

Spirit teacher – A nonphysical disciple or Master who accepts responsibility for training a personality or Self in spiritual growth. A Spiritual Teacher operates at a higher level of capability than a **Spirit guide.**

Spirit world – A general name given to all nonphysical planes of existence. This term is associated with Spiritualism and Spiritualists who believe they communicate with the spirits of deceased persons.

Spiritual – 1) Refers to the Life essence in each person and object. 2) The higher, most essential aspect of a person, as compared with material or carnal aspects.

Spiritual family – A group of persons in physical and nonphysical bodies who have formed Loving relationships in physical embodiments and/or the Interlife. Members of one's Spiritual Family provide Loving care and guidance to a person in physical life.

Spiritual growth – The natural process of evolution for all beings. For a person, it means a process of maturation that includes individualization first, then integration of all elements of the personality, and finally unification of personality with Soul.

Star of origin – The star where a **Soul** is created by its **Monad** and educated in its home civilization of Souls. At some point in its growth, a Soul chooses to leave its star of origin and travel to other star systems for reasons of promoting its evolution and assisting planets in their evolution.

Subconscious mind – The intermediate level of consciousness in a personality, generally residing between the **Outer Self** (conscious mind) and the **High Self** (superconscious mind). It contains **Subconscious Selves** as individual expressions of will and mind.

Subconscious Selves – Selves residing in the subconscious level of mind in a personality, including **Basic Selves** (Male Self and Female Self), **Judge Selves** (Mental Judge and Astral Judge), **Body Self,** and **Somatic Selves.** Monitor indicates that additional Selves might also be found.

Subtle energies – Energies or forces beyond the present measuring capacity of our technology, or too subtle for our meters and sensors. Such energies might be physical or nonphysical, but we do not yet have instruments to identify, measure, and categorize them scientifically.

Superconscious mind – The highest level of consciousness in a personality. Monitor identifies the High Self as the most accessible aspect of our superconscious mind.

Sutratma – A Sanskrit term for the stream of Life force from Soul to the personality and returning to Soul – literally a person's "life-line." When the

High Self withdraws the sutratma from a person's physical body, the body dies. The seven major chakras are aligned periodically along the sutratma and draw Life force from it to create the four bodies of the personality – mental, astral, etheric and physical.

Synchronicity – A term coined by psychologist **Carl Jung** for coincidences that have meaning for a person or Self, yet have no other apparent connection. Synchronicities can convey a message to us or call our attention to a lesson we need to learn. According to Monitor, our **High Self** often creates synchronicities to teach us through manipulation of external events when we do not pay attention to its internal messages to us.

Tao – 1) As expressed in the ancient Chinese book, *Tao-te Ching (Book of Tao)*, attributed to Lao-Tse, pictograms suggest "teaching" and "the way humans should follow." In Taoism, it represents the most beneficial way of living in harmony with Tao, the source of Life behind all material appearances. 2) The name used by an extensive group of **Spirit Teachers.**

Telepathy – Communication from mind to mind via thought transmission from one being's mental body to another being's mental body.

Time – A person's or Self's awareness of the duration and sequence of events that it experiences. The multiple levels of awareness in a person's mind produce multiple time awarenesses. 1) "Physical time," as measured by clocks. 2) "Psychological time," an Outer Self's awareness of the duration and sequence of events. 3) "Subconscious Self time," experienced by Subconscious Selves. 4) "Superconscious Self time," experienced by our High Self. 5) "Soul time," experienced by our Soul, and so forth.

Time streams – Monitor says that an **Outer Self** in a physical body normally accesses only one forward-moving, linear time stream of awareness that we consider "past, present and future," yet our **Subconscious Selves** in etheric, astral, mental bodies have access to multiple time streams, so they perceive a broader expanse of time than the Outer Self. Our **High Self** and Soul in causal bodies perceive even greater expanses of time. An Outer Self can receive transmitted perceptions from Subconscious and Superconscious Selves that relay information from time streams beyond the physical plane, producing precognition (knowledge of the future) and retrocognition (knowledge of the past).

Transformation – Transformation suggests a significant positive or desired change in a person, Self, or other being. Transformation requires learning that results in significant change of perspective, values, and behavior. Transformation occurs both in consciousness and matter.

Transition – 1) Generally, a change of circumstances for a person, Self, or being. 2) In relation to physical death, a change of awareness from a physical body perspective to an etheric body perspective to an astral body perspective. In referring to physical death, some persons prefer the more positive connotation of "transition" instead of "death" because transition suggests that a dying personality moves into *another* normal state of existence, while "death" suggests that a person's life ends with physical body breakdown.

Translation – When used in regard to the attainment of spiritual mastery, "translation" refers to the intentional process whereby a personality translates their physical body into an etheric body. The physical body disappears in a blaze of light and is absorbed into the etheric body as a code that can be activated again when needed.

Transmutation – In terms of a personality or Self, "transmutation" refers to the intentional conversion of negative (lower) states of consciousness (for example: desires, emotions, thoughts, intentions) into positive (higher) states through the application of Love and Wisdom.

Truth – The experience of a personality, Self, or being when it achieves an accurate match of its perception to the perception of another being. Truth is experienced in an increasing scope of experience, leading to our development of mental capability for attaining direct contact with what Monitor calls "Master thought forms" in the higher levels of the mental plane. Our experience of "truth" involves our synthesis of Power, Love-Wisdom, and Intelligence (the three primary attributes of Divinity) inside our personality, and demonstration of that synthesis externally in interaction with our Planetary Being.

Unconscious mind – A term employed in psychology to designate parts of the personality other than the Outer Self or "conscious mind." Carl Jung extended this concept to include the "collective unconscious" of humanity.

Universe – The entire Creation of **God,** including the world of forms and Life without form. It includes all **planes of existence:** adic, buddhic, causal, mental, astral, etheric, and physical.

Universal Being – God, the Creator, both inside and outside the world of forms.

Universal energies – Divine creative energies emanating from the **adic plane.** These energies express through both consciousness and matter.

Vibration – Periodic motion of matter and energy in the **planes of existence.** Monitor says that physical matter has the densest, most complicated, patterns of vibration compared to the higher planes of existence. Etheric matter has less complicated patterns of vibration. Astral, mental, causal, buddhic, and adic matter have successively simplified patterns of vibration. The vibrations of one plane affect the others.

Vibratory forces – 1) Physical vibratory forces include heat, sound, light, electromagnetism, etc. 2) Nonphysical vibratory forces include forces active in etheric and higher planes and between all the **planes of existence. Subtle energies** might include physical and nonphysical vibratory forces.

Vortex or vortices – Specific places on the planet (such as the Sedona, Arizona area) that produce subtle energy effects on people. Sensitive persons perceive funnels of subtle energy in those locations, especially where **ley lines** intersect. Vortex effects can be positive or negative for humans. Positive effects include enhanced ESP, sense of energization and wellbeing, physical and emotional healing, and communication with nonphysical beings. Negative effects include disorientation, nausea, and debilitation.

Yang – A Chinese word that indicates the masculine aspect of the universe. Monitor describes it as a configuration of energy that radiates from a central source. Its complement is **Yin.**

Yin – A Chinese word that indicates the feminine aspect of the universe. Monitor describes it as a configuration of energy that moves from the periphery to the center. Its complement is **Yang.**

Yoga – An ancient process for attaining union of diverse elements of consciousness and matter in a personality by performing regular physical and mental exercises. The word "yoga" means "joining" or "union" in Sanskrit.

Zodiac – In astrology, the sky is divided into twelve sections or "signs" which are given names and symbols to represent the vibratory influences associated with them. The twelve signs now include constellations of stars in Aries,

Taurus, Gemini, Cancer, Leo, Virgo, Libra, Scorpio, Sagittarius, Capricorn, Aquarius, and Pisces.

Index

astral energies 208, 316
astral environment 208
astral existence 27
astral expression 177, 227
astral field 208
astral form 293
Astral Judge Self 198, 268
astral level 247
astral movement 240
astral perception 154, 242
astral plane 27, 79, 124, 125, 126,
    133, 136, 145, 146, 147, 172,
    190, 193, 194, 197, 198, 211,
    216, 227, 230, 240, 242, 243,
    246, 247, 248, 259, 288, 289,
    292, 293, 301, 316
astral realm 288
astral senses 119
Astri 249
astrological influences 40
astrology 40
Atlanteans 181, 187, 226
Atlantic Plate 229, 236
Atlantis 181, 187, 196, 226, 227, 228,
    229, 244
Atlantis, rising of 229
atoms 58, 72
attention 2, 21, 28, 50, 60, 62, 65, 66,
    69, 70, 75, 79, 80, 83, 85, 96,
    97, 102, 110, 112, 113, 116,
    136, 143, 163
attention, conscious 78
attention, focus of 66
attitudes 79
attunement 67
autistic 30
autonomic nervous system 14
Avatar 79
average number of lifetimes 191
avoidance 74, 87, 108
awareness 3, 9, 26, 33, 34, 61, 65, 66,
    75, 78, 80, 83, 137
awareness, higher 13
awareness exercise
    sleep 2

awareness of God 34
A Course in Miracles 25, 28, 118

B

babies 52
ball court 250
Bank of Credit and Commerce Inter-
    national 251
baptism 316
Basic Self 287
Basic Selves 198, 249, 254, 264, 280,
    287, 296, 304
Being 1
being 94
being-to-being communication 219
beings from space 209
beings of Light 210, 257
beliefs 137, 142
Bering Strait 244
Bible 45
Bimini 226
Bird Tribes 272
birth 30, 52
Black Mountain 248
blindness 129, 152
blockage 68, 156
blow hole 250
body 119, 123, 304, 305
body, love of 305
body-mind 31
body/mind awareness 51
body as bad 27
body as telephone to God 27
body awareness 50
Body Consciousness 29, 57, 106, 138,
    166, 237, 269, 276, 296, 298,
    299
Body Consciousness dream 298, 299
Body Self 284
brain 120
brain chemistry 120
brain functions 264
brain stem 157
Britain 226
British Isles 227, 229, 238

mind 268
Conscious Mind 28, 60, 62, 118, 119, 120
conscious mind 53, 67, 75, 95, 125, 126
consensus reality 131, 167
contact of Being 83
continuity of consciousness 16, 53, 125, 140, 141, 145, 277, 280
cooperation 276
cord of fear 257
corpus callosum 264, 265
corpus callosum, severed 264
corruption 251
cosmic being 73
Cosmic Identities 59, 217, 219, 223
Cosmic Identity 4, 6, 11, 73, 139
Cosmic Tree 4
couple dreaming 287
courage 113
Course in Miracles 27
Creation 76
creation 58, 64, 176
creation, conscious 61
creative change 78
creative energy 58
creative force 274
creative mode 78
creative process 67, 114
creative thinking 264
creativity 57, 58, 59, 61, 65, 66, 67, 68, 69, 71, 75, 78, 80, 83, 87, 88, 90, 92, 93, 94, 96, 99, 100, 102, 103, 105, 110, 111, 113, 114, 115, 161, 228, 264, 275
creativity blocked 113
creativity of prayer 68
Creator 4, 6, 9, 12, 23, 27, 38, 58, 63, 68, 69, 73, 74, 77, 80, 82, 90, 92, 104, 139, 170, 177, 187, 189, 190, 212, 213, 216, 217, 219, 220, 223, 264, 267
crop circles 47, 238, 239
crown chakra 316
cruelty 24

currents of consciousness 24

D

dance 275
Dark Ages 65
deafness 129, 152
death 28, 41, 89, 105, 121, 140, 216, 242, 292
  conscious 140
death of past patterns 306
desire 8, 14, 22, 24, 27, 39, 48, 51, 74, 78, 79, 88, 107, 113, 115, 139, 160, 168, 177, 179, 191, 198, 208, 212, 216, 217, 227, 239, 240, 247, 249, 266, 282, 316
destabilization 251
destiny 110
destruction 90
destruction of the physical form 266
devas 60, 73, 79, 229, 305
devastating winds 208
devic being 129, 164, 230
devic consciousness 295
devic dreams 298
devic kingdom 47, 169, 208, 228, 236
devic lives 305
devic qualities 294
devotion 268
dialogue 114, 250
dinosaurs 230
disability 30
disagreement 72
discernment 127, 148
diversity 59
Divine assistance 274
Divine Feminine 100
Divine Fire 47, 316
Divine Fire of Mind 278
Divine force 123
Divine Help 317
Divine Love 304
Divine Lover 100
Divine Mind 278
Divine Mother 307, 308

310, 311, 312, 313, 314, 317, 318

Himalayas 248
Hindu tradition 90
Hohokam 183, 210, 226
holy relationship 306
homeostasis 65, 121
Hopi 183, 184
house 276, 278, 299
house, symbolism 295
humanity 47
human being 118, 119, 124, 129, 222, 224, 293
human beings 223, 228
human body 227
human consciousness 73
human evolution 302
human existence 74
human form 123, 124, 129, 131, 235
human kingdom 245
human mind 125
human personality 261
human sacrifice 210
human sensory mechanism 120
human structure 118
human thinking patterns 32
hypnosis 287

I

Ibez 43, 181
identity 3, 4, 6, 13, 111, 115
identity forms 3, 26
illness 105, 106, 109
Illuminati 251
illumination 264, 311, 312, 317
illusion 79, 85, 86, 88, 90, 92, 115, 142, 172, 273
illusions 309
image 110
imagination 124, 135, 169
immigration 227
immune system 26, 51
improvisation 61
Indian 180, 181, 182
individuality 224

individualized group consciousness 43
individuation 58, 101
indwelling Life 246
indwelling Life essence 124
infinite compassion 34
infinite knowledge 34
infinite mercy 34
infinite power 34
information 236
initiation 316
initiatory activity 236
Inner Earth 246, 247
inner Life 168
inner life 131
Inner Selves 170, 243, 281
inner Selves 275
insane 30
insomnia 14
inspiration 264
instinct 7
instinctive mind 237
integrated personality 81
integration 99
integration of masculine and feminine energy 224
intellect 44
intellect, intuitive 76
intellectual mind 237
intelligence 43
intensity 42
intention 5, 63, 68, 158
intention, conscious 58, 78
intention, self-centered 63, 68
intention, universal 68
interdependence 43
interlife 106
internal power 160
internal resistance 25
international group of financiers 251
intuition 43, 44, 76, 81, 100, 137
intuitional mind 237
intuitive guidance 44
intuitive mind 81
investment of being 58, 77, 78

priorities 132
prior embodiment 296
probes 238
prophets 302
protection 71
protection prayer 71
psychological research 2
psychology 1, 43, 302
psychology, evolution of 302
purification 47, 278
purifying agent 278
purpose 5, 74
Pyramid of Cheops 246

Q

qualities 59, 62
quarks 72

R

races 182
radiant beings 228
radiant Life 246
rain 300
rays 189, 190, 209, 219, 286
re-embodiment 106, 292
reactive mode 78
reactivity 89, 102
reality 14, 110, 117, 118, 121, 123, 124, 133, 136, 147, 168, 172, 179
reality, creation of 131
recalcitrant Conscious Mind 112
relationship 213, 214, 295
relationships 84, 291
religions 212
resistance 41, 75, 114, 156
resistance to body 26
resistance to learning 13
restriction 78, 291
retarded 30
rhythm of creativity 88
risk 79, 83, 88, 89, 115
river 283
rock art 186, 209

role model 107

S

safety 108, 251
Saturn 169
satyr 228
Science of Mind 109
scientists 72
sculptor 61
sculpture 61, 110
second wave of Souls 194
Sedona 210, 211
seismic activity 220, 236
selectivity 71
self-acceptance 307
self-awareness 24, 32
self-centered emotions 316
self-defeating emotions 316
self-doubts 308
self-imposed limitations 291
self-worth 308
selfknowledge 309, 317
Selves 90
senses 26, 112, 116, 119, 122, 123, 124, 133, 134, 135, 136, 139, 143, 146, 147, 148, 151, 165
senses of perception 120
sense of feeling 135, 136
sense of hearing 135, 136
sense of sight 135, 136
sense of smell 136
sense of taste 136
sense of touch 149
sensitivity 110, 223, 261
sensory loss 152
sentimentality 34
separation 115
service 153, 179
Seth 85
sexuality 283
  rejection of 50
sexual abuse 48, 50
Shadow Self 195
Shakespeare, William 16
shamans, magicians, sorcerers 45

CPSIA information can be obtained
at www.ICGtesting.com
Printed in the USA
BVOW06s0346180118

505435BV00001B/137/P